GENEROUS BETRAYAL

Generous Betrayal
POLITICS OF CULTURE
IN THE NEW EUROPE

Unni Wikan

The University of Chicago Press
Chicago and London

UNNI WIKAN is professor in the Department of
Social Anthropology at the University of Oslo. She
is the author of numerous books, including *Behind the
Veil in Arabia; Managing Turbulent Hearts;* and *Tomorrow,
God Willing*—all published by the University of
Chicago Press.

The University of Chicago Press, Chicago 60637
The University of Chicago Press, Ltd., London
© 2002 by The University of Chicago
All rights reserved. Published 2002
Printed in the United States of America

11 10 09 08 07 06 05 04 03 02   1 2 3 4 5

ISBN: 0-226-89684-6 (cloth)
ISBN: 0-226-89685-4 (paper)

Library of Congress Cataloging-in-Publication Data

Wikan, Unni, 1944–
   Generous betrayal : politics of culture in the new
Europe / Unni Wikan.
      p. cm.
   Includes bibliographical references (p.) and
index.
   ISBN 0-226-89684-6 (alk. paper) — ISBN 0-226-
89685-4 (paper : alk. paper)
   1. Europe—Ethnic relations.   2. Immigrants—
Europe—Social conditions.   3. Minorities—
Europe—History—20th century.   4. Racism—
Europe—History—20th century.   I. Title.

D1056 .W55 2002
305.8'0094—dc21

                    2001043722

In memory of my grandmother
Emma Olsen (1885–1967)
and to the future of Nasim Karim,
Nadia, and "Aisha"

When a man is subject to violence it is called torture,
but when a woman is subject to violence it is called culture.
NASIM KARIM

It was at the expense of their culture that European individuals gained, one by one, all their rights. In the end, it is the critique of tradition that constitutes the spiritual foundation of Europe.

We will never resolve the difficulties facing us by allowing the need to abolish privileges to become the prerogative of one civilization alone. We cannot limit the practice of individual rights only to those we identify with the West.

ALAIN FINKIELKRAUT

There is nothing in the history of the world to indicate that women will not value more freedom when they actually come to experience it. The absence of present discontent, or felt radical desires, cannot wipe out the moral significance of . . . inequality if individual freedom—including the freedom to assess one's situation and the possibilities of changing it—is accepted as a major value.

AMARTYA SEN

Contents

Acknowledgments

At the end of a long journey I trace my steps back in time to a place north of the Arctic Circle where I grew up. The most profound influence on my life was my *mormor,* my mother's mother. It was she who first taught me about social welfare—not by way of words but by her own example. She was the most generous woman I have ever known, but also the most courageous and outspoken. It was this rare combination of qualities that was her distinction. As a child I remember fleeing her kitchen at times when she received what was perceived to be the scum of society in those days—the poorest and most decrepit, some of whom were Sami (or Finn, as we called them). They smelled strange and had a threatening air about them, which frightened us children. I also remember going with her into some of their squalid sheds to give them food and clothing.

This was at a time when social welfare was still a non-word. But my grandmother practiced social welfare and social justice by the force of her convictions. Among the first cohort of teachers to graduate from the world's northernmost teacher's college in 1905, in Tromsø, she braved the fierce North Atlantic ocean in an open rowboat for ten years to bring education to children in remote schools in the Lofoten islands. After that, she settled in Ibestad (also an island, but more benign), where she was elected the first woman to the municipal council (*herredstyre*) in 1922. She remained a member for twenty years.

She was never afraid to speak up, never. She dedicated her life to social service and social justice, changing the world for the better in her place and time.

But for my grandmother's example, I might not have had the courage to step out into the minefield I knew "the immigration debate" to be when I entered it. And there was no dearth of warning from friends about what

I would be in for. But my grandmother had taught me not to suffer social injustice silently and not to be afraid of the powers that be, but to stand up for my own convictions.

Emma Helmine Justine Olsen died in 1967, eighty-two years old. She had been baptized Emma Helmine. But in her time "every" little girl had three names, and so she added Justine to be just as good as all the others. It was the one concession to vanity that I knew her ever to make. Was it fortuitous that the name she chose for herself is one that means justice?

I dedicate this book to her—in memoriam.

After eighteen years on an island north of the Arctic Circle, life took me to Egypt, Oman, Bali, and Bhutan for anthropological fieldwork. The imprint of those experiences is strong in this book, even if not apparent to many of my readers. "The man should have his freedom, but not at the woman's expense," said Umm Ali in her abode in a poor area of Cairo. "God helps him who helps himself," said another Muslim, Huriya in Bali, Indonesia. "And does the rat beget lions for children?" quipped Suriati, another Balinese, when a rich man had mocked her lack of education. "Tibet was colonized by China . . . , but we have been colonized by our own government," said Angey, a poor village woman.

Each in her own way, these women give testimony to themes and concerns that reverberate through this book. When I make a case for universal values, it is because they, and others I know, have taught me to see beyond culture to some common existential concerns that we share as human beings. Foremost among these is a concern for freedom, equality, and social justice.

Closer to home, my debts to many people and institutions are profound. I would like to thank in particular Nasim Karim, Walid al-Kubaisi, Sükrü Bilgiç, Farid Bouras, and Mustapha Laatiaoui. Special thanks to Nasim Karim, for permitting me to reprint material from *Izzat—for ærens skyld* (Oslo: Cappelen, 1996) in chapter 13; and to Sükrü Bilgiç, for permitting me to reprint "Fra ei ung, utenlandsk jente til de norske sosialarbeidere" (*Det Nye Oslo*, 1993) in chapter 15; translations of both are mine.

I am also deeply indebted to Inger-Lise Lien, Ottar Brox, Kåre Hagen, Hege Storhaug, and Thomas Hylland Eriksen. Thanks also to Afzal Abbas, Mohammed Bouras, Ann Christine Eek, Eva Khan, Marianne Knudsen, Ellen Rojahn, and Sara Rosenblatt; and to Leidulv Digernes, Arne Ruth, Hans Fredrik Dahl, and Bertel Haarder.

Members of the press have given me much inspiration and useful materials, especially Peter Normann Waage, Olga Stokke, Inger Anne Olsen, and

Karin Westrheim. A special thanks to Per Egil Hegge for invaluable critique and support at a crucial point. I would also like to thank Per Ståle Lønning, Nils Gunnar Lie, and Sverre Tom Radøy.

As always, I am much indebted to our librarians, Nancy Frank and Frøydis Haugane. To Roger Grace, manifold thanks for keeping me sane by sorting out my computer problems.

Thanks also to the numerous individuals and institutions—too many to mention—that over the years have encouraged and facilitated my engagement and learning by inviting me to talk to various audiences or run day-long seminars, and by consulting with me on critical issues. What I have learned from this is invaluable, as teachers, social workers, child care workers, health workers, physicians, politicians, and others have shared their experiences with me and challenged my mind. I offer my thanks to everyone, though I cannot give all their names here. A special thanks to Åsta Bjørnør, Gunnar Mandt, Trond Herland, and Åse Kleveland.

Some of those I would most have wanted to thank must remain anonymous. Among them is "Aisha," but there are others whose trust in me I deeply appreciate.

A special thanks to Rune Gerhardsen, former chairman of the Oslo city council, for engaging me to work on two action plans for immigrants in 1996. Also thanks to the Ministry of Child and Family Affairs for hiring me to do the situation analysis in preparation for the government's action plan regarding youth and children of immigrant background in 1992. But for that experience, I might never have taken the path that eventuated in this book. A special thanks to Michel Midré and Lise Grette.

My students have also taught me a lot and sharpened my comprehension. Particular thanks are due Grete Aspelund, Lára Benjnouh, Celine Blom, Christine Johansen, Camilla Kayed, Marianne Lund, Gro Mikaelsen, Mohammad Ali Samiei, Therese Sandrup, Vivien Wrede-Holm, and Ingvild Østby—all of whom have done research on immigrants or their children and shared their insights with me.

My work has also gained immeasurably from the feedback and encouragement I have received, as a lecturer, from academic audiences in many European countries—from the anthropology department at the French School in Rome; the history department at the European University in Florence; the history department at École des hautes études en sciences sociales in Paris; the anthropology department at the London School of Economics; the Frobenius Institute at the Wolfgang Goethe University, Frankfurt; the Association of Danish Anthropologists' biannual meeting in Ålborg, Denmark; the Association of European Anthropologists' biannual meet-

ACKNOWLEDGMENTS

ing in Barcelona, Spain; the anthropology departments at the University of Trondheim, the University of Bergen, and the University of Oslo, all in Norway.

In the United States, I have been privileged to be invited to lecture and discuss the issues at (in chronological order) the department of anthropology, George Washington University, St. Louis, Missouri; the department of anthropology, Boston University; the Leverett House senior common room, Harvard University; the American Anthropological Association meetings, San Francisco; the department of anthropology, Harvard University; and the department of social medicine, Harvard University.

In addition, I have benefited greatly from my participation in the interdisciplinary working group "Ethnic Custom, Assimilation, and American Law," under the auspices of the U.S. Social Science Research Council. Over the three years that the group has been in operation, with biannual meetings, I have had occasion to meet with some of the best minds I can envision and to gain immeasurably from their knowledge and erudition. A very special thanks to Richard A. Shweder, Hazel Marcus, Martha Minow, and Frank Kessel, initiators and organizers. To Rick in particular I owe a huge debt for constantly challenging me with a generosity of spirit that is rare in these times.

I am also very grateful to Jonathan Friedman and the Guggenheim Foundation for inviting me to join the working group "Globalization and Transnationalism" that met biannually for two years. Again, the sharp minds and extensive knowledge of the members, as well as the constructive character of the debates, helped clarify and enhance my own grasp of many issues.

My thinking on the issues framed in this book has matured during two periods of residence at Leverett House, Harvard University—in 1995 as a visiting scholar at the department of anthropology and in 1999 as a visiting professor at the department of social medicine. I am grateful to my colleagues in both departments for the congenial environment they offered, both mentally and socially. A very special thanks to Arthur Kleinman, who has been my mentor for more than ten years, and also to Joan Kleinman for friendship and inspiration.

The community of Leverett House deserves special thanks. I am deeply indebted to John and Judith Dowling, former co-masters, for inviting me to join the House, and to Howard and Ann Georgie, present co-masters, for extending the invitation. To tutors, students, and staff alike, my thanks for providing me with a sense of home and company—of freedom as a social commitment. And to Judith Murciano-Goroff, senior tutor, my deep-felt thanks for her example and inspiration.

Without David Brent, senior editor at the University of Chicago Press, I should never have accomplished what I have. But for his encouragement, guidance, and friendship, writing would have been much less of a pleasure, publishing much more of a pain. To Margaret Mahan, my copyeditor, thanks for superb work; thanks also to Christine Schwab.

Last, to my family: As ever, my husband, Fredrik Barth, has been my companion in work, tirelessly discussing every aspect of every issue, and bringing his own unique insight into it all. For ceaseless encouragement and support, and for keeping me alive by serving me dinner every night, my deep-felt thanks.

But without Kim, our son, who said, "Mama, do it!" at a critical point when I would have chosen to lie low in the immigration debate, my life would surely have taken a different turn. For sustaining me through the minefield and cheering me up when I almost fell, my warmest thanks; and to his Anniken as well for being Kim's life force.

Finally to my mother, Bibbi Wikan: deep-felt thanks for everything.

Introduction: A Personal Odyssey

My stakes in the story that eventuates here are high. In 1995 I set myself the task of trying to make the Norwegian government change its policies regarding immigrants and their children. Much has been achieved, thanks to the efforts of people who had gone before me as well as others who engaged themselves, though there is still a long way to go. And writing this book is part of that effort: to try to ensure that the issues are conceptualized clearly and remain prominent. I am hoping thus to capture the attention not only of Norwegians but also of members of other plural societies—politicians and public of diverse origins—who are concerned with social justice and the future of an increasingly shared world.

Talking to audiences in various countries on the themes discussed in this book, I have met with a surprisingly similar reaction: resonance. What I tell about Norway rings a bell in Italy, France, Spain, Portugal, Sweden, Denmark, Britain, Germany, and the United States. Though I might expect to be told that the Scandinavian situation is unique, that the problems faced there are particular—which must to some extent be true—this is not the message I get from the audiences I have met. Rather, their response is resounding: the Norwegian situation and the issues I raise in analyzing it are of general import. So are the case materials I use to give them a human face. They carry a message that is valuable for all to hear—and to think about and learn from—however different the particulars of the situation in individual countries. The basic goals are the same: to create a well-functioning multicultural society committed to social justice and individual liberty.

And the task, we all know, is difficult. The way ahead is thorny and the issues have to be rethought. Battles will have to be fought, and some compromises will be hard to swallow. Yet there is no alternative—which is why the lessons from Norway have general relevance. Much as Norway is far from realizing a socially just and equitable society, the Norwegian experience regarding immigrants reveals both the perils of silencing crucial human dilemmas and the gains to be had from dealing with them—even when painful.

Not everyone will agree with me. The story I tell attests to a contestation of voices and some fierce disagreements. But that is precisely as I have said: in immigrant matters (as in most of human life) there is no smooth sailing. The issues we must face—and "we," of course, includes both natives and immigrants—are heartrending, painful, and dangerous. Racism and stigmatization may follow in the wake of a frank assessment of the situation, as when the facts reveal a disproportionate use of public assistance among some immigrants, and natives react with consternation and anger. Thus the balance between concealment and open discussion is especially sensitive when racism and discrimination are at stake, leading many well-meaning people to feel that a lid had better be kept on the turmoil—disclosure presents excessive risks.

This is not my view. And it is not the view I have advocated through my years of engagement in Norwegian public life with the aim of securing social justice and a better quality of life for immigrants. On the contrary, my view was—and is—that "unless we describe reality, we will awake one day to a reality that is indescribable."[1] Understanding the situation is the first step toward any effective social action or public policy. Silencing is the enemy of social justice, as of freedom of thought and expression.

There have been efforts to silence me in Norway, some of them very painful. I knew I must be prepared for the worst when I went public with my analysis in 1995, shattering a silence that it was in many people's interest to maintain and voicing views that were considered unspeakable. What has perplexed me are adverse reaction from some academics, especially in the United States, to the issues I raise. What troubles me is not so much their disagreement in some of the matters I raise as the sense that certain issues should not be spoken of. Political correctness is an ailment of our times, especially within liberal academia. And my odyssey is not politically correct; on the contrary, it is an effort to transgress the bounds of a conspiracy of silence that, as I wish to show, has been wreaking havoc with the lives of many immigrants and their children. The children's fate and future are foremost on my mind. For, as two Pakistani fathers in Norway said, "Our generation will soon be gone. It is our children who will continue to live here. Please don't punish them for our failure to dare to address the problems."

Courage is needed by all of us—working in consonance.

My book is also this: an attempt to give courage to fellow academics and others who might have wanted to do something about the state of affairs but are reluctant for fear of public opprobrium. It does work; it is possible to do something. Be prepared for the cost. It is going to be painful. But so is every effort that requires exertion. If the effort more than repays the cost, it is by virtue of the exhilarating sense of accomplishment that follows from putting one's knowledge to work and achieving worthwhile results. Indeed, I would go further and argue that this is the duty of all social scientists: we should put our knowledge to work out there in the world. Applied anthropology has been seen as a second-rate enterprise in some academic circles, and there are many, especially among our students, who hesitate to take it up for fear of their career prospects. I hope that by going public with my own adventure in this field, in Norway, I can give heart to students and colleagues who might opt for public engagement. Having spent most of my life in academia, enjoying a relatively successful career, I can nevertheless attest that nothing has given me such satisfaction as the tough engagement of the past few years. True, I have been beaten symbolically, so my body ached. And I have wept (for myself) on two occasions. But the satisfaction was worth every bit of the pain. And I encourage others to go on.

Whatever success my work achieved owed much to the efforts of many others who engaged themselves, or worked separately from me, on similar issues. Together and apart, we managed to get things going. I would also like to thank my opponents and, to a degree, my enemies. Without them, the issues would not have been so sharpened. Without them, there would have been less need to think critically through and refine the points of the debate. Without them, the solutions—if so they may be called—might have been more difficult to arrive at. And in the end, some of our points of divergence and even our critical differences have sorted themselves out beyond ourselves, through the force of circumstance. Some of us who would never have expected to join forces now find ourselves in the same camp. The reader will find examples of this throughout the book as I relate the Norwegian experience as I perceived it. Others may write their own stories, and some already have done so.

This is how it all began for me. In August 1992 I received a phone call from the Ministry of Child and Family Affairs, asking me to do a consultancy job. It was urgent—it had to be done within two weeks—and consisted of performing a "situation analysis" of children and youth of immigrant background in preparation for the government's action plan, to be launched (as I understood) five months hence.[2] I would have at my disposal all available research reports and statistics relevant to the task. And I would be assisted by a working group consisting of a member from each of the different ministries (Finance, Health, etc.).

I was baffled. Two weeks! I had a full-time job at the university and could hardly request leave: my students needed me. On the other hand, the job sounded interesting—the more so as I would get to see all the existing material on immigrants, some of it confidential. And the official who called me implied that I was the only person fit for the job. He referred to a brief talk I had recently given at a meeting convened by the minister of child and family affairs at which a few invited people had been asked to give their opinion on the most urgent policy issues concerning children. My five-minute contribution on Muslim children and families had made headlines when a journalist from a major newspaper, *Aftenposten*, printed an interview under the heading *Still krav til innvandrere*—an essentially untranslatable phrase which means, "Make demands on immigrants, require them to do their part; don't just treat them as if they were helpless, pitiful, mere victims." Indeed, it is disrespectful *not* to hold people to account.

It seems so simple now in retrospect. But at the time it was like throwing a bomb. "Make demands on immigrants!" A friend, an anthropologist, called and said, "Please, Unni, be careful, or you'll be labeled a racist." Perhaps I was. All I know is that today nearly everyone is saying those words, even the most pro-immigrant, pro-multicultural, antiracist people. Immigrants themselves say so. But I believe I was the first in Norway to utter them publicly, or at least (against my better judgment) to have them printed. I had consented to the interview. I had said the words, along with many others. What I was not prepared for was to have them stare back at me in the headlines of a prominent newspaper.

But it was my intercession at that meeting, which had been convened by a cabinet member, and perhaps those very words, that had resulted in my being urged to do a situation analysis. The government was alarmed, said the official. The situation appeared very difficult for many children and youths. Would I please accept the assignment?

So I assented, and we struck a compromise. I would be given a month to do the job, not two weeks. And, as originally offered, I would be given all the assistance I required from the Ministry of Child and Family Affairs and a working group of members from all the other ministries. Their participation was essential for the recommendations we were to make: there was a tough political battle ahead, and bringing out the different opinions was crucial.

To make matters clear: I had—and still have—no political affiliation. I have never been a member of any of the seven political parties in Norway, nor would I be. My assignment was purely professional. I was recruited as a scholar knowledgeable about Islam and Muslims (the great majority of immigrants in Norway, as in the rest of Western Europe, are Muslim), who also had wide experience of working among Hindus and Buddhists.[3] I had no research experience among immigrants in Norway, but few did. My credentials were those of a scholar who could be counted on to do a solid job but who might come up with some controversial conclusions—if the materials seemed to warrant it. The report, I believe, was not expected to be bland.

Nor was it. But the end result was. When the Ministry of Child and Family Affairs finally launched their action plan in January 1996—three years after I had been led to expect it to appear and making nonsense of the urgency of my assignment—it was hardly recognizable. And it was bland. This is not just my own judgment but that of many others—teachers, social workers, child welfare workers, and concerned citizens—who found little of use in the action plan. What the situation analysis I had helped write contained that—if acted upon—could improve conditions for youths and children had been watered down or deleted. And the reasons seemed to me all too clear. The authorities were not ready to engage in the battle that must ensue if our recommendations were put into effect. For they challenged the power of men to define the good of women and children; and they challenged the power of the authorities and the parents—acting in collusion in many cases to adjudicate the best interests of the child. Basically, the situation analysis had concluded that a misconceived "respect for their culture" on the part of Norwegian authorities was playing into the hands of certain spokesmen, who then took the opportunity to ascend to a position of power far beyond what they had held "back home." The position of women, accordingly, had been undermined and eroded. The greatest losers were the children, but the mothers and the whole family suffered.

Når overmakten blir for stor was the title I had given to the situation analysis—again an untranslatable phrase into English, evoking the image of being over-whelmed by impersonal forces, alluding to the twin powers to which children are subjected through the complicity of the government and parents, acting in concert to respect "the culture."

No wonder, you may say, the government got cold feet. No wonder their urgent action plan was held up. But for me the result was fortunate. Thereby I was compelled, as I felt, to take action myself. Something had to be done—that was clear from the materials I had been given to study in order to prepare the situation analysis.

My most significant finding had been how little we knew; there were masses of papers and other materials but little substance. The exceptions were a few qualitative studies of small samples of respondents.[4] But overall, studies—especially statistical studies—were lacking. One was left to guess about the situation of immigrants in Norway on the basis of a few sound qualitative and quantitative studies of small samples of respondents and masses of haphazard, indirect material. "Inspired guesswork" was what one had to resort to, and for this my training as an anthropologist comes in handy.

The second major finding was even more disturbing. It appeared not only that we knew pitifully little about the immigrants' situation in Norway—more than twenty years after they began to arrive—but also that such knowledge itself was unwelcome. Reading through the materials I had been given, I had the uncomfortable feeling of staring into a black hole that was there, not as a matter of accident, but as the result of some hidden agenda. It seemed that knowledge was considered dangerous; that our paucity of knowledge was not accidental but even convenient—not perhaps by anyone's design but because of unspoken fears that our "colorful community" (*fargerike fellesskap*) would suffer if uncomfortable truths were brought to light.

In retrospect I realize that this was not just a Norwegian predicament. All over Western Europe, to varying degrees (and surely in the United States too), similar fears have expressed themselves in reluctance to face up to the facts of the case regarding immigrants and their children. Hence a complicity of silence. But there were victims along the way. For one cannot formulate responsible social policies or take effective political action in the absence of knowledge. The antiracist banner had forced the authorities to seek cover where they hid in the hope that problems would go away or sort themselves out. That, at least, is how I interpreted the situation. And it was because I saw no sign that the government would change its course, an impression forced upon me by the dismal fate of the action plan, which seemed never to eventuate, that I decided to take action. Some of the things I did, and how I proceeded, are set out in later chapters. Here let me just mention some central features of my engagement and the results to which it led.

In the fall of 1995 I published a book called *Toward a New Norwegian Underclass: Immigrants, Culture, and Integration.*[5] It was intended to stir up attention. And it was bound to do so by its mere title. For "underclass" was an unspeakable word in Norway at the time;[6] and to link it with immigrants, as I did, was all the more provocative. In the book I argued that the government was compromising the welfare of immigrants by practicing a policy of welfare colonialism that undermined people's capacity for self-help.[7] Putting people on welfare for life was not a respectful way of treating them, I argued. It eroded both their self-respect and the respect accorded them by society. In the name of charity, harm was being done, and it was detrimental to everyone—children, adults, immigrants, natives. The whole society suffered, for our common future was one.

But my argument went further and was an indictment of the government's self-serving purposes. Selling out to the antiracists (as I argued between the lines, avoiding too blunt an argument), the government was terrified of doing anything that might elicit accusations of racism. Anyone familiar with Norway (or the other Scandinavian countries at the time) knew how little it took to be branded a racist; it was as if any observation or characterization of immigrants (or of a single immigrant) that was not positive was per se racist.

But how to get a serious discussion going under such circumstances? And how to break the silence that interdicts social action? As I have said, constructive action requires knowledge; and knowledge requires assessments from many points of view. It was in an effort to break the silence that I wrote my book. It resulted in a clamor beyond anything I could have expected. But it also rallied support for my stance from many quarters. Best of all, the discussion got going, and now there is no turning back.

So I accomplished what I had intended: to help break the silence. But it is essential to point out that without the efforts of many others who engaged themselves to bring about changes, my own endeavors would have mattered less. In the aftermath, Norway has come a long way in addressing issues and trying to deal effectively with problems that had been shoved under the table. Some of the more significant of these will be discussed in the book. But first, to convey something of the political climate at the time, let me speak of the clamor.

"Norwegian fundamentalist in scientist's garb" was the headline on the front page of the Marxist paper *Klassekampen* for their review of my book. That did not disturb me too much. But I wept when I read in the liberal national newspaper *Dagbladet* that I had argued that everything bad comes from Islam. It was the most unjust, unfair rendering of my argument that I could imagine. Having spent years of my life learning about Islam the hard way—by sharing people's lives in some less than pleasant places—and then taking that knowledge and putting it to work by publishing books intended to enhance understanding of Muslims,[8] I could not help feeling sorry for myself. My consolation was that my friends in the Muslim world would have rallied to my defense. Also, when I asked a couple of media-versed friends whether I ought to write a rebuttal, their response, independently of each other, was the same: the comment must have been a printer's error, for it made no sense. That comforted me, though hardly reassured me.

But life sometimes brings opponents together. And so it was with the *Dagbladet* journalist and me. Having fundamentally the same agenda—to better the lot of immigrants in Norway with regard both to their material welfare and to their sense of social respect—but coming to it from different perspectives, we have in time become friendly, while still disagreeing on some points. With hindsight, I must grant that his reading of the book may have been marred by my failure to express myself clearly.

The second occasion that brought tears was more serious yet had an even more positive effect. I present it here as a morality tale, serving both as warning and encouragement. The national newspaper just mentioned, *Dagbladet,* announced on the front page that the leader of the antiracist movement in Norway, Khalid Salimi, had accused me of being an ideologue (*ideologisk premissleverandør*) for the rightist party, *Fremskrittspartiet* (the Progress Party). Not only that, but Salimi claimed to have received letters threatening his life from people who invoked me in support of their racist stance. To the newspaper's defense it should be said that they had tried to reach me for a comment to be published alongside the article, but I was away.

I was mortified. The accusations seemed to me outrageous.[9] True, the leader of the Progress Party had—at the party's national convention a few days earlier—quoted a passage from my book. But it was a passage I myself would have chosen. It is a passage that sums up the essence of my argument, that it is the children's future, first and foremost, that is at stake. The excerpt, referring to the situation analysis I had done, describes "children's double powerlessness," in relation to parents and the authorities.

As I understood the situation, the authorities and many parents were involved in a shared design [*et slags spill*] aimed at respecting "their/our culture." But in the process, the children were forgotten. For it was not of course their culture that was entailed, but a culture defined by eloquent men. Norwegian authorities were supporting the powerful—at the expense of children, many of whom suffered serious consequences in the long run. (Wikan 1995a:47–48)

Could this be offensive? Was this ultraconservative? Clearly not. What made it unpalatable to the antiracist movement was the Progress Party leader, who was quoting this passage. And since the words were mine, since I was the ostensible author, that made me unpalatable to them also. It was a harrowing experience to me. And it has a lesson to teach us all. We do not own our own words. They pass out of our ownership on publication. There is no such thing as copyright with respect to how one's words or utterances can be used by others, orally at least. So there I was, and such are the conditions under which we must operate.

Going public with words, printing, publishing, appearing in the media is a risky business. We may be misused. We must expect to be misused. But what is the alternative—to keep silent? Silence is easier. It makes for a more pleasant life. But if academics—who are really so privileged and protected, relatively speaking—do not dare or care to speak out, then who will? Invoking scientific neutrality is no excuse, as I see it. Not taking a stand on public issues is itself a political stand; it is not a neutral position. And, as I shall demonstrate in chapter 19, there are occasions and instances where we academics are in a better position than the people for whom we speak to plead their cause, simply because we have less to lose. Their costs would be too high.

It is fashionable these days to say that the "natives," whoever they are, should speak for themselves. And it is true, they should. But some cannot, and this book shows why they cannot. Yet I include examples of some who did, and the terrible price they paid. I tell of others who contend they would, that they wish nothing more than to exercise their freedom of speech, but that if they did so, they would lose their following and thus their ability to reason with and influence their community. Reform is going to take time, they say. So, for the time being, would I please do them the favor of speaking up on their behalf, raising issues that they support, though they can't do so publicly. On the contrary, some of them will publicly come out against me, criticize me for my opinions, casting me as an opponent and sometimes even as an enemy.

This is in the nature of the game of politics. And I have learned to play it, not because I wanted to but because it seemed to offer the only feasible way to achieve things. I had never envisioned myself as an advocate, a public figure, or a political player. When I entered the fray, it was from a sense of obligation as a citizen and an academic.

Doing anthropology is an enormous privilege, as I see it. It provides a unique opportunity to learn about life and the world—constantly acquiring new knowledge. Should we not, must we not, repay the world for this privilege by putting that knowledge to work in whichever way we can? Of course, this is what most anthropologists do as a matter of fact. I am simply arguing that there is a way that not many—indeed, too few—have chosen, a way that offers unique and challenging opportunities for positive influence. It is one I would have chosen over and over again, were I to live my life twice.

Let me return to my experience of being accused of ideological demagoguery for the far right and of supplying racist extremists with fuel, even leading to death threats. How does one deal with that? My reaction to the latter was anger. I know people who have received threats to their lives but have not announced it in the press. These are people who, to my mind, had more reason to be afraid than the then leader of the antiracist movement in Norway. But the accusation of being an ideological demagogue was painful and thus more difficult to deal with. Anger is an easy emotion, you can get it out; but when one is very deeply hurt, as I was, the pain lingers.

For the media, of course, the incident was *Gefundenes Freschen*—a scoop. Here were the ingredients for a great debate; and so I was asked—once again—to appear, this time in a prime-time radio debate with my opponent, Khalid Salimi. At first I rejected the invitation, refusing to meet a man who had shown such lack of respect for me; but the journalist (who I knew was a serious person) urged me to change my mind, pointing out that the purpose of the debate was to get my view across. I acquiesced, but I warned that if Salimi so much as whispered "ideological demagogue for the far right," I would walk out. It took no time at all; the debate had hardly begun when he uttered those memorable words. And I walked out. Fortunately, the radio debate was not being carried live. The panel of journalists finally persuaded me to proceed. But I had made my point, I would take no nonsense. In a debate, you have to show your opponent a minimum of respect, or the whole effort falters. And I was needed as an opponent, as a foil for the antiracists' ammunition. I was in a sense indispensable at the time. So Salimi changed gears. The debate proceeded in a civil fashion—in part because the panel pressed Salimi to be clear about the points on which he differed with me and the practical alternatives he had to offer. In the end, we seemed not so far apart after all.

I had learned a vital lesson—to demand a reasonable level of respect. So when the Students' Antiracist Movement (SOS-Rasisme) at the University of Oslo asked me to meet Salimi in a three-hour debate soon afterward, I agreed—on condition that there would be no accusations of my being affiliated with the Progress Party. If there were, I would walk out.

I am happy to report that the whole debate was constructive and amicable. That was the last time that Salimi and I met in public debate; he was soon to step down as leader of the antiracist movement. From what I read in newspapers, I have the impression that he and I are really very much on the same line now, as indeed we ought to be. For there is really no discrepancy between what we want to achieve. Circumstances have caught up with us. Issues that were formerly unspeakable have now become explicit, even commonplace. And although, understandably, there are basic disagreements among actors on the Norwegian scene about which way to go and what is best, the era of concealment and silence is over. Indeed, that has been one of the most satisfying results of my engagement on immigrant issues—to experience a watershed in Norway as to what can be said and what cannot be said. If one looks back no more than three or four years, it is striking how issues that earlier would have been labeled racist, were one to voice them, have been forced into the open and are now politically clean and speakable.

This new openness is thanks to the many people who engaged themselves, together and separately, to break the conspiracy of silence. In particular, two types of actors who are often overlooked are teachers and social workers, who have grass-roots experience of problems, and journalists. Without a publicly committed watchdog press that counts several eminent journalists who dare where most academics would not, and whose research on critical social issues could stand as an example to our students, much less would have been achieved.

My book relates a journey partially traveled. It describes a process that is still under way. It will never be finished, for a society worth living in—Eric Hobsbawm's phrase and a leitmotiv of this book—is an ideal ever to be pursued though perhaps never to be realized for everyone. There will be winners and losers in any society. My concern has been to ensure that Norway will see who these are, who is what, and that it will proceed to take action to better the lot of those who are prone to lose.

My government must be commended, I believe, for having learned a lesson; it has shown itself capable of learning from mistakes and of moving in what I perceive to be the right direction. It is now prepared to recognize that immigrants are a mixed lot of unique individuals; that "culture" is not sacrosanct; and that every inhabitant of Norway should have the protection of the law. Moreover, Norway is now ready to stand up for human rights, over and above "culture"—to recognize that culture and power go hand in hand and that the protection of weaker members of a group may involve some hard battles. Although the Ministry of Child and Family Affairs was not ready to even consider such battles or problems back in 1992 when they engaged me, and the long postponement of the action plan indicates how sensitive they felt the issues were, in the end I am proud of my government for what has been achieved.

That does not mean that we can rest satisfied. The problem of how to reconcile human rights and cultural rights is still with us, as with all plural or multicultural societies of a liberal democratic nature. The question, how free should the exercise of culture be? continues to trouble us, if not in principle, then certainly in practice. And to provide some sort of equal opportunity for immigrants and their children remains an ever-present challenge—in Norway as elsewhere. There is still much to do to ensure the welfare and dignity of immigrants and their children, but a significant transformation is under way. Such is the story I shall relate.

The materials on which this book is based derive from many sources. Much of the groundwork was laid through countless talks with hundreds of individuals I have met over the years. They include immigrants of all ages and stations in life and many different nationalities. I have had discussions with social workers, teachers, principals, child welfare workers, refugee consultants, health care workers, doctors, and nurses; I have spoken with members of the Norwegian cabinet, representatives of Parliament, members of the Oslo city council, local politicians from all over the country. I have spoken with journalists and radio and TV reporters and appeared on their programs and debates; I have consulted with lawyers and policemen, judges and witnesses, and attended court cases both as a special witness (or "culture expert") and as a lay person. I met many of these people at talks I have given and at seminars; others approached me independently for advice or to share their stories; some I sought out myself. Since 1995 I have spent practically all my free time in such pursuits. Though exhausting, as I became the hub of so much information and many people depended on me, the experience has also been extremely fulfilling.

I should mention two particular engagements of very special importance. One is my work with Youth Against Violence (*Ungdom mot vold*)—an organization founded and led by Farid Bouras and Mustapha Laatiaoui (and that I have served as chair of the board since 1995). The association has afforded a unique window on various viewpoints and positions.[10]

A second special learning experience arose when in 1996 I was invited by Rune Gerhardsen, the chairman of the Oslo city council, to work on a white paper regarding immigrants and their children in Oslo. This task involved five months of close collaboration with politicians and bureaucrats to develop two action plans, one for adult immigrants and the other for children and youth. It taught me a great deal about practical policies and political economy.[11]

In addition to the wealth of data I gathered by these firsthand experiences, I have drawn on a number of secondary sources: newspaper reports; statistics; research by other social scientists; and stories provided by other authors—Nasim Karim, Sükrü Bilgiç, and Hassan Keynan—of immigrant experiences in Norway and beyond. I also borrow extensively from the insights provided by other scholars who have nothing to do with Norway as such, yet are deeply enlightening and relevant to my work. Eric Hobsbawm, Alain Finkielkraut, Slavenka Drakulić, Amartya Sen, Sadik Al-Azm, and Martha Nussbaum convinced me that the issues I am dealing with are general, human issues.

This book was written mainly over a period of nearly three years (early 1997 until October 1999). It took so long because writing had to be combined with continuing action. I gave literally hundreds of public and professional lectures, wrote op-ed articles, engaged in public and media debates, and so forth, all the while attending to my university commitments in my "real" job. But this means that even now, as I am writing, history unfolds. I could not keep up, for I never had a complete set of material to draw on. While this sometimes seemed cumbersome—I often wondered what tense I should I use, how to qualify assessments so as to be properly nuanced, and whether I could keep up with the chain of events—I now see it as an advantage. The story I relate is a story on the move, an unfinished narrative. Some literary theorists argue that it is the ending that defines the narrative; without an ending, the author would not know how to proceed (Kermode 1966).[12] I thought I knew how to proceed, but the end result is not what I could have envisioned. I could not have imagined, for example, that Nadia's story would unfold as it did and bring the responses it did. I could not have imagined the rash of robberies by children that took place during 1998–99, involving boys as young as twelve. I had warned in an earlier book (Wikan 1995a) against youth violence among boys of immigrant background, predicting that it would increase and be hard to combat. But I had not imagined how extreme the developments would be, or that the youngest of the young would be involved—recruited, it seems, because they cannot be punished, they are too young, below the minimum age for prosecution.

All this and more, I did not envision. It is important that the reader keep this in mind. The story I relate is of history on the move; hence different impetuses and premises are laid for action on the part of particular individuals as well as on that of agents of the state. Take Nadia's case, related in chapters 21–22, as an example: the verdict against her parents could hardly have been worded as it was if it had been issued two or three years earlier. The time would not have been ripe. This is also an advantage of using Norway as my case: the scene is more transparent, the line of developments easier to trace than in larger, more complex societies. Thus we can also more easily trace the precipitates of later events in the unfolding narrative.

Indeed, as this book goes to press, new and astonishing events are taking place in Norway. Suddenly there is a torrent of testimonies regarding forced marriage. One girl after another comes forth with her horrendous story, though only one, so far, under her full name. The floodgates are open, but how did it happen? Why now? Some of the causes are explicable, others not.[13] What is certain is that there is no turning back. Events have been set in motion that will indelibly set their stamp on Norwegian history and mark a turning point in the lives of many people.

What will come of it all remains to be seen. But the changes are momentous. Once again, events have outstripped me. But that is as it should be. Think of this when you meet Noreen and Nadia, or hear the story of Aisha; remember that they have helped beat the path for the positive developments now under way. Indeed, they said so themselves, Noreen and Nadia: it was to help others be spared from their own miserable fates that they chose to go public with their stories.

My book opens with Aisha's story. Her story provides me with a natural point of departure, for it was through her story and my engagement with it, starting in April 1996, that I came to understand issues regarding citizenship, social justice, gender, and the law that have preoccupied me ever since. Aisha's story shows clearly what remains to be done, how far we still have to go. And this is largely what the book is about: the issues lying ahead. So this book is different from my earlier book *Toward a New Norwegian Underclass*—which was written for a Norwegian public and was intended to stir a Norwegian imagination. It assumed a great deal of context, and played upon associations that a Norwegian readership could be expected to provide. *Generous Betrayal* is the story of a story, an attempt to provide an overview of a political process in Norway over the past few years that is matched or paralleled in much of Western Europe. It is above all an attempt to go global with this story of events—to lift it from the Norwegian context and share it with others who may learn from the Norwegian experience. In so doing, I do not mean to divest my analysis of its singularity and embeddedness in a particular political and historical situation. On the contrary, with Michael Walzer I believe that context and contingency are crucial. In his book *On Toleration* (1997:3–4), Walzer writes:

> Procedural arguments won't help us . . . precisely because they are not differentiated by time and place; they are not properly circumstantial. The alternative that I mean to defend is a historical and contextual account of toleration and coexistence, one that examines the different forms that these have actually taken and the norms of everyday life appropriate to each . . . We must consider as well how the arrangements are experienced by different participants—both groups and individuals, both those who benefit and those who are harmed . . .
>
> Comparisons across arrangements are morally and politically helpful in thinking about where we are and what alternatives might be available to us.

This is the contribution of the Norwegian story: that it offers a sufficiently contextual account to help others think through what alternatives are available if social justice, individual liberty, and tolerance are primary goals. And by showing how actual human beings were affected, the issues become more compelling, more difficult to ignore. But in thus lifting the story out of the Norwegian experience, I also make a case for universal priorities and universal values. I argue for a universalizing discourse that would recognize the basic integrity of the human being and the indispensable value of respect for human rights. Even more than that, I argue that such values are rooted in lived experiences in a wide range of societies; thus calling them universal is not a plea for a Westernized discourse. On the contrary, it is in keeping with deep-seated longings and desires and entrenched values widely shared throughout a plethora of human societies. The form such values may take in lived experience varies, depending as it does on social and political arrangements. Hence a case for universal values can also be tolerant of difference. What a multicultural welfare society cannot do— or, rather, must not do—is distinguish between natives and immigrants, or the children of immigrants, in how it protects and supports their basic human rights.

Aisha's story shows how far we still must travel to reach that goal.

WELFARE FOR WHOM? | I

Some words of Eric Hobsbawm, renowned historian and author, can serve as a fitting preamble to this book. Hobsbawm ended a lecture to students at a Central European university by telling them something he himself had been taught before he began to teach:

> "The people for whom you are there," said my own teacher, "are not the brilliant students like yourself. They are the average students with boring minds who get uninteresting degrees in the lower range of the second class, and whose examination scripts all read the same. The first class people will look after themselves, though you will enjoy teaching them. The others are the ones who need you."

He continued:

> That applies not only to the university but to the world. Governments, the economy, schools, everything in society, are not for the benefit of the privileged minorities. We can look after ourselves. It is for the benefit of the ordinary run of people, who are not particularly clever or interesting, . . . not highly educated, not successful or destined for success, in fact, nothing very special. It is for the people who, throughout history, have entered history outside their neighborhoods as individuals only in the records of their births, marriages, and deaths. Any society worth living in is one designed for them, not for the rich, the clever, the exceptional, although any society worth living in must provide room and scope for such minorities. (1993:64)

Such is the message of this book: Modern states are all, to varying degrees, welfare societies. A welfare society is worthy of the name only if it caters to the well-being of its neediest members. Is Norway up to the test?

My angle on this problem will be culture and identity politics. I shall explore the way certain European nations and their publics cope with the challenge posed by the new immigration that is rapidly changing their face and future. How is Norway managing to craft a new plural society in which immigrants and their descendants can live and be respected as equal human beings? Let me begin by way of a story.

2   *A Tale of Two Would-Be Survivors*

She was fourteen years old, a Norwegian citizen, born and raised in Norway. Suddenly in 1996 she was taken out of the country to be married in her parents' original homeland. She feared the deportation and fought it with all her might. She lost; and she lost with what appears to have been the consent of the child welfare authorities, who forced her back to her parents after she had managed to escape to a foster family with which she had previously been placed. Because of the problem of finding someone from her parents' ethnic minority,[1] the foster family was ethnically Norwegian.

The girl, let us call her Aisha, had thrived with her new family. She begged to be allowed to remain with them, backed by her teachers, who had witnessed her suffering from mistreatment by her parents and kin. To no avail. Convinced that children should remain "in their culture," the child authorities did not pause to ask what *is* in effect the culture of a girl born and raised in Norway. Rather, they assumed that they knew, as if culture were determined by birth and parentage, not by experience and learning. And so Aisha was brought back to her parents by force when they insisted on having her back and promised to treat her well—vows Aisha did not believe in the least.

The last anyone in school heard from her was a frightened whisper into a mobile phone before the phone went dead. Two days later the family was out of Norway. The parents came back from time to time. Aisha alone was gone.

To throw Aisha's story into relief, a comparison with her father is in order. Twenty-five years earlier, when living in his native land, Aisha's father had faced a situation not unlike Aisha's own. He too was threatened with an assault to his freedom and identity—not from a forced marriage but from forced loss of his job. Because he drank heavily, he was fired, and he had meager prospects for new employment.[2] Thus unable to provide for his family and reap respect in society, he looked for an escape. And he found it in the prospect of life in a welfare society that takes care of a man's needs whether he works or not.

He journeyed to Norway and made his career as a social welfare client. He did well. Residing now with his family in an elegant section of the capital city in an apartment supplied by the state, he managed to save some money and invest in property in his native land. Thus he recouped his honor and expanded his freedom, even raising his prospects in the marriage market: he could leave his first wife, the mother of his son, and marry a woman twenty years his junior. He continued to drink and spoke no Norwegian, but that is beside the point.

The story of Aisha's father would be a success story, were it not for certain uncomfortable facts. Aisha was not an only child; she had five brothers. The eldest died of an overdose of drugs. Another became what in Norway is called a *versting* (from the adjective for "worst"), meaning an incorrigible juvenile delinquent. Two younger boys, when only seven and ten, already had a history of violent, antisocial behavior, even as their mother was expecting yet another child.

Aisha was a would-be survivor who tried to break out from this vicious circle. As her father had done twenty-five years earlier, she looked for an escape when faced with a threat to her freedom and identity. Like him, she had been socialized to think that she mattered as a human being and that her personal welfare counted. In his case, it was his Middle Eastern upbringing that had instilled such ideas in a man; in hers, it was her education in a Nordic welfare society committed to the premise that all humans are equal, irrespective of gender and rank, that had formed her thinking. Father and daughter thus had similar compelling concerns and took similar steps to safeguard their welfare and identity. He escaped to a foreign land to start life anew. She solicited a foster family to have a new beginning. He won, she was defeated. And she lost at the hands of the same nation that saved him—not a traditional Muslim society but a modern European welfare state, *her* country, one with which she identified but he did not.

Norway prides itself on its humanitarian values. Indeed, it was those values, realized in the form of practical social policies, that enabled her father to come as an alien and reap the fruits of a welfare system to which he had contributed nothing. This is the essence of a truly socialist and humanist state: that it gives to each according to his or her needs, not according to his or her contributions. Yet when Aisha's welfare was most at stake and her protection urgently needed, this same society let her down.

Aisha did not want to be sent to a foreign land. All she wanted was to be able to lead the life of a normal Norwegian fourteen-year-old—to go to school, see her friends, and be protected from mental and physical abuse. Such rights are written into the Norwegian constitution. Such should have been her rights. Yet when Aisha tried to plead for her welfare, she ran up against resistance of the most impervious kind: she did not receive the backing that would have permitted her to continue her education; she was deprived of her freedom of movement; she was deprived of the right to decide whom and when to marry; and, by being forcibly reunited with her family, she ended up as an involuntary bride.

Thus she was doubly deprived of her citizen's rights. Forced marriage is illegal according to Norwegian law.[3] So is depriving a child of a primary school education. Aisha was, in effect, granted fewer rights than her father, who has been able to ride the Norwegian system with considerable success. It is a tragedy that the same nation that rescued him has so subverted Aisha's efforts that she could now be considered a missing person.

Though presumably living somewhere, somehow, Aisha is out of reach, incommunicado. She cannot get in touch with any of her former friends, nor they with her—and not, presumably, because she wanted it that way: the letters she wrote and was able to send before her departure from Norway all burn with a scathing accusation: "Do they think I'm lying?" She refers to her abortive efforts to alert the child welfare authorities to her story of physical and mental violation at home and to the plight that was in store for her.

The child authorities are not callous. They care for this girl and are concerned that they may have done her harm, now that it is too late to help. Her parents assure them they have nothing to fear: Aisha is happily going to school in their homeland. "Happily!" snorted a young man of the same ethnic heritage. "That's what they always say to convince their daughters they have nothing to fear by going on vacation to the parents' homeland! The girls panic, of course."

Whether in school or married, Aisha is not likely to be happy. Or why does she not get in contact with any of her former friends, this affectionate young woman who always used to keep in touch by letters or telephone? To her teachers, Aisha is a missing person, and not because she wanted it that way but because she was forcibly deprived of her human rights, including the right to her own body.

WELFARE FOR WHOM?

Can Aisha, then, not be rescued? Is there no hope of helping her regain her freedom and identity? As a Norwegian citizen, could not the government intervene on her part to undo the damage done by the child welfare authorities' sins of omission?

Apparently not. We have tried, her school and I, to appeal her case to the highest state powers.[4] To no avail. Everyone who heard her case was deeply distressed at her fate. Many did not think such things could happen in Norway (though they should know, for Aisha's story is not unique, and other such stories had been featured in the press). Her case has been heard even by the minister of child and family affairs and the minister of culture— responsible women with deep humanitarian concerns. And yet there was nothing they could do to help this girl. Aisha was a lost child whose tragic fate might help *others* be protected from similar misery. But as far as she was concerned, there was nothing to be done—after the fact.

Aisha, when it all happened, was only fourteen years old. At such a tender age, a child is seen as belonging to her parents. If they decide to take her out of the country, so be it. There is little the Norwegian government can do— after the fact. Only if the authorities had realized the danger beforehand and acted to prevent her deportation could she have been saved. This is the lesson they are now drawing from Aisha's case and others similar to hers: that they must act before it is too late.

The troubling question is, what does it take for a child to be heard? Why were Aisha's efforts to alert the child authorities fruitless, though she used all the means at her disposal? She did not just scream and cry; she pleaded and begged; she ran away from home, at one point even taking to the streets where she was fortunately caught before making a nuisance of herself. She had witnesses in her teachers, who have described her wretched performance in school while she was living with her parents, her subsequent blossoming after she was removed to a foster home, and the physical violence against her by kinsmen right outside the schoolyard. If Aisha had come from a family known to be well functioning, the child authorities might understandably have thought she was best off living at home. But such was not the case. Aisha's family was known, not just to the child authorities but to many people of her parents' ethnic minority, to be deeply dysfunctional. And yet her pleas went unheard: "Do they think I'm lying? . . . I hate the child authorities!! I thought they were there to help children. But *I've* been betrayed!" Aisha's pain reverberates through letter upon letter written to trusted teachers and friends before her departure from Norway.

Aisha, a Norwegian citizen, born and bred in Norway, is missing. But her status as such is nowhere recorded except in the hearts and minds of friends who care for her deeply. Only if she resurfaces at the Norwegian embassy in the country where she now lives, with a complaint that she has been forcibly married, will she again be counted as a person in her own right by her country of citizenship. But the likelihood of this happening is not great. Aisha's silence speaks louder than words and signals that her freedom of movement and expression has been effectively suppressed.

3   *A Modern Form of Sacrifice*

How can a society be wedded to humanitarian principles and policies, yet sacrifice the welfare of a young female citizen while extending generous support to a male who was a misfit in his own society and continues to be so in Norwegian society? This is not, of course, to say that a citizen born in Norway should have priority over naturalized citizens, nor to vilify a man who may have had his own reasons for succumbing to alcohol. But it is to highlight a basic human inequality and lack of social justice exemplified by Aisha's case.

Aisha's story is unique, as is any individual life. But the pattern of culture, power, and pain that accounts for her plight repeats itself in other forms over and over, and not just in Norway. Why does it happen? What is at stake? And who are the main protagonists?

Aisha's story is the story of a modern form of sacrifice, the one being performed on the altar of culture. Its high priests are state authorities and institutions who act in conjunction with spokesmen of "the culture" to ensure compliance with traditional mores. The objects of sacrifice are minors, often girls but also boys and other weaker members of the group who are not given a say but compelled to do as "culture" bids. How power enters into the picture is rarely asked. If it is asked, the answer is often overlooked because acting on it would be uncomfortable and perhaps dangerous.

The principal of Aisha's school and other members of the staff who stood up for her were physically threatened by some of her relatives. Some valuable equipment in the school was broken by these people. This is not an unusual reaction but part and parcel of patterns of behavior that emerge with increasing frequency in the "colorful community"—*fargerike fellesskap*—that is an epithet for the new Norway. Ask any principal, teacher, or social worker (as I have), and they will be able to report how they, or others they know, have been subject to verbal or physical assault by immigrants, usually men, who claim their rights are being violated. This is not to say that ethnic minorities alone engage in verbal or physical abuse, nor to paint all with one brush. But asocial behavior by immigrants, whether not occurring or—for the past two decades—not written about, is now being increasingly reported in the news media.

"Culture" is the coinage used to express and claim minority rights, and it is backed by hard sanctions. Physical force, or the threat of such, may not be necessary to compel compliance. A little word, just six letters long, does the job just as effectively: "Racist!" Nor need the word be spoken. It hangs like a specter in the air, palpable if invisible, and frightens people into accepting acts that they deeply deplore and that may strike at children like Aisha.

Why were the child authorities so reluctant to heed Aisha's pleas for help? It was not from lack of humanitarian concern or from lack of commitment to the basic tenets of "the rights of the child" or the equality of the sexes. I have spoken with some of the persons concerned, not about Aisha for that was too painful for them to discuss, but about other cases like hers, and I am convinced of their deep moral engagement. I venture the interpretation—based on talks with these officials as well as other professionals (child care workers, teachers, social workers, etc.)—that the one abiding fear that keeps many well-meaning and deeply caring persons from intervening on behalf of the child is the fear of being called a racist.

"Racist" has become a "deadly word"—to borrow a metaphor from Favret-Saada (1980). It pierces the heart of the well-meaning Scandinavian, whose cherished identity is that of world champion of all that is kind and good. Norway, the richest of the Scandinavian nations, is the most generous dispenser of aid to the developing world (measured per capita), and its humanitarian organizations have a long and venerable history. These are just some of the indices of an ethos that places a very high value on kindness, goodness, and charity. Add that belief in the equality of all human beings, irrespective of gender, age, and other factors, undergirds Scandinavian societies, and it is the more understandable why "racist" would strike so hard.[5]

But there is a price to be paid for such high morality, and it is paid neither by those who pride themselves on supreme tolerance toward immigrants, professed as "respect for their culture," nor by those who cry "racist" to claim or enforce such respect. It is Aisha and others like her—persons in a weak bargaining position—who pay the price of the cultural politics played out in Norwegian everyday life. Such politics proceed as if society consisted of a majority pitted against a minority, with racism and discrimination a property of the majority only. But this is a gross misrepresentation with dire consequences for individual lives. First, "the minority" consists of numerous ethnic groups with their own axes to grind, with respect both to one another and to the majority. Second, there are minorities within minorities, persons like Aisha or Noreen, or Sara, of whom we will hear later—who, even in their own ethnic group, are not regarded as persons in their own right. The question, Who pays the price (of being doubly disadvantaged) and what is the cost? is rarely asked. And so Aisha's pain and the pain of numerous others translate into the language of "respect." But for what? Sacrifices on the altar of culture are made time and again, every day, openly and in concealed ways. But when state institutions that are there to protect and promote the welfare of *all* members of society buy into this rhetoric of respect, it is time to call out. That is why I have chosen to foreground Aisha's case.

Cultural politics sealed the fate of this fourteen-year-old who was not allowed to be what she felt she was—a person in her own right. She was defined by her roots, or rather those of her parents, as belonging to a particular ethnic group and predestined to perpetuate its traditions. How she herself felt about thus being pigeonholed was not a relevant issue for those who determined her fate. Rather, the decision to bring her back to her biological family was predicated on the premise of "right" and "wrong" identities. Her foster family was of the wrong kind. It belonged not to her parents' ethnic minority but to the majority of Norwegians—with which, by all the evidence, Aisha herself identified.

But such was not her right. By aligning herself with "the majority," the girl transgressed the limits of propriety and property. She breached a boundary held in place by the "best-interest doctrine" embraced by a collusion of powers—parents and representatives of the state. Not just in Norway, but other places as well, social workers have been found in some instances to come down squarely on the side of the "national interest," thereby sacrificing individual lives and welfare.[6] This is the more likely to happen when an ideology of communal welfare celebrating the sanctity of the ethnic group or other collectivity supersedes concern for the individual. As Alain Finkielkraut notes, "It takes very little to reduce individual identity to collective identity, to imprison people in their group of origin, without ever calling on the laws of heredity" (1995:90).

So it was with Aisha. "Culture" did the trick. And it was "culture" that sealed her fate, making a mockery of her human rights, her citizenship, and basic human liberty.

Aisha had to step back in line and "put her uniform on."[7] What next happened we need not rehearse. Perhaps if she had been placed with a foster family of the "right" ethnic kind, she might have been spared her final outcome. But by placing her with a Norwegian family—for want of finding someone from her parents' ethnic minority—the child authorities laid themselves open to accusations of racism. Concerned to set the record straight, they were relieved when Aisha's parents requested to have their daughter back and promised to treat her well. Aisha's own desperate protests and the warnings by her teachers that a forced marriage probably was in store for her (a cousin had warned her) were brushed aside as unwarranted suspicions. Did the child authorities not know that forced marriage is a common sanction against youth, especially girls, of Asian or African descent who reject, or at least rebel against, their parents' culture? Were they perhaps reluctant to think such bad thoughts of people who, in other contexts, bear the brunt of racism in Norway? Did they perhaps fear that they might be racist themselves if they had listened to the warnings?

I ask these questions because child welfare workers with whom I have talked consistently report that they are unable to offer the same protection to children of immigrant background as to other Norwegian children. Worse, they are aware of accepting acts of mistreatment of children of immigrants that they would not dream of tolerating with regard to "Norwegian" children. This lands them in a deep moral dilemma. Equality, irrespective of race or ethnic background, is sacrificed on the altar of culture. Children's rights and welfare are sacrificed on the altar of culture. Citizenship is sacrificed in all but a nominal sense. And the losers are primarily females. Let a comparison between Aisha and her father illustrate.

The tragedy of her fate—and his good fortune—came about in part because she misjudged her time and place, whereas his assessment of his prospects was perfect. He came to Norway as a man, an adult, subject to no one's bidding. He had freedom of movement; he was physically strong. He knew that Norway, like many other West European nations, was obliged to offer social welfare to anyone who resided in the country, whether a citizen or not. What mattered was to gain access; once that was achieved, the rest would take care of itself. Not a Norwegian in any sense of the term for his first ten years in the country, Aisha's father was nonetheless treated *as if he were a citizen with full citizen's rights,* denied only the right to vote at national elections.[8] For the rest of his life he can continue to reap the fruits of membership in an affluent welfare state, without being required to make any contribution.

Aisha might be thought to have had a better point of departure. She was born in the right place. But she was born in the wrong body—she was a girl. Now if she had been a regular Norwegian, that would have been no great detriment. Norwegians have an enviable record for gender equality. As a Norwegian citizen, born and bred in Norway, Aisha may have thought the authorities would stand by her when her rights as an equal human being were violated. But she was wrong. For she was only an *as-if* citizen. Unlike other Norwegian girls who would be protected by both law and custom from a forced marriage, she was protected by the law only. And above the law in many cases looms custom or culture, if not in name, then certainly in practice.

Culture is a way of distributing pain unequally in populations, observes Veena Das (1990). Her words deserve to be heeded. Membership in society has its price, but the price is unevenly distributed. Those with the power to decide what is to count, and for what, will usually define custom or culture in such a way that it serves their own interests. The result may even be "a moral economy of systematic injustice," as Arthur Kleinman warns (1998). But if this is the case, then respect for "the culture" is a flawed moral principle. It is necessary to ask, What does that which I am now respecting do for the welfare of the weaker members of the group? Such questions are necessary to prevent sacrifices on the altar of culture—performed in the name of charity.

THE NEW NORWAY | II

Norway is a country of four and a half million people, spread over a distance from north to south the same as that from London to Sicily, or Maine to Florida. The coastline is so jagged that if it were stretched out, it would reach halfway around the Equator. And the distance from the North Cape to the southern tip of Norway is as great as that from the southern tip down to Rome. The land is long and plentiful, with great expanses and empty spaces. It is also harsh and inhospitable in some ways, with long, dark winters, especially up north. The ruggedness of the landscape and the long distances also mean that people live, in many ways, in different worlds. The fisherman's wife in the far north and the businessman down south do not have much in common. Characteristic is the departing remark of an au pair from the north who had served with a family in the capital: she said she was so happy to be going home again "where the people are normal!"[1]

A lack of "normality" was also what I found when I first came to Oslo as a student in 1965.[2] "Down south" was a different country with foreign mores and a rather condescending attitude to northerners. So I moved as soon as my studies permitted to Bergen, in the west—a town also down south but on the coast. With a long history of trade and communication with the north, mainly by sea, the people of Bergen were much more like us. And I understood why my grandmother had thrived when she worked in Bergen as a housemaid in her youth. The Bergen people and "we" resembled each other; we spoke "the same language," if entirely different dialects; and we were equal, and regarded each other as such. At the time of my studies in Oslo, it was not unusual for ads for rental apartments to include the wording "Not for northern Norwegians."

This is to say that the common notion of Norway as a highly homogeneous country is an overstatement, to put it mildly. Norway is and has always been culturally complex and variegated, for cultural pluralism is not just a matter of differences in ethnicity and religion—though Norway had its share of that too. It also pertains to region, rank, class, gender, age, and more. Hence, what is new in Norway is not cultural pluralism as such but the particular form it takes: the ethnic and religious complexity that marks present-day Norway is a new fact of life that poses its own challenges.

The new Norway is home to people of least 158 different nationalities; this number has been reported for Oslo, the capital. Oslo, a city of only 500,000 people, thus equals New York City in the degree of complexity shown. In Oslo, as in Miami or Los Angeles, about one in every three children in primary school speaks a foreign language as his or her mother tongue.[3] And the proportion is steadily growing.[4] The number of languages now spoken in Oslo exceeds one hundred, and it is not uncommon to find thirty or forty different mother tongues represented in a single school.

A graphic illustration of the situation in another Scandinavian country was furnished by a young German I met who recalled (with a twinkle in his eye) how he used to travel to Sweden in summer to meet blond Swedish girls. But now they are becoming rare, a vanishing species. He had a point. With one in every five Swedes now being of immigrant background, and one in seven of non-Western origin, blond girls will indeed be on the decline—in Sweden as in other Scandinavian countries. Nevertheless, as Astrid Suhrke has observed,

> A striking feature of the immigration debate in contemporary Europe is the vehemence with which governments and citizens deny that their states, in contrast to the USA, Canada, and Australia, are immigration countries. Yet this is evidently a case where "the lady doth protest too much." In fact, Europe west of Russia and the Ukraine now has about the same proportion of foreign-born persons as the United States and Canada together. (1996:vii)

With 158 different nationalities represented in Oslo alone, what then is the ethnic makeup of Norway today? Nobody knows, for ethnicity is not a matter of hard facts. It pertains to people's self-identification and identification by others, as cultural markers are seized upon and made relevant in interaction (Barth 1998). What counts as an ethnic label in one context—Pakistani, for example—may be broken down in other contexts; Pashtuns, Punjabis,

Baluchis, Gujeratis, and Sindhis, for example, distinguish themselves as different *kinds* of Pakistanis. What we can say with certainty, however, is that the ethnic complexity of present-day Norway vastly surpasses the range of nationalities reported. Present-day Norway is thus markedly different from the way it was until the mid- to late 1960s, when only five ethnic minorities were recognized—Tinkers, Tater (Gypsies), Jews, Kvæns (Finnish speakers), and Sami. The Sami (formerly known as Lapps) are an indigenous population of fishermen and reindeer herders living mainly in the north and speaking a Finno-Ugric language.

The new immigrants started arriving in the late 1960s. In Norway, unlike Germany or France, for example, there was no institutionalized effort either by government or by private agencies to recruit guest workers for cheap manual labor. Rather, immigration seems to have been initiated from abroad, primarily from Pakistan, as people looked for new prospects in the West (Storhaug 2000).[5] We need not here go into the flows and mechanisms— the push-and-pull factors—that spiraled immigration once it had started,[6] since these have been well documented in a number of works on Western Europe (e.g., Harris 1995; Lewis 1994; Rogers 1985). What concerns us here is the present situation and the political maneuvers by the government and other key actors, immigrants included, to deal with the challenges posed.

The present naturally has its history, which needs to be understood for an appreciation of the situation. But to deal practically with the problem of creating "a society worth living in" requires another approach—a sharp focus on the predicaments and life situation of people differently positioned within the larger society, a "history according to winners and losers" (Scott 1985).

That's why Aisha's case interests us. She provides a fleck of a history not often told in the story of the new immigration, whether to Europe or the United States. The usual story has able-bodied *men* in the key roles. Also, when the focus is on families, their fate is thought to depend on the career and life situation of the male head of the family. Little do we hear of children, especially girls, and how they cope with the immigrant experience, for research on the so-called second generation is sorely lacking. A few studies and first-person narratives, however, suggest that migration to the West may not be an unmitigated blessing for the children who, in many cases, lose more than they gain (Heide-Jørgensen 1996; Kumar 1997). On the basis of extensive studies in the United States, Carola Suárez-Orozco (2000) observes that "the pressures of migration are profoundly felt by the children of immigrants."

Such testimonies are important to counter a notion, common among Western liberals, that it is good per se to be an immigrant, if you consider the alternative—living in a Third World country. But what do we actually know of children's and women's experiences? Where are the Aishas in the vast literature on immigration? And where are the likes of Fatima, her mother? Of immigrant mothers in Norway, for example, we know little except that a great many, perhaps most, never learn to speak Norwegian however long they live in the country and that many suffer from a variety of ailments connected with seclusion, isolation, and a feeling of loss of respect from their children, whose lives are lived in a different world, of which the mother understands little.[7]

The usual immigration story also has a majority pitted against a minority or even minorities pitted against one another; it has culture against culture or even contestations within cultures.[8] But it seldom explores what "a culture" is at the practical policy level, or how official policies and practices at the institutional level interact with everyday politics at the micro level to produce winners and losers. So Aisha's case is relevant also for the writing of history.

She belonged to an ethnic group—or her parents do—that entered upon the Norwegian scene in the early 1970s. They came in what is known as a chain migration: early labor migrants sent word and helped finance the journey and entry of kinsmen and close friends. At the beginning of the twenty-first century, this group, including the second generation, counts about 5,000 people, most of them living in Oslo. According to a 1991 study, more than 70 percent of men aged fifty to fifty-four in this group lived on disability pensions (Grünfeld and Noreik 1991). This is partly explained by the costs incurred in hard, double-shift, physical work that many of them did at the beginning of their stay in Norway, and partly by the high unemployment rate for non-Western immigrants even at a time when unemployment for Norwegians is declining (it reached a low of 2.4 percent in 1999). But that is not all. The ethnic group to which Aisha's father belongs has a poor employment record by comparison with many other ethnic minorities.

The great majority of immigrants to Norway, as to most of Western Europe, came from the Middle East, North Africa, and South Asia. They are Muslim, an identity they underscore.[9] In Norway, Pakistanis constitute the single largest national minority, whereas Turks predominate in Denmark and Germany, Iranians and Kurds in Sweden, and Algerians in France. With approximately nine thousand Norwegian-born children, the Pakistani minority now totals about twenty-six thousand, most of them settled in Oslo. Until recently the Vietnamese were the second-largest minority with nearly fifteen thousand, of whom almost four thousand were Norwegian-born. They have now been superseded by Bosnians. Next in line follow Kosovo Albanians, Yugoslavs, Tamils, Turks, Iranians, Moroccans, Chileans, Polish, Somalis, Indians, and Iraqis (Bjertnæs 2000:15, 20).

Of Western immigrants to Norway, Danes and Swedes make up the largest proportion. But they present no problem. "The problem" is connected with Third World immigrants, of which Aisha and her family present an especially difficult case. Most immigrants manage better than they, and some do extremely well.

Why, then, focus on the difficulties? My answer is simple. A society worth living in is not one in which a disproportionate number of immigrants fall way behind the host population with regard to standard of living or quality of life, or both; it is not one in which the rights of the child and gender equality apply mainly to the majority population; nor is it one in which the emergence of an ethnic underclass is acceptable. Facts presented in the next chapter will show Norway grappling with a multiethnic situation that is grave in terms of the prospects offered for equality and dignity to all citizens, even when material circumstances may be exceptionally benevolent. This is not just a Norwegian phenomenon; it is a problem in all of Western Europe.

True, Aisha's family is extreme in some respects. But the plethora of problems they faced is unfortunately not uncommon. Many families struggle with some of the same problems, or with other problems of an equally grave character. In short, being an immigrant in Norway—or the child of immigrants—is a precarious existence. Some win. But many fall by the wayside.

Tabulating the number of immigrants in Norway relative to the population at large depends on how "immigrant" is defined—and also on how reliable the measures are. Indeed, failure to specify what is meant by "immigrant" is a weakness of many studies, making comparison across countries or societies difficult.

In Norway, an immigrant is defined as a person with two foreign-born parents. By this criterion, there were about 244,700 immigrants in Norway in 1998, making up about 5.5 percent of the population (Bjertnæs 2000). But almost one in ten Norwegians (9.8 percent of the population) had a foreign background, either being born abroad or having one foreign-born parent. This proportion is low compared to that in Sweden, about 20 percent of whose inhabitants were of immigrant background in 1996 (SOU 1996:55). Of those, 11 percent were of non-Western background, compared to only 3.5

percent in Norway, reflecting Sweden's more liberal policies with regard to refugees. But the tables are turning. And if the figures for Norway seem low, appearances are deceptive. Suhrke shows that "Norway has an immigration rate which belies its self-image as a country of overwhelmingly home-grown citizens. The gross immigration rate in Norway in the early 1990s was about 0.3 per cent per capita (excluding asylum seekers), or equivalent to the per capita rate of the principal immigration country in the modern world, i.e. the United States" (1996:vii). Moreover, Norway has been experiencing the most rapid increase in political asylum seekers of any European nation; from 1997 to 1998 it rose by 308 percent, compared to 200 percent in Italy, the second highest. Sweden and Denmark, by contrast, experienced an increase of only 45 percent and 0.8 percent respectively (*Aftenposten*, December 17, 1998). We shall come back to the question of what accounted for Norway's unequaled popularity during this period.

As we have seen, an "immigrant" in Norway is defined as a person with two foreign-born parents; this is the definition used for general statistical purposes. This means that a person who has never immigrated but was born in Norway of foreign-born parents is still defined as an immigrant. The government has recently tried to undo the unfortunate implications of this practice by suggesting that the term be used only for persons who have themselves immigrated, whether they are children or adults. Under such a definition, Aisha would not be considered an immigrant.

Official definitions are matters of politics, and the definition of immigrant is no exception. Reducing the number of immigrants by a definitorial sleight of hand serves the government's interests in a situation of considerable public resentment against the new immigration. This is true of Norway, as of the United States, Canada, Australia, and many other countries.[10] Yet I welcome the move. It is in line with what I have argued publicly and repeatedly, that any child born in Norway has the right to be considered just that: a nonimmigrant. The government's suggested usage would grant this right, but it also raises problems that could backfire in terms of children's welfare.

If children of immigrants are not statistically marked, it will be impossible to follow their life trajectories and study how they fare through time. Effectuating measures to help them cope and attain equality with other Norwegians may thereby become more difficult.[11] The writing is already on the wall: precautionary measures are needed. On the other hand, singling out children with *two* foreign-born parents as "immigrant," while including those with *one* foreign-born parent as "nonimmigrant," is also problematic.[12] Excluded thereby are numerous children with *one* foreign-born parent whose life situation and needs may be very similar: these are children living in ghetto-like environments and having one parent who is a newly arrived immigrant. They may be as marginalized and struggle with the same kinds of problems as do many of those with two foreign-born parents.[13] A note on marriage patterns is in order here.

Marriage establishment in Norway, as in much of Western Europe, follows a characteristic pattern: the great majority of immigrants marry an imported spouse (as did Aisha's father). This practice pertains not just to the first but also to the second generation, in marked contrast to the United States. We will return later to what the pattern portends. Suffice it here to note that with each new parental generation there will be a re-creation or reinforcement of tradition.

Recognizing that "immigrant" is an unfortunate term in many respects, efforts have been made to replace it with more appropriate labels that would not be stigmatizing but would be respectful of the person's special standing: "distant-cultural" (*fjernkulturell*) and "foreign-cultural" (*fremmedkulturell*) are used of persons with non-Western background, whereas "minority-lingual" (*minoritetsspråklig*) refers to anyone with a foreign mother tongue. The former two terms, however, perpetuate the very problems they sought to avoid, as is evident from the following example.

In 1998 the respected newspaper *Aftenposten* reported the good news that new recruits to the police college included nine foreign-cultural students—this after years of efforts to attract such recruits. The report was denounced by three of the "foreign-cultural" students, who were as Norwegian as anyone else: they had been adopted as babies from the Far East and never known anything but Norwegian culture. What distinguished them was simply their foreign looks. Here "culture" is confounded with "race," and a child is taken to be an "immigrant" simply because he or she looks different from the natives.[14] It was this same logic that worked against Aisha. Years of exposure to Norwegian society counted for naught as she was ordered to join the ranks of her like-looking though not like-minded parents, whose life styles were light years away from hers.

With increasing recognition of the detriment done to children and others by labeling them in ways that deny them their individuality and hence their ability to grow and change, official institutions now tend to use the more neutral "minority-lingual" instead. It is meant as a term of respect and makes no claims regarding a person's cultural identity except to say that his or her mother tongue is not Norwegian.[15]

Ironically, the term used by many youngsters to refer to themselves is one that subverts these efforts at incorporation and reinstates the categorical divide; *utlending*, "foreigner," is their term (Blom 1998; Mikaelsen 1998). Thus they mark their position as marginal, making a claim to authenticity while leaving the question of "culture" unspoken. Others use hyphenated identities—for example, Norwegian-Pakistani—or, depending on context, call themselves either Pakistani or Norwegian. And many others feel like the girl who said, "It's not that I am Pakistani or Norwegian, I just want to be myself."

Most of the immigrants in Norway, as in Europe generally or in the United States, settle in the capital or in a few other large cities. Oslo, with half a million people, has only 11 percent of the national population but 35 percent of all immigrants.[16] In 1999, immigrants accounted for 17 percent of the city's population; almost 50 percent of all non-Western immigrants lived in Oslo. The degree of concentration differs, however, with Vietnamese, Bosnians, and Tamils, who are spread throughout the country, whereas people from Africa, the Middle East, and South Asia tend to congregate in the capital and its environs.[17] As Brox (1998:103) observes, there is a "glaring contrast between the officially formulated decentralisation goals and the seemingly 'spontaneous' tendency of immigrants to form urban concentrations." Because these concentrations are not random but occur in lower-middle-class areas that are becoming more and more "ethnic" as immigrants move in and native Norwegians move out, a ghetto-like situation results (which will be dealt with in more detail later).[18]

Aisha's family was an exception to the rule: they lived in an upper-middle-class part of the capital; their rent was paid by the municipality. The great majority of immigrants in Oslo make do with much more modest circumstance, living in relatively modest housing in the inner city or lower-middle-class suburbs. This physical congregation has implications for identity politics as well as for language learning and the immigrants' prospects of integration in the wider society.[19]

As previously noted, about one-third of the children in primary school are now of immigrant background. But their distribution is uneven. In some districts of the city (according to a 1998 survey), 80 percent of the children aged five to nineteen are of non-Western background.[20] In some primary schools, such children constitute 95 percent of the students. The principal of one such school estimated that 50 percent of the children hardly spoke a word of Norwegian when they began school, though they had been born and raised in Norway.[21] This very poor knowledge of Norwegian is a cause of grave concern, not only for society in general but also to many of the parents.

Clearly, then, Oslo has a "ghetto" problem that concerns the public and politicians alike. For although the term "ghetto" is unjustified if strictly defined as "an urban slum where one ethnic minority is the majority"—the largest ethnic group, Pakistanis, does not comprise more than 30 percent of the population in any one district (Blom 1997:45)—still, the complex of problems associated with "ghetto" in popular usage is rampant in some parts of Oslo, as well as in Drammen, a neighboring town.[22] And the "problem" is growing. The state has tried to restrict the influx of immigrants to the capital by a steered use of public welfare, but the policy has been unsuccessful. Oslo continues to receive most of the non-Western immigrants and the proportion is steadily increasing.[23] Thus there is reason to be particularly concerned with developments in Oslo.

Norway instituted a halt to immigration (the "immigration stop") in 1975, shortly after similar moves by Germany, France, and some other European nations. Yet a 1995 study found that 67 percent of all immigrants in Oslo had arrived since 1985; 23.7 percent were children born in Norway to immigrant parents; and only 9.3 percent had arrived before the "immigration stop" (Djuve and Hagen 1995).[24] Norway shares with other European countries the experience that the immigration stop did not halt the influx of immigrants. What it did was change the face of immigration, not its substance. Brochmann (1996:27) comments: "European immigration policies since the early 70s have been based on the assumption that it is possible to put an effective halt to immigration. In fact, the 'stop policy' has *not* been a success in any of the countries in question, and several *unforeseen consequences* have appeared."

Among such consequences is the diversion of would-be immigrants from the labor migrant circuit to the political asylum–seeker circuit, much more expensive for the host countries. Immigrants needed to find new ways when they could not come as migrant laborers; family reunification, political asylum, residence on humanitarian grounds, and the like provided some outlets, or rather inlets, for people who are now, as then, economic refugees in many cases—though many are also real political refugees. Freeman (1994:28) makes the point:

Contemporary discussion of immigration in Europe is dominated by questions of political asylum . . . Since 1989, hundreds of thousands of persons have sought asylum in Western Europe but also in the United States, Canada, and Australia. By any fair assessment, the great majority of these persons, however desperate their plight, are economic rather than 'convention' refugees.

Brochmann (1996:30–32) concurs:

> The possibilities of entry as an asylum seeker have made the "stop" policies less than effective, in turn obscuring the traditional distinction between the "economic" migrant and the "political" migrant/refugee. Information flows to areas that are "producing" asylum seekers tell that four out of five of these migrants manage to stay in Europe even though they have been refused status as refugees.
>
> The point is that the different streams of migrants are connected and influence the actions and movements of one another. After the door was closed for *labour* migrants in the early 1970s, the only *legal* entry was through the asylum path and arrangements for family reunion . . . Presumed control of one gateway may consequently divert the flow into a new track.

This takes us back to a puzzle left unanswered: What accounts for the dramatic increase of political asylum seekers to Norway during 1997–98, compared with other European nations? At first glance, Norway might seem to have many disadvantages. It is located at the northernmost tip of Europe; it is a cold country (in more than one respect, many would say) and less cosmopolitan than Sweden or Denmark. Geographic position alone should be enough to disqualify Norway as an asylum seeker's preference: by European conventions, persons seeking political asylum must do so in the country in which they first set foot. And from most places it is impossible to get to Norway without making a stop somewhere else. There are no direct flights from Asia and North Africa. Traveling by land or sea, as most political asylum seekers do today, is even worse: Norway is at the end of the line (except for Russians and a few others). So why go to all that trouble of trying to get there?

Political asylum seekers are pragmatic, like most people. Norway may not be their preference in absolute terms; given a free choice, most would probably head for the United States or Canada.[25] But Norway is a good alternative: it is *accessible* in ways that other Scandinavian nations have not been recently. Making it to Norway can also be a stepping stone in a further migratory career that will eventually take them to where they want to be—if all goes well.[26]

Of signal importance was the announcement by a Christian Democratic coalition government, on assuming power in October 1998, that it would pursue a more humanitarian immigrant policy than the previous Labor government had done. Instantly, the news spread through the grapevine, and the number of political asylum seekers multiplied.[27] There are also economic advantages to making it to Norway. Even if asylum is not granted, the chances are that the seeker will return to the home country considerably better off than when he or she left it, thanks to the benefits received during the time it takes (years in some cases) to have an application reviewed.[28] I know "failed" asylum seekers who have been celebrated like heroes on returning to their families; and some try again, under new identities. But the hope is of course that they will be allowed to stay and shape a new life in the West.

To maximize their chances of staying, many political asylum seekers take care to disguise their route of travel: they rid themselves of all travel documents before presenting themselves at a police station in Norway. Almost none arrive by air, lest their place of origin or transit be known. In 1998, about 90 percent of asylum seekers in Oslo arrived without any identification. Disguising one's identity is a strategy designed to prevent deportation from the country in which asylum is being sought, for if asylum is refused, residence on humanitarian grounds will have to be granted. It was such prevarications that led Fuglerud, who has done extensive research on Tamils, to conclude that "increasingly, migrating has now become not just a passage from one place to another, but a consciously planned act of subversion" (1999:59).

In 1998, most political asylum seekers to Norway came from Somalia; in 1999, most were Kurds from Iraq. Tellingly, the number of Iraqi refugees to Europe as a whole has been stable over the past three years, whereas Norway has had an increase of 1,300 percent. The Danish police has issued a cry of alarm. "Laughs at Norway" is the headline of a newspaper article based on an interview with a Danish chief of police (*Verdens Gang*, February 22, 2000). But "the laughter is mixed with concern. For Norway's benevolent asylum policy leads to major pressure on neighboring countries as well." The police chief complains, "We have turned into a kind of a hotel for Kurds on the way to Norway." The critical difference that marks Norway as an asylum seeker's dream in this case is that Norway offers the prospect of permanent residence and family reunification, whereas Sweden and Denmark grant only temporary residence and do not offer family reunification. But one nation's leniency may become another's nightmare, which is why Norway may eventually be forced by the European Union to modify its policies. Besides, internal pressure is building up as the Norwegian government is becoming increasingly aware of the adverse consequences of its own intended charity. Agents who smuggle refugees into the country earn exorbitant sums;[29] and a large number of refugees are operating with false identities or refusing to offer any identification to maximize their chances of staying in Norway.[30] The general benevolence of the government is beginning to wear thin.[31]

Aisha's father was fortunate; he could arrive simply and easily as a labor migrant, though he proved incapable of holding onto a job. He could cross borders openly, present himself at the passport control with an official visa, and apply for residence. He did not have to mask his identity or throw away his passport and travel documents to deceive state officials or even countrymen whom he could not trust.[32] He was bona fide, in contrast to many who are equally needy or eager to get to the West but must make use of subterfuge at an exorbitant price. So, too, most of his countrymen in Norway have found an easy way in. Most of them originate from the same city in their homeland, and most are doing well: the savings they make from work or as welfare clients they have invested in buildings or businesses back home. But when they now want to extend their connections "back home," or help kinsmen get to Norway, family reunification is the means. And it is in this perspective that the marriage patterns of the younger generation—their children—must be seen. Marriage provides a visa for would-be immigrants who cannot claim political asylum status or can do so only with great difficulty. Men from the homeland of Aisha's father who would try must attempt to pass as residents of another, politically turbulent country. Family reunification is easier. If Aisha plays her family's game, she can help bring in a new immigrant when she turns eighteen. All she need do is to present him as her spouse, and he is automatically granted entry. As Portes and Rumbaut observe, "governmental attempts at reversing well-established immigrant flows do not generally have the intended effect because of the resistance of dense social networks linking places of origin and destination" (1996).

Amersfoort and Penninx (1994:141ff), writing from the Netherlands, concur: Once under way, migration movements achieve their own momentum. The migrant population already settled exerts a great deal of influence on the subsequent development process. The scope for regulating secondary migration is therefore very limited, due to the fact that family unification and family formation have become vested rights.

This then is the situation: Norway now has a multiethnic population of more than 150 different nationalities, most of them congregated in the capital, where one out of three children in primary school is of immigrant background. The number is steadily rising. How do these immigrants and their children fare? What does Norway do to accommodate its new populace in ways that cater to their dignity, equality, and welfare? This is the key question of this book. Let us look at the facts.

5   *Dangerous Facts: What We Were Not Supposed to Know*

Until the fall of 1995, not much was known about the situation of immigrants in Norway. Such knowledge was considered dangerous; knowing the facts might trigger racist responses in the Norwegian population—or so it was presumed. What the politicians themselves really knew about the situation is not clear. But my understanding is that they too—and not just the public—were relatively ignorant regarding the factual situation of Norway's new inhabitants from the Third World. The cover-up meant that no one really knew much. Newspapers, for example, were expressly forbidden to mention a person's ethnic or immigrant background in reports on criminal cases lest a bad image be projected.

Typical of the times was the reaction against the head of the Norwegian immigration bureau (*Innvandrerdirektoratet*) when, in 1990, he went public with the results of a study of employment and the use of social welfare among refugees in Trondheim, Norway's third largest city. Although the aim of the study—unique for its time—was to discover how refugees fared in the long run and what their prospects were for employment and self-help within the existing system, the reactions of the news media and the intelligentsia toward the director were so fierce as to compel him to resign.

What did the study show? An unemployment rate of 52 percent for refugees who had been in the country for five years or more. But even those who were working could not support themselves in most cases: 90 percent of all refugees in Trondheim received some form of social welfare, with dramatic effects on the city's budget. Constituting only 1 percent of Trondheim's population at the time, refugees consumed 27 percent of its social welfare benefits (*Dagbladet,* October 4, 1990).

Was Trondheim then a special case? The director of immigration thought not. The indications, he said, were that the situation in Oslo was similar. Posterity has proved him right.

The results of the Trondheim study might have been to mobilize the nation in a concerted effort to ameliorate the situation of refugees, so as to enhance their prospects for employment and thus for self-respect and social esteem. But such was not the case. Attention was diverted from the real issue to that of the moral standing of the director of immigration, who was accused of inviting racism by going public with the results. The real issue—how refugees fared through time and what could be done to improve their situation was forced underground for another five years.

Immigration debates at the time had one salient feature: they hovered around the question of how many more refugees Norway should admit (immigration proper having been halted) and not on the issue of people's welfare once in Norway. Conspicuously avoided was the question, what kind of life do we offer to those already here? Public debates proceeded as if all immigrants and refugees should consider themselves lucky just to *be* in Norway. It was as if human dignity, welfare, equality—all these essentials of a well-lived life—did not count in regard to immigrants; or else, as if they could be reduced to a matter of mere material support, along with freedom from political oppression and freedom of expression, which went as a matter of course. To me it seemed as if an underlying premise of the whole nondebate was a condescending view not just of life in the Third World but of the people coming from there; it was as if they were all presumed to be so poor and pitiful as to be content with anything Norway might choose to offer. In consequence, the moral standing of Norwegians could be judged in terms of their stance on the quota or "border question": how many more refugees would we accept—which is why the debate on potential newcomers came to take precedence over the fate of actual immigrants in the country.

As in Aisha's case, the deadly word "racist" loomed in the background or was explicitly spoken in every public debate. The protagonists were so eager to judge each other's moral standing as revealed by their stance on the border/quota question that it seemed to be forgotten that getting into Norway was not the only issue. But how do you discuss the fate of people about whom next to nothing is known and about whom you are not supposed to know much lest the facts (as it was presumed) prejudice a population susceptible to discrimination and racism?

I entered this debate one evening just before the municipal elections in September 1995. To grill the leaders of the seven political parties on the issue of "immigrants," two of Norway's leading television reporters had got them together and lined them up for a two-hour debate. And most Norwegians probably settled down to watch the spectacle.[33] Two guests were invited to present views or pose questions from the audience. One was a man originally from Bosnia, Mladen Citanović, who had lived in Norway for twenty years and presented himself emphatically as Norwegian, not Bosnian. I was the other, invited because I had a book on immigration coming out that had just made headlines in a major newspaper. We were told we would each be given two minutes to speak at an unspecified moment—which meant that we could not prepare.[34] We had to play it by ear.

My fellow Norwegian, formerly Bosnian, had nonetheless prepared his lines. He had one burning question for the politicians, and he was not going to lose his chance. "Why is it that if a Norwegian won't let his daughter marry an immigrant, it's called racism, but if an immigrant won't let his daughter marry a Norwegian, it's called culture?" he asked. The politicians were speechless, at a loss for a response, so that he turned to me afterward and asked, "Do you think they didn't understand my question?" We agreed that they probably *had* understood, but did not know what to say because the matter he raised was too dangerous to consider.

I was luckier; my intercession did elicit a response, perhaps because it was easier to deal with. We were halfway into the debate, and the seven party leaders had done little more than accuse one another of being more or less racist (as revealed by their respective stances on the "border/quota question") when I was given the floor. I said I was dismayed at hearing them sing the same old tune when there was an urgent issue to consider—the welfare of immigrants *once in Norway*. When would they come to that? Stop telling the public, I urged them, that immigrants have a *claim* to respect, and ask yourselves instead what Norway is doing, what *you* are doing, to provide immigrants with opportunities to *earn* respect—for themselves and from others. Are we able to offer a decent and dignified life to the people—or just welfare colonialism? What does the record show? And I listed some of the facts I knew that indicated that Norway was about to develop an ethnic underclass—a marginalized, socially deprived, and partly stigmatized group of easily identifiable citizens. I used the word "underclass" on purpose, knowing full well that it was unspeakable at the time in a country where social equality is a national slogan.

It was like dropping a bomb: The politicians scrambled not so much for their defense as for a point of view that would address the matter. For the next hour this uncomfortable question was the focus of the debate and thus aired nationwide:[35] What kind of life do we offer our new countrymen and -women? An answer, of course, requires hard facts. And thus raising the matter of the welfare of immigrants is a way of pressing for an assessment of facts that could possibly backfire by stirring anti-immigrant responses in the population at large. On the other hand, who will pay the price of concealment? How can we fashion effective policies to deal with the issue if the facts of the case are not known?

All is not well in the "happy country" as the French newspaper *Le Monde* dubbed Norway in 1996. Let us look at what we now know about the situation of immigrants and refugees in Norway. Because most of the new immigrants come in the capacity of refugees (a term inclusive of political asylum seekers), or as relatives on the family reunification scheme, I begin with what is known of refugees. I then proceed to consider the situation of non-Western immigrants in general. Unless referring specifically to refugees, I use the word "immigrant" to refer to both immigrants and refugees—in accordance with common usage. We should keep in mind that the majority of immigrants in Oslo are recent arrivals, only about 9 percent having arrived before the "immigration stop" of 1975.

Norway pursues a policy of decentralization in regard to refugees that is presumed to further their integration. Refugees are settled in municipalities throughout the country, which receive an integration bonus (*integreringstilskudd*)[36] for five years for that purpose. After five years the integration process is supposed to be completed.

Experience shows otherwise. Many, if not most, refugees end up in Oslo within four or five years after their settlement in Norway.[37] Is this because opportunities for work are better in Oslo? How do they manage the higher cost of living, especially for housing, in the capital? Let us look at some facts.

The unemployment rate among refugees in Oslo was 60 percent in 1995, even higher than the 52 percent found in the Trondheim study five years earlier that forced the director of immigration to resign. The Oslo rate was determined by a study of persons from six different ethnic groups with six to seven years' residence in Norway (Djuve and Hagen 1995).[38] The study was commissioned by the Labor city council in 1993 but kept secret until after the elections in 1995 because the findings (and perhaps the study itself) were too explosive, immigration being the central issue of the elections. The debate on the issue of the immigrants' welfare in Norway, launched in the media and in my book, published in October 1995, helped facilitate publication of the Oslo study in November 1995.[39] The study lent full support to the conclusions I had drawn on the basis of random evidence and inspired guesswork. The situation was indeed as grave as I had argued, in some respects even worse, warranting fully my use of the term "underclass" (which the authors themselves used) to call attention to the life situation of many immigrants in Norway.

What did the Oslo study show? Not just an unemployment rate of 60 percent for refugees with six to seven years' stay in Norway but also that 20 percent of those actually employed worked only part time; no more than 20 percent of the refugees had full-time jobs. Nor did the prospects of employment increase with the length of a person's stay in the country, as had been expected. The study showed that those who failed to find work during the first three to four years would most likely remain unemployed. The first few years were critical.

Likewise in Sweden. A study commissioned by the Swedish Department of Labor in 1995 found an unemployment rate of 81 percent for refugees with five years' residence in the country (SOU 1996:55). With its stronger economy and much lower unemployment, Norway should have done better.[40]

The Oslo study also investigated the use of social welfare benefits. More than 40 percent of the refugees depended on public assistance as against only 7 percent of Norwegians.[41] Moreover, 33 percent of refugees had social welfare as their main source of sustenance as against 3 percent of Norwegians; and, once on social welfare, they tended to remain there. For 41 percent of them, social assistance had become a permanent feature of life in Norway (Djuve and Hagen 1995:10–12).[42]

Other statistics corroborate these findings. Whereas non-Western immigrants make up 13 percent of Oslo's population, they consume 37 percent of the social welfare budget; and though the number of recipients has not risen over the past few years, their total consumption has increased dramatically because of large families. The same pertains to refugees nationwide. The use of social welfare *per person* rose 9 percent from 1995 to 1997—this at a time when the use of such assistance for Norwegians has been declining.[43]

But the finding of the Oslo study that alarmed me the most concerned the fate of children: Whereas only 4 percent of native Norwegian children lived in families where neither the father nor the mother was employed or undergoing education, 50 percent of refugee children did. In other words, *50 percent of the children of refugees lived in families where neither of the parents was at work or in school.* If children tend to inherit the life situation of parents, this augurs ill for their prospects in Norway.[44]

Ethnic minority status is not fate; it does not condemn an individual to an underclass position. But it can become fate unless auxiliary measures are undertaken to compensate people for handicaps, and opportunities are provided for them to develop and use their capacities. Self-help is to be encouraged but with a realistic view to the structural constraints people face in realizing their potential. Norway is doing poorly in these respects.

I have focused on unemployment among refugees in Oslo. What about the situation of immigrants, not just refugees, in general? At first glance, immigrants might seem to fare better. Unemployment among first-generation immigrants (including refugees) was down to 8.1 percent in 1997 as against 2.5 percent for the overall population. But when we look at non-Western immigrants in particular, the situation worsens. Africans had an unemployment rate of 15.8 percent and Asians 11.5 percent. East Europeans too fared badly, with 13 percent unemployed. Nor does the official figure encompass all those actually unemployed but only those who had registered as such at a municipal labor office. Also excluded are those engaged in some kind of temporary, makeshift work under the auspices of the municipality, which pays their wages to induce employers to take them on.

Oslo does not have the highest unemployment rate for immigrants in Norway. The situation in some counties in the far south is even worse. Immigrants in many areas do better, however, especially in the far north, where Tamils are employed in the fish industries and have an employment rate of nearly 100 percent.[45]

Not only do non-Western immigrants have an unemployment rate many times higher than native Norwegians; they are also, as noted above, much more likely to be living on disability pensions. A study of Pakistanis, Turks, and Moroccans found a rate three to five times higher than that for native Norwegians: "We can only conclude," note the authors, "that labor immigrants in the age group forty to fifty are increasingly pushed into the ranks of disability pensioners" (Grünfeld and Noreik 1991).[46]

In sum, immigrants and refugees fare badly with respect to employment in Norway. In the best case, Asians and Africans are five to six times more likely than native Norwegians to be unemployed; in the worst case, up to twenty times more likely—as was reported for refugees in Oslo in 1995. Thus Norway must be said to have failed to integrate immigrants in the labor market and to offer them the prospects for self-respect and social respect that follows from self-help and gainful employment.

The Norwegian situation bears comparison with what is occurring in some other European countries. In Denmark, in 1995, 35 percent of non-Western immigrants were unemployed, compared to 4.5 percent of native Danes (Haarder 1997:87). Turks, the largest ethnic minority, had an unemployment rate of 41 percent (Djuve 1999:20). In Denmark, as in Sweden, the integration of immigrants into the labor market has greatly deteriorated over the past few years (20–22). In Great Britain, in 1991, four times as many Pakistanis as whites were unemployed (28.8 percent versus 8.8 percent; Lewis 1994:22). In the Netherlands in 1995, 41 percent of Turks and 27 percent of Moroccans were registered as unemployed as against 6 percent of the Dutch. And this is only the tip of the iceberg, as the figures do not include all those who are not working and are receiving benefits under the Sickness Benefits Act or the Employment Disability Act (Eldering 1997:337).[47]

The European situation contrasts unfavorably with that in the United States. In 1990, the percentage of the foreign-born population in the United States that was in the labor force was nearly identical to that of the national average (Portes and Rumbaut 1996:66–67). "In the aggregate, native children and second-generation children are remarkably similar with respect to the labor force status of their household heads" (Jensen and Chitose 1996:98). A *New York Times* article points to part of the reason:

> [while] men in their prime working years are not faring much worse in Europe than in the United States . . . in America, which excels at absorbing new workers, other groups like the young, immigrants, and women are faring much better. Now the American economy is absorbing workers with the least education and the lowest skills. (May 19, 1999)

Other studies corroborate the picture of an emergent ethnic underclass. Let us look at education and Norwegian language proficiency.

Fifty percent of boys of immigrant background drop out of high school as against 30 percent of native Norwegian boys.[48] Girls manage far better; Aisha is a case in point. One study commissioned by the Ministry of Education found no difference in the school achievements of girls of immigrant versus native background, though the rate of enrollment for daughters of immigrants is much lower. This is in keeping with what has been found in other European countries. But, as with Aisha, the achievements of many of these girls do not count for much in the long run. The majority are married at a young age to an imported bridegroom. Secondary education is devalued by many of their parents, who believe a girl's marital chances may suffer if she is better educated than her prospective groom.[49] Modesty is also an issue. When a girl reaches puberty, many families fear for the threats to the family honor posed by her associating with boys outside the family.

Marriage by import also has grave consequences for the children's language learning. Because most children, even the grandchildren of immigrants, grow up with at least one parent who is a first-generation immigrant, many have next to no knowledge of Norwegian when they begin school. And even after nine years of elementary school, many have insufficient Norwegian to secure a job.

Among the dangerous facts still be to be uncovered is the Norwegian language proficiency of born and bred Norwegians of immigrant background who have been through the Norwegian primary school system. But the situation is alarming. The principal of one inner-city Oslo school estimated that 60 percent of minority-language children in his school graduated after nine years without a proper command of Norwegian. Another observed that some Norwegian-born ninth-grade students in his school needed mother-tongue translators in order to take their Norwegian oral examinations. "Everyday talk is okay, but a Turkish pupil who speaks fluent Norwegian can get by without understanding what's written in the textbooks" (*Verdens Gang*, August 30, 1997). That they are able to graduate at all may be in part because standards are lowered for them—unofficially, of course—as some teachers indicate. And not just in Norway. A Swedish boy, Mehmet, in a newspaper interview entitled "The School Betrays Us New Swedes," attests that he had the same grammar in ninth grade as he had in sixth grade. "We have never been given the chance to learn anything from it; never had any tests or any requirements" (*Sydsvenskan*, February 7, 1997). Anyone who wishes may still proceed to secondary school, but many teachers feel that students are being cheated. Many of the youngsters have such poor command of Norwegian that their comprehension suffers gravely; nor do they stand much chance of getting a job in due course.[50]

A recent study of higher education has revealed a disturbing fact: the proportion of children of immigrants—the second generation—in higher education declined by 5 percent during 1994–97. The decrease was especially high for second-generation males aged 19–24. During 1994–97, the rate of enrollment of both first- and second-generation immigrants declined, whereas it increased slightly for the population at large (Bjertnæs 2000: 32–33).

Many immigrant parents complain that the situation is deteriorating, that they themselves learned Norwegian better than their children who were born in Norway. One Turkish mother approached me in tears, complaining how her Norwegian-born daughter had learned Norwegian so poorly that she could have no future here. If things did not change, said the mother, she saw no choice but to move back to Turkey, since Turkish was the only language her Norwegian daughter had mastered. The mother had good reason for concern, for her daughter had been placed in a Turkish-only class, against the wishes of 92 percent of the parents whose children shared a similar fate. Although unusual, this case bespeaks a misguided humanism that undermines some children's prospects in Norway.[51]

Among the causes of the inferior education received by many immigrants are the growing segregation of immigrant communities and changing patterns of communication.[52] Wherever more and more immigrants move in, native Norwegians tend to move out.[53] Of particular concern to Norwegian parents is the academic quality of schools; hence some of those who value a "colorful community" while the children are small move away once education becomes "serious," that is, when their children enter fourth or fifth grade.[54]

In one case that caused a public stir, a mother felt compelled to use the media to draw attention to her daughter's plight: The daughter (of a Pakistani father) attended an inner-city school in which 60 percent of the students were of immigrant background. The problem was not the students but the fact that many of the teachers—themselves immigrants—did not know basic Norwegian, even though hired to teach general subjects. When the mother's appeal to the school authorities yielded no action, she felt compelled to move out of Oslo. Her case made headlines and caused public debates that were echoed in Parliament. A Norwegian child is debarred from learning Norwegian in a Norwegian school because the school authorities do not require teachers to know the language! How can this be? Norway has state public schools. What are the state's obligations toward this child? And what of children of non-Norwegian nationality whose future lies in Norway—should they not be able to learn the national language?

Native Norwegians are not the only ones to worry. A Pakistani father went so far as to declare in a public meeting: "My child is not *my* child, he is a Norwegian!" His was a desperate cry to alert the authorities to their neglect of children like his, "as-if" Norwegians, and to beg them to take responsibility. No one knows how large a proportion of children complete primary school as virtual illiterates, nor have the authorities dared to find out—so far. I have challenged them repeatedly in public, simply because we need the figures in order to compel the authorities to take action. Under the status quo, more and more children in Norway, be they citizens or not, graduate as second-rate citizens in terms of linguistic competence.

Deteriorating linguistic proficiency also mirrors changed patterns of communication. As several parents have pointed out to me, there was no satellite TV when they arrived in the country; all they had was one Norwegian state channel. Today, the choices are legion. Many youngsters have told me that their parents never watch Norwegian-language channels. Obviously this hampers the children's exposure to the language.

In sum, increased segregation of immigrant communities and changing patterns of communication contribute to making Norwegian harder to learn for the children and grandchildren of immigrants than it may have been for their forebears. Increased unemployment and marginalization also play a role. Add that Norwegian as a language has no international prestige or usefulness, and it becomes the clearer why, for people to have an incentive to learn it, there must be some "bonuses" built into the system. Under the status quo, these seem to be lacking to large extent.

The Norwegian situation highlights dilemmas and challenges facing small-language nations in the context of the new immigration. For a contrast, consider a study of Bradford, the British city with the highest proportion of non-Western immigrants. The study found that "there is an increasing number of local Muslims whose first language is English and who have only a smattering of Punjabi and Urdu" (Lewis 1994:183). Even in 1985–86, "most of the times, parents were at a loss to understand their children because they have given up speaking their mother tongue" (179). Likewise in Miami, the American city most heavily affected by recent immigration, "children of immigrants not only possess widespread competence in English but also demonstrate an unambiguous preference for it in everyday communication." Among Hispanic minorities, presumably the most resistant to abandoning their mother tongue, "the shift toward English is massive, with up to 96 percent of U.S.-born adults adopting it as their main or only language" (Portes and Schauffler 1996:28). This is a far cry from the situation in Scandinavia and other continental European nations.

So much for language. There are other alarming facts. Child custody cases are soaring among immigrants. In Oslo, where non-Western immigrants make up 13 percent of the population, they are concerned in 50 percent of child welfare cases. Violence against women is a related concern. In 1999, 69 percent of the women seeking refuge in shelters in Oslo were of immigrant background, a figure up from 50 percent in 1995. This need not mean that immigrant men are more violent than others. A lack of social networks that would enable women to seek help in trouble could be part of the problem; but that in itself is cause for concern.

Drug abuse is also becoming serious. Recent studies show an explosive increase among boys of immigrant background.[55] Moreover, drug abuse is not something immigrants bring with them from where they came. It is a Norwegian-developed affliction: a response to life in "the happy country." Aisha's eldest brother is an especially tragic case: he died from an overdose. Although it has long been known that immigrants and their descendants are disproportionately involved in the drug trade, the fact that drug abuse is also unusually high among them is a recent finding that adds to the picture of the troubled circumstance in which children of immigrants find themselves.[56]

Finally, there is violent crime. Developments over the past couple of years have impressed upon citizens, natives *and* immigrants, the need for urgent action to stem a frightening tide of violent crime involving youngsters of immigrant background as culprits. Whereas native Norwegians predominate with regard to theft and property crimes,[57] immigrants figure heavily in regard to violent crime. Recent statistics from Oslo show them to be involved in 70 percent of reported cases. Similar observations are made in Sweden. The chief inspector of police in Oslo, who had previously been careful *not* to draw attention to immigrants, has now sounded the alarm: the situation is grave, and concerted efforts are needed if it is not to get out of control. Boys as young as twelve operate in gangs and randomly attack young children and youth, even in daylight, even in the center of town. The victims are usually native Norwegians. Statistics put out in January 1999 showed "ethnic" boys to be the culprits in 80 percent of cases. Given that boys of immigrant background make up only about 25 percent of their age group in Oslo, their disproportionate involvement in violent crime is exceedingly high.

It is a measure of the extent to which Norway has slowly come to *acknowledge* the problems involved in creating a viable multicultural society that both the King and the prime minister, in their talks to the nation on New Year's eve, 1998, made a plea for concerted action to help stem the tide of ethnic youth violence. Three years earlier, when I published my book *Toward a New Norwegian Underclass,* such matters were so unspeakable that if a criminal happened to be an immigrant, the media were forbidden to mention it.

The picture I have drawn is set largely against the backdrop of Norway's capital city and the surrounding area, where most immigrants settle.[58] We have seen that the prospects for work are not especially good in the capital, where refugees at least—the great majority of immigrants—had a 60 percent unemployment rate in 1995. How then do they provide for themselves? How can immigrants afford to live in the capital, where the cost of living—especially for housing—is exceptionally high? (Oslo was ranked as the fifth most expensive city in the world in terms of ordinary living expenses in 1998 and 1999.)[59] The answer has already been given: social welfare comes to their aid. And that also answers the question why the government's policy of decentralization has proved dismally unsuccessful.

Norway is a welfare state with a thriving economy, thanks to vast resources of North Sea oil and gas. At the beginning of the twenty-first century, Norway is the second-richest country in the world, in terms of per-capita income, after Switzerland. Since the Second World War, the country has had a nearly unbroken line of Labor governments committed to building a democratic socialist society premised on the equality of all citizens and the provision of welfare for all.[60] Differences between rich and poor were supposed to be minimized by a system that imposed extremely high taxes on the better-off while helping the less fortunate to rise also through other leveling mechanisms: Free health care and education were provided along with general welfare benefits—ranging from aid to the unemployed, the retired, the aged, widows, single mothers, and so forth—to simple social assistance (*sosialhjelp*), which covered household expenses such as rent (*bostøtte*) for those in dire need. Thus, if a family has no source of income or cannot manage on the income earned to cover normal household expenses, the social welfare system comes to their aid.

You do not have to be Norwegian to be entitled to social assistance in Norway. All needy people staying in the country may receive help. Refugees, for example, are provided with anything they need in the way of material welfare immediately upon their arrival in Norway. A nurse from Bosnia who came as a labor migrant twenty years ago commented ruefully,

> My sister-in-law and her husband have been given everything for free: flat, furniture, clothes, bicycles for the kids, everything, whereas my husband and I had to work for every penny. We took out a mortgage to buy our flat and pinched and scraped to make ends meet—but *they* won't have to do a day's work! And they are not poor at all!

Her bitterness was fuelled by the fact that she had suggested to her sister-in-law, also a nurse, that she take a job; there is a critical nursing shortage in Norway. But the sister-in-law reckoned that it did not pay: she made as much money sitting as home as she would by working.[61]

The nurse's complaint is echoed by that of a Tamil immigrant:

> The asylum seekers will never learn the real value of things . . . Today they can go to the West and get everything for free. An asylum seeker being settled today will be given for free what I struggled for twenty years to achieve. They have become corrupt. They have become like Norwegians. (Fuglerud 1999:123)

That liberal welfare policies may backfire is obvious. A *New York Times* article headlined "Where joblessness is a way of making a living" reports that "in Sweden, unemployed workers can collect nearly 80 percent as much if they are working, compared with 50 percent in the United States" (May 19, 1999). The same pertains to Norway, as was vividly brought home to me once in New England, where I met an Afghan shopkeeper who, on hearing I was from Norway, burst out to my American friend: "D'you know that in Norway they earn 80 percent as much if they don't work as if they do!" He clearly thought it ridiculous. Also, in the European welfare states, in contrast to the United States, there is no limit to the duration that people can be on public assistance. The *New York Times* article, drawing on interviews with several well-known liberal economists, concluded that "in Europe, there's no longer much stigma attached to being out of work . . . Europe's cradle-to-grave safety net has become self-defeating."

The conclusion is an overstatement. Many people do feel stigmatized when out of work. Both their self-regard and their social esteem suffer. But the complaints by the Bosnian and the Tamil should warn us to beware of the unintended consequences of a cradle-to-grave safety net as well as the sense of inequity that stems from immigrants' seeing their brothers and sisters among the refugees being unduly privileged.[62]

Refugees are in a special position. Others, like the original labor migrants or their relatives joining them on the family reunification scheme, are expected to provide for themselves. But these too will be helped if there is a blatant need.[63] This policy has helped earn Norway a reputation as the most generous country in the world among Pakistanis in Oslo (Lien 1997:68).

In other words, you don't have to earn a living to be able to live moderately well in Norway, which is not to say that many do not suffer on the public assistance given, which varies among municipalities and also with the individual official hearing one's case. However, it is also possible to do very well—as did Aisha's family. With the money they derived from two sources—child benefits (*barnetrygd*, which rises exponentially with the number of children one has) and social assistance (which paid their high rent)—the family income placed them at a good middle-class level.

The political economy explains why most refugees manage to settle in Oslo despite the higher cost of living there. The expense is further defrayed by a welfare measure that in some respects actually *favors* immigrants. The advantage is due to the difference between unemployment benefits (*arbeidsledighetstrygd*), which most unemployed native Norwegians will receive, and the social assistance given to immigrants in a similar position. The former is nationally standardized; the latter varies according to cost of living, local ideas about minimum standards, and the professional ideas prevailing in the local welfare office.[64] So a person receiving unemployment benefits does better to stay where the cost of living is less. With social assistance, one has greater freedom of movement. "Even if the municipal welfare office tries to usher [immigrants] into inexpensive flats, they will in principle have their housing costs *refunded*. This means that their household economy will be unaffected by moving to more expensive areas" (Brox 1998:15–16).

To earn the right to the kind of insurance entailed by unemployment benefits, a person must have had regular employment in Norway for a certain time. Most immigrants are not in that position, which is why they depend on the municipally managed social assistance—with consequences that thwart the government's efforts to keep immigrants dispersed.

> The social assistance system in principle neutralizes the variation in living costs that might have motivated immigrants to stay away from the capital. This must especially be the case with the way in which housing costs are refunded. We may safely conclude that as long as the social assistance system is used to secure the welfare of immigrants, Norwegian politicians will have no chance to see their goals for immigrant settlement pattern implemented. (Brox 1998:15–16)[65]

Receiving social assistance is one thing, however, and there is unanimous political agreement in Norway that immigrants are entitled to it. But should *moving around* on social assistance be a person's unrestricted right? The question has arisen from a concern for the movement of immigrants to the capital and its environs, where the cost of living is higher and the social problems are greater. To stem the tide, the Oslo authorities attempted to deny persons who had been granted social assistance in one municipality the right to such assistance elsewhere. But the attempt was largely unsuccessful. Is "the right to travel" not a human right? Appealing their cases, immigrants usually win.[66] And so the flow to the capital city continues unabated,[67] increasing its share of unemployed and unemployable human capital.

For this was another dangerous fact brought out by the Oslo study: that refugees in general had a level of education far below that of native Norwegians, not high enough to be really attractive on the labor market. Contrary to the image of the typical male immigrant presented by the news media— that of a highly educated person whose qualifications are depreciated by racist Norway—the Oslo study gave another picture: most refugees have had only eight years of schooling—even less than a Norwegian primary education.[68] That will not get them far in a country where education is very highly valued, and even twelve years (including secondary school) is not enough for most jobs. This is not to underestimate the problems faced by many highly qualified immigrants from discrimination and racism.[69] But with a double handicap—a relatively low level of education and poor proficiency in Norwegian—many immigrants are likely to end up unemployed.[70] Particularly distressing under these circumstances is that relatively few—even those who had been pursuing their education in their homelands—choose to continue their education in Norway. Recall the finding that 50 percent of the children of refugees in Oslo had neither parent either at work or at school.

Social assistance was never meant to be a permanent arrangement for anyone. It was intended as an emergency measure, something to help people get over a crisis, not as a replacement for the *fattigkasse* ("poverty chest"), which provided sustenance for the poor in earlier times. With the development of the welfare state, poverty was meant to be eradicated. Now, however, 50 percent of immigrants depend on social assistance as their regular means of sustenance. This means, as Kåre Hagen (1997) has pointed out, that half of them are living on the *fattigkasse*. Had this been the case for native Norwegians, there would have been a national outcry. But when it comes to immigrants, other standards apply. So Norway covers its failure to help immigrants live respectable lives by placing half of them on the dole for life, an easy way out for a rich country in a difficult human situation.

The picture is not uniformly bleak, however. My presentation of dangerous facts may convey the impression that immigrants are all of a piece and are equally exposed to unemployment and marginalization. This is not the case.

Among facts that I too do not know how to deal with is the fact that different minorities manage very differently. Unemployment among refugees in Oslo ranges between 12 and 88 percent, depending on the ethnic group: Tamils and Chileans have the best employment record, Vietnamese and Somalis the worst. Iranians and Kurds have a medium score; Pakistanis do better but not nearly as well as the Tamils.[71] What can Norway do with such facts, given that they are considered dangerous?

The fundamental value on which Norway rests is that of equality of all human beings, irrespective of gender, race, rank, and the like. Hence official Norwegian policy regarding immigrants is based on equal, not differential, treatment, although it is recognized that special help may be needed in some respects to facilitate their prospects for self-help and integration into the larger society.[72] But how do we deal with the fact that minorities are not all of a piece but show significant differences when it comes to their prospects for self-help?[73] Should Somalis, or Vietnamese, or Iranians, say, be the beneficiaries of affirmative action to help them manage on a level with Tamils and Chileans with regard to employment? The Norwegian answer would be no; basically, "equality" means equality of opportunity, not of results. But if nothing is done to reduce these differences, the result will be one that Norway can hardly live with. As Kåre Hagen (1997) has argued, Norway has pursued a policy of equality with regard to immigrants, but the result has been *massive social inequality* among the different ethnic minorities. This is the problem we now have to confront: Equal treatment produces social inequality.

What Norway will do remains to be seen. For the time being, the problem is silenced, though it is constantly brought to the fore in workshops and conferences dealing with immigrants, sometimes by immigrants themselves. Because the term "culture" is a non-word with regard to immigrants' performance in the labor market, we are in a bind. There is probably a fear that it might be racist even to suggest that some minorities had a "culture" that set a greater value on working than did others. Though if one were to take culture seriously, that is precisely what one would have to be prepared to find.[74] Replacing "culture" with "structure" might be a way of getting around the problem. Research in the United States shows that there are significant differences among (and within) minorities with respect to structural properties such as class, education, and social networks that affect people's employment prospects. Similar studies are lacking in Norway. Wishing the problem away by making sure differences will not show up in statistical surveys seems to be the solution currently favored. Meanwhile, inequalities will continue to grow.

The fear of knowing certain things about ethnic minorities is not just a Norwegian phenomenon. In the Netherlands, according to Marlene de Vries, "it is almost taboo to inquire into the possibility that members of a minority group might also be impeded in their emancipation by aspects of their very culture" (1990:1). Lindo (1995:144) follows suit: "Until now, anthropologists in the Netherlands have hardly addressed the question of what brings about differences in success among minority groups, and what role the cultural or ethnic dimension may play in this process." [75] Gibson, reflecting on research from Canada, Israel, France, Britain, and the Netherlands on the school performance of ethnic minority youth, observes that although relevant research has been undertaken in each of those countries, "the analysis has centered for the most part on explaining the disparity that exists between the minority and dominant group students, rather than on exploring and explaining the variability that exists among the different minority groups" (1997:322). Such hesitance is understandable.

"Asking yet again what ethnicity or 'race' has to do with school performance has its dangers," warns Anderson-Levitt (1997:316) in her foreword to a collection of essays on minorities and education. "And yet . . . we would have to be blind not to notice that in spite of individuals' strategies of resistance and thousands of success stories, we can predict with some regularity which racial and ethnic categories encompass disproportionate numbers of students failed by the system." This is just the point: "failed by the system." So too with performance in the labor market, we can predict with some regularity which ethnic minorities will be marginalized, whether in Norway or other European countries. I believe the reluctance of some European governments to initiate research into the causes of such disparities has something to do with their own responsibility in the matter. In Europe, in contradistinction to the United States, the welfare of immigrants is a *public* responsibility. This, and not just the fact that the United States has a much longer history of immigration, may account for European sensitivity to research on disparities *among* ethnic minorities. Europe's cradle-to-grave safety net may also play a role. Inequities can be masked; but masking has its price.

I have argued that Norway is about to acquire an ethnic underclass; and my analysis has been substantiated and supported by such distinguished Norwegian researchers as Brox, Hagen, and Djuve. Our conclusions rest on the fact that although many immigrants are materially well provided for, their average standard of living is far below that of native Norwegians, and many suffer additionally from a complex of problems associated with an underclass. An extremely high rate of unemployment is just one index; an extremely high reliance on social welfare is another. When the population so affected is also ethnically and visibly distinct from native Norwegians, the seeds of conflict are sown. Some Norwegians regard these foreigners as "milking the system." As Brochmann (1996:137) has observed, "the [immigration] stop has channelled immigrants into routes that are more costly for the authorities, and this in turn gives grounds for opinions that they come 'to exploit our welfare state,' resulting in increased hostility." Immigrants, in turn, resent being thought of as freeloaders, when they want nothing more than to work. Both populations want the situation changed, and both are concerned with the problems following in the wake of unemployment, welfare dependency, and marginalization.

Again, the situation in Norway is not unique:

> there is currently a growing opinion in all EU [European Union] member-states that marginalization of immigrants carries heavy risks of social unrest and ethnic conflicts, particularly when also parts of the national population feel economic strains. As a consequence of this understanding, integration policies now rank high on the agenda in EU countries. (Brochmann 1996:125)

It may be argued that I have drawn too dark a picture of the situation in Norway. Using the term "underclass" may be inappropriate in economic terms: the standard of living of many immigrants in Norway is clearly much better than what the Norwegian side of their lives reveals.[76] It is expensive to keep up two homes in two continents, as many do; and many participate in an informal economy that is less than transparent. Moreover, as Philip Lewis points out (1994), "the deprivationist perspective is clearly inadequate and does not begin to do justice to the complex and differentiated picture now emerging." His reference is to Great Britain, but his words have relevance beyond. Surely, there are positive trends and signs of hope in some respects. Moreover, every observation I have made could be stood on its head. Rather than saying that 50 percent of children of refugees in Oslo live in families where neither the mother or father is at work or at school, one might have noted that half of the children do *not* live in such families.[77] This is true, and yet I stick to the picture I have drawn.

A society worth living in is not one with a stark discrepancy between the life situations of the "host" population and the "guests." It is one in which those who need the government are, to cite Eric Hobsbawm, the less privileged, whose voices are usually silenced. To those who argue that giving the facts as I do is likely to incite racism and discrimination in the population at large, I answer that not doing so could be worse: racism and discrimination are more likely to grow if the differences noted above are not remedied. A recent study showed half of the Norwegian population to have an ambivalent or a negative attitude toward immigrants; and one-fourth could be described as hostile (Aardal and Valen 1995). Fear of racism, real as the problem is, has done enough damage to the lives of people already, without frightening us into acceptance of a scenario unworthy of Norway or any country—that of a growing "ethnic" underclass.

The problem in Norway lies not in such facts as we have but in how little we know and how little we have been allowed to know. Even the word "problem" does not exist in the politically correct parlance; there are only challenges, no problems, in the colorful community.

Any policy to deal with a practical life problem must address the problem in all its complexity, which means facing up to the facts. Aisha is only one of many victims of Norwegian integration policies. Along with many children, she is paying the price for the adults' failure to face up to the situation. As poignantly expressed by the two Pakistani fathers cited earlier, "Our generation will soon be gone. It is our children who will continue to live here. Please don't punish them for our failure to dare to address the problems."

Daring to address the problems that is the heart of the matter. The problems are manifold, and they cannot be wished away. But before we consider possible solutions, let us ask, Why did things go so wrong?

6   *Silence as Political Cover-Up*

Norwegian immigration policies were based, in my view, on three unrealistic or even utopian premises about society and human nature. First, as Norwegian politicians never tired of telling the natives: immigrants have a claim to respect (*krav på respekt*). But this is spurious and has dire practical consequences: Immigrants, like anyone else who enters a foreign land, cannot just claim respect, they must earn it. In no society that I know can you come, uninvited, and demand respect. This is not to deny the inherent worth of the human being who needs to be respected, but to point to a simple fact of life: it is by being placed in a life situation where you can *show your good qualities* that you deem yourself worthy of respect.

By riding on the slogan "claim to respect," Norwegian authorities made it easier for themselves. The onus was not on them; they need not cater to the welfare of immigrants beyond handing out social welfare and being generally tolerant and antiracist. This may be a slight overstatement. The government did offer immigrants a minimum of lessons in Norwegian (750 hours for refugees and 500 for other foreigners) and some opportunities for training and work. But overall, it did not face up to the fact that the way to practice respect for immigrants was by helping to provide them with opportunities whereby they could develop and use their competence and hence earn social respect.

That immigrants have a claim to respect, regardless of how they behave, and Norwegians a simple duty to grant it to them, was a first failed premise of Norwegian immigration policy. In principle the premise is right; in practice, it is not how humans behave unless they are ideologically committed to multiculturalism, which most Norwegians—and probably most humans—are not. It takes more to make a multiethnic society work than simply telling the natives that uninvited visitors have a claim to respect while placing the latter on the dole—and thinking this will make them grateful and loyal citizens.

For that was a second failed premise of Norway's integration policies: that being on the receiving end of a gift relationship will engender feelings of loyalty and gratitude. Or, to put it more bluntly, that living on social welfare will elicit good feelings in the person concerned. This is as unrealistic as it is simpleminded. True, there are those who bless Norway for its generosity, and some (among immigrants as among natives) who are quite content not to have to work for food and shelter. But gratitude is likely to be short-lived when people experience the price to be paid for living on the dole. Loss of self-respect and social respect is common. Being suspected of having come to take advantage of the system is a further hardship.

Talks with numerous immigrants convince me that inferiority and bitterness rather than gratitude are what many of them feel.[78] It was most strongly expressed to me by a man from Ghana who said he hated the Norwegians for putting him in the position he was in; he had lived twenty years on the dole although he was a tough, able-bodied man. His hatred of Norwegians was so fierce that it made me shiver, and it was not in the least tempered by the material affluence he had enjoyed for twenty years without having to work for it. Was this a way to treat humans, he fumed, relegating them to animal existence? True, *animals* have only material needs! And although I did not hear it so strongly expressed by others, it is evident that many incline toward sharing his view. Talks with youths of immigrant background bring out a similar, consistent pattern: many are ashamed to admit that their fathers are not working.

Life on social welfare engenders neither self-respect nor social respect in many cases. And self-respect (which is dependent also on social recognition) is a powerful human need.[79] Unless this need is reckoned with *also in regard to immigrants,* we are in deep trouble.

A third failed premise of Norway's immigration policies concerned the idea of "culture." The premise was that immigrants should abide by the laws and basic values of Norwegian society, whereas Norwegians should respect "their culture." On paper this looks fine. In practical life, problems arise that open the way for power abuse and cultural fundamentalism. The concept of "culture" at the base of these policies was hollow: it rested on the assumption that to each culture there is a single people that speaks with a common voice; ordinary human contention, not to speak of oppression and power abuse, were absent from this rosy notion of culture. Hence any spokesman could speak on behalf of "the culture"; and many did. *Culture and Truth* is the name of a well-known book in anthropology (Rosaldo 1989). And mistaking culture, as professed by any spokesman, for the truth was precisely what afflicted Norwegian immigration policy. No wonder Aisha could not be heard. She did not fit in under this formula.

Was *her* culture ever respected? Was she ever given a say? To quote Veena Das (1990) once again, "culture is a way of distributing pain unequally in populations." Thus a policy based on "respect for their culture" begs more questions than it answers. Worse, it risks adding to the pain, allying itself with forces to which it should be opposed in a society worth living in.

Norway should have been a society worth living in, not just for Aisha, but for all those immigrants and refugees who made it to this fortunate land, as well as their children. If we have failed to provide the life conditions that would cater to the welfare of all too many of them, it was not because of material want. The country is rich, indeed so rich that handing out social welfare becomes an easy way—a cheap way—out of a difficult human situation. But by paying its way out to the refrain of "immigrants have a claim to respect" the government did not just belittle the worth and dignity of immigrants and their children. (We know from our own personal experience that material surplus does not make for happiness, so why should it for them?) It also nurtured the reactions it would most want to avoid such as bitterness, anger, disloyalty—all born of feelings of inferiority and wounded self-respect. And it also nurtured contempt among many. As one Pakistani said, "The problem is, Norwegians are so gullible and we are so clever. We should stop being so clever" (Lien 1997).

Norway does not merely have a large immigrant population. It has a population of immigrants that in large measure live their lives on the margins of society in what promises to be a permanent underclass for many of them.

To sum up my critique of Norway's immigration policies, let me borrow some words from the late Israeli premier, Yitzhak Rabin. On the eve of his receipt of the Nobel Peace Price in Oslo in 1994, Rabin was asked, "How do you feel about the situation [in Israel]?" He answered, "I don't deal with feelings, I deal with problems."

The Norwegian government, by contrast, has dealt with feelings rather than problems with regard to immigrants. It attempted to place "the problem" *in the hearts and minds of people* rather than out there in the real world where practical social policies are called for. The politicians talked as if antiracism, nondiscrimination, and respect for "their culture" would do the trick of integrating immigrants into Norwegian society. But the tactics backfired, as indeed they must—for they were based on unrealistic and utopian notions about human nature and society.

Naturally, Norwegians should be antiracist and nondiscriminatory in their dealings with immigrants as with all others. But no amount of good feeling on the part of Norwegians will ever solve the problem of massive un-employment among immigrants—in a society where higher education and facility in Norwegian are required for most jobs. Nor will good feelings and a tolerant attitude on the part of natives work miracles in the form of "integrating" immigrants who in many cases want to be separate and remote; and who have all the more reason to want to be so when they feel shunned by a labor market that spurns their qualities.

The "problem" needs to be redefined as anchored out there in the real world rather than in the hearts and minds of people. It is linked with an unmerciful political economy in which qualifications and higher education are in fact needed for most jobs. As Kåre Hagen has observed: Norwegian society is in reality capitalist and competitive. By sending contrary signals to refugees (the present-day immigrants) in the ways we receive them—acting as if all will be served on silver platters—we are doing both them and ourselves a disservice. The fact is that they will have to work and work hard if they are ever going to make it in society. Those are the rules of the game even in this welfare society.

Rather than exonerating the government, this puts the responsibility squarely on the government's back. For it is in the nature of the Scandinavian nation-states that the welfare of immigrants is a *public* responsibility. In the past,

> If Finnish frontier farmers starved, or [Italian] stone masons died from work-related diseases, it was their problem and God's will. Today, the government will be blamed if immigrants have welfare problems, just as the government is responsible generally for the welfare of the native population in a social-democratic state. (Brox 1998:104)

But how will we know whether immigrants have welfare problems if the facts are not available?[80]

This is the crux of my critique—the silence regarding facts was the government's way of avoiding blame. As long as the facts were not known, it could not be held to account. The government acted as if concern for the immigrants was the overriding reason for silence regarding their life situation— and perhaps this was in earnest. Negative images might nourish xenophobia and racism. But in effect, the cover-up veiled the government's own failure in immigrant matters. As long as the facts were not known, the government could not be blamed for policies that did not work. But neither could *effective* policies be enacted.

It might be said in the government's defense that it did not realize the immigrants had come to stay. They would return to their original homelands, it was presumed, once they had made enough money for a decent level of living back home. Hence there was no need for assembling facts on their lives in Norway; the original labor migrants were not regarded as immigrants but as temporary guest workers. It was a myth that proved remarkably resilient.[81]

One wonders what sustained this myth. Was it wishful thinking? Or was there anything to indicate that, given the deteriorating conditions in most Third World countries and man's natural inclination (or so it seems) to seek to acquire wealth, guest workers would ever choose to relinquish life in the West? If Western governments ever harbored such expectations, they have long since been proved wrong. The statistics on immigrants as far back as the mid-1970s, when European countries put a halt to immigration, are unequivocal: there was a rush to get one's family into Europe before it was too late.[82]

Thus the evidence has long been overwhelming that immigrants have come to stay—or sojourn, to be more exact. Some strike roots in the West, but many stand with one foot in each camp, enjoying the material welfare of the West but living emotionally and spiritually "back home," as do Aisha's parents. This means that increasing integration will not follow as a matter of course; there is resistance built into the system. But the writing has long been on the wall: it was clear that immigrants would remain in Norway and their numbers would grow; so knowledge about their life situation was essential for effective policies to be enacted that might further their welfare. It is my argument that by discouraging or even forbidding the collection and publicizing of such knowledge the government covered its own failure with regard to immigrants. Whatever its stated aim, the *effect* was to protect the government against criticism: silencing served as a political device in the government's, if not the immigrants', best interests.

Norway is now trying to make up for twenty-five years of relative neglect of immigrants, neglect not of their material needs so much as their need for self-respect and social respect. These depend on being provided with opportunities to develop one's capacities and to show one's worth by using one's competence and qualifications. To effectuate policies to help immigrants cope, the problem needs to be located where it belongs: out there in the real world. And it needs to be addressed, not concealed. As David Grossman notes: "Unless we describe reality, we will awake one day to a reality that is indescribable" (*Aftenposten*, January 1996).

This is the scenario that is now haunting Norway, and this is why I have advocated facing up to the facts.

A young girl, Aisha, was sacrificed on the altar of culture in Norway in 1996. How many more tragedies like hers there are we cannot tell. Aisha was sacrificed in a big way: she lost her freedom, her country, perhaps even herself; she certainly lost the power to decide about her own body and sexuality; and she probably lost her "culture" as well; for however one thinks about it, it is difficult to avoid the conclusion that Aisha was not a traditional Middle Eastern girl. She was steeped in different mores by virtue of her childhood and education in a modern European welfare state wedded to principles of equality and democracy. These must have gotten under her skin—or so it seems, from the letters she wrote that I have been able to read.

But if Aisha was irretrievably sacrificed, there are others who become subject to "small" sacrifices, time and again, every day. Some of these have become known to me through the media, by way of personal calls, through third persons, and so forth. They may be schoolchildren (especially girls) who are not allowed to do this or that, like participating in physical education or class outings, and not because they themselves don't want to, or the school does not consider their participation obligatory; but because some parents invoke "culture" to forbid their children from participating, and some teachers may be afraid to cause offense and to elicit verbal or physical assault.

In child welfare cases, "culture" often wins out even when there is over-whelming evidence that the child is suffering abuse in the home. Child care authorities I have spoken with are unanimous in their admission that forms of child abuse that would never be tolerated in the case of native Norwe-gians are sometimes accepted when committed by immigrants. For fear of not respecting "their culture" and hence being labeled racist, the authorities have been reluctant to intervene with immigrants—although, since the late

1990s, there is finally some evidence of change. (Nadia's case, which we will hear later, marked a turning point.) Aisha paid the price of such fear: "I *hate* the child authorities!" she wrote in a letter to a teacher. "I believed the child authorities were there to help children, but I was completely wrong!! I feel they have deceived me."

Is this just a child's reaction to a reality that grown-ups understand better? Aisha feared that this is what they thought:

> Can't they understand that I can't move home again? They said I needed help! Then for what? I don't understand!! Do they think I'm crazy?! I feel deceived, I'm afraid to move home again!

Had she read official policy documents regarding immigrants, passed by the Norwegian Parliament in 1987, she would have known that the law was on her side. I refer to a proposition titled "Goals and Objectives for Immigration Policy" (Stortingsmelding 1987–88). This important document, however, is worded so as to invite misconceptions. The law is clear, but the implications are not. Let us consider it in some detail.

Norwegian immigration policy has been based on the twin premises that "we" should respect "their culture" whereas "they" should abide by the laws of the state. This is putting it crudely, of course. The Norwegian "we" now encompasses thousands of people who once belonged in the category "they," yet who now count themselves as Norwegians in addition to their membership in a minority group. The document states that in the case of a conflict between Norwegian law and the immigrants' culture, the law prevails.

> Immigrants stand in the same position as other inhabitants when it comes to respecting the laws and norms of our society, regardless of personal views. There are fundamental values [*evalueringer*] on which there exists political agreement in Norway, such as the value of democracy, gender equality, and the rights of the child. This implies a clear restriction of freedom of choice for all inhabitants . . . Freedom of choice cannot be interpreted to mean that immigrants can choose to stand entirely outside of Norwegian society, for example by refraining from learning Norwegian or acquiring any knowledge about Norwegian society. (Stortingsmelding 1987–88:49)

Official Norwegian immigration policy is based on the three core values of the French Revolution: freedom, equality, and solidarity. Whereas immigrants (like all others) are restricted in their freedom to stand above the law, the principle of *true equality* between immigrants and natives also entails that immigrants "shall be able to maintain a separate cultural identity and live in harmony with their surroundings." So as not to invite misconceptions, however, the government's 1987 immigrant policy declares,

> The formulation "freedom of choice" brings to mind a more comprehensive freedom than what has been intended. The core of the policy regarding immigrants is that they shall be able to participate in society without being required to assimilate culturally . . . A more accurate formulation of the intention entailed in the principle of freedom of choice is *respect* for the immigrants' language and culture . . . [However,] in relation to the goal of real equality, the principle of respect will have to be subordinate.

So in other words, integration, not assimilation, is the purpose. To that end, immigrants have the right to maintain a separate cultural identity and to demand respect for their culture. However, if this culture comes into conflict with Norwegian law and the basic values on which Norwegian society rests, then culture must give way. The superordinate goal of real equality for all citizens, regardless of race, creed, gender, or any other status, entails clear delimitations on the practice of culture—in Norway as in every welfare state or liberal democracy.

Such is the spirit and the political intent of Norway's immigration policy. But what is the practice and the effect? The story of Aisha indicates that practice may be far removed from the humanitarian principles and goals embedded in Norwegian state policy. Nor is Aisha's case unique. How many girls like her must be counted as missing, no one knows. Many of these cases of disappearance are effectively covered up; and nowhere is there a record of them. But many people have, as I do, knowledge of individual cases.[1] There are also some stories that have found their way into the media after a girl has managed to escape. One concerns Nasim Karim, now a friend of mine, who was able to escape after being forcibly married in Pakistan and was almost beaten to death because she tried to refuse the marriage. She managed, against all odds, to make her way to the Norwegian embassy in Islamabad and, with the embassy's help, to flee the country. She has paid dearly for her quest for freedom by becoming an outcast from her community. Her story is told in chapter 13. As in Aisha's case, Nasim's tragedy came about after the child welfare authorities had reunited her with her family, which had mistreated her. But in her case, nevertheless, there is a kind of happy ending if with tragic overtones. Aisha's case, as far as I know, is only tragic. It is Aisha's father and Nasim's father who are the victors in the "immigrant story." Both made a great deal of money and have invested in property in their homelands; both live in good housing in the best part of their respective towns in Norway; both have significantly increased their freedom of movement and action as well as their status and prestige, though Nasim's father did suffer a loss because of his daughter's intransigence and the public affront to his honor. How Aisha's father was affected by her recalcitrance and forced marriage, I do not know.

Let us turn again to some of the dilemmas, or contradictions, inherent in Norwegian state policy. We have seen that immigrants have a right to "maintain a separate cultural identity" but that "respect for the immigrants' language and culture must be subordinate to the principle of real equality." First, to whom do the policies apply? Who is the quintessential "immigrant" government has in mind? Is he or she a first-generation immigrant only, or are the children of immigrants also included? If so, when does an immigrant cease to be an immigrant—how many generations does it take? Next, the matter of identity: what *is* the identity of a girl, or a boy, who has grown up in historical circumstances different from those of the parents? Is it the distinct cultural identity of persons like Aisha or Nasim that the Norwegian Parliament has in mind when it passes an official policy to the effect that "immigrants shall be able to maintain a separate cultural identity"? Clearly not. This whole official policy has been based on the premise that to each people there is one culture and one identity. Thus people were packaged in boxes, which made them easier to contain. But the contents spill over, unruly and angry, for they do not fit the formula. And so we have Aisha and Nasim, and numerous other young people, many of whom (especially girls) suffer quietly at home because they were prepackaged by Norwegian authorities acting in conjunction with parents into "cultures" that did not fit the children's lived experience.

Misconceptions or distorting language that have bedeviled anthropology for decades still ride official European immigration policies, at least in Scandinavia. I refer to those notions known as essentialist in current anthropological theory: that to each people a single culture belongs, which compels all the people to abide by its mores, on which they agree. Thus there is consensus, no contestation, welfare and harmony that "the culture" is supposed to further, or "it" would not be there—or so it is presumed. This notion of culture has timelessness built into it; it is static, unmoving. Nor is identity a problem for the people. It is given, bestowed by culture. In this view, it does make sense to say that "immigrants should be able to maintain a separate cultural identity"—as did the Norwegian Parliament.

There is hope for the future, however. In their most recent policy statement on immigrants, of February 1997, the Norwegian government appears to have learned a lesson. Rather than speaking in broad categorical terms as if immigrants were all of a piece, it now foregrounds the individual—as it would in the case of native Norwegians. Under "Goals and Principles" the government now states that

> Everyone, irrespective of background, has the same right to be regarded as an individual and not just part of a group, or religious congregation. All children and youth, irrespective of background, must be able to shape their own identity and future. (Stortingsmelding 1996–97:8)

We see that the notion "separate cultural identity" has been replaced by "own identity"—a clear turn away from the rights of the collectivity, what we might term cultural rights, to the rights and liberty of the individual, his or her human rights.

These are new, constructive signs on the part of the Norwegian government, indicating that it was not in vain that some of us raised a battle cry on behalf of individuals of immigrant descent who were being treated as if they did not exist apart from the group. But the shift in Norwegian policies in the direction of human rights rather than cultural rights is also in line with what is happening in the international arena: the fundamental conflict of principle between collective rights and individual human rights is giving way to an increased recognition of the harm that may be perpetrated by society *on* the individual, and hence of culture as a potentially oppressive force.

The United Nations Convention on Human Rights, which most modern states have ratified, initiated what Michael Ignatieff calls "a juridical revolution in the value we accord the human person." Whereas before the Second World War, only states had rights in international law, "since 1945, the rights of individuals against the state and also against the family and society have received international legal recognition" (1999:10). But this has implications for "culture" too. Since no modern state can declare itself above human rights, the rights of the individual must take precedence. This is why we find in official documents relating to cultural pluralism in countries as diverse as Norway, Australia, or South Africa, surprisingly similar, almost identical wordings.[2] All are committed to respecting culture, but not to the extent that culture trumps the law. In principle, the moral individualism at the base of the Convention on Human Rights accords to each human being the inviolable right to have her dignity respected.

We have come a long way over the past couple of years in recognizing the integrity and autonomy of the individual human being, whether a Norwegian or not. But there is still a long way to go in realizing these principles in practice.

Perhaps the critical concept is "identity," a currently fashionable concept that is both vague and imprecise. I doubt that many people, myself included, really understand what it means.[3] But it has something to do with a person's cherished idea of what and who he or she is, though this idea is moving, changing. People do not project the same identity in all contexts, nor over time in the same kinds of context in their own lives. Identity is to some extent situation-specific and strategic.[4] Take the incident recounted to me by a Turkish professor. When boarding a plane for Frankfurt at the Istanbul airport, she spotted two attractive young girls clad in the latest fashion and elegantly made up. They were as modern as could be and delighted in their own appearance. Shortly before landing in Frankfurt, she noticed two women draped in black from head to toe, whom she had not seen entering the plane in Istanbul. Then she realized: they were the same girls preparing for their landing in Frankfurt.

So much for identity. Where is it lodged? In the latest fashion or the Islamic mode? The answer, of course is, both. Though one cannot tell from the case of those two girls which identity, if any, has priority.[5] Suffice it to note that power enters into the picture. If there had been no father or brother or husband waiting for them in the Frankfurt airport (or a mother or an aunt for that matter), what might the girls have done? It is of course entirely possible that they might still have chosen to "veil" in order to distinguish themselves from the Germans, or to escape negative sanctions by countrymen who are more concerned with "their women's" purity abroad than back home.[6] The lesson of the story is simply that there is no single, distinct, collective cultural identity that immigrants, or others, should be able to maintain, and that is unchanging across time and context. Rather, immigrant policies in *a society worth living in* must make room for people to craft identities that cater to their own well-being while respecting the equality of other human beings.[7] The Norwegian Parliament said as much: "There are fundamental principles on which there exists political agreement in Norway, such as the value of democracy, gender equality, and the rights

THE POLITICS OF CULTURE

of the child. This implies a clear restriction of the freedom of choice for all inhabitants."

A fourteen-year-old girl, Aisha, stands as witness to the hollowness of this official policy. She was right; she should have had the protection of the child welfare authorities. But when they did not dare to help her, it was not from lack of concern but from lack of appropriate knowledge and the courage to act on it. They did harm in the name of charity.

8   *Culture and Accountability*

After years of public lecturing in Norway on issues related to culture, immigrants, Islam, and the like, one thing was painfully clear to me: "culture" had become an obstacle to understanding, a stumbling block; and the more people struggled to avoid it, the more likely they were to get caught. It was as if "culture" unmercifully trapped well-meaning, caring individuals who wanted nothing more than to do the right thing and live by high principles; but in their efforts to do precisely that, they were hooked by the very concept to which they looked for guidance. And so many felt not just lost but let down and bewildered.

Why did their efforts to do the right thing fail so pitifully? Why, when they tried to do the best, were the results often the opposite: accusations of racism; suffering on the part of individuals, especially children; and infringement of human rights? And how to get out of the trap?

This is where anthropologists are sometimes called upon and where the received wisdom of our discipline serves us so poorly. "Culture," more of it, must provide the answer: knowing more about culture, understanding it better, taking courses in cross-cultural communication, learning about Islam, Muslims, Muslim culture, and so forth—this must be the way. I received more requests for talks than I could answer. And it was from talking to various audiences on these matters that the realization slowly dawned on me: culture was not the answer, it was the problem. But if culture was the problem, then so were anthropologists.

If "culture" failed to deliver the promised results, it was not just because people were lacking in knowledge of "it," or of the hundreds of cultures that make up the new Norway. (If these were indeed as different as was assumed, how could anyone hope to acquire sufficient knowledge?) Rather, it was because the concept was both over- and underrated. It was believed to be a magic key to understanding, hence overrated; simultaneously, the complexity of the notion and the problems it poses for understanding were, naturally, not widely understood, hence underrated. But if "culture" was the problem, then so were anthropologists. For "culture" was our thing, the merchandise by which we lived. Yet we had not sold it responsibly and had thus failed to enlighten the public on the merits and *de*merits of our product. We had been keeping our qualms to ourselves while acting outwardly as if our merchandise were safe and good—for all purposes.

But the truth of the matter was that anthropology had been undergoing an existential crisis since the mid-1980s, brought about by the realization that "culture," our key concept, was inherently dangerous. In the words of the late Eric Wolf, a distinguished and highly respected anthropologist, culture carries "a heavy burden of rage and shame" (1994); and historian-cum-anthropologist James Clifford called it "a deeply compromised idea" (1988). It can be misused more than most concepts for dreadful personal and political ends; and it was all too clear to many anthropologists that our discipline had played a part in promoting an understanding of "culture" that facilitated such abuses. Wondering how things could go so wrong, several anthropologists had concluded that the concept must go; it was beyond salvation, too damaged by the wreckage it had wrought (Abu-Lughod 1991; Ingold 1993). Others argued for not throwing the baby out with the bathwater but for retaining the valued insights of "culture" by replacing it with other, less compromised terms (Barth 1994b; Bloch 1994; Fardon 1990; Kahn 1989; Keesing 1994; Paul 1990). Yet others would keep the concept as it was, arguing that anthropologists could not be held responsible for how the world misused their idea. Our profession required the term however much the public profaned it.

We need not enter into this professional debate here. Its relevance for now is simply that while these painstaking discussions were going on, the public was presented with "a bright face," to use a Balinese expression (Wikan 1990). Outwardly, many anthropologists continued to act as if all was well within our discipline; and naturally so, for our livelihood was at stake. But meanwhile, the very insights that were being discarded in anthropology continued to lay the foundation for much public policy and professional practice *outside* our discipline, often with disastrous effects—as was increasingly clear to me from my exposure to hundreds of audiences of politicians, teachers, social workers, child welfare workers, and others, all out to get a grip on that supposedly most fundamental and useful concept—culture.

Talking with these audiences, I had the harrowing experience of realizing that people's commonsense reactions were sometimes ahead of the anthropologists' belated understanding of "culture." Yet they dared not act on their intuitive knowledge; standing in awe, even fear, of the concept "culture," they lost their bearings. This is not to say that the public's (to use a general label) understanding of culture was as thorough as that which was crystallizing within anthropology—naturally not—but to point to an important insight: from their practical dealings with immigrants and their children, many professionals had a gut feeling regarding "culture" that corresponded with what anthropologists were coming to in theoretical terms and from other points of view. Unaware of the debates within our discipline, however, and impressed with the "bright face" that anthropologists presented to the world, they ignored their own sensible reactions and placed their trust in an outmoded model of culture that was being discarded by anthropologists.

No wonder listeners were thrilled with my revelations of the current rethinking of the concept of culture. It seemed to give them a lifebuoy, something to grasp and hold on to, in the hurly-burly of daily trafficking in immigrant matters. And they should know; for they bought our wares. They used anthropologists again and again to enlighten them on what they needed to know in order to "respect the culture" of immigrants. They were do-gooders, in the best sense of the word, wanting to do the right, the just and the good. What could I deliver to help them cope with what for many were daily contradictions that drained their energies and nurtured a feeling of failure? They deserved to be told the truth.

So I told them the story of "culture" that unfolds in the following chapter, and for which the story of Aisha has paved the way here. The reactions of my audiences were almost palpable: gratitude and relief. Perhaps the one statement I made, a single sentence, that made the most impact was "kultur har *ikke* krav på respekt"—culture is *not* entitled to respect in and of itself. It meant that one was not a racist for not liking or accepting everything that was propagated in the name of culture. It was possible, indeed commendable, to stand back and ask: But what is that which I am now respecting doing to the welfare of a particular person? Or of other members of the collectivity? Or: If I respect this, *who will suffer the consequences?* In other words, respect for individual welfare and integrity may require that "culture" be demoted or resisted or actively opposed, lest individuals suffer insufferable consequences.[8]

Also, the insight that "culture" did not just refer to time-honored traditions but to an ongoing, creative process made a profound impact on these audiences. For it meant that the ancestors or parents did not have a monopoly on culture. The *children* had to be reckoned with and *their* special experiences and knowledge accepted as an integral part of culture. Moreover, if "culture" did not constitute the objective truth but was more like a point of view, then *women* were suddenly *in* the picture. Women ought to be given a voice and asked to speak for themselves.

These were some of the points about "culture" that I espoused—to the audiences' delight. The most palpable reaction was, as I have said, gratitude for a newfound sense of trust in one's own gut reactions. Next came the plea: I must get the politicians' attention. This is how the following essay, originally published on the op-ed page of the newspaper *Aftenposten*, came to see the light of day. I realized that this was the best way of going public—to publish a statement on "culture" in a respected newspaper that all politicians in the capital (including members of Parliament) were bound to read. But it was no easy choice. The essay lingered on my desk for nearly four months before I submitted it—after much deliberation. What was the problem? I knew I had to do it, or someone did. But how could I formulate sensitive professional arguments in a language entirely jargon-free and accessible to a broad public without compromising professional standards and alienating my colleagues? Putting an op-ed piece in a Norwegian national newspaper requires the writer to submit a manuscript of no more than four double-spaced typewritten pages. Would it be possible to render a professionally adequate exposition of that most complex of anthropological notions "culture" within this format in a way that appealed to a broad public, yet appeared truthful to my colleagues? Even more was at stake. For it was a question of exposing professional secrets, so to speak, of taking the concept of culture apart, yet doing so in a way that engendered (renewed) trust among customers and clients rather than making them turn their backs on our trade. Or else, I might be accused of having sold out and compromising anthropology in the public eye.

When eventually I chose to run the risk, after numerous rewritings of the essay to be as clear as possible and yet cover my back, it was because I felt I had no choice.[9] Someone must speak out, and I was probably better qualified than most to do it, thanks to a combination of professional and personal circumstances. It was a matter of trying to halt a process that was, as I saw it, deeply misguided and wreaking havoc on the lives not only of all too many immigrants but also of native Norwegians who were grossly misled about the state of affairs. For the sake of our common future, "culture"— the culprit—must be identified and drastically rethought to serve better uses.[10]

THE POLITICS OF CULTURE

The essay was published on the op-ed page of *Aftenposten* on January 4, 1995. Translated from the Norwegian, it is presented below as chapter 9.

9   *Culture—A New Concept of Race?*

My purpose here is to draw attention to how "culture is loose on the streets" of Norway. The expression is not mine. I take it from the anthropologist Paul Bohannan, who thus characterizes a phenomenon of our times: Culture has run astray. And it is now being used helter-skelter to promote all kinds of special interests. [11]

But can a concept that has gone astray function as a suitable frame for the encounter between immigrants and Norwegians? My own answer is no. And I shall propose an alternative that can better facilitate mutual respect and understanding.

First, two examples of how culture is loose on the streets in Norway: As a culture expert—an anthropologist—I receive frequent calls from people who are dealing with immigrants and refugees. One type of question is of this nature: "He has beaten his wife (or children), but he says *it's his culture*. What are we to do?" The callers are social workers. A different type of question comes from a lawyer who phones and says: "I have this client. He has beaten his wife (or murdered a man or something), but I think it's his culture . . . Would you please appear in court as an expert witness for the defense and say that?" And when I say I will not, this is not a matter of culture, the lawyer then proceeds: "But do you think we can find *somebody else* who will say this is his culture?" To which my answer is "Certainly!"

The lawyer has hit the nail on the head: culture is not a thing, a material object; it is just a concept, an abstraction. But because many people clearly think of it as a thing, "culture" becomes amenable for use in defense of all kinds of special interests. Whoever can gain credence for the claim that "this is my culture" or "this is his culture" has the upper hand.

But "culture," like most other concepts, can be filled with various kinds of contents, depending on one's vantage point. Whereas one Muslim may claim that he *must* beat his wife to defend his honor, another will deny that this has any legitimacy. Both can invoke "culture" in support of their view. For in most societies discord prevails about what is to count and for what—though some people have the power to enforce their views on others.

This power aspect is prominent in Norwegian everyday politics, where some people benefit from the aura surrounding "culture." As poignantly expressed in the realistic essay "From a Young Foreign Girl to the Norwegian Social Workers," "You never asked *me*!" Written by a father, Şükrü Bilgiç, the essay is a scathing attack on a social policy that sacrifices the interests of Muslim girls on the altar of culture. By letting themselves be lured by the concept of "culture," Norwegian authorities have actually helped men attain a position of power far beyond what many of them held "back home." By mistaking for the Truth what are actually particular points of view professed by some spokes*men*, Norway has sided with the strong against the weak and vulnerable.

But what *is* "culture"? Is there no universal definition? The answer is no. In 1954, two well-known anthropologists set out to explore how many definitions were in use. The answer was 156—some thirty years ago. Since then, no one has repeated the exercise. What many anthropologists agree on today is that culture refers to the *sum* of learned or acquired (as against innate biological) knowledge and experience among a collectivity of people. We used to say that such knowledge (which includes values) must be *shared*, and that it was *transmitted* from one generation to another. But this has proved untenable—for reasons of great practical relevance for Norwegian immigration policy.

What would it mean if we said that there must be agreement in a population on knowledge and values for a culture to count as such? The question would logically be: Among how many people? A thousand? A hundred? Ten? Two? The question is unanswerable. Rather, as Strauss and Quinn (1994) have argued, "culture" comprises all knowledge and experience embraced by a group or collectivity of people. Culture refers to the *total* sum of such knowledge, which means that children's experience is part and parcel of culture.

Second, why do we no longer underscore *transmission* from one generation to another as the distinguishing mark of culture? To take an example, my mother, my son, and I have lived in different times and places and thus have different experiential knowledge. Would it make sense to say that only my mother's knowledge, as transmitted to me and then to my son, should count as culture? What then of *my* knowledge, which I have accumulated as part of *my* lived experience? What of my son, and what is uniquely his?

To say that culture refers only to traditions and values that have been transmitted from one generation to another is like bowing to ancestors at the expense of children (and adults) whose life experience is very different. And it means freezing culture in time. In reality, culture is always changing, for humans learn as long as they live. Hence Norwegian or Pakistani "culture" must *also* include the children's lived experience and reflect a splendid multiplicity of views. But is this an insight we bring into play when thinking of immigrants?

Take youth as an example. Would it ever occur to Norwegians to try to learn about Norwegian youth culture by asking the fathers? Of course not. We are proud that "our" youths have the ability and will to think for themselves and shape their own identity. But when it comes to youths of immigrant background, we operate with another model: *They* should have their spokes*men* and abide by reified traditions "so that they don't lose their [that is, the fathers'] culture." But if this is so important, why not require the same of Norwegian youths?

We are guilty of applying a double standard, but we do not see it because "culture" is something we apply to "them" but not to ourselves. And here we are at the heart of the matter. We are about to make "culture" into a new concept of race. But the misuse I want to arrest is one that both natives and immigrants are guilty of, and it is unintended. It is a matter of doing harm in the name of charity.

What is racism? It is to treat people condescendingly because of ethnic or biological attributes. "Culture" functions in a racist manner if it is a model of humans we apply only *to "them" but not to ourselves* and if this model implies a *derogatory view* of the Other. And this is my contention: Whereas Norwegians generally regard other Norwegians as individuals with a different character and the ability and will to think for themselves, immigrants are largely perceived as *products* of culture. They are perceived as caught in the grip of culture and therefore unable to exercise independent judgment. But they are thereby deprived of motivation and intention, yes, even of folly and stupidity—basic human traits. It is disrespectful and really quite degrading.

Unfortunately, immigrants themselves often contribute to such degradation. By constantly invoking "culture" as explanation (and excuse) for their behavior, they belittle themselves as acting, thinking, willful human beings; and they run down the very qualities that have brought them here: initiative, courage, perseverance. For it is the resourceful ones who emigrate; the truly disadvantaged remain at home.[12]

I am not alone in issuing a warning. In anthropology today there is an ongoing existential debate about the value and future of the concept "culture." Some well-known scholars advocate getting rid of the concept altogether. It does not do the job it was meant to do—fostering interpersonal understanding and building bridges between people. On the contrary, as a cursory glance at the world shows, "culture" has become a tool, or weapon, for pursuing particular interests and building barriers between people. Other anthropologists argue that "culture" has come to stay but it must be reworked to serve better uses.

Why did things go so wrong? The reasons are several; let me mention one in particular. Anthropologists advocated a concept of culture that focused almost exclusively on differences between people. Who talks about "culture," for example, when a Pakistani acts like "us"? "Culture" has become a label for the exotic and strange, yes, only for the exotic and strange. It does not refer to commonalities among people, to what a Balinese priest formulated thus: "Hindus, Buddhists, and Muslims, they are completely different— exactly the same!" This "completely different, exactly the same-ness" is poorly conveyed by the culture concept. It cannot build bridges between people. A concept that only tells us how strange the Other is may well make for a colorful community [*fargerikt fellesskap*], but mutual respect is more important. Yet that can only be if we take one another seriously as human beings, which means holding one another to account as responsible persons.

"Antiracism means working for the rights of the individual," wrote Khalid Salimi, leader of the Antiracist Center in Norway: "The challenge that a plural society presents us with is to regard others as individuals, not as specimens of groups" (*Dagbladet,* October 3, 1994). This is in accordance with current anthropological theory. Can we then throw the "culture" concept overboard? No, in my opinion and in the opinion of many, perhaps most, anthropologists. But we can use the concept with sensitivity and care. Culture is not a box to put people into and thus to contain their differences as if they were all of a piece; and no amount of courses in cross-cultural communication will ever solve the problem of interpersonal understanding. What is needed is, rather, mutual respect based on a conception of others as different *and* similar. There, and there alone, lies our hope for a well-functioning, multicultural society.

No person is a *product* of either culture or religion. What distinguishes us humans is that we can, and will, think for ourselves and that we have a splendid ability to learn—if we will. Take the ability of immigrants to make use of the Norwegian social welfare system. It has nothing to do with "their culture." The whole system is entirely foreign to the world from which they came. And yet many learn in a minimum of time to master an intricate repertoire of knowledge and techniques. Just so impressive is the human being, just so flexible, in spite of his or her "culture."

Let this insight provide the basis for our efforts to craft a well-functioning multicultural society: The culture discourse has failed. Talks with numerous immigrants as well as Norwegians convince me that "culture" has become a holy cow that breeds impotence, intolerance, and irresponsibility. Many immigrants complain that "culture" is used to stereotype them, erode respect for the individual, and deter integration. Norwegians, on the other hand, complain that "culture" is used as a weapon to brand them "racist," whereas it also serves to protect "us" from addressing "their" problems: call it "culture" and you are excused! It is time to stake out a new course and place personal responsibility and learning ability at center stage. Indeed, it is disrespectful *not* to hold people to account [*Det er respektløst å ikke stille krav til folk*].

The critique of the culture concept that is engaging anthropology must be applied with equal force to the situation of immigrants in Norway. Otherwise the result will be racism—wielded in the name of charity.

10   *Cultures Don't Meet, People Do*

If cultures can collide, they can also meet, or so it is commonly assumed. Indeed, the phrase *kulturmøte,* "meeting of cultures," is much used in Scandinavian languages. But the idea is misleading and may have a number of negative effects if used as a basis for public action.[13]

Cultures cannot meet, for "culture" has no agency. It is just a word, a concept, and concepts do not meet. So talking as if cultures could do this or that—meet, collide, or clash—begs the question of what drives people. It is people, not culture, who have the power to act. And it is people, not culture, who can change life for better or for worse.

Why belabor this point? Because it makes a difference how we use words. You can *do* things with words, as the philosopher J. L. Austin noted long ago (1975 [1962]). I am struck by people's proclivity to talk as if culture were endowed with mind, feeling, and intention. Nor is this just a layperson's way of speaking. Academics, anthropologists included, are as likely as anyone else to talk this way—as if culture had taken on a life of its own.

I want to root out such usage. It can be disastrous in its implications. Place agency where it belongs, with human beings who have the power to act and who can *use* that power for good or ill. True, every one of us is a child of culture in the sense that we are deeply affected by our social environment and the models *of* and *for* life that we have acquired in the course of living (Geertz 1968; Shore 1996). But cultural models are not sui generis. They derive their force or power—their impetus—from their ability to give direction to, and mobilize, *human* energy. "We are no longer content to say that people do things simply because that's their culture or because they've been conditioned by society to do those things," says Robert Paul (1990:30); we have to invoke "an acting subject full of hopes, fears, desires and plans" (1990:4).

This acting subject is in motion; he or she is a feeling, thinking individual with the ability to adapt to new circumstance and respond to changing situations. Culture cannot do such things, for culture is a thought construct. It refers to values, norms, and knowledge that we associate with a collectivity of people. But *what* is to be included in the concept depends on one's vantage point. There is no authentic formula, no naked truth. *People* can think about culture and formulate *their* truth—depending on their perspective. Is it legitimate for women to work outside the home or not? Are children to be brought up to learn to choose for themselves, or is deference to their elders' judgment an ultimate goal? These are some of the issues on which people in the poor quarters of Cairo, where I did fieldwork for a number of years, disagreed with one another. *Both* views are part of the culture of the people. But not all persons will have an equal chance to gain credence for their views. Culture and power go hand in hand, in every society, at all times. And in all societies, children and other weaker members of the group are more likely to be the losers.

If people "of different cultures" are to meet, it must be as people, as persons, for it is only thus we *can* meet. And then the stage is set for something that can foster mutual respect and understanding—or struggle. Talk of "culture," and the picture that springs to mind is one of difference, divergence, and distance. Talk of "people" or "persons" instead, and the picture is one of humans who struggle with some of the same compelling concerns and who therefore—despite all difference—can resonate across time and place.[14] A man in Bhutan put it beautifully: "Our customs are different, but our lives are the same." He was speaking in the midst of agony. A member of an ethnic minority of Southern Bhutanese of Nepali origin, he was threatened with expulsion from his homeland. And he invoked that self-same idea that is at the base of all interpersonal understanding: that life exposes us to a common set of trials and tribulations—despite all differences (Wikan 1994a).

Culture is a layer, a lens through which life is perceived and handled, but we are ultimately vulnerable to forces beyond our reach. Custom or culture can lessen the blow, but it can also exacerbate it, as when Sara, Anna, and

Noreen—whom we shall meet later—are made to pay for being females in ways that most other Scandinavian girls are not. But Scandinavian girls are not spared the agonies of *other* life experiences that can cause deep feelings of loss, betrayal, and pain. In this sense, our lives are the same, as the Bhutanese man reminded me.

When children "of different cultures" get along as well as they often do, it is because they behave as persons, as individuals. They are in motion, not trapped in rigid positions; and they relate to one another as human beings, not as exemplars of "culture." Research on children of different ethnic background in Norwegian primary schools and kindergartens bears testimony to this: "ethnic" is not an important label for them. Children sometimes protest the tendencies of their elders to operate with such labels (see, e.g., Aspelund 1998; Lund 1998; Østby 2001).

"Culture" is a grown-up concept. And it is a Western concept that has spread like wildfire all over the world in recent decades. I, for one, grew up in a world without "culture" as the sum total of a people's lifeways. "Culture" for us referred to the fine arts—of which we had little, north of the Arctic Circle. There were people up there who were different from "us," namely the Sami. But they were not regarded as having a different culture. *Customs* was the word we used. In retrospect I have come to think that maybe this was a more benign way of perceiving—which is not to deny the harm done to the Sami by discrimination and stigmatization at the hands of the majority of Norwegians.

Much has been gained by marking and celebrating Sami culture as the distinct heritage of the Sami people. But something has been lost. People of Sami origin themselves are torn by discord as to what constitutes their culture and who has the right—and the duty—to abide by it (Hovland 1996). With "custom" as one's tool, identity politics is harder to play. For custom refers merely to an aspect of people's activity; it does not encompass the whole human being. Nor does custom imply that a person is stuck, once and for all, in his or her ways. It is in the nature of customs to change. Furthermore, custom, unlike culture, is not usually spoken of as an agent, something with the power to act. Perhaps this is where the contrast with "culture" shows up most clearly: whereas "culture" is constantly featured as an agent, with custom the intentional being is rather a person. So custom is less engulfing. It holds out the hope that people can meet *with* their differences. With "custom" you can be on the move; like baggage, you can carry it or discard it. With "culture" you are tied to your roots.

As noted, several prominent anthropologists argue for getting rid of the concept of "culture" altogether; we are not served, they contend, by a concept that works against its own purposes (Abu-Lughod 1991; Ingold 1993). Others caution against discarding it altogether. Substituting "culture" with "knowledge/experience" is one way to salvage the concept, some suggest (e.g., Barth 1994b; Bloch 1994). Replacing the noun with the adjectival form, as in "cultural values," is another (e.g., Keesing 1994; Paul 1990; Wikan 1996a). These suggestions are not just of academic interest. They stem from a deep sense of disquiet regarding the suffering that can be inflicted, and steadily *is being* inflicted, by the arbitrary use of a concept of "culture."

The advantage of using "knowledge/experience" is that one steers clear of essentialism and reification: it goes without saying that people have different experiential knowledge depending on their background, and also that the lifeworld of children offers a different perspective from that of the parents. Hence one can preserve the idea of commonalities as well as differences within a collectivity. And the definition of reality promulgated by the powerful is reduced to just that: one attempt among many to get a grip on reality and a frame for action. Likewise, to avoid the noun "culture" (which easily becomes "the culture") in favor of the adjectival form is to recognize that there are innumerable cultural differences in outlook and lifeways among people who also have much in common. It also counteracts the idea that there is an objective reality behind the word "culture," and that this reality is lodged in a homogeneous group of people who are in complete agreement on values and norms.

"Culture" refers to norms and values that are contested and contestable. Even the most traditional societies, however isolated and small, have been marked by disagreement and strife regarding values and norms. When this has not been obvious in Western representations, it reflects more on "us" than on "them." Westerners have cherished a romantic idea of primitive societies as characterized by harmony and consensus; and scholars have studied such societies by talking primarily with a few chief informants, mainly eloquent men. But in so doing, they have been running their informants' errands—as Norwegian authorities did when they thought they could get an objective view of the "culture" by listening to the "cultural authorities."

"Culture," by playing up the exotic and dramatizing differences between groups of people ("of different cultures"), disguises differences within one group ("of the same culture"). But this practice makes us seem both more different and more similar than we are. Gender, age, class, education, and other distinctions recede in the face of "culture." Instead it consolidates a contrast between two groups, two cultures. It is this presumption that underlies the expression "collision of cultures" (Fadiman 1999). And it is also, paradoxically, this notion that informs the idea of "the meeting of cultures." For behind that hopeful phrase lurks a silent suspicion: it's going to be hard; will it work, given that people (cultures) are as different as they are? In a multiethnic society one has to hold out hope. I think hope is better served by supplanting a notion of difference with one that heralds the commonality of humans.

I have pointed to some problems regarding the culture concept. Let us briefly recapitulate:

- Culture is a concept, not a thing; although it refers to real phenomena, it has no autonomous or material existence.

- Like most concepts it can be filled with various contents; there is no objective definition. There is, however, broad consensus in anthropology that culture as an *analytic* concept refers to the "distinctly human"—that is, to knowledge and experience people acquire by virtue of their membership in society.[15] Hence, children's experience of the society where they live is as much part of culture as that of the adults.

- Culture has no agency—only humans and other sentient beings have the power to act.

- Neither does culture have any power—beyond what people attribute to it.

- Culture is often portrayed as if it were immutable, whereas all human activity, all conceptual activity, is subject to change; hence all cultural things change.

- Culture is often portrayed as if it possessed uncontested and uncontestable authority, whereas authority actually rests with those who hold power. Some people have the right—or seize the right—to define what is to count and for what, and the result, the authoritative "truth," is often called culture. Culture and power go hand in hand, in every society, at all times.

- Culture is an exoticizing device. It plays upon and exaggerates differences. Thus culture easily becomes a distancing strategy. Culture is usually taken to mean difference, not difference *and* similarity.

Cultures Don't Meet, People Do

- By exaggerating external differences, internal differences between the members of the group are downplayed; and the picture that emerges is one of cultures (plural) at odds with one another. In reality there are numerous important differences internally as well as ties that connect (or can be used to connect) externally.

- Culture plays down the internal differences among members of a group and thus gives a false picture of homogeneity.

To conclude, "culture" covers up the complexity of human existence, the fact that we are all both children of "our culture" and unique individuals—as the Balinese priest put it (Barth 1993), "completely different, exactly the same."

GENDER AND IDENTITY POLITICS | IV

Sara did not live to see herself make headlines in the Swedish newspapers. She died, fifteen years old, at the hands of her brother and cousin. The crime for which she paid so dearly was that of wanting to be Swedish. That she had lived in Sweden since she was ten did not lessen her mortal sin in the eyes of her murderers. She had to pay with her life. And so Sara's mother lost two children—also a son, only sixteen, who had been like a twin brother to Sara (they were only eleven months apart) until he was transformed into her murderer.

Sara's mother tells how Hassan had threatened to kill Sara a couple of weeks before the deed. Sara, he said, was a whore who slept with Swedish boys. "And what about you, don't you sleep with Swedish girls?" asked his mother. Yes, but that was completely different, said Hassan. He was a boy; and in any case he would never dream of sleeping with Iraqi girls (girls of his own kind). It was just with Swedish girls, with whores, that he did it (*Dagens Nyheter*, February 7, 1997).

Three days after the murder, Sara's mother, in a singular act, severed her ties to her son. She collected his belongings, clothes and audiocassettes and all, and carried the lot to the place where Sara had met her death, on a mound of snow close to their home. There she lit a fire and lingered, her laments punctuated by quiet weeping, until the last shred had been consumed. It was her way of saying, You are dead to me, dead like Sara.

When Sara's story came to feature so prominently in the Swedish media, it was not just because of the brutal killing of a young girl by her kinsmen. She gained fame posthumously because she opened Sweden's eyes to a kind of crime that happened not infrequently but had so far been hushed up by the news media. There had been some ten similar attacks before, it now turned out, two of them within the five months before Sara's death on December 15, 1996. But they had received short shrift so as not to incite racist feelings in the population. In this, as in so many matters, the antiracist slogan won out: it dictated reactions to violations of human rights and even to crimes, and it silenced the question of who pays the price of concealment and "tolerance." So Sweden had let the years pass by with little attention paid to the plight of girls of immigrant background. Until Sara opened everyone's eyes.[1]

A fifteen year-old girl had to pay with her life before the country was shaken. And the crime for which she died, according to the evidence, was only that of wanting to enjoy the normal freedom of Swedish girls—the freedom to go dancing, for example. On the eve of her execution, she had attended a party in an Iraqi restaurant with friends. Because there was not enough room in the car that was to take her friends home, she boarded a bus, presumably unaware that her brother and cousin had hidden inside. They had repeatedly threatened to kill her, and she was afraid, so afraid that a week earlier she had received police escort home from a disco. Indeed, Sara lived in constant fear and sometimes spoke of the threats against her life. But who can understand, who can fully believe a fifteen-year-old who says that her kinsmen are going to kill her?[2] Sara's warnings were not taken seriously, and she had to pay the price of her courage. As several girls of immigrant background told reporters, Sara did only what most of them would want to do, but she did it openly. Unlike them, she did not live her Swedish life behind the backs of her male kinsmen. She insisted on her right to freedom; she lived by the force of her convictions and the mores of the country where her future should have been.

The impact of Sara's case was heightened by the force of circumstance. In the course of the two months after her death, Sweden was shaken by two further crimes that took the unique imprint of Sara's case and threw it into relief. Two more women of immigrant background were brutally attacked by their kinsmen. One survived, paralyzed from the waist down. She was a Turkish girl who was stabbed twenty-one times in the back by her brother. The other, a Lebanese woman, was killed by her ex-husband. And their offenses, for which they must pay? They were the same as Sara's. In both cases the attacker justified his deed in the same way that Sara's brother Hassan and her cousin Tareq had done: the victim had become too Swedish, and this constituted a mortal offense to the family's honor.[3]

"Honor" was also at stake in two other cases in the fall of 1996, between four and five months before Sara's death. Varna, a mother of six, was murdered by her husband, also from Iraq. Her offense? She had allegedly talked to another man. But in addition she had testified to what doctors, social workers, and neighbors had already detected (and her children had confirmed)—that her husband beat her severely and often, even while she was pregnant.[4] Although Varna, in fear, withdrew her testimony, the man was sentenced to six months in prison. When he was released after three months for good behavior, he went straight home and killed his wife in their children's presence. He then took the children with him to the police and gave himself up. As the Iraqi-born psychiatrist Riyad al-Baldawi notes, "To report oneself is part of the deed. Such deeds are meant to be known."

More fortunate was a seventeen-year-old girl of Kurdish descent, whose brother tried to kill her. She survived, though badly bruised. The brother was only sixteen years old. Thus, in a six-month period, at least five young women of Middle Eastern background were murderously attacked in Sweden by their kinsmen. Two survived—barely. Three were between fifteen and seventeen years old; two were in their early twenties.

But it was Sara, and not Varna or the others, who changed the record, the discourse. For what reason, I cannot say for sure. Clearly, it mattered that Sara's story was amply covered by the media. But Varna's story too was told in at least one major article (*Expressen*, September 1, 1996). Perhaps it was simply that the time was ripe when Sara met her death—but not when Varna did—for the nation to fully recognize their plight. But there were two other factors as well, I believe, of relevance.

Sara was easier to empathize with than Varna. She touched the hearts of everyone, for she was just a girl who wanted to live like an ordinary Swedish girl, and she had the courage of her convictions. She braved fierce resistance; she stood up for her goals. And she was slaughtered in cold blood for wanting to be—simply—a girl in a civilized nation. Varna's case was more idiosyncratic. Her story was too complex and harder to fathom. A mother of six at the age of twenty-six, she suffered the most violent abuse from her husband and then denied it, though the evidence was plain. There is no hero in this story, only a deeply pitiful woman whose only act of subversion, if her husband is right, was having talked with another man. So Varna is ensconced in the exotic realm, a traditional Middle Eastern wife cum victim. But Sara stands forth in her willful recalcitrance, claiming to be heard, battling for a voice. And heard she was in Sweden posthumously, as few other women, leaving her impact on the nation.

Sweden has been extremely generous—more generous than Norway, until recently—in opening its arms to immigrants and refugees. One in every seven of Sweden's inhabitants has origins in the Third World. The majority of newcomers are from the Middle East. So were the culprits in the cases above: Hassan and Tareq came from Iraq, as did Varna's husband; the two young men who paralyzed their sisters short of killing them were from Turkey; the man who killed his ex-wife was from Lebanon. All those men were enjoying the freedom and social justice of a liberal welfare democracy. But freedom for whom? This was the question that Sweden was now forced to consider. What should be the limits to tolerance? Who has the right to "become Swedish"? How to respond to the idea that becoming Swedish is a sin when it is precisely by *being* Swedish that the nation has been able to develop as it did and offer freedom and social welfare to immigrants from other countries?

As in Aisha's case, the discrepancy between the male's and female's prospects as "immigrant" is thrown glaringly into relief. Sweden has not so far had any case of a female killing a man for becoming "too Swedish." The mere idea sounds absurd. Being "too Swedish" or "too Norwegian" can be a criminal offense only for girls, though boys may also sometimes meet with sanctions from their family.[5] Indeed, a common complaint from girls of immigrant background in Norway is that boys of their kind are given free rein to indulge their freedoms; that's why, some girls say, they would not dream of marrying such boys: they have no manners and no morals. But when girls like Sara or Aisha assert *their* rights to enjoy the liberties incumbent on all citizens in a modern welfare state, even the child welfare authorities often fail to stand by them. Let us consider the two girls by way of comparison. The similarities are striking.

Sara, like Aisha, had a history of coming under the care of the child welfare authorities. She too had been mistreated by her father and subjected to physical and mental abuse. Like Aisha, she had been placed temporarily in a foster home, where she thrived and wanted to remain. But she too was forcibly removed from it and reunited with her family. Aisha, as we know, was returned to her natal home, whereas Sara was placed in the custody of her father's brother. Both Sara and Aisha stood in fear of their custodians. Both tried to escape by running away to their foster families, and both were brought back by force, Sara even with police escort.[6] Both Sara and Aisha feared for their lives, albeit in different ways. Aisha had received threats that she would be deported from her country and forcibly married; Sara had been warned that she would lose her life: "Don't think that you are going to escape death just because your mother did!" Sara's uncle is reported to have said, according to her testimony to her friends. (Sara's mother had divorced her father in Sweden.) And many people, not just Sara and her mother, had heard her brother brag that he was going to kill her.

But when Sara, like Aisha, *acted* on the threats by appealing to the authorities for protection, her fears were brushed aside. "Do they think I'm lying?" Aisha had cried in outrage. "Can't they understand that I can't move home again? . . . I'm afraid to move home again!" She was right. She had reason to be afraid, just as Sara had: the evidence is that the very man in whose custody the child authorities had placed Sara—her uncle—had plotted her murder along with her father and other kinsmen.[7] Her brother and cousin were just the willing executioners.[8] Indeed, the cousin was her custodian's son.

Was, then, the crime against Sara motivated by culture? Can such crimes be culturally explained? This was a key question raised by the respected journalist and lawyer Jesús Alcalá, in the major Swedish newspaper *Dagens Nyheter*. Through a series of articles, Alcalá did more than anyone to ensure that Sara's case received proper national attention. He was also to file a charge against Sara's father and uncle for complicity in the crime after the police had failed to heed the import of testimony by the uncle's ex-wife, that the family had already been plotting Sara's murder a year before the deed.[9]

To the question, can such a crime be culturally explained? Alcalá answered yes, culture was at its base. This elicited critiques from people who took his stance to be conducive of racism. But before we ponder the complexity of the issue, let us listen to his argument.

In an article named "Not a murder, an execution," Jesús Alcalá contends, "The murder of Sara was no 'usual' murder, if such there are. It was an execution. A fifteen-year-old girl was sentenced to death because she wanted to lead and choose her own way in life" (*Dagens Nyheter*, February 10, 1997). Alcalá points to the fact that Sara's murderers had repeatedly threatened to kill her because she didn't care about her honor, she was a whore, and she brought shame on the whole family. "Honor" and "shame" figured prominently in their vocabulary, and not as jargon but as lethal passions. The boys claimed that culture had nothing to do with the murder—it was an accident, they said; they had merely been a bit mad at Sara and wanted to scare her, when a belt they were threatening her with caught hold, and she was strangled. But their words are not credible. The menfolk in Sara's family abide by an old-fashioned culture imbued with "honor" and "shame." In such a culture, as Alcalá argued, the woman does not count for much relative to the man. She should abide by his wishes and be the repository of the family's honor. This view of the prerogatives of the male rests on a deep depreciation of woman that is culturally endorsed: in short, there *are* cross-cultural differences in the way women are perceived, and there are even cultures where a murder is not a murder if the victim is a woman—hence the title of Alcalá's piece, "Not a murder, an execution." In some places, killing a woman who transgresses the strict norms of propriety is considered a manly act, which resurrects the family's honor.

To this, Alcalá's critics replied that it is dangerous and wrong to argue as he does. There are in Sweden today about 85,000 people from the countries from which the culprits of the crimes that had gained such notoriety came. Most of them live by the law and condemn such crimes. Also, as some underscored, Sweden has its share of indigenous wife abusers. Violence against women is nothing exotic, it is a common problem, and it is this that should be addressed, not the culture of specific culprits. Indeed, when Swedish men are found guilty of violence, it is explained in individual or structural terms. So why call on "culture" just because the perpetrators are immigrants?[10]

But Alcalá also received support from many quarters. Jan Hjärpe, a highly respected authority on Islam, put it bluntly: "True, Swedish men also kill their wives—but they are not applauded for it" (*Sydsvenskan*, February 11, 1997). As Hjärpe wrote, a crucial difference between these immigrant men and Swedish men is that the former come from societies where the family or clan commands supreme loyalty; the head of the family has certain judicial powers over all its members; and the family's honor depends crucially on the sexual modesty of women. Hence the applause when the men avenge an affront caused by female misdemeanor. This pertains even though the crimes were committed by deviants, and were in no way normal behavior.

Several immigrants supported this view. Among them were Nalin Baksi, a Kurd who is now a member of the Swedish Parliament, and Ferryal Messo Bolos, from Syria. As Ferryal said, "Defending the family's honor makes one a hero" (*Sydsvenskan*, February 12, 1997). Some immigrant women with firsthand experience of working with other immigrants also came out in support of Alcalá's stance: hidden violence, they said, was a pervasive and growing problem in many homes. Women usually do not dare to complain for fear of reprisals; nor will neighbors or relatives speak out. The fear of reprisals silences everyone, except for a few courageous souls like Sara. But the price they paid for their convictions will act as a deterrent to others who would have wanted to stand by their freedom as these women did.

Alcalá deserves credit for his courage and eloquence in raising these issues. Idris Ahmedi from Kurdistan said in an interview, "The researchers kid themselves when they ignore the culture. They are afraid of nurturing racism. But the debate becomes meaningless if we do not talk openly. Culture and tradition play a major role, and they are slow to change" (*Hufudstadsbladet*, March 8, 1997).

Yet I also must agree with Alcalá's critics: it *is* dangerous to argue as he does, not least because the notion of "cultural crime" is already being invoked by some lawyers and those they defend who argue that a defendant's acting according to "his culture" may be considered a mitigating circumstance. Thus Alcalá's argument can be turned on its head and used to excuse crimes rather than to hold people accountable. Moreover, I agree that to label Sara's murder "cultural" is to run the risk of stigmatizing a whole people ("of the same culture"), many of whom would distance themselves as emphatically from the terrible deed as would you or I. And yet we cannot do away with "culture" in our attempt to make sense of what was at stake.

"Honor and shame" are part and parcel of many societies, in the Middle East and elsewhere. In some societies "honor crime" even receives official backing as justifying atrocities against women (Shaaban 1991; Stewart 1994). Thus, there is ample evidence that the problems Alcalá identifies, and Hjärpe and others underscore, are genuine and cause tremendous suffering for females in many societies. There is also no denying that culture has traditionally played a part in justifying such crimes, and that it does so even today, among some people, in some places.[11]

Times are changing, and more and more people are speaking out. Middle Easterners in Europe and elsewhere represent a plethora of perceptions and practices. That is not the point when we look at Sara. The point is that her murder—and the assault on many females in Scandinavia and elsewhere—is justified with reference to an honor-shame complex that is deeply rooted in the hearts and minds of people. If men are perpetrators in most cases, culture is the tool they use to target their victims and justify their crimes.[12] A vast literature testifies to the prevalence of the problem.

Jesús Alcalá has a point, and it is important. He fears that Sara's murder will go down in history as a singular case, an individual tragedy, when there are, as he writes, "many Saras. Let us not betray them." He asks: "What shall we do with Sara? What responsibility do we—did we—have for Sara?" And his answer is that Sweden must not sleep any longer. Sweden must wake up to the painful reality, the hard fact, that there are numerous women of immigrant background who struggle as Sara did and they have been forgotten or ignored. This is not to say that all should or would want to take Sara's path to personal freedom. Alcalá writes:

> Among Muslim women—even in Sweden—there are surely many, perhaps a majority, who only want to stay at home and find it totally in order that the man should make all major decisions regarding family and society. This can be well and good. But we are talking about those women who do not want to subject themselves to this kind of order. In short, what shall we do with Sara? What responsibility do we—did we—have for Sara?

Alcalá believes that there are "cultures that are, how to put it, better than others in the sense that they are less oppressive and more tolerant toward the individual, regardless of gender." To those who hold that saying so is dangerous and inducive of racism, Alcalá replies that criticizing inhuman aspects of a cultural tradition is not the same as belittling a whole people. Silence is much worse. It would mean assenting to outrageous offenses that are perpetrated in the name of culture. "We place ourselves in an impossible situation if we try to make human freedom and human rights subject to negotiation, depending on political and religious context." Further, Alcalá writes,

> I believe that all humanism presupposes the individual perspective. We must all try to become something else and more than the sum of received and unreflected assumptions in the society in which we happen to be born. Neither our desire to be diplomatic nor Hassan's and Tareq's traditions must be allowed to cover up or excuse the murder of Sara.
>
> The idea of the integrity and basic value of the human being rests on the premise that the individual has a right to respect also beyond her membership in a group, even in the absence of friends who share her views (*meningsfrender*), even in her recalcitrant independence, even in her solitude . . .
>
> There are many Saras. Let us not betray them. (Alcalá 1997b)[13]

12   *Anna and Others: Religion Is Not the Culprit*

The stories of Sara and others told in the last chapter may give the impression that the "cultural" factors at work in the crimes against them stem from

Islam or the Muslim tradition. But such is not the case, according to Dr. Riyadh al-Baldawi, an Iraqi-born psychiatrist, now living in Sweden. With his wife, psychologist Fatima al-Baldawi, Dr. al-Baldawi has done research on the psychosocial problems of several families of Middle Eastern background in Sweden. Lending support to Alcalá's argument that cultural factors are indeed involved in crimes like the above, Dr. al-Baldawi notes that behind the kinds of problems that plague Sara's family (divorce, alcohol abuse, violence against women, male delinquency, etc.) one commonly finds a pattern rooted in patriarchal family structure. In the patriarchal family, all power rests with the male head of the family, but the eldest son in particular is obliged to serve in his stead and defend the family honor, if necessary. Daughters, on the other hand, rank lowest in the family hierarchy, and are very strictly guarded.

But it is tradition, not religion, that is at bottom, according to Dr. al-Baldawi. What is at stake are age-old traditions and customs. It is when this family structure meets an entirely different society with completely different gender norms that a catastrophe like Sara's can occur. What we see is a battle for power (*Dagens Nyheter*, December 19, 1997).

Fatima al-Baldawi adds that "people from that part of the world regard Sweden as a female-run country. They meet only women at the social welfare offices, in school, at the employment offices, and such places." Indeed, when Hassan and Tareq, Sara's murderers, gave themselves up to the police and were met by a female official, they refused to talk to her. It was beneath their dignity. A man had to be called so that they could speak to an equal (Alcalá 1997b).

The testimonies by Dr. Riyadh and Fatima al-Baldawi are corroborated by Anna, speaking three weeks later in another context but on the same theme. It was in the aftermath of Sara's death, but by then the Turkish girl had also met her tragic fate, and other stories, previously less noted or even concealed, had been revealed. They were now seen to form a pattern— the kind of pattern the al-Baldawis observed, with alcohol abuse, violence against women, male delinquency, and so forth—rooted in a battle for power as a patriarchal family structure is challenged by the rule of law and the men's self-respect is struck at its core. But however strongly the al-Baldawis contended that religion was not the culprit—the problem lay with tradition and custom—the suspicion lingered among many that it could not be wholly so. Or was it accidental that the culprits in all the above cases were Muslims? Yes, it was, says Anna—a Christian of Syrian descent. So this is where her story comes in.

Anna was seventeen when her story appeared in the press, two days after the Turkish girl had been brutally attacked by her brother and paralyzed from the waist down. It was Anna herself who contacted the newspaper *Expressen* and asked that her story be heard. In all essentials it resembles that of the Turkish girl—and of Sara—except that Anna is still alive and walking. But she feared for her life, especially as the child welfare agencies—applying the "best-interest" doctrine—wanted to reunite her with her family or, at least, tell them where she was living (Anna had been placed in foster care after reporting her family for repeated violence against her). As Anna said, "If I am forced to move home again, I'll run away. For the punishment is bound to come, sooner or later. One never escapes one's family" (*Expressen*, January 10, 1997).

By going public with her story, Anna hoped for support and understanding: "It isn't at all unusual that immigrant girls are mistreated and threatened with death by their fathers and brothers! You Swedes could just not imagine how things are with us!" Now with Sara and all the others whose tragedies had surfaced, she knew she could count on a believing audience. And she had a specific point to make: Don't just believe that it's Muslims ("bad guys," "fundamentalists") who do such things. In Anna's view, "the Christians in our homelands are worse than the Muslims." One need not buy into her generalization to take the point: don't blame religion. The problem is rooted elsewhere. And if you delude yourselves into thinking Islam is the culprit, you'll never be able to help the likes of me, Anna.

That she needed help and had long been in need of help is evident from what she told of her upbringing. I present her story here because it mirrors themes and complaints that appear with increasing frequency from girls of Middle Eastern and South Asian background in Scandinavia; and also from dedicated teachers, social workers, child care workers, physicians, and others who deal with such girls and are perplexed and distressed at much of what they see, wondering how to help. How to help the girls without infringing on "their culture" or inviting the rage of their male family members is how the problem is often posed. Realizing that "their culture" is not necessarily that of the girls is a first step. Helping girls to find their voice is a good second step. Without support, without "adults to rely on," as Anna puts it, too many girls may find, as she did, that they can hardly manage any more the quest for freedom and the right to speak for themselves. So listen to Anna's voice. The problems to which she points, family abuse and the denigration of women, may have diverse roots and take various forms, but they are often found in patriarchal family structures wedded to an "honor and shame" complex.

Anna is a Swedish citizen. She came to Sweden when she was four and has never returned to Syria. Nonetheless, she doesn't feel as if she is living in Sweden. She is imprisoned by walls of isolation and control that her family has erected around her. The family's honor is all-important. Those who contravene the rules cast shame on themselves and the whole family.

> "Think of what the people will say, just think what they will say about our family!" These are the words I've been raised on . . .[14]
>
> For girls, everything centers on getting married and being a virgin at marriage. That's why girls are very strictly guarded all the time. (*Expressen*, January 10, 1997)

Anna herself has been forced to be examined by a gynecologist so that her family can check that she is still a virgin.

In Anna's case, her family's strict adherence to traditional norms has nothing to do with marginalization in the labor market.

> My family has worked all the time while in Sweden. But as soon as they come home, they shut out everything connected with a Swedish way of life. They never watch Swedish TV, only Arabic cable TV. I have never been in the home of a Swedish family. I don't have a single Swedish girlfriend.[15] If I should dare even to glance at a Swedish boy, my father would kill me . . .
>
> My mother has beaten me more than my father,[16] but he hits harder. Beating is part of our upbringing. My brothers beat me too, they have my father's permission. "Don't you talk to me in that voice," they may say, and knock me to the ground. All the men in our family have the right to beat me, those are the rules. And they are proud to do it! . . .
>
> I have never been allowed to go outside and play like other children. As soon as I was big enough, I had to take care of my younger siblings and do housework when I came home from school. "Girls must always be kept busy, for if they don't work, they will want to go out, and then they might bring shame on the whole family." That's how the males reason in my family.

In the town where she lives, Anna has a large family spanning several generations. So there are always some relatives around to keep an eye out and to make a fuss if she so much as smiles at a boy from school:

"Have you had sex together?" they will ask. Then there will be a thousand questions. "We know you greeted that boy outside the store! Why did you do that? Do you know him? What have you been doing together? Have you been sleeping together?"

She says she will probably marry some day. But it is inconceivable that she could marry a Swede. Just as inconceivable as that she could marry a Muslim:

> The best thing, according to the family, is to marry a relative, like a cousin. But it must be somebody the whole (extended) family can accept, otherwise there will be quarrels and discord . . .[17]
>
> What a girl fears the most is being forced to travel to her parents' homeland and be married against her will. My parents have threatened me with that many times.

Even though Anna has grown up in a conflict-ridden family, she has always attended school regularly and has gotten good grades. Her longing for the right to a life of her own she has kept to herself.

> There are no adults to trust, so I keep mostly to myself. But I dream about an ordinary Swedish life and hope that I shall have time to get myself an education before I am married . . .
>
> But now that I have brought shame to the whole family [by telling this story], I don't know what will happen to me . . .[18]

She implores us:

> Listen to me, I have grown up here and been educated here. I have had to learn Swedish ways and to follow Swedish law. I have had to learn to respect people and to show them respect—while I grew up in a family where beatings were a normal and natural part of upbringing. Because of the men's power and control I have not had the same opportunities to have friends my age as Swedish girls do.
>
> . . . My life since childhood has been like this: going to school, coming straight home, looking after the house, taking care of my younger siblings, cooking, laundering, caring for babies. This since I was six years old.
>
> . . . I'm grateful for the upbringing I have had. Still, I wish I could have had a childhood more like other children, and could be a normal teenager. With us, it's not unusual for girls to be married off at the age of ten or as soon as they reach puberty. To be a virgin when married is a

must. Otherwise, the whole family is disgraced. To this day a bloodstained handkerchief must be displayed to the groom's parents after the wedding night as proof of the bride's virginity.[19] That's why we are absolutely forbidden to use tampons.

I have grown up in Sweden, I feel like a Swede inside, but there is a bit of the old as well. All I ask is to be able to live my life as a Swedish citizen and a free human being, not as a slave bound by religion. I will fight for my right to live as a Swedish citizen. But at times the evil powers seem overwhelming and I feel as if I cannot bear it any more.

Now the social welfare authorities want to reveal my secret address to my parents. Also, they are thinking of dispensing with the rules of discretion and giving my parents information about me that is harmful.

Swedes harbor the prejudice that Muslims are mean [hårda], but Christians are not just mean, they are rabid.

Thus spoke Anna. Her words should be taken for what they are, a lament, a rhetoric of complaint. Doubtless there are multiple truths—many different versions of the truth—in her case, as in any family relationship. But she draws attention to problem complexes that have reverberated throughout this book since our first meeting with Aisha.

What girls dread most is being forced to travel to their parents' homeland and to be married against their will, says Anna, in line with the young man who commented on Aisha's fate. Indeed, by the late 1990s the problem of forced marriage had become so prevalent and well publicized in several European countries that Norway, for one, has issued warnings to girls over fifteen not to travel to their parents' homeland if they fear such a fate.[20] Once the girl is out of Europe, there is little that can be done to help her— as we have already seen with Aisha. Anna's contention that parents use the threat of forced marriage as a disciplinary measure is testified to by many young girls I know, although with the attention that forced marriage is now receiving in several European countries, it may be that parents will become less prone to use such threats, so as not to scare the girls into seeking protection from the state.[21]

Anna's remark that she would never be allowed to marry a (native) Swede or a Muslim reminds us of Mladen Citanović's question to Norwegian political leaders in the TV debate in September 1995: "Why is it that if a Norwegian won't let his daughter marry an immigrant, it's called racism, but if an immigrant won't let his daughter marry a Norwegian, it's called cul-

Anna and Others: Religion Is Not the Culprit

ture?" With Anna, however, it was not even a question of a Muslim's being forbidden to marry a non-Muslim—a common enough scenario, since Islam is generally understood to veto such a marriage for females[22]—but of a Christian's being forbidden to marry a fellow Christian—that is, a Swede. To refuse to see this for what it is is to nurture the forces that breed ethnic and religious cleavages and undermine basic personal liberty.

Anna's description of a childhood spent in hard work and under strict control is in line with reports from many corners regarding the lives of many Asian and African girls in Scandinavia: coming straight home from school, doing housework, attending to siblings, providing company for mother—an often desperately lonely woman who knows little of the wider society, doesn't speak the local language, and rarely leaves her house. Here a daughter comes in handy. A girl is her mother's lifeline to the world. But at what cost? The loss of a quite ordinary, normal childhood is how Anna phrases it. Research shows that girls of immigrant background in Europe are often much more strictly controlled than their agemates of similar socioeconomic level in their countries of origin. Evidence from the United States points in the same direction.

Whereas time moves forward in Pakistan, Turkey, and other places from which immigrants hail, it seems to stand still or even move backward among many in their present abodes, where there is a revival and reinvention of tradition. Sükrü Bilgiç (2000:49) provides an example based on the research of Esma Ocak: in some villages in Turkish Kurdistan (where there is great cultural diversity), girls as young as twelve to thirteen had boyfriends—and their mothers knew; it was regarded as a natural thing. But in Norway, Bilgiç observes, similar behavior would be inconceivable among Turkish Kurds. Moreover, whereas in Turkey the sexes are allowed to meet and mingle at festivities and weddings, in Norway strict sex segregation is practiced by the very same people. Hence what is permissible and honorable in Turkey becomes taboo and shameful in Norway.

From Denmark, Gülsum, a Turkish Dane, tells the story of how she was ousted from her family in Denmark when she married a Dane. Not even when the couple had a child would the Turkish grandparents relent. But when Gülsum and her husband visited relatives in Turkey, they were welcomed with open arms (cited in Mørck 1996). So too with a Tunisian-French couple in France; they were ousted from the wife's family in France, but heartily welcomed by her relatives in Tunis (Benjnouh 2001). What is acceptable or even prestigious among people in Turkey or Tunisia may be an affront to their countrymen in Europe, especially if they are from the countryside. This is a point noted by many scholars. The clash is not between an "immigrant" culture and a West European culture but between an urban and a rural way of life. Since many of the immigrants to Western Europe hail from rural districts in their homelands, what they impart to their children are mores and values that have long since disappeared, or that are on the point of disappearing, among modern people in their native lands.

"Tradition," however, does not affect all equally. It is females, primarily, who are affected. This is the irony that the stories of Sara and Anna bring out, as do those of more ordinary, uneventful lives: there is a discrepancy between the female's and the male's positioning in time. Whereas she is confined more strictly than ever so as to stay pure and clean and to avoid contamination from the West, he savors new freedoms and breaks new ground. Discos, alcohol, and "whores" at night, sports, outings and other activities in the day are the indulgences of many males who watch their females with an eagle eye.

Such behavior is often explained with reference to the male's very difficult life situation, which includes unemployment and psychosocial problems linked to the immigrant experience or the ordeals that preceded it. Marginalization, discrimination, or even racism add to the pains of encountering "a female-run country," as Fatima al-Baldawi called it. One's absolute authority and power as a male is challenged by a society that sets a high value on gender equality, and sides with women, as many men feel. Overdramatization of authority and power may be a natural response to a profound challenge to one's person and identity. Dr. al-Baldawi warns: "it is important that the social agencies do not uncritically take the side of one party. One must look to the whole family: even the often degraded man or father must be met with understanding" (*Dagens Nyheter*, December 19, 1997). The stress and the traumas are perceived to afflict the male deeply, and hence one can also understand why outlets for frustration and aggression are needed.

But what about the Saras and Annas? What remedies do they have? Anna has given her answer: none. Bilgiç (2000:104–5) observes, "The girls have to bow their heads for the authorities. Because they have no other choice, they appear to accept the situation with equanimity." He makes another important point: that because the practice is for "immigrant" youths to live with their parents until they are married (and often afterward), the parties have to contain the stresses that might otherwise be released by the youngsters' moving out. Anna and the al-Baldawis remind us that it is a given who will have to carry the main burdens. As Anna said, "one never escapes one's family."

Anna, the Assyrian Christian, went to the press to ensure that Swedes would understand that Islam is not the enemy. Christians may be just as bad. Unless Swedes realize that, they will never be able to help girls like her, a Swede who wants to live as a citizen in a civilized nation, not as a slave bound by religion. But what *is* the relationship between culture and religion?

Anna seems to confound the two, as if they were one and the same. And naturally so. She has grown up in a community where religion is used as the justification for moral behavior in general. "Right and wrong" depend on religion in her world, and religion is constantly invoked to encourage good behavior and justify punishment for wrongs. This is the case all over the Middle East, and among Middle Easterners in Scandinavia.

Dr. al-Baldawi takes a different view. Religion and tradition are different, and should be separated. Religion should not be blamed for violence inflicted in patriarchal traditions. The problem is power abuse, not religion.

Can his view and Anna's be reconciled? Yes, they can. People generally speak to a purpose, and if we look more closely at what each of them wants to achieve with their messages, their differences can be resolved. People like Dr. al-Baldawi, an adult intellectual living in a multicultural Western society, will constantly be called upon to defend Islam against blame for all kinds of atrocities carried out in the name of religion by fundamentalists and others. Salvaging religion from the contaminating influence of inhumane practices becomes important. It is increasingly done, in my experience, by liberal Muslims in the diaspora. It is a way of protecting one's own identity and all one holds dear. And it is a way of showing that religion and change are not incompatible: rather, a living religion necessitates change (see al-Hibri 1999; Nussbaum 1999).

But for Anna, as for Sara, religion appears the archenemy. Sara said she wanted to leave Islam when she became an adult. Anna called Christians she knew "rabid." For these two girls, and many others, religion becomes a prison. No intellectual attempt to separate religion from tradition can help them: together they make up inseparable parts of the patriarchal practice that denies them the freedom they long for. For their family, religion and tradition *are* one and the same; and that is what the girls have to deal with.

Different stakes, different experiences and positions, explain these apparently different views of the role of religion versus that of tradition. Ultimately, however, the al-Baldawis and Anna seem to me to have a common project: to try to break the spell that intimidates public authorities and public opinion and makes them complicit in violence waged in the name of either culture or religion. What is truly at stake is neither religion nor culture; it is the rights of individuals, the limits of control and compulsion legitimately vested in groups, be they family, ethnic communities, or nations.

13   Noreen's Story: The Price of a Narrow Escape

Noreen's story is told in the book *Izzat—For the Sake of Honor* (1996), by Nasim Karim, a Norwegian of Pakistani descent. Noreen is a fictional character, but her story mirrors that of the author, whose experience has become well known through the press and the broadcast media in Norway.[23] Noreen faced the same fate that Anna spoke of and Aisha experienced. She was married by force, betrayed by her own father—whom she had adored. She managed to escape, but the price she paid was excruciating: she lost her family and community. The author became an outcast who has lived in hiding much of the time since she came back to Norway in 1992; and she has suffered severe mental and physical distress. In 1996 she even had a fatwa issued against her, and fled the country for a time in fear for her life.

Yet she has not allowed herself to be silenced. She has spoken up time and again, launching a crusade against forced marriage and other forms of violence perpetrated in the name of culture. She has become a spokesperson for numerous girls of immigrant descent in Norway who are afraid to speak up. Nasim is ostracized in many circles. She has been severely criticized by certain members of the antiracist movement for painting a hurtful and wholly inaccurate picture of women's plight in Pakistan. One critic even accused her publicly of having produced a pack of lies. But she stands her ground with eloquence and conviction. She became the first girl in Norway to have her forced marriage annulled by the courts.[24] Indeed, it was thanks to her that forced marriage came onto the political agenda in Norway. Nasim's case resulted in the reinstatement of a section against forced marriage as part of the Norwegian marriage law in 1995. The section had been canceled two years previously because it was deemed superfluous. It took Nasim's case to convince Parliament and the judiciary that their optimism had been premature. Posterity has proved that the 1995 law is still not strong enough to address the facts we have before us, as we shall see when we revisit Aisha's case

It was when Nasim spoke to some members of the Norwegian Parliament that I heard her utter these memorable words: "When a man is subject to violence, it is called torture, but when a woman is subject to violence, it is called culture."

Here is Noreen's story, drawn from *Izzat—For the Sake of Honor*. Noreen was the daughter of Pakistani immigrants to Norway and the apple of her father's eye. She lived with her parents and siblings in a town just outside of Oslo, in comfortable circumstances. Her father had come as a poor man from Pakistan in the late 1960s; one pair of pants and a worn shirt (which he keeps to this day in an old suitcase and occasionally displays to his children) were all he had in the way of clothes. Through hard work and frugality—which is the point of the old clothes display—he managed to build a considerable fortune. Prematurely retired and receiving disability benefits, he suffers no material distress, for he owns several buildings in Norway and Pakistan. But the satisfaction he enjoyed materially was not to bring him the honor and prestige he craved. This is where Noreen comes in. It was she who wrecked his life, his honor, and his health because she did not want to go along with the life plan he had intended for her—one that, in her own words, would have made her the wife of a poor, illiterate peasant in a backward village in Pakistan.

It is to Nasim Karim's credit that she sympathizes with the father, depicting him as his own worst enemy. She regards him as both a victim and an offender. But there are no impersonal forces in her account, no "culture" that compels people to do its bidding. Rather, there are individual persons, like the father, brother, uncle, and other Pakistanis, who have the power to *choose* but consistently use this power to further their own ends at the expense of others. Culture is the coin they use to justify their actions—if "justify" is the right word. In their view, actions performed to protect the family honor are automatically just. But it is *people*, human beings, who perpetuate the charade, giving honor the power to destroy lives. Noreen reflects:

> For many years I have been depressed about the traditions in my part of the world. I have seen all too many girls married against their will—not just Pakistanis but Iranians, Turks, Moroccans, and Indians. These are the same traditions and rules that are being deployed everywhere. The same notion of honor, *izzat,* is invoked. The girls cry while the parents say "we are obliged." "Obliged"—it seems so cheap . . . Why can't they just say it as it is: "We have to destroy your future. You mean less to us than our honor."
>
> . . . Everyone knew I was being forced to marry and that it was illegal according both to the Qur'an and to Pakistani laws; yet no one did a

thing to help me. No one tried to talk sense into [my father] or stand up for me. The whole atmosphere seemed to imply that what he was doing was right. But it was not right, nor can it ever be right to destroy another human being's life. No one has the right to do that. (Karim 1996:14–15)

And the destruction of a life it would have been had not Noreen managed to escape. After the wedding she thinks,

> My father has destroyed me. He has taken his own daughter's life. He has married me to a poor relative in a village. I am to cook on a fire, fetch water from the well, and wash clothes in the river. I shall live in a dilapidated house without electricity, I shall be raped, and I shall deliver my children on an earthen floor. My father has given a man the right to rape me. My life has no meaning any longer. I want to die. (120)

Suicide was often on her mind during the months leading up to the grim finale, her wedding. This is how she describes it:

> Three hundred people stand watching as a corpse is brought in by her father. No one does anything to help me, though everyone knows I'm being forced. They know it is illegal and yet they let it happen. The thought of suicide is stronger than ever, and I know that if that so-called husband of mine ever so much as touches me, then it's the end, then I shall kill myself. (118)

On three earlier occasions she had tried to do precisely that, once by swallowing an arsenal of pills, once by driving at top speed and crashing her car (injuring a pedestrian but escaping relatively unharmed herself), and once by trying to jump off a cliff. Each time, especially the last, she was brutally beaten for her defiance. In a chapter titled "Torture and Submission" she describes how her father and brother beat her almost to death—under the eyes of her aunts, uncles, and cousins, who were unable to help.

> One of my aunts cries but dares not intervene. I look at them with despair, begging mutely for help, but they avert their eyes.
> "You wanted to kill yourself, but I'm not going to let you die so easily. I'm going to make you suffer for it," I hear Papa say.
> Tears are streaming down my face, but I keep quiet from fear of what will happen if I emit a sound. Papa unbuckles his belt and starts beating me. I want to cry out with pain, but dare not. I pray desperately to God for help, but again no God is there for me. No one, neither God nor

human, prevents what is happening. They keep beating, kicking, cursing, and tearing my hair. At regular intervals they stop and ask,

"Now, are you going to obey? Are you willing to be married?"

I have only one thought in my head. This is a battle they are not going to win. I will not give in! They get the same answer each time:

"Never!"

Their assault continues, worse than before.

One of my uncles, who is very religious but who has forgotten for the time being that the Qur'an forbids marriage by force and that it gives girls the full right to refuse, says, "If she will not be married, we shall kill her!"

My brother, who is standing beside him, joins in:

"Yes, let's do that, let's kill her," as if it were the easiest thing in the world, as if I were just a glass they could break.

My grandfather bends over me:

"Do as they say or they will kill you, bribe the police and get away with it!"

"Get out the pistol," says another uncle.

I am frozen with fear. I realize that they mean what they say. They're going to kill me. I don't believe Papa will let them do it, but there are many of them, and they can go against his will. It's no longer a question of what he wants but of what the family wants. That's probably the way it has been all the time—Papa has done what the family thought necessary to save his honor. I'm a threat to his honor, and therefore to theirs. My feelings are in full revolt. I am frantic and furious at the same time, and I know only one thing: I can't let them win. I won't let them kill me. *They* are not to decide if I am to live or to die. I don't know that I want to live, but if I'm going to die, I shall die by my own hand, not theirs. I'm going to show them who decides.

"No, no, don't do it! I shall do everything you say! Don't kill me, don't kill me!" I implore them.

I give in. After being hit, kicked, whipped, and cursed for six hours, I give in. I know I have agreed to their destroying my future so that I can save my own life—and save the last remnant of my self-respect.

I gave in because I was alone and there were too many of them. I shall never forget how they forced me to sit by Papa's feet and hug his knees and beg for my life. That I can never forget. (109–11)

Having granted her the right to live, Noreen's father gives her the right to choose her own husband from the extended family. "You can choose one of these five boys," he says, showing her their photos, "for I don't want to force you." Not force her? Does her father no longer see the difference between freedom and force? Noreen wonders. They might as well have asked her to choose her own executioner. She refuses to choose, thus retaining a vestige of self-respect. But they continue to press, and in the end she randomly chooses someone called Hussein:

> I have never felt so small and so humiliated. They have abused me physically and mentally for hours in front of my own family. This feeling of being small, dirty, and helpless will remain with me forever. (III)

Noreen's ordeal has a kind of happy ending. She manages to escape after the wedding and prevent consummation of the marriage by using menstruation as an excuse (Islam forbids sexual relations during menstruation). But when her alleged period persists for eight days, her in-laws become suspicious, and she herself grows desperate. So she conceives a plan that she executes in masterly fashion—though with a good deal of luck. Feigning severe stomach pain, probably connected with menstruation, she asks to be taken to the doctor in the nearest town. Before leaving, she collects all her wedding jewelry and puts it in her bag, realizing it might be needed to bribe the police and buy herself a ticket to Norway. After reaching the town and while walking to the doctor's office, she tells her husband, who is escorting her, that she needs to talk to a friend who is working in a beauty salon. "Men are not allowed in, so please wait outside. But instead of just standing there and waiting, why don't you go and buy me a handbag?" Noreen suggests. Naive and in love, Hussein does as she says. Noreen enters the beauty salon, where there are six girls, all of them acquaintances. They are alarmed when they see her, but she tells them, "Relax. I know what I'm doing. I'm going to escape. Just give me fifty rupees and a veil to cover my face with." They give her what she asks, and one of the girls also exchanges clothes with her. Then they help her drape the veil so that her face and hair are completely covered. "If my husband comes, tell him I'm in the toilet and that I shall have a haircut afterward. Tell him to go to the tailor and get some clothes for me, and if he creates an uproar when he gets back, tell him I'm gone and you don't know where I am," Noreen exhorts them.

Bidding the girls farewell, Noreen panics, realizing that in Pakistan a human life is not worth more than a 200,000-rupee bribe to the police, and that her family will gladly pay that much—if she gets caught.

She is both lucky and ingenious. She manages to catch a bus to Islamabad and make her way to the Norwegian embassy—which is closed. But she inveigles a guard to give her the ambassador's private address, and reaches the house at midnight. The ambassador is home, but the Pakistani guard refuses to let her in. Showing him her Norwegian identification card, which she happens to have in her bag (though not her passport, which her family had confiscated), she finally gains entry. "It must be important," says the ambassador when he sees her. She tells him her name, says she is a Norwegian citizen, and describes what has happened to her. "Do you realize that your father and brother may be prosecuted for what you have told me?" the ambassador asks. Noreen hesitates:

> Pictures race through my head. I see Papa's and Amir's pale faces; I see Mama and [my younger sister] Imran crying and relatives turning their backs on them in the street. I see Papa and Amir with flails in their hands, myself in my wedding dress. My face turns hazy, it changes, the corpselike skin takes on Imran's face. I must prevent them from destroying her too. I have only one answer. "Yes, I am aware of that, but they have to take the consequences of their actions." (156)

Noreen is invited to stay overnight in the ambassador's residence, and the next day she is given a new passport. But she must pay for the ticket to Norway herself. She sells her jewelry, which fetches more than the price of the ticket. Escorted by an armed guard from the embassy, she is taken to the airport the following day, and safely boards a plane for Norway. "On a summer night in 1992, British Airways flight 736 finally lands at Fornebu (Oslo international airport). After ten months and twenty-eight days in Pakistan I am back in the same Norway that I left behind. But nothing will ever be the same" (5).

She is met at the airport by two policemen and secretly escorted to the Shelter for Women in Oslo. She does not even go through passport control, because the ambassador has warned the airport authorities that her life might be in danger.

> It's a terrible way to come back to Norway. Instead of being greeted by my family at the airport, I am met by the police. Instead of going home, I am driven to the Shelter. No one is happy to welcome me home again, no one offers me a meal or wants to hear how I have been . . . I get a room and sit there all by myself, thinking about what has happened. (8)

At night she calls the child welfare authorities in her home town and talks with the person who oversaw her case when she was under their care before going to Pakistan. The official says she is sorry, but they cannot help her any more because she is too old now—two months past eighteen.

But when they returned me to my father's custody, their talk was different. Then they said, "If anything happens to you while you're in Pakistan, we will help you." "If anything happens—" . . . Well, I'm back, and now they cannot help me and don't even want to. I'm alone. (9)

She muses about the child welfare authorities:

How many girls' futures will they destroy before they understand what is at stake? . . . That once they have taken girls of immigrant background into their care, there is no turning back. Even today they make the same mistake; they blame the collision of cultures and lack of resources, capacity, and knowledge. In my case, the psychologist concluded that the problem was not due to a collision of cultures; yet this was what the child authorities hid behind. Perhaps it is true what has been said—that culture has become the new concept of race . . .

Because of this, many girls who might have had a future end up as housewives and birth machines, uneducated, jobless, and devoid of opportunities. They become prisoners in their own homes. There were so many of us who tried to call on help before it was too late, but only a few who got it. The system let us down. "Collision of cultures," the child welfare agencies said. It was so simple, so easy to blame that, whereas *doing* something for us was much more difficult. What could we have done? they ask me now, when I accuse them of having betrayed people like me. Yes, what could they have done? Perhaps they could have saved us from a forced marriage; not returned us to our parents' custody once they had taken us away, because we could not possibly live with them; heeded our cries of despair. Most of the girls who experience what I did never manage to escape. I know how lucky I am, after all . . .

But my struggle for identity is not over. I want to be remembered not as a fallen girl without morals but as a girl who accomplished something in life. I know it will be difficult to fight for my values, but someone has to lay the foundation. If I lay the first stone, perhaps others will follow. I have already had my marriage annulled by the Norwegian courts. Very few of us come that far.[25]

Perhaps I have managed to convince Papa that I am right. I have at least prevented him from making a new Noreen of my sister . . .

Many people may think that in his struggle for honor my father lost against his own daughter. But that's not how I see it. Papa did not lose against me—he just did not manage to convince me that his thoughts and actions were right. Don't let it be a matter of winning and losing. Neither of us won. Both of us lost. (72–73, 142–43)

With these words, Nasim ends her story of Noreen and her book *Izzat*. Five years after her return to Norway, Nasim herself finally left—to pursue her studies in England. She missed Norway and suffered qualms of conscience at having left her cause, her mission. But practical considerations favored England, at least for the time being.

I last saw Nasim in December 1997, shortly before she gave birth to a daughter. She had hoped to revisit Norway with the child's father.[26] But on applying to the Norwegian embassy for a visa for him, she was warned that there had been a threat on his life a while back. They chose not to go. When eventually she returned with her daughter, it was alone. To this day, her history haunts her.

I hate the first-person plural. But it is only now, seeing it in my own writing, that I realize how much I hate it. My resistance to it is almost physical . . . I can smell the scent of bodies pressed against me in a 1 May parade or at the celebration of Tito's birthday on 25 May . . . I can feel the crowd pushing me forward, all of us moving as one, a single body— a sort of automatic, puppet-like motion because no one is capable of anything else. I can feel the nausea; there is no air to breathe and I want to get out of the crowd, but my movements are restricted to a step forward or backwards in a strange ballet choreographed from a podium up above. Exhausted, I can't do anything but allow myself to be carried along until it is all over. (Drakulić 1996:2)

Thus writes the Croatian journalist Slavenka Drakulić. And we should listen to her words for the light they shed on the lives of Aisha, Sara, Noreen, Anna, and others; for although Drakulić's text emanates from a particular political context, it embodies a cry of protest against the suppression of individual liberty that transcends political regimes. At stake is the individual person's inalienable right to think for herself and speak for herself—without fear of persecution. A subtle means of denying this right is legitimizing only the first-person plural, hence her cry, "I hate the first-person plural!"

I grew up with "we" and "us": in the kindergarten, at school, in the pioneer and youth organizations, in the community, at work. I grew up listening to the speeches of politicians saying, "Comrades, we must . . ." and with these comrades, we did what we were told, because we did not exist in any other grammatical form. Later on, I experienced the same phenomenon in journalism. It was the journalism of endless editorials in which "we" explained to "us" what "we" all needed to understand. More neutral forms of language, not as direct as "we," were used later on, but still in the plural. It was hard to escape that plural, as if it were an iron mould, a shirt, a suit—a uniform. First-person eyewitness reports were not a popular genre of journalism precisely for this reason. In such pieces, the reporter can't claim that "we saw it," only that "I saw it." He can avoid referring to himself altogether, but he is still by definition present in his story. Writing meant testing out the borders of both languages and genres, pushing them away from editorials and first-person plural and towards the first-person singular. The consequences of using the first-person singular were often unpleasant. You stuck out; you risked being labelled an "anarchic element" (not even a person), perhaps even a dissident. For that you would be sacked, so you used it sparingly, and at your own risk. This was called self-censorship.

That hideous first-person plural troubles me for another reason, too. I saw at first hand how dangerous it can be, how easily it can be infected by nationalism and war. The war in the Balkans is the product of that "us," of that huge, 20-million-bodied mass swinging back and forth in waves, then following their leaders into mass hysteria. Individuals who were against that war, who saw it coming, where could they turn? To what organization or institution? There was no organized political alternative. The individual citizen had no chance to voice his protest or his opinion, not even his fear. He could only leave the country—and so people did. Those who used "I" instead of "we" in their language had to escape. It was this fatal difference in grammar that divided them from the rest of their compatriots. As a consequence of this "us," no civic society developed. The little there was, in the form of small, isolated and marginalized groups, was soon swallowed up by the national homogenization that did not permit any differences, any individualism. As under communism, individualism was punished—individuals speaking out against the war, or against nationalism, were singled out as "traitors."

How does a person who is a product of a totalitarian society learn responsibility, individuality, initiative? By saying "no." But this begins by saying "I," thinking "I" and doing "I"—and in public as well as in private. Individuality, the first-person singular, always existed under communism, it was just exiled from public and political life and exercised in private. Thus the terrible hypocrisy with which we learned to live in order to survive is having its backlash now: it is very difficult to connect the private and public "I"; to start believing that an individual opinion, initiative or vote really could make a difference. There is still too big a danger that the citizen will withdraw into an anonymous safe "us."

The difference between "we" and "I" is to me far more important than mere grammar. "We" means fear, resignation, submissiveness, a warm crowd and somebody else deciding your destiny. "I" means giving individuality and democracy a chance. (Drakulić 1996:2–4)

Drakulić's words mirror, in many ways, Aisha's, Sara's, and Noreen's experiences. One need not be subject to a communist regime to experience the nausea of an oppressive "we." Life in a welfare democracy may be as conducive to the suppression of individual liberty—in certain circumstances. Noreen, Sara, and Aisha all lived the pain of such circumstances.

How does a person who is a product of a totalitarian society learn responsibility, individuality, and initiative? By saying "no." Indeed, this is what the three girls did. "But this begins," writes Drakulić, "with saying 'I,' thinking 'I' and doing 'I'—in public as well as in private." This is precisely what the girls did. They refused to give up their individuality. They spoke up, they stood up for their convictions—in public as well as in private. Though thereby they deprived themselves of the security and comfort of belonging to the group. They took the risk, not of being labeled "anarchic elements" or even dissidents, but of suffering an even worse fate: Aisha was treated like a chattel ("merchandise" is her word) and married off against her will; so was Noreen, though she managed to escape after almost being beaten to death; Sara was actually strangled to death. They were traitors, dissidents, criminals in the view of those with the power to decide over their lives.

A fatal difference in grammar divided these girls from many of their compatriots. And from this difference flowed a set of actions of importance beyond all grammar: By saying "no" to "we," the girls rejected "submissiveness, a warm crowd and somebody else deciding your destiny." By standing up for "I," they insisted on giving individuality and equality a chance.

When Aisha and Sara lost, it was because of the betrayal of a humanitarian welfare state that did not accord them the individuality to which they were entitled. Perceived as *belonging* to their fathers' ethnic groups, Aisha and Sara were submerged in the great "we," where submissiveness and somebody else deciding your destiny is the norm, or even an iron rule, for females. The rest is history. But we would do well not to forget.

A Fatal Difference in Grammar

Slavenka Drakulić could count on a receptive audience in the West. For the "fatal difference in grammar" she evoked has been shown to be a subtle device masquerading as solidarity, whereas it was in fact a means of combating liberty and democracy—in communist countries. But what happens when that same device is used in liberal democracies? Who will then listen? And who will have the courage to speak out? Noreen did, as we have seen, but hers is a rare courageous voice. Others who have tried have also paid the price of their convictions; and many have reneged and backtracked.

Drakulić was fortunate in that she spoke out against something everyone was ready to condemn, which is not to detract from her achievement but merely to draw a stark contrast: Young girls, or boys, who speak up against the suppression of individual liberty waged in the name of culture have had a hard time being heard. For communism is an enemy, while culture is supposed to be a friend. But to whom?

Let us see how Sükrü Bilgiç, originally from Turkish Kurdistan, imagines a young immigrant girl speaking, had she been given a voice. Originally published in Norwegian in 1993, his documentary essay won a prize. A schoolteacher and the leader of a youth club for years, as well as the father of three children, Bilgiç came to know many young girls well and to empathize with their plight. He wrote this essay to draw attention to their problems. The point he makes in a poignant, evocative form is the same as was made in sharp analytic language by the Indian anthropologist Veena Das (1995:73): "We witness . . . an alliance between the state and social work as a profession, which silences the voice of victims by an application of the 'best interest' doctrine." "From a Young Foreign Girl to the Norwegian Social Workers" is the title of Sükrü Bilgiç's essay.

> Do you know me? No, you're right, you do not. I'm a young girl who came here with my family as a child. I'm that girl you discuss in your workshops and conferences, and use as an example in your meetings.
>
> But you don't know me . . .
>
> How could you possibly know me? Without ever listening to me, without asking me, without attending to my world, you set yourselves up as judges over my future . . .
>
> You won't get to know me by way of theories, books, hypotheses, and examples, or by trial and failure, or by leaving it all up to chance.
>
> For I'm something new . . .

Except for a few journalists who have savored our exotic atmosphere and taken our pictures to embellish their newspapers and make them look interesting . . . , nobody has ever asked us any questions.

Have you ever asked me?

It was always my father who declared himself a Muslim who was the source of your judgments.

It was always father's bad temper . . . that made you recoil. You feared that he might cause an uproar. And this betrayal you have disguised to this day by calling it cultural differences, religious differences, or differences of customs.

I tell you the truth!

You have always been afraid of my father. That's why you always ask him and not me.

Not me!

You have made me a prisoner of his primitive world.

You have taken me to inhabit my mother's limited world view.

Never my own!

. . . In a country that prides itself on the emancipation of women, it is my father and mother and elder brothers who are given responsibility over my future. Not me.

And you support them with all your heart.

They say: she should go to Qur'an school.

And you support them.

They say: she should attend a sewing course.

And you support them . . .

They say: she must wear the headscarf.

And you support them.

They say: she must not walk hand in hand with a Norwegian boy in the schoolyard.

And you agree for fear of being called racist.

You never asked me.

Did you ever ask me if *I* wanted to walk hand in hand with a Norwegian boy?

In a country that prides itself on being modern and civilized, you have imprisoned me in the Dark Ages.

Get this into your heads! All the people around me, children and youth, enjoy immense freedom.

But I'm a prisoner of my family's traditions because you support them, from fear.

From fear of my father, you never asked me any questions. Recoiling from his sense of honor, you did nothing to find a solution to our emotional and sexual problems and conflicts.

You showed me no way out of the problems I struggled with. You had no suggestions, you took no steps.

From time to time *I* become the object of your judgments. But it's always my parents' outdated values that are your reference point . . . and this pertains to all of you, social workers, teachers, psychologists, sociologists . . .

Let me give you some examples.

Because my father wanted it, Qur'an courses were started . . . Because my mother wanted it, courses in sewing and cooking were started. And these things you announced proudly in the newspapers and called them important measures [*tiltak*].

But nobody asked what I wanted.

You want me to adapt to Norwegian society? You think I do that by living in seclusion and attending courses in the Qur'an and sewing and cooking?

No!

Have you ever asked me what I wanted to do?

No!!

Because my father is hotheaded!

Because my mother is old-fashioned.

Because my older brother is rash and violent!

. . . But I remain silent. For I'm alone.

Have you ever thought about me?

Oh yes, you have. In your eyes I am "that poor little thing" [*en stakkar*]. But do you do anything about it?

No.

Because when you consider me, you always think of my father's bad temper, my mother's traditions, and my brother's rage. You never perceive my soft, dreaming, and sensitive world. For you never give me any other role than this "poor little thing."

Even the most daring of you never did more than show pictures of sexual organs and ads for condoms, and give AIDS information. To me who did not even have the freedom of holding hands with a boy, you started giving courses on family planning!

You didn't dare to take the least step to increase my freedom—all the while deceiving yourselves, and me, by talking about different cultures, different traditions, and different religions.

In a world where anyone can kiss in public, where all the media—movies, TV, and videos—portray love and sexuality in intimate detail, and where Norwegian youth can switch sweethearts every other day as if it were the most natural thing . . . , I am forbidden even to glance at a boy. Now what d'you think of that? In which conference will you take that up? . . .

I ask you!

. . . What kind of social order is this?

Tell me, you men and women, how do you accommodate such contradictions within your framework of values?

Give me an answer!

It's enough!

Enough conferences!

Enough seminars!

Enough fear of my father!

Enough sympathy with my mother!

Enough siding with my brother!

Listen a little to me too! . . .

For I'm furious!

I despise your duplicity.

As long as I keep within the confines of my home, left to my own destiny, without doing you or the Norwegian society any harm, you're not going to give a damn about me or free me from this prisoner's existence, of that I'm sure.

Now I wonder: When are you going to put me on your agenda as you have with my brothers? When are you going to start talking about me? When are you going to take up my problems?

Oh, I know . . . !

When I start stealing!

When I start breaking windows!

When I run away from home!

When I injure someone!

When I start carrying weapons!

When I commit a robbery!

When I form a gang!

"You Never Asked Me!"

Khalid was a boy of Pakistani descent who also tried to forge an "I." He fought to get around another obstacle as well—poor learning conditions imposed by his ghetto-like environment, and in this sense he also went against official Norwegian immigration policy for its failure to give him a chance.

Khalid's problem was that he did not learn Norwegian properly, though he had lived in Norway all his life and was now seventeen years old. Still, his Norwegian was so poor that he was often hard to understand; he spoke with a very strong accent and had a weak grasp of vocabulary. A bright young man, he had made earnest efforts to learn. His handicap was the consequence of official Norwegian language policy practiced in a particular environment: Khalid had received bilingual education from the start on the grounds that a solid knowledge of one's mother tongue is essential for learning another language—in his case Norwegian. But there was an additional hitch: the "mother tongue" in which he had received mother-tongue instruction was not, in fact, Khalid's own.

Khalid, like most "Pakistanis" in Norway, is from Punjab, and Punjabi is his mother tongue. Yet many children like him have received mother-tongue instruction in Urdu. The difference between Urdu and Punjabi is something like that between German and Dutch, and it is questionable whether "mother tongue" education in German would have helped, say, a Dutch child to learn better English. So too with Khalid and others like him. From the start, Khalid had to cope with three languages in school—Punjabi, Norwegian, and Urdu—leaving him not even fluent in two, but "three times half-lingual," as Tor Aase, an expert on Punjabi immigrants in Norway, puts it (1992).[1]

Khalid's predicament was even worse, however. From early on, he had to cope not just with three languages but with five. In addition to Punjabi, Urdu, and Norwegian there were Arabic and English—Arabic in Qur'an school and English as a foreign language from the third grade in primary school. Hence Khalid, a young man living in a relatively deprived environment with parents who were nearly illiterate, was required to cope with four languages from age seven (the school entry age in Norway) and five from age ten. No wonder he became three times half-lingual. That he had little chance to practice Norwegian in his local community did nothing to enhance his facility in the language.

Why did the authorities default on their obligation to provide proper mother-tongue instruction? After all, children were entitled to it by Norwegian law on the grounds that such knowledge would further their general cognitive development as well as their ability to learn Norwegian. The answer is complex, but strands of the explanation follow.

The authorities, like the parents, want the best for the children. But they also don't want trouble with the parents. Parents in general take pride in the national language of their native homelands; it gives status and esteem to know that language well. Many parents, being illiterate or nearly so themselves, are the more concerned that their children should acquire fluency in the parents' national language.

What Lewis (1994:65) writes of Britain pertains to Norway as well:

> Many Muslims from South Asia consider a knowledge of Urdu vital for the preservation of religion and culture, not least because it remains the lingua franca of the majority of South Asian Muslims. It is the language in which an enormous amount of Islamic literature is written, and into which a large part of the rich store of Islamic scholarship in Arabic and Persian has been translated. In this context any initiative which seeks to keep knowledge of Urdu alive is of great importance.

The same holds true for Arabic, another prestigious minority language in Norway that is being taught as a mother tongue to children whose real mother tongue is different—the vast majority of Moroccans who are actually Berbers. So most parents report that the *national* language of their original homeland is their children's mother tongue, though the children may actually be speaking another language at home. The school authorities often know they are being misled, but feel there is little they can do, other than express their concern and hope to remedy the situation.

As the following case shows, it is sometimes difficult to determine a child's mother tongue. Children themselves may be confused, as was brought home to me on this occasion. I was visiting a Moroccan Berber family when I casually asked a seven-year-old who was chatting with her younger brother, "What language do you speak?" "Arabic," she answered. But it was not Arabic. Her father, seeing my confusion, quickly intervened "Moroccan! Say you speak Moroccan!" But I think the girl, who was bright, had probably been taught since kindergarten that Arabic was her mother tongue. No wonder she came to think that Berber is also Arabic. Or perhaps she knew the difference between Berber and Arabic but had learned to answer "Arabic" when asked by a Norwegian what her mother tongue was.

In any case, the authorities are stuck with teaching what the parents report as the children's mother tongue, even though they may know better.[2] Undoubtedly some children benefit by learning several languages early, becoming truly bilingual or multilingual. The little girl I talked to might be among them; she comes from a well-situated family that sets great store by the children's education. Not all are so fortunate. As Portes and Rumbaut observe, on the basis of extensive research in the United States, an important distinction needs to be made between "elite" versus "folk" bilingualism, or "fluent" versus "limited" use of two languages: "The positive evaluations in the literature [on bilingualism] are built on a considerable body of evidence concerning the performance of fully (or 'true') bilingual children. By contrast, little research has been done on limited (or 'semi-') bilinguals" (1996:201, 206–7). Social class is a key factor "that can determine the proclivity of immigrant families to promote home language retention *and* scholastic achievement among their offspring" (223). Evidence from the Netherlands on children of Pakistani, Turkish, and Moroccan descent points in the same direction.[3] Statistical evidence from Norway is not available, but it is likely that here too a great number of children are semi-bilingual or, as Aase puts it, three times half-lingual.

In Norway, Khalid was among the losers. His knowing Urdu might well have added to his parents' status in Pakistan and Norway, but it hardly helped him to make it in Norwegian society.[4]

Khalid appears to have realized as much. And so he decided to take the matter into his own hands. He would improve his Norwegian by changing schools and becoming a pupil in a place where he would be obliged to practice his Norwegian. It meant he would face long commutes every day, and expose himself to the trial of having to make new friends in a place where he would be—at least initially—an outsider. But he must have judged that it was worth the effort.

Now there may have been an additional reason why Khalid wanted to change schools, though I cannot be certain. It is clear that he did have a girlfriend and that his family was furious about it, but whether he had her when he changed schools, or only afterward, I do not know. Be that as it may, Khalid was up against two odds: he wanted to learn Norwegian properly, and he wanted to choose his own girlfriend or fiancée. To both objectives he said "I." He stood out. He struck an independent course. A brave young man who had the makings of an everyday hero, he was nonetheless defeated on both counts.

Khalid's choice of the new school did not turn out happily. His classmates were receptive to him and wanted to include him. But it was not so easy. Khalid spoke a broken Norwegian, almost incomprehensible at times. His body language too was awkward. Understandably, his classmates had the impression that he might not have been very bright. None of them could really fathom, I believe, how even a clever young man could become a "loser" in Khalid's circumstance. The fact that there was another boy of Pakistani descent in the class, with whom he was compared, also worked against Khalid.

The other young man, Shahid, spoke flawless Norwegian and had none of the gestures so characteristic of Pakistani-Norwegians raised in the inner city. His body language too was "Norwegian." Indeed, Shahid was so well adapted that his classmates said, "Shahid is Norwegian," a point of pride to Shahid, though he also cherished his Pakistani identity. Shahid's parents had made a clear decision as to their children's future: they were to learn proper Norwegian and be well integrated in the society. So the family settled in a "Norwegian" neighborhood, and the children were encouraged to have Norwegian friends. Shahid's classmates were particularly impressed that his father sometimes even spoke Norwegian with him when they rode the tram.

But Khalid had no such support on his home ground. On the contrary, he was under severe strain in his personal life because his family was strongly opposed to his "becoming Norwegian." On one occasion he even had to seek refuge in the principal's office because a relative of his showed up at the school, threatening to injure him because he had a girlfriend.

The girlfriend was not "Norwegian"; so that was not the problem. She was of Pakistani descent. But Khalid had chosen her himself, against the family's wishes. In other words, Khalid was not just struggling to learn Norwegian and make new friends in a new environment. He was also fighting pressure from his family, who insisted on his retaining his Pakistani identity, and that in a very traditional form. Khalid was caught between a rock and a hard place, whereas what he needed was full support, from all sides, for *his own* project: to forge a new role; to be Pakistani in a new way, far removed from his family's outmoded perceptions; to become a Norwegian-Pakistani of a kind; and to make a future for himself in Norway.

No wonder both his verbal language and his body language got tangled up and that he could be perceived as dumb and a bit odd. When one thinks of the pressure this brave young man was under, it is only natural that it should express itself in some discordant ways.

Shahid, Khalid's Norwegian-Pakistani classmate, is not alone in being privileged. One of his counterparts is Aamir Javed Sheikh, a successful businessman and politician, who came to Norway when he was seven years old. He attributes his fluent Norwegian to the fact that he was the only immigrant in his school.

> I first attended Kampen school with many immigrants. There I was placed in a purely Pakistani class. I had little contact with Norwegians and did not learn the language. And so I changed schools. It worked out well . . . I had a mother tongue instructor both at Kampen and at Veitvedt [the new school], but they were no good in Norwegian. It was not by that instruction that I learned Norwegian, but because of my Norwegian schoolmates. (*Aftenposten*, August 9, 1994)

As Aamir tells it, he learned about Norwegian culture in his friends' homes, while they learned about Pakistani culture in his.

But Khalid, our everyday hero, was not among the fortunate. With all the odds against him, he struggled for his human right—the right to shape his future in the country where he was born and raised, through no choice of his. Coming to Norway had been entirely his parents' decision, and yet now they wanted him to behave as if they had never migrated. They would not even allow him to make his own choice of a "Pakistani" bride. Pakistani she must be, but of their choice. I hate to think what they might have done had he been seen with a "Norwegian."

What has become of Khalid, I do not know. He vanished from my horizon four years ago. His classmates reported that he seemed to give up during the last year of high school—after two years of diligent effort. He was probably unable to graduate because of poor attendance. During his final year he attended school only intermittently and obviously suffered grievously from problems at home. But of this I am sure: he will remain an "immigrant" or a "foreigner" for the rest of his life, one of the many who make up Norway's new ethnic underclass. It is a tragedy for himself and a shame for Norway that a valiant young man who made a bid for his own future should be condemned to failure because society has made him a functional illiterate.

Who says that illiteracy is not widespread in Norway? The concepts of "foreign-cultural" and "minority-lingual" have become a sedative. Yet we are dealing with Norwegian children, born and/or raised in Norway—children like Khalid who were never given a chance.

As Alain Finkielkraut has noted (1995:106), "It was *at the expense of their culture* that European individuals gained, one by one, all their rights. In the end, it is the critique of tradition that constitutes the spiritual foundation of Europe."

We shall have much to answer for if we deny Europeans of non-European descent this same right to contest and transcend their culture—as Khalid tried to do. Nor is principled support enough. Khalid's story shows some of the massive forces working against human freedom and dignity—forces that must be combated, be it at the cost of being labeled racist. It is a small price to pay compared to what Khalid and Sara and Noreen and countless others go through.

17   *Overcoming the Odds: Somali Women in Norway*

Khalid, Sara, Anna, and Aisha are among the losers in "the immigration experience." But all is not equally bleak. For others—and not just men—life in Norway may grant both freedom and opportunities. As the Somali sociologist Hassan Keynan, who now lives in Norway, observes, disasters sometimes generate unexpected opportunities. Many Somali women, for example,

> glow with inspiration and exuberance and talk about their newfound freedom with poetic eloquence. "I feel I have undergone a miraculous process of recreation and renewal," says one woman now living in Norway. "I am a new person, blessed with a full and fulfilling life. It's magic." (Keynan 1995:25–26)

How did it happen? Keynan gives an incisive analysis of the changes brought about in Somali women's lives as a consequence of civil war and famine and the subsequent emigration by many as refugees to the West. The effect has been to dislodge traditional gender roles—to the women's advantage. This is how Keynan describes the traditional situation:

> Somali "culture" allows and equips men to dominate women, who are systematically relegated to a subordinate, marginal existence. The roots of these inequities lie in a patriarchal tradition, which confines women to house-keeping and procreation, excludes them from positions of power

and influence, and denies them access to resources and means of making an independent living. This tradition imposes severe restrictions on women's intellectual and social development, and stifles their creative skills and energy. It also discourages them from openly expressing their thoughts and feelings . . .

Somali culture has established elaborate myths, folk literature and traditional discourse to rationalize and sanctify patriarchy. It is in oral literature that men's campaign against women begins . . . "A breast that contains milk cannot contain wisdom," says a well-known proverb. Poetry, a national institution of great power and influence, portrays women as incapable of rhyming one word with another and therefore as unworthy of having a meaningful voice. The ideal woman is the silent woman whose words and ideas are limited to her immediate circle of children and other women. (Keynan 1995:27)

What propelled Somali refugees down the road of change, with particular consequences for male-female relations? Keynan emphasizes four factors. First, prolonged civil war and famine in Somalia removed many of the men from their families and placed additional burdens on women. Female-headed households have proliferated. Second, more than a million Somalis, one-fifth of the total population, were forced to flee the country. Most of them ended up in refugee camps in neighboring countries, but many sought asylum in the West. The majority of the latter were women and children, so that women have played a more prominent and visible role. Third, there are indications that "Somali women have shown greater resilience and resource-fulness than men in coping with the trauma of civil war and famine at home and the anxieties and uncertainties of refugee life abroad" (Keynan 1995:27). Fourth, and most important, "new possibilities seem to have opened up for women refugees, especially where the country of asylum provides adequate economic support, protection from gender-based inequities and understanding and tolerance toward migrants" (27).

According to Keynan, Norway has provided the very conditions needed for Somali women to thrive. Most significantly, women have found a voice. They are now able to speak for themselves, and they have begun to demand and defend their rights, in private and in public. They have become more assertive in areas traditionally dominated by men. For example, men can no longer run the affairs of the family as they wish, nor can they take a second or third wife on a whim. "The patriarchal discourse is slowly being demystified; the lifting of the oppressive and dehumanizing burden of patriarchal dogma is seen by many women as a wondrous intervention designed to celebrate their humanity, dignity and talent" (27).

Anyone familiar with Somali women in Norway knows that they generally arrive with, or are later reunited with, a great number of children, their own as well as the children of relatives in many cases.[5] With the help of the welfare state they are provided with adequate economic support. Norwegian newspapers occasionally present reports of Somali women with their numerous children lodged in cramped quarters in a hostel at an exorbitant cost paid by the municipality. The message is that this is unworthy of human beings and wasteful for the state, since renting an apartment would cost a fraction of that amount. Nonetheless, and this bears mention, the rent *is* being paid, as it would not be in a non-welfare state. And by being featured in the media, replete with photographs, many a Somali woman manages to achieve what she sought—a place to live, an apartment in a real neighborhood. By drawing attention to the family's plight, the media often manage to work a solution.

I do not know if Somali women are exceptionally adept at working the social welfare system. But they have a reputation, among people I know who deal with immigrants, of being very clever at it. Perhaps a lifetime of subjugation in a starkly patriarchal system has taught them various survival techniques, which they now put to good use and are amply rewarded for. But whether one is "working" the system or not, Norwegian social welfare benefits are especially advantageous to mothers with many children—as many (if not most) Somalis have.[6] Also, as single women, many do not have a husband or male custodian appropriating what they get,[7] unlike many women from other countries, who are rarely single. Moreover, with the resilience and resourcefulness learned in coping with daily life in civil war and famine, many Somali women succeed in finding work in Norway whereas the men are generally unemployed. Somalis top the statistics on unemployment among immigrants in Norway, with only 14 percent employed in 1995. Also in Sweden, and elsewhere in Europe, Somalis have the highest unemployment rates.[8]

I do not know if the unemployment statistics capture most of the work that women do, or how much of it takes place within the informal economy. Keynan observes that most of women's work is in areas like child care, health, food processing, catering, and cleaning. Furthermore, "many have also established small family businesses that deal mainly with women's and children's clothes, jewelry, cosmetics and special types of incense widely used by Somali women. The result is that many households now have women, not men, as breadwinners and heads of family" (1995:27).

How do Somali men react to the changes taking place? Keynan poignantly describes their profound sense of discomfort and apprehension.

> Many believe that the changes taking place in gender relations are too radical and too destabilizing. They view the growing empowerment of women as a serious threat to their authority and dignity and, by extension, as a threat to the moral and cultural norms and traditions of Somali society. They complain about humiliation and lack of respect, marginalization and expulsion, orders being given by their wives, loss of family coherence and values, and confusion and disorientation in the way children are brought up. Many men admit that they are no longer able to cope with these pressures and humiliations. It is reported that some are sinking into depression and have started drinking heavily. (1995:27)

Some Somali women, exasperated with the men, have asked me to urge the Norwegian authorities to stop funding the "cultural cafés"—meeting grounds financed by the state to facilitate the maintenance of minority culture and identity. What function do these cafés serve? ask the women, who regard them as places for daydreaming and escapism, where men can sit and discuss Somali clan politics, thinking they are doing something important. Sitting there keeps them from looking for work, real work, and from building a life in Norway.

Obviously this is a rhetoric of complaint, not an objective assessment of the situation. Many Somali men, as the news media have effectively shown, are struggling hard, against heavy odds, to land jobs and make it in the new Norway. So it is a one-sided picture that the women present to me, but it should be noted for the story it has to tell. According to Keynan, some Somali men complain about the effects on children of the changes in male-female relations, alleging that children are becoming confused and disoriented. Whatever the cause, Somali boys in Norway have indeed become a problematic group. Teachers and others who deal with minority children consistently single out Somali boys as the most difficult to handle. And recent police reports on violent crime among children in Oslo single out Somali boys. A number of measures are now being taken to halt such negative developments. But the fact that the media have now actually gone public with the Somali case is a sign that the situation is now regarded as very serious, almost out of control. Otherwise, the ethnic identity of the offenders would have been suppressed.

There is therefore cause for concern, but also for satisfaction—satisfaction that many Somali women are able to make it in the new society and throw off the oppressive mantle of patriarchy, but concern that losers along the way are men and perhaps also male children, at least for the time being. Perhaps this is the way it had to be, given the men's former extreme privileges, which are now being eroded. But for men's self-respect and social esteem to be retrieved, it will not do to go on social welfare and sit in cafés talking politics. As Keynan said in another context, though the point pertains to Norway too: "The Finnish society's most important task is not to hand out money to the Somali refugees. It is to explain the rules of the game in the society, and to do it so clearly and distinctly that they cannot be misunderstood."[9] The social welfare system may occasionally work against people's own best interests by making it all too easy for them to settle into a state of passivity, depression, or worse. On the other hand, unless the host society, in this case Norway, is able to offer Somalis real opportunities for work and self-respect, they may be forced to become social welfare clients for life.

The 1995 Oslo study of refugees (discussed in chapter 4) found that most Somalis came from the privileged classes and were accustomed to having servants and enjoying a high social position.[10] In other words, some may feel that they have a claim to respect by virtue of who they are rather than what they do (a common human proclivity). They may also consider themselves above doing menial work, as do most Norwegians, and so they turn down jobs that other minority groups, such as Tamils and Chileans, are glad to accept. Unfortunately there are few nonmenial jobs available for immigrants other than the highly educated; and Somalis, according to the Oslo study, rarely had more than eight years' education. It will be interesting to see through time how Somali men, as opposed to women, cope under these circumstances. Will the changes in gender relations that Keynan has identified continue to be buttressed, or will more men change their attitudes (and perhaps even learn from the women)? For the present at least, Somali women seem less status conscious and better prepared to find new ways of adapting to society, while the men tend to grieve for what they have lost, leading them to cling all the more tenaciously to their Somali high-class position. Or perhaps it is not so much their high class as their relative position within the clan hierarchy that is at stake. The result is increased cleavage between the sexes and increasing marginalization of men. If this situation persists, Keynan warns, the men may reinforce clan traditions in a bid to regain what they have lost, and women may lose some of their advantage. The result will be the increasing isolation of all parties, accompanied by greater discrimination.

With this brief glance at male-female relations, the question arises, why are Somali women apparently more able than women of many other ethnic minorities to exert their independence in Norwegian society and gain a new sense of personal liberty? The description Keynan gives of Somalis in Norway, based on firsthand observation, would clearly be off the mark for Pakistanis or Turks or Moroccans in general, according to the evidence we have so far. Rather than a newfound sense of freedom, a tightening of the reins is what many women of these minorities experience. The felt threat of Norwegian society often leads the men to intensify their control of women and to keep them even more secluded than they would "back home." In the same vein, men generally usurp even the tasks and responsibilities that women traditionally had in the public realm and that sustained their respected position. This leads to a weakening of women's traditional sphere of influence and increased powerlessness for many.

I think it crucial that so many Somali women came to Norway alone, unaccompanied by a male guardian. Most women from the Middle East and South Asia came after their men had arrived, as wards of male custodians—husbands, fathers, brothers, uncles. The man would immediately take charge upon arrival in Norway, and Norwegian authorities played up to him. The myth of Muslim women as generally submissive and docile became a springboard for males to enhance their prestige. Norwegians thought it natural, for example, that women did not come to school for parents' meetings but stayed home and let the men perform all public functions. This was in keeping with the Orientalist picture of Muslim women that many Norwegians held, a picture that men played up to not just because it served their personal interests but because if they did not, they might be regarded as not proper Muslims. In Western Europe in general, the idea of a "Muslim" identity has been crystallized by perceptions and *mis*perceptions on the part of Europeans as to what constituted a real Muslim, and Muslims then felt that they had to act up to that identity. The result was a self-fulfilling prophecy. Rather than being empowered, as were many Somali women, many Muslim women from South Asia and the Middle East were indeed disempowered, even relative to their position in their countries of origin.

"A breast that contains milk cannot contain wisdom," says a Somali proverb. An Arab proverb is similar: "We women are like goats, we know nothing."

But the Omani Arab women who told me this also said, "Men reign, but women rule," and "Even when the man *has* the right, the woman is *given* the right" (Wikan 1991a).

Woman's position is rarely unequivocally good or bad. Subjugation in some respects may be counterbalanced by influence and even power in others—as Omani women's reflections about their own position clearly show, and as Somali women demonstrate in their lives both in Norway and back home. The challenge of any society is to give women—and men—the privilege of enjoying freedom and equality in keeping with their human dignity. But then "culture" may have to go, as Keynan (1995:27) lucidly shows: "Somali 'culture' allows and equips men to dominate women who are systematically relegated to a subordinate, marginal existence." Such a culture is not in keeping with human dignity—which takes us right into the heart of the problem of what is—or should be—the relationship between freedom and tradition. How to secure individual freedom and human rights within a multicultural society? This is the question to which we now turn.

In his book *The Defeat of the Mind,* Alain Finkielkraut explores the historical circumstances giving rise to ethnic identity politics and its pernicious consequences in today's world, primarily in Europe. Like Slavenka Drakulić, Finkielkraut is struck with the *grammatical* form of such politics.

> Left to themselves, the formerly colonized became their own captives, stuck in a collective identity that had freed them from the tyranny of European values. No sooner had they said, "We won," than they lost the right to express themselves in anything but the first-person plural . . . If there was no place for the collective subject in the logic of colonialism, there was no place for the individual in the logic of identity politics . . .
>
> The individual, a false reality, was abolished: everyone was like everybody else, the bearer of the same identity; the mystical body of the nation had absorbed each and every soul. (1995:69–70)

But Finkielkraut's vivid images simplify. Everybody was not the bearer of the same identity, as we have seen with Noreen, Sara, Aisha, and others. The power to represent their identity was strictly vested in certain individuals only—those of the right sex and age. In Somalia, Pakistan, Vietnam, Turkey, Ghana, and other states from which immigrants came, gender inequities were perpetuated even as freedom was being sought and celebrated. Yet Finkielkraut's point stands for the sake of his argument: the individual, a false reality, was abolished, as was the right to say "I." Aisha, Noreen or Anna are not persons in their own right from the point of view of identity politics. They are merely *examples,* to cite the girl writing her letter of complaint to the Norwegian social workers (see chapter 15); or, according to Finkielkraut: the individual is "nothing more than an interchangeable representative of a particular class of beings" (1995:75). The tragedy of such politics with regard to immigrants in Europe is to substitute tolerance for humanism.

> Attempting to minimize the brutal experience of leaving home, we turn immigrants over, bound hand and foot, to other members of their collective community living abroad. In so doing we end up limiting the application of the right of man only to societies identified with the West, believing all the time that we have expanded these rights by giving peoples of other traditions the chance to live by the laws of their own cultures. (107)

How did this happen? Finkielkraut locates the roots of identity politics in the German romantics' preoccupation with *Volksgeist,* the national spirit or soul of a people that was the unique imprint of their character and the source of their deepest pride. Discredited later in the nineteenth century as crippling development by steeping the mind in tradition, and also as breeding discord between peoples by celebrating their differences at the expense of their common humanity, the idea of the Volksgeist was nonetheless revived in a new guise after the Second World War: the concept of culture, propagated by UNESCO with the aid of anthropologists, replaced the Volksgeist as the vessel of a people's soul.

The intentions were good. The idea was to honor the humanity and dignity of previously colonized people by respecting their traditions, customs, and ways of being. Thus "culture"—which formerly had been used in its adjectival form, "cultured," meaning civilized, enlightened, and had been regarded as the hallmark of the colonizers in contradistinction to the colonized—was divested of its elitist notions and given a plural form. Redefined as the total body of knowledge and traditions of *any* people, "culture" became "cultures," and consequently a major transformation took place. In Finkielkraut's words: "No longer was it a matter of opening others to reason but of opening ourselves to the reason of others." Europeans were no longer seen to represent civilization but "were just one more culture, another variation of human being, as passing and perishable as the rest" (Finkielkraut 1995:57, 60). With this transformation of a key concept came the birth of modern identity politics.

> With the support of the philosophy of decolonialization, the concept of culture, the symbol of the imperialist West, broke away, moving over to represent the societies it had previously nurtured with condescending attention. The theme of cultural identity permitted the colonized to stop

being mimics, allowing them to replace the degrading parody of the invader with the affirmation of their cultural difference, to turn into an object of pride what they had been taught to be ashamed of. (Finkielkraut 1995:67–68)

Thus a revolution of thought accompanied the political work of decolonial-ization: man—that "unitary concept of universal significance," to quote Ed-mund Leach (1969:68)—gave way to diversity, and thus was born *the cult of time-honored beliefs*, in Finkielkraut's words (68), a cult more insidious than rule by an external invader when it becomes transfixed as a person's identity. In her book *Désenchantement national*, Hélé Béji shows how cultural identity, which was a means of resistance under colonial rule, became an instrument of subsequent repression.

> When it is a matter of defining myself against the physical presence of the invader, the force of my identity dazzles and reassures me. But once my identity takes the place of this invader, or, rather, my own (national) effigy sets itself up as the authority and surrounds me, in all logic I should not have the right to challenge it. (Béji 1982:118)

Anthropologists were key movers in this game, according to Finkielkraut, and many anthropologists would agree with him. A draft for the Declaration of the Rights of Man submitted by the American Anthropological Associa-tion to UNESCO in 1947 included this sentence: "The individual realizes his personality through his culture, hence respect for individual differences entails respect for cultural differences." Again, the noblest intentions were expressed, but the effect (or the execution) was about "as clumsy as that of a bear stepping on the face of the sleeping gardener in its attempt to chase away a fly."

> At the very moment the Other got his culture back, he lost his freedom: his personal name disappeared into the name of the community; he became an example, nothing more than an interchangeable representative of a particular class of beings. While receiving an unconditional welcome, the Other found that he no longer had any freedom of movement, any means of escape. All originality was taken away from him; he was trapped insidiously in his difference.
>
> Those who thought they had left behind the idea of abstract man in order to embrace the real human being had, in effect, done away with the space that existed between individuals and the collectivities from which

they came, a space that anthropologists in the Enlightenment period had insisted upon preserving. Under the guise of altruism, they turned the Other into a homogeneous bloc, destroying the individual realities of others. Out of love for the Other, they deprived the former colonies of experiencing European democracy. (Finkielkraut 1995:75)

These words are in accord with Drakulić's view of the preconditions of democracy: turning the Other into a homogeneous bloc requires her or him to say "we," to speak in the first-person plural. But " 'we' means fear, resignation, submissiveness . . . and somebody else deciding your destiny. 'I' means giving individuality and democracy a chance" (Drakulić 1996:4).

Saying "I" is not to celebrate individualism as the unbridled exercise of selfish ends. Individuality must be distinguished from individualism (Cohen 1994), and it is in defense of individuality that both Drakulić and Finkielkraut speak. Respect for the individual integrity of the human being was born of the modern period in Europe. The "right to reject one's uniform" (Bloch 1976:104) was instituted. No longer were human collectivities conceived as totalities that assign to individuals unchangeable identities; they were now thought of as associations of independent persons having both the right and the ability to choose affiliations. Or, as Finkielkraut (1995:104) puts it, "either people have rights or they have uniforms; either they can legitimately free themselves from oppression, or their culture has the last word." Replace "culture" by "roots" or "rank" or "class," and the message is the same.

It is this right that enables a poor man's child to rise in the social hierarchy or an "untouchable" in India to discard an otherwise stigmatized position. Unfortunately, respect for individuality prompts some members of the upper class, be they Norwegians or Somalis or Iranians, to expect esteem simply by virtue of who they are. In a liberal democracy, however, "who they are" depends not on "where they came from" but on "what they do." Hence the political economy of a capitalist welfare state exacts a price in the form of requiring each individual to prove his or her worth by doing, not just being. Respect for individuality is thus not an unmitigated good, any more than are most other noble principles. But it has shown itself of superior value for the exercise of democracy and human rights. And that is why Drakulić, Finkielkraut, and other humanists deplore the grand "we" that parades as solidarity while suppressing individual liberty.[1]

Aisha, Sara, Anna, Noreen, and Khalid exemplify the price individuals may have to pay for trying to throw off the mantle of oppression. And do not think their plight was simply that they were children of immigrants, caught "between two cultures." Though individuality is prized in the West, it would be erroneous to think that the notion of the individual is peculiar to the West. Research on languages worldwide has shown that the concept of "I" is universal, as is the concept of "person" (Wierzbicka 1993). Everyone, everywhere, has a unique sense of her or his individuality. In Robert Paul's memorable words: for each one of us, "life is being lived uniquely and for the first time" (1990:4).

So when Europeans speak up for individuality, they need not fear that they are being ethnocentric or racist, although some do. As Alain Finkielkraut so pointedly phrases it (1995:106), "many Europeans recognize that Europe and Europe alone ranked the individual above all else. But they apologize immediately for having done so."

How can human dignity be given a chance if people are not allowed to think for themselves, act for themselves, and educate themselves in the sense of striving for greater knowledge? Finkielkraut is devastating in his critique of anthropologists and UNESCO for inhibiting such developments. True, UNESCO, as the United Nations agency for education, science, and culture, continued to stress the importance of culture and education; but the fact that culture was no longer seen as something acquired but as given by birth had far-reaching consequences. In Finkielkraut's view, it actually reversed the educational process. Because the integrity of the group was now regarded as more important than the autonomy of individuals, education no longer sought to provide students with the tools to think for themselves and choose among the many beliefs, values, and opinions that made up their heritage. Instead, it plunged them headfirst into the pool of tradition:

> Where once there was "I," now there was "We." Instead of having to cultivate myself (thereby getting out of my own little world), now I have to rediscover my culture, defined as "the whole range of knowledge and values which were not specifically taught but which every member of a community nevertheless knows." This is what Enlightenment thought called lack of education or prejudice. (Finkielkraut 1995:82–83)

Another pernicious feature of subsuming the individual under the collectivity and defining both by virtue of their culture is that it is racist, as I argued in chapter 7. If individuals are seen as drawing the substance of who they are from the group (or culture) to which they belong, is that not really the equivalent to saying they are products of race, a now discredited concept? I have shown how the concept of race is alive and well in Norway, cloaked as "culture." Finkielkraut (1995:79–80) makes the same general argument:

> We believe we have since discredited the concept of race, but have we really made any progress? Like the racists before them, contemporary fanatics of cultural identity confine individuals to their group of origin. Like them, they carry differences to the absolute extreme, and in the name of the multiplicity of specific causalities destroy any possibility of a natural or cultural community among peoples . . .
>
> In replacing the biological argument with a cultural one, racism has not been wiped out, it has simply been returned to its point of departure, to square one.

A similar point is made by social historian Walter Benn Michaels. In his book *Our America: Nativism, Modernism, and Pluralism* (1995), Michaels shows that the replacement of race by culture, and of superiority by diversity, was neither as simple nor as liberating as it might seem. The new emphasis on culture and diversity led, paradoxically, to a greater obsession for distinguishing people by their origins. Indeed, *it makes no sense to talk of people's abandoning or betraying their culture unless they are tied to that culture by some unspoken biological link* (Star 1997). Michael also shows, in line with Finkielkraut, that it was the cultural pluralists who proved to be the most committed to the idea of human difference and hence of separation. Thus the functional equivalent of race entered through the back door; it was kicked out only to slide back in, in the guise of culture: back to square one, in Finkielkraut's words.

But what does it mean to elevate culture to this position and celebrate diversity as if there were no human nature, or no commonality in human experience? Cross-cultural communication becomes difficult, as I have argued before. Anthropologists, with the best of intentions, have contributed to the problems. In Roger Keesing's words, we have been dealers in exotica (1989). Indeed, the critique that Finkielkraut launches against anthropologists has been made as forcefully by renowned scholars from within our own ranks. But it would be hard to beat Finkielkraut's poignant characterization of the loss to humanity perpetrated by an exoticized view of man, which demotes the commonality of human experience. Invoking Goethe, who once had the exhilarating experience, on reading a Chinese novel, of feeling great resonance with his own works rather than the sense of strangeness he had expected, Finkielkraut draws the following conclusion:

What gave Goethe pleasure in this book was the possibility of coming into contact with people from another civilization without having the discovery of their difference diminish the meaning of communication. *Having no pity, the social sciences dispel this illusory sense of closeness, interrupt the conversation and return everyone back home.* (1995:97; emphasis mine)

Speaking of culture only in the plural is like incarcerating people in space (Appadurai 1988) or requiring them to inhabit the place allotted to them and not move beyond it (Finkielkraut 1995:99). But in so doing one "refuses people of different periods of civilizations the possibility to communicate about values and meaning beyond the limits of the place where they first appear" (1995:101).

To put this in a language more akin to what Nasim Karim and Sükrü Bilgiç use, "culture conflict," "collision of cultures," "differences in religion," and "differences in tradition" are the terms used to deny people the right to move beyond the place allotted to them. And such language has been used as a straitjacket to protect a modern welfare state like Norway from facing up to the existential human dilemmas of immigrants and their children. "Call it 'culture,' and you are excused" (see above, p. 83). In Norway, as the writer Walid al-Kubaisi, a refugee from Iraq, has observed, criticism of one's own tradition has been the privilege of native Norwegians only; immigrants were perceived as traitors to their own people and to the cause of a "colorful community" if they ventured the same (1996).[2] Other immigrants have made the same complaint.

As with Slavenka Drakulić in Yugoslavia, so also with writers like al-Kubaisi in Norway until the late 1990s. They likewise were under pressure from the larger society to stand in line and keep their uniform on. But this is also racism, as the distinguished Syrian philosopher Sadik Al-Azm (1995) points out; it reflects a derogatory view of other "cultures" (and the people who come from them), as if they could not withstand the kind of criticism deemed essential in Western societies for the promotion of human welfare—in which case human welfare will have to go. For above it, Culture is enthroned.

Multiculturalism is the position that all cultures are of equal value and should be granted equal respect; hence all should have an equal place within the colorful community (Glazer 1997).[3] But if people are presumed to prefer their own kind and to take pride in their own distinctive roots, how can they be expected to grant each other equal respect? Multiculturalists try to resolve this conundrum by preaching cultural relativism. People must be taught to respect other cultures and see the value of their traditions and products. And the place to begin is in school: teach children that all cultures are equally deserving of respect. As we have seen, this position has informed Norwegian immigration policy, and it is one for which Aisha, among others, paid the price. Equally worthy of respect—or you are a racist! The deadly word has been used to make people subservient to cultural relativism in many cases where culture was *not* worthy of respect.

In Norway, Walid al-Kubaisi and Nasim Karim have been among the most vocal critics of multiculturalism and cultural relativism from within the ranks of "immigrants." And they have been bitterly attacked in the news media by some antiracists. Their alleged offense, for which they have had to stand ad hominem attacks in the media, is that of sacrificing respect for "their cultures" in favor of ego trips serving their own personal ends, such as quest for fame and money. Al-Kubaisi has even been dubbed Norway's Salman Rushdie, not to flatter him but to warn him that his life too is in danger.[4]

Finkielkraut is not subdued in his critique of people who descend, as some do, to this kind of dehumanization.

> Supporters of multicultural society demand the right of everybody to wear a uniform . . . In a singular feat of reasoning, they present as the ultimate achievement of individual freedom the absolute dominance of the collectivity . . .
>
> Tolerance vs. humanism: this is the way we might subsume the paradoxical critique of ethnocentrism that ends up defining people by their culture.
>
> Born out of the struggle for the emancipation of peoples, cultural relativism has become a celebration of servitude. (1995:176, 108, 103)

Who pays the price of such generous betrayal? We all do, but some more than others. Nasim Karim's fate will not have to be shared by the most vocal antiracists in Norway, simply because they are men. This spares them the risk of certain atrocities (though it exposes them to others). Aisha's fate likewise cannot be shared by a male, for though forced marriage may be inflicted also on male youths and cause them great suffering, it is easier for them to escape through divorce or even plural marriage (Kayed 1999); nor will a man be subject to rape in marriage. Again, gender makes itself felt.

But in the view of some media-friendly antiracists in Norway—whose voices are actually being heard—culture is not a problem. By an ingenious and subtle move, problems related to "culture" are redefined as exceptions, unique happenings, or individual events. Don't generalize, is the slogan. True, there are some individual cases of forced marriage, to take that example, but they are rare. There are no problems, only challenges. And the way to handle challenges is to look at individual cases.

This is true in a sense, and yet entirely wrong. If "forced marriage" is reduced to individual cases, then "patriarchy" or "subjugation of woman" in the West would have stood little chance of ever coming on the political agenda. Individualizing suffering and particularizing problems is a way of rendering them nonthreatening. There are "only" individual cases, so the polity need not concern itself with them.

Antigeneralization is a strategy pursued by many multiculturalists in Norway, most of them elite men (whether natives or nonnatives) in comfortable positions, who paradoxically advocate the cause of individuality, but with disastrous effects for individuals less favorably placed. The particular brand of individuality here at stake is one that insists on regarding persons as persons, as individuals, not to be encompassed by the group; but as individuals, these persons have no general problems deriving from their culture; all such problems are linked with the new society, life in the immigrant country. Therefore, while Drakulić spoke of the shared human predicaments of individuals trapped in a totalitarian regime, and Anna, the al-Baldawis, and Keynan spoke of the shared predicaments of females trapped in patriarchy, the new individualists, as one might call them, see generalization as stigmatizing, dehumanizing, and racist. Culture is sacrosanct, and so is the individual. And since individuals realize themselves through their culture, a critique of the latter is tantamount to racism, except so far as Westerners are concerned. But that takes us back to square one—individuality subsumed under culture or the collectivity.[5]

To give Finkielkraut the last word (1995:114): "What is the use of challenging Tradition if it only leads to replacing custom with the indispensable authority of Culture?" As he points out,

> It was at the expense of their culture that European individuals gained, one by one, all their rights. In the end, it is the critique of tradition that constitutes the spiritual foundation of Europe.
> . . . We will never resolve the difficulties facing us by allowing the

need to abolish privileges to become the prerogative of one civilization alone. We cannot limit the practice of individual rights . . . only to those we identify with the West.

. . . The apostles of multiculturalism have quite consciously destroyed the spirit of Europe, making prosperity the only attraction Europe has left. (1995:176, 108, 103)

"To fear someone is to grant him power," notes an Indonesian friend of mine. And it is my argument that identity politics rests on a structure of fear. It is not tolerance so much as deep-seated distrust and apprehension that nurtures identity politics. But the question of who is the subject and who is the object of fear has no obvious answer. It is not just the weaker members of collectivities who suffer the pangs of fear, as might be inferred from my discussion so far. The leaders, the spokesmen, are themselves often trapped. Nor is the object of fear just "the Other"—that anomalous, distrusted, discredited nonmember of "my" people. Equally, the object of fear may be a person's own people—the very ones who are the bestowers of loyalty and solidarity. This is of course nothing new. It is well known from family studies that the sources of love and affection are often also objects of fear and distrust.[6] But the connection needs to be brought out in relation to identity politics because it goes against the public rhetoric and shows the forces at work on tough, able-bodied men.

In so doing, I also hope to render identity politics less threatening, more divided, by showing some of the existential dilemmas involved that are not often disclosed. The public face and the private heart may be at odds. And it is important to say so with regard to immigrants—though it should be wholly unnecessary. We know it to be the case for human beings generally, so why should it not be so for them? Yet tell me if the message of the following case does not come as a surprise to you.

Arriving at a radio studio for a debate with a prominent Muslim spokesman, I took a seat in the waiting area with my opponent-to-be, who was visibly distressed. He had been interviewed by one journalist after the other that day in connection with a conflict in one of the schools, and was probably exhausted by now and also quite angry. The issue was whether Muslim girls could be required to swim as part of their physical education in school. The protagonists were a father and a school principal. The father insisted that his daughter be exempted on the grounds that girls' swimming was against Islam. The principal refused, maintaining that physical education was an integral part of the Norwegian school system, and vital to bodily health—for girls as well as boys. As neither party would give in, the conflict escalated and was picked up by the press. At some point the Muslim spokesman whom I was to debate was brought in. He had taken the father's side, naturally, telling the media time and again how it was wholly against Islam for girls to swim, and criticizing the principal—and the Norwegian school system in general—for intolerance and discrimination. No wonder he seemed distressed now; it was late in the afternoon, and he would have to go through his routine one more time, now against an opponent who, as he was aware, knew Arabic and might have read the Qur'an.

Since we were both early for our debate, we had some time to socialize beforehand—something moderators dislike or even actively resist as they do not want rapport to build lest the temper of the debate suffer. But we had been placed in an interior waiting room where no one could see us and interfere. Hardly had I sat down before the Muslim leader disclosed the source of his distress: "But *I* am not against girls swimming!" he burst out. "I think this whole issue could have been solved." I was quite taken aback, since I had heard him reiterate the contrary attitude time and again that day in the media. "But why don't you say so?" I asked. "I can't," he answered, "for then they will think I am not a Muslim."

I never had the time or the wits to ask him who "they" were—members of his congregation, other Muslims, "the Norwegians," or who? For at this point the door to our enclosure was opened, and we had to take our seats for a live debate. It proceeded very amicably, to the moderator's surprise. But I did not have the heart to go out against the man; I was so stunned and moved by his revelation: "For then they will think I am not a Muslim."

Why do I make so much of this little incident? First, because it is not atypical, and second because it has a general point to make about identity politics. Let us look first at the incident's unexceptional character: Over the past few years I have been contacted several times by immigrant spokesmen who plead the same predicament as my fellow debater: "*I* am not against . . . (this or that), but I can't say so. Please would you [meaning me] do it?" The request has usually come before a TV or radio debate in which they knew I was to appear, perhaps because they too have been invited but have declined. And so they appeal to me to present their case—under cover, of course, or the sanctions against them would be too great. Without exception, the stance they want me to convey is a liberal one that favors greater integration of immigrants—for example, by requiring them to learn Norwegian, or to be more tolerant of their daughters' desire for an ordinary life. For me it is no problem to say so; for them it is a risky business. Standing out from the crowd, going against the majority (of the minority) has its price, as we have already seen with Sara, Anna, Nasim, Khalid, and others.

But it applies to the powerful as well—those who, in Veena Das's (1990) conception, are the distributors of pain by being the purveyors or custodians of culture. I want to qualify that statement and show that the argument of "culture" can be self-destructive. Where identity politics are being played, everyone may be constrained and even disempowered, even those who appear to set the rules of the game. For it may be difficult to see who they are. The game becomes addictive, all-consuming. The stakes become higher and higher. And as the risks loom consequently larger, it becomes the more important to keep control of all the players. Moreover, with identity politics, impersonal forces take the place of the referee, holding people in thrall so that they behave according to script. "Think of what the people will say," said Anna; that was the sword that hung above her head throughout her upbringing. Yes, just think of what people will say. There is every evidence that extremely strict control over opinion is wielded in many immigrant communities, and that physical sanctions, ostracism, and psychological terror may be employed, not just against individuals but also the families of those who might try to opt out. Shaming, disgracing, and assaulting are powerful measures used.[7] But it is not always easy to know who the perpetrators are. "The people's talk"—gossip and slander—is everywhere and all around; it becomes almost an impersonal force, compelling people simply to join—and to strike at their very own.[8]

So my first reason for telling this story of my encounter with the Muslim leader is that it is not atypical: he is not alone in experiencing a painful discrepancy between private heart and public face, and being called on to take a public stand that actually conflicts—at least at the time—with what he "really thinks." But if such is the case, then the postures assumed in identity politics must be taken with a grain of salt. And this is the second reason why I have chosen to foreground the case. The fronts are not as solid as they might seem; boundaries are blurred as some men suffer the consequences of having to take an uncompromising stand in public (identity politics are by definition uncompromising) while covertly searching for ways to build bridges, even by calling on an unlikely ally like me. I become a spokesperson for persons who would not dream of aligning themselves with me publicly since it would compromise their own political standing, but who are quite content for *someone* to say the things I do. Even those who play the game of identity politics may be deeply disturbed to think of its consequences.

As I have said, I never did find out who "they" were who might think my fellow debater was not a Muslim if he had said that swimming for Muslim girls was okay. The point is that *he* saw some such scenario and acted accordingly. To "be" a Muslim meant, as he saw it, to take a firm stand in the eyes of the world. Whatever Muslims in Norway said was against Islam, he too would publicly be against it—with only a few exceptions. He was not among those few leaders—in this case imams—who publicly defended the fatwa against Salman Rushdie. (They later regretted their stance when the Oslo city council threatened to withdraw its financial support of their mosques on the grounds that the state would not support religious congregations that condone murder.) But he was prepared to go a long way to defend actions with reference to Islam so that no one could question his good faith.

So it was that this man, whom I came to know in time as a moderate man, a humanist, and a bridge builder between congregations, nonetheless stood forth in the media as a religious conservative, relentless in his defense of questionable positions or behaviors with reference to the Qur'an. I know from reliable sources as well as from my own subsequent acquaintance with him, that there was—or is—a discrepancy, a painful discrepancy, between his private view of Islam and his public performance. Himself a victim of identity politics as well as its perpetrator, he is highly confined in what he can permit himself to say—in private "I," but in public only "we." The problem is that Norwegians hear only the "we" and take it to mean "I"; the public stance is conflated with the private self—in the case of immigrants.

The next time I was supposed to meet this Muslim leader in a radio debate, he chose to withdraw. Again it was at the end of a long day; again the issue concerned Muslim girls. This time the point of contention was whether female nurses working in homes for the elderly could attend to male patients. The precipitating case involved two young nursing students who claimed that they should be spared the indignity of having to wash or in other ways come into contact with the private parts of males. Their stance created an uproar at the nursing school, and this same Muslim spokesman was called on again. He reiterated what the girls and their fathers had said: that it was against Islam for female nurses to be required to attend to male patients. Sex segregation must prevail for Muslims even in hospitals and nursing homes. It was written in the Qur'an.

Imagine the clamor in the Norwegian media that day, of which I was unaware as I sat at my office desk until the phone rang and a journalist was at the other end. Informing me of what was going on—there had just been a heated one-hour debate between the Muslim leader and a representative of the chancellor of schools in Oslo, where neither would budge—I realized I would have to do my part one more time: enough of using the Qur'an to legitimize this and that. I had lived in many Muslim countries. In no place did female nurses or physicians refuse to treat male patients (or vice versa). Nowhere does the Qur'an say that compassion and aid to reduce pain and save lives should be limited to one's own sex. For once I was not just annoyed but was really quite upset. And I looked forward to saying so in no uncertain words. Not that I was the only one to do so. Kari Vogt, a respected professor of religion with Islam as her specialty, had already made the point on another channel: Islam enjoins compassion. Islam is merciful.

Perhaps he had heard her and realized he had gone too far, or perhaps he had other reasons. But in any case, the Muslim leader chose to abstain from the debate with me. Instead he sent a Norwegian female convert who was entirely in line with both Professor Vogt and me: thus he extricated himself from an impossible situation, without compromising his standing vis-à-vis his congregation: Islam is merciful, but he did not say so; Islam is compassionate, but he did not say so; all he said was that sexual segregation is enjoined by Islam; hence, females should be protected from seeing male patients' private parts.

On another occasion I received a call from a man who is known to be an aggressive Muslim traditionalist. He wanted my advice on what to do about certain illegalities in regard to family reunification. He was distraught, he said, for he knew that such abuses were common among his countrymen; indeed, he had masses of evidence that he intended to go public with in due course, for the practices were detrimental to the whole society, to our common future. These were words he used. Meanwhile, could I help?

I was surprised. Not so much at the illegal practices he brought up, but at his clearly deep-felt concern and also that he should choose to contact me. But perhaps I should not have been. For there had been an incident, as I now remembered, a year or so earlier, when after a TV debate he had turned to me the moment the lights were switched off and said, "Professor Wikan, I have to talk to you!" Then he told me of his private dilemmas and turmoils, and urged me to cooperate with him to help combat customs and practices that undermined young people's freedoms and life prospects. And these were customs, practices, that he had just defended in that same TV debate.

I remembered it now when he called again. Because we had both been busy, all too busy, neither of us had taken the initiative to follow up on that conversation. Or perhaps he had expected *me* to? Or perhaps he had been content to see that I did follow up on the issue publicly, along with others who also tried to help, and that we were having an effect? The problem for which he now wanted my cooperation was a trickier one.

As it happened, this telephone conversation took place only a few days before I left the country for an extended stay abroad, so there was not much I could do for the time being. But I noticed, after I was gone, that information had been leaked to the media regarding parts of the problem complex he brought up, resulting in a number of well-researched, excellent articles bringing the problem to public attention. And I wondered: might it be he, or might he be one of those who spoke with the media—under cover? He would have to do it under cover in any case lest he lose his influence and ability to work on the minds and hearts of those he wished to sway.

As with the other Muslim leader mentioned earlier, this young man strikes me as pitiful in all his outer self-assurance. To a considerable extent he is trapped. He has to play the game of identity politics, and it is one where the identity in question is not negotiable. It is frozen, rigid. There is little room here for accommodation on determining, for example, what a Norwegian-Pakistani or Norwegian-Turkish identity should entail. Liberal intellectuals often argue that "Norwegian" no longer means white Protestant native; it encompasses all other nationalities and religions that are found in Norway today. From an idealist perspective, that view is fine. But for many immigrants it goes against the grain: they want no part of this Norwegian identity, though some of them may in fact have Norwegian citizenship; they want to be able to stand apart and resist an influence from the host society, just as the parents of Aisha, Nasim, and Khalid did.

The dilemmas faced by the two men I have described, and others like them, result from the kinds of processes that Finkielkraut and Drakulić so lucidly describe: where, for the sake of the collectivity, people lose the right to speak in the first-person singular. The community behaves as if it were under siege; and the result is to stifle public, democratic debate and freedom of expression. Appiah (1994:162–63) brings out the point well when he notes that "between the politics of recognition [or identity] and the politics of compulsion, there is no bright line." Or, to put it more strongly, demanding that people play strictly according to scripts that mandate the proper way to express an identity is destructive: "It is at this point that someone who takes autonomy seriously will ask whether we have not replaced one kind of tyranny with another."[9]

In identity politics, "culture" and "identity" have come to stand for each other—a point also noted by Appiah (1997). This interchangeability was vividly brought home to me on one occasion. Walking out from a TV debate on forced marriage with a man who had been insisting, more or less, that the practice was nonexistent among Pakistanis and that those of us who argued otherwise were racist, I turned to him and said, "Why do you talk like that? You know the problems as well as I do!" He looked surprised, then countered, "What would *you* do if you were abroad and people criticized Norwegian culture?" It was one of those enlightened moments when pieces of a puzzle suddenly come together.[10] I realized there and then that the man—a highly educated politician who had lived in Norway for twenty years—simply assumed that I would have done the same, defended "my culture." It was a matter of standing up against the "Other." He might not even have believed me had I told him that I am a fervent critic of many aspects of Norwegian culture, at home and abroad. But the other insight I gained from our brief interchange was even more important: "culture" was the catchword that silenced the dialogue. He did not think of forced marriage (or so it seemed to me) as a form of behavior, a practice, that some people engaged in. No, if it was practiced, then it was a matter of culture, and thus the issue was closed.

Pondering our conversation in retrospect and juxtaposing it with what I know from other sources, I have come to the following conclusion, which I think holds an important observation: "culture" vs. "society" is the contrast with which many immigrants operate. "The Norwegians" have "society" whereas "we" (the immigrants) have "culture." And naturally so. The same contrast is applied by many members of the host society. An example: when in 1992 I helped revise a textbook for high school on "society and the individual," I discovered that the word "culture" appeared only three times in a span of 280 pages, in connection with immigrants and Sami. It was evidently not needed to educate students about "the Norwegians."

TOLERANCE VERSUS HUMANISM

The terms "culture" and "society" are not comparable. "Society" is secular, referring to manmade practices and institutions, whereas "culture" is sacrosanct, connoting identity and authenticity. By eliminating "society" from the discourse about themselves, immigrants may attempt to make themselves inviolable. Forms of behavior that are discreditable in terms of equality and social justice become the harder to combat. They may even recede from view, becoming invisible—as was the case with forced marriage in the example above.

But it is important to note that this entrenchment into "culture" is not just of the immigrants' making. It also comes about through the host society's attitudes and reactions to them. As the renowned author Amin Maalouf (himself an immigrant from Lebanon to France) has noted, the worst one can do is to create a feeling of guilt toward one's own culture. In a world in which there is pressure on all identities, where identity can no longer be taken lightly, it is imperative that the host society show some sympathy toward the culture of immigrants. If immigrants feel you are being hostile, then going on the defense is a natural reaction (as it commonly is with human beings). So this may have been precisely the reaction of the politician who denied all knowledge of forced marriage. Ethnic identity politics is born as much of fear and anger at the other's felt (or imagined) hostility as of pride in one's own heritage or "culture."

But "culture" does more than fend off criticism of certain elements worthy of criticism; it can also mask positive developments in the direction of human freedoms. This comes about from a felt need to protect the sanctity of one's own culture, hence to portray oneself as more traditional and authentic than the facts of one's own life indicate. Let us take an example.

Love marriages among second-generation South Asians in Norway are a sensitive issue and known to be rare. But a young Norwegian-Pakistani journalist, Noman Mubashir, had managed to persuade two couples he knew to tell their story, thinking it might help others who wished to follow in their footsteps. A year later he joined the production team for "Migrapolis," a TV program dealing with multicultural issues. Planning a piece on love marriage, he sought out the two couples he had interviewed earlier, only to be turned away: they had faced too many problems by going public with their stories, being perceived as betraying their families and culture. Noman Mubashir finally turned to me, having asked a dozen couples he knew to volunteer for the program and met with the same response: love marriage must be disguised as arranged marriage. Did I know anyone more forthright?

I did not. At stake are loyalty to the parents and respect for their feelings and traditions, but also fear of the contempt and rejection of society.[11] Acts expressing individual autonomy must be covered up, and the impression must be given of submitting to hardbound tradition.

What most surprised him, the journalist told me, was that even youths who were entrepreneurial and independent-minded, who *had* gone their own ways, would feel compelled to deny it publicly. But perhaps the reason was precisely, as I have come to think in retrospect, that they had already risked so much, challenged so many pillars of "culture" (and religion) that the best way to save face was to abide by tradition in word if not in deed. After all, honor *is* a question of face and appearances, of taking a public stance. Why jeopardize honor when there is no need to?

In Europe generally, ethnic identity politics hinges on the behavior and demeanor of females: women and girls. We have noted several examples already—swimming, attending to male patients, and forced marriage (though the latter also afflicts males). Wearing the Muslim headscarf in school and work settings is another common example, though it has not become politicized in Scandinavia as it has in France and Germany.[12] As a rule, then, the defense of cultural practices is likely to have a much greater impact on the lives of women and girls than on those of men and boys. In Shachar's words (2000:13), "females are asked to shoulder a disproportionate share of the costs of multiculturalism." The point is substantiated by the response of a Muslim leader to the question, "In what respects is there an absolute limit to what Muslims can accept in the Norwegian society?" He answered, "I can mention three examples: Muslim girls cannot participate in school dances; at weddings, females and males cannot sit together unless they are relatives; Muslim women must consult male physicians" (*Aftenposten*, October 22, 1995).

The issues are sensitive because gender equality—an entrenched value of modern democracies—is at stake. The position of Islam in the matter is highly disputed. Some argue that gender equality is inscribed in Islam,[13] others that it is not against Islam,[14] others that it is "profoundly threatening to the Muslim hierarchical order" (Mernissi 1996:110). Muslim leaders in Europe who subscribe to the value of gender equality, not just in word but in deed, must walk a tightrope between their constituencies and the host society if they are to have effect. It must be remembered here that Muslim leaders depend on their constituencies for their position: they can be fired, and most likely will be, if they do not abide by the standards and values that their congregations are ready to accept. The following example illustrates the dilemma.

I once met a Muslim leader in a court case to which we had both been summoned as witnesses. As it happened, our testimonies differed widely; and I heard harsh criticism of him from many Norwegians who had followed the media accounts of the case. The man appeared as a hardcore fundamentalist, insensitive to the plight of young girls of Muslim parentage trying to find a modus vivendi in Norway. But as the case drew toward an end, he contacted me privately. Please, would I cooperate with him? Please, would I come with him and talk with the parents who were charged in the case, in an effort to try to dissuade them from launching an appeal. (He expected them to be found guilty, as they were.) On our way to their house, he talked about his sympathy for their daughter. He felt genuine compassion for her, and shared with me his concern that many parents were doing their daughters grave harm by insisting that they live a traditional Muslim life, in Norway. The parents will have to change, but it will take time; unfortunately, it is taking too much time. And he talked about the harm such parents were doing not just to their daughters but to themselves and the Muslim community. Everyone suffered. And antagonism between Muslims and non-Muslims was bound to grow as each party accused the other of intolerance and inhumanity. He would do all he could to work for integration. But his hands were bound, in public. He must move with extreme caution, and work behind the scenes, lest he antagonize his constituency.

On reaching the family's house, we were heartily welcomed. To my surprise, during the long hours we spent there, the Muslim leader chose to keep a very low profile. Gradually I understood that I was supposed to brave the issues—heeding my step, allowing the family at each point to save face, and giving myself a chance to backtrack if there were signs I had gone too far. I was being used as an intermediary who could be made to carry the blame if things went wrong. That was perfectly acceptable to me. It allowed the Muslim leader to remain above the fray, in a position of authority and respect, without compromising his standing in the family's eyes. And that is what he must do if he is to carry out his work.

As it turned out, we did not succeed in our endeavor this time—which only strengthened our cooperation. Other forces are working on the minds and hearts of families like this one, exhorting them to take an uncompromising stand vis-à-vis "the Norwegians." And naturally so. With the decay of ordinary decency that they perceive around them, little wonder "the Norwegians" appear to embody vice and license. The problem is only that some of these "Norwegians" may be their nearest and dearest; their own children—persons like Aisha or Nasim or Khalid who are opting for the right to say "I." "Most of the violence that is perpetrated against children takes place right in the heart of the family," says Jacob Jervell, a respected Norwegian professor of theology. "We should recognize, therefore, that children have the right to self-ownership."[15] Appiah (1994:159) makes the same point: "As children develop and come to have identities whose autonomy we should respect, the liberal state has a role in protecting the autonomy of children against their parents, churches and communities."

But this thinking, for many Muslims and non-Muslims alike, goes against the grain. The conflicts entailed in the immigrant experience are therefore bound to be painful and hard. And the "work of culture" (Obeyesekere 1990) that must be done by Muslim leaders who—in their hearts of hearts—condone a humanitarian stance committed to the equality of all human beings is excruciatingly hard. For they must work on several fronts simultaneously, balancing on a razor's edge between the demands of their constituencies and the sensitivities of civil society. As with the Muslim leader, by now a friend, who sought my help, the cost is a deep sense of loneliness; a feeling of not being able to show his true face and therefore meeting with unjust criticism from like-minded people, people committed like him to freedom and social justice.

Telling parts of this story to fellow Norwegians I have sometimes met with a reaction akin to contempt: But why are they such cowards? Why don't they speak up? Being two-faced is not a condition that Norwegians condone; but this is what the story seems to convey: the picture of a man who changes his appearance according to the exigencies of the situation.

It is important to arrest this impression. For what is at stake is a different kind of consideration, much more fundamental. It concerns not just the character or career of this man—or men like him—but the future of our multiethnic societies: what is the best course if one wishes to achieve integration and mutual tolerance or respect?

Let a story illustrate. In 1997 there was an uproar in a school in Oslo that again made headlines in a major newspaper: A father was furious because the school authorities had introduced, ahead of time, a new curriculum on religion and world views (*livssyn*) that had just been passed by Parliament after much controversy and heated protests from many quarters that it amounted to indoctrination of Christianity. On this issue many religious and nonreligious Norwegians had joined ranks with Muslims. But the curriculum had been passed, and was supposed to be introduced in January 1998.

This particular school, however, had wanted to begin the curriculum a semester early, at the beginning of the school year, and so had sent out letters to all minority-lingual students' parents, asking them if they had any objections. As none were voiced, the school proceeded with the new curriculum. That was when the father took action. He had not been asked, he claimed—and perhaps he had not, either because the letter was lost or because he could not read or understand what it was all about. He called on an ally and spokesman, a Muslim leader, who alerted the newspaper; the conflict was thus brought to the fore, and the father's voice appropriately registered. In a major newspaper report, accompanied by a photo of the two men in the school yard, the school was criticized for its oppressive action and its attempt at premature indoctrination.

One would have thought that the father would then have demanded partial exemption for his daughter from this class, this being a parent's right. But he did not. He let his daughter continue[16]—again a dramatic contrast between public face and private heart, a turnabout of sorts, if one takes the public clamor at face value. But I do not think it should be taken at face value—any more than the behavior of the two Turkish girls who appeared in Istanbul airport in Western fashion only to reemerge as "veiled" in Frankfurt should be taken at face value. Human beings are complex and composite. And the pressure of identity politics is such as to compel many a man and woman to wear a public garb that is at odds with their privately felt longings and desires—or the desires that might be expressed in other public settings where identity politics are not at stake.[17]

As Amin Maalouf (2000) warns, we must get rid of "the old notion of identity," which is a straitjacket, and embrace instead the more sensible idea of identity as made up of many elements. Belonging to a community should be one aspect of a person's identity, for people have a need to belong, but it never encapsulates the whole human being.

"Prosperity is the only attraction Europe has left," sighs Alain Finkielkraut (1995:107). Certainly, the attraction of Europe to many immigrants is not what many of us would like it to be: it is not freedom of speech and expression; it is not democracy and human rights; it is not gender equality or the rights of the child. Or, if it is, then the evidence is veiled, unclear. What many of us who work closely with immigrants see, on the contrary, is a pattern more in line with the plight of the Muslim spokesman described

The Politics of Fear

above—intensification of social control; severely curtailed freedom of speech and expression; loyalty to clan and kinsmen rather than to civic society; a politics of fear. What are the implications in terms of a dialogue between persons "of different culture"?

Clearly, the matter is more complex than many of us would like to think. Inge Eidsvåg, former rector of the Nansen school in Norway, has pointed out that dialogue may deepen the divide—it is not a given that mutual understanding will ensue. He is speaking from experience, having been instrumental in bringing together ex-Yugoslavs of different ethnicity at the Nansen school in an effort to bridge gaps by opening up a dialogue. Often, the result was the opposite—the intensification of conflict.[18] Evidence presented in this chapter accords with Eidsvåg's experience. It may sometimes be better *not* to bring people together but to let them air their differences separately or privately, or both. This may be especially true when the parties are unequal or perceive themselves as such, a point Eidsvåg also notes. Where identity politics are at stake, dialoguing in public is often destined to reiterate the division, as people feel compelled to take an uncompromising stand against the Other (or "they will think I am not a Muslim").

Under present circumstances, mutual understanding can best proceed, I believe, by avoiding the public posturing and working behind the scenes. This is not an ideal stance, but an argument from necessity (Walzer 1997:xii). It may sound as if my position here goes counter to my argument: that silence is the enemy of effective social policies. But I see no contradiction here. I am merely cautioning against the kind of dueling that inevitably leads people to entrench themselves and hence affirms the apparent enmity between "us" and "them."

It is to be hoped that this argument from necessity will soon become obsolete, that liberal democratic forces will work toward a more constructive form of dialogue. For that to happen, the Norwegian government must also change gears in its immigration policies. At present, the political economy underwrites a politics of ethnic identity. To understand just how counterproductive this is, let us turn to a consideration of ethnic versus civic citizenship.

20   *Civic Liberty and Liberal Democracy*

Ethnic diversity and liberal democracy are contradictory, if applied as equal principles of human association. So argues Liah Greenfeld in "Democracy,

ethnic diversity, and nationalism," originally presented at a Nobel Sympo-
sium in Sweden in 1997. The two cannot logically be combined because
"the *rights of communities and rights of individuals cannot be ensured in equal measure;*
either the former or the latter must become subordinate." This has profound
consequences for public policy.

> When formulating public policy to deal with ethnic diversity and to pro-
> mote liberal democracy, it is very important constantly to keep in mind
> which one of these two sets of rights—often antithetical in their conse-
> quences as well as logical implications—one wants to uphold. Plainly
> put, cultural validation and empowerment of ethnic identity and ethnic
> diversity endangers liberal democracy. However heretical in the current
> political climate this may sound, the best way to assure that such democ-
> racy will thrive within *ethnically diverse populations* may be by rejecting the
> principles of ethnicity and ethnic diversity and, instead, encouraging civic
> identities and commitment to pluralism, or diversity, of a civic nature.
> (Greenfeld 2000:29)

Greenfeld's position accords with the argument of this book. As Michael
Ignatieff points out,

> Rights are only meaningful if they confer entitlements and immunities
> on individuals; they only have force and bite if they can be enforced
> against institutions like the family, the state and the church. If rights sim-
> ply become a catalogue of desirable virtues and agreeable compromises
> between individual and social purposes, then they have no clear meaning
> at all. The Universal Declaration is not a charter for the good life . . .
> It is simply a statement of the entitlements individuals can legitimately
> claim from the authorities which rule them . . . Rights language can-
> not be parsed and translated into a non-individualistic, communitarian
> framework. It presumes moral individualism and is nonsensical outside
> that assumption. (1999:36–37)

We have seen in our discussion of the politics of fear how important it is
to foster civic identities and commitment to diversity of a *civic* nature in a
plural society. It is important to reiterate this point for it goes counter to
present policies in some vital respects—in Norway as in many other European states. To wit, in 1996 the number of immigrant organizations in Oslo
totaled about 280—in an "immigrant population" of approximately 80,000
(comprising first and second generations). By now the number has probably

increased. The membership and leadership of these organizations are pre-dominantly male. Some of them count some females among their members, and a very few, specifically committed to women's issues, have female leaders. But, overall, the organizations are male led and male dominated. And they are proliferating.

What are the purpose and function of the immigrant organizations? That varies, of course. Some are dedicated to helping children and youth do better in life and at school, for example by offering help with homework and organizing games, trips, and other extracurricular activities. Others work to the good of women in various ways. Yet others function as cultural centers for like-minded countrymen, helping them to maintain a sense of their own ethnic identity and to solicit resources from the state based on that identity; this is their entitlement. The state is committed to give financial aid to immigrant organizations, hence marking oneself as an immigrant is a way of making financial claims on the state.

At a special meeting in 1996 I gained a rare, if discouraging, insight into the inner life of some of these organizations and their interrelations. The occasion was a sad one: Oslo had been ridden by a series of gang rapes involving immigrant men as culprits and native (Norwegian) women as victims. The police had had a hard time trying to investigate the crimes, as immigrants would not cooperate. Given what was said in the previous chapter on the politics of fear, this is not surprising. As one man from Gambia said in the meeting to be described, he would never report on one of his own countrymen, even if he knew he was involved. The notion of countryman is important here. The Gambian had lived in Norway for twenty years, and still counted his own people, ethnic Gambians, as his countrymen commanding his full support—as against the Norwegians, his fellow citizens.

To try to mobilize support for the investigation and to show the commit-ment of immigrants to the social contract, one major figure in Norwegian politics, Aslam Ahsan, originally from Pakistan, sent an invitation to all 280 organizations, enjoining them to come to a joint meeting to discuss the mat-ter and evolve a plan of action. To ensure that all received the message, he also telephoned every one of them. The result? About forty people, all men, showed up. But the most disconcerting fact was the nature of the discus-sions. Rape—the ostensible reason for the meeting—was barely mentioned. Only two representatives, in addition to Aslam, spoke to that issue. The rest wanted to talk about politics, their politics, divisive politics, and how Nor-wegian society was letting them down. It was in this context that the man from Gambia announced that he would never report a countryman to the

Norwegian police, even if he knew him to have committed a rape—a point he repeated on Norwegian TV the next day. Indeed, if a TV crew had not been present at the meeting, I wonder how many representatives there would have been. With the potential publicity, there was at least some incentive to show up.

I would not make much of this story were it not that I think it illustrates an important general point. The combatants—for such they were—had more important things to do than to mark a commitment to law and order, or to take a stand against violence and rape. Identity politics took the better of them. In many cases, their internal divisions and external animosities are their raison d'être.[19] That was one reason why so few showed up, I believe. Why give Aslam Ahsan the credit for having summoned a successful meeting, adding to his stature among "the Norwegians"?[20]

The essence of the argument I am making is that the Norwegian state underwrites ethnic identity politics—which will come as no surprise to you at this point; we have already seen it in many contexts. The immigrant organizations and Aslam Ahsan's abortive attempt to get them to act and speak out against the rape of Norwegian girls provide just one example of civic liberties gone astray (presuming here that commitment to a social contract is part of such liberties). For it is not fortuitous that immigrant organizations foster the separate distinctive interests and identities of their members in many cases; that is what they are for: indeed, it is thought-provoking that many of their members are long-standing residents of Norway with Norwegian citizenship. When does an immigrant cease to be an immigrant? We have raised that question before. It surfaces here again as a logical appendix to a situation where ethnic identity continues to be the main criterion of organization membership for many immigrants in Norway, and where the state encourages the proliferation of such organizations through its financial aid. But at what cost? Commitment to pluralism, or diversity, of a civic nature seems to suffer, as is apparent from the very low degree of participation of immigrants in nonimmigrant organizations and their low, and declining, participation as voters in local elections.

To return to Greenfeld's argument: to have a full grasp of her line of reasoning, some of her terms need to be made clear: ethnicity, democracy, and civic rights. "What do we mean when we speak of 'ethnic diversity'?" she asks. On the face of it, the term refers to nothing more than a plurality of ethnicities within a society, or the existence within it of physical and cultural differences such as those of religion, language, and race: "In this sense, 'ethnic diversity' is both ubiquitous and innocuous." When these differences are not marked symbolically, we call societies homogeneous. The judgment is in the eye of the beholder. For, as Greenfeld points out, the same measure of diversity may be *perceived* differently.

> Not every society attaches cultural significance to ethnicity and ethnic diversity and regards them as the core of its members' fundamental identity . . . When a *modern* society does not attach cultural significance to the ethnicity of its members and does not regard it as the foundation of their identities, the identities that are cultivated are rather civic, they have to do with one's acceptance of the values of one's society and achievement in their framework. In this case, ethnic diversity is highly unlikely to have any political significance. Many modern societies, however, do attach to ethnicity great cultural significance and . . . allow it to become an important political force. (2000:25–26)

The social significance attached to cultural differences is rarely proportional to their "objective" magnitude. As Barth (1998) and others have argued, cultural differences only create identities when they are stressed as emblems of group membership—that is, when people themselves make an issue of them.[21] This may strike both ways. Such differences may be emphasized or ignored, depending on the situation. To take a case from Norway, Somalis in Norway are uniformly perceived as just that, Somalis, from the point of view of most Norwegians. But this is not how Somalis perceive themselves. According to Hassan Keynan, clan association is the relevant attribute; Somalis distinguish themselves by the hundreds, whereas the notion of Somali is foreign to their self-identification.[22] This, of course, has practical relevance for Norwegian social policies vis-à-vis Somalis. Problems in getting some of them to cooperate become more understandable in this light; and although it is not appropriate for a *Norwegian* state to substitute the clan identity of some citizens for their national identity, it does make sense to realize that "Somali" is an externally imposed identification.[23]

Likewise with Pakistanis in Norway. As Lien has shown in her important longitudinal study, Pakistanis operate with a host of nesting, variably inclusive, ethnic self-identifications. Whereas the farthest a knowledgeable Norwegian might go would be to distinguish between Punjabi, Baluchi, Pashtun, Gujerati, etc., according to their languages, many Pakistanis regard subcaste identification (*biraderi*) as the most salient group identity in a number of contexts. With supreme *cultural* significance accorded to these social identifications, their import is magnified[24]—as disclosed in the response of some people to Lien's presumption that racism was a problem for them in Norway. Oh, no, they countered. Norwegian racism was nothing compared to what they encountered among their own countrymen in Pakistan and Norway. Norwegians were too naive to practice real racism (Lien 1997).

The point is that ethnic membership does not coincide with national membership, as is often presumed, nor need it be embraced as constitutive of personhood. Ethnicity is a constructed difference and, as such, variable both in its salience and its boundaries. Slavenka Drakulić (1993:50) brings this out in a poignant passage:

> Along with millions of other Croats, I was pinned to the wall of nationhood—not only by outside pressure from Serbia and the Federal [Yugoslav] Army but by national homogenization within Croatia itself. That is what the war is doing to us, reducing us to one dimension, the Nation. The trouble with this nationhood, however, is that whereas before, I was defined by my education, my job, my ideas, my character—and yes, my nationality too—now I feel stripped of all that. I am nobody because I am not a person any more. I am one of 4.5 million Croats . . . One doesn't have to succumb voluntarily to this ideology of the nation—one is sucked into it.

Drakulić's complaint feeds into the point we have made, that ethnic difference may expand or contract in importance and inclusiveness, depending on human volition (or the volition of power holders). At this point in her life, Croatian takes precedence whether she likes it or not. For many Pakistanis in Norway, on the other hand, their subcaste identification takes precedence and it is subcaste that is used to account for their need to bring marriage partners for their children from "back home." Pakistanis in Norway will not do, nor will Muslims of other nationalities, though in other contexts these identifications may be salient.[25]

Likewise with Kurds, for example. Kurds from Turkey, Syria, Iraq, and Iran will not intermarry. Though members of one imagined community, "the Kurds," which takes precedence in certain contexts, in other contexts they are deeply split among themselves into clans and cleavages that compel absolute loyalty; in other words, they are all too human.

"The definition of an identity as ethnic presupposes a belief that a person's inclinations, attitudes, and behavior are determined ascriptively, by the group to which one is born—which, in effect, means genetically—they are given, so to speak, in the blood" (Greenfeld 2000:26). Indeed, "it makes no sense to talk of people's abandoning or betraying their culture unless they are tied to that culture by some unspoken, biological link" (Star 1997). And it is not just culture that can be used in this way; religion is another candidate. How often I have heard Pakistanis in Norway say that they are Muslim first, Pakistani second, and Norwegian third. Why then can they not marry other (non-Pakistani, non-same-biraderi) Muslims? There is no prohibition in Islam on a Muslim's marrying a Muslim.

We have also noted that "Muslim" may be an imposed definition, an identity enforced by a host society practicing what a Pakistani editor in Norway has called "misconceived humanism." Take the incident recounted to me by an Iranian refugee in Norway. When she was in Iran, "Muslim" was not a salient part of her identity. In fact, she did not know much about Islam. But in Norway, everyone kept saying to her, "Oh, you're a Muslim!" So in order not to appear ignorant, she bought herself a Qur'an and started reading. "And now," she says, laughing, "whenever I feel uneasy, I say, 'But I'm a Muslim!' "

A similar complaint has been voiced by Omar Dhahir, an Iranian in Denmark. He has described how he fled from Iran because he is a communist and an atheist who was persecuted for his convictions. To his surprise, Danes all want to know about his relationship to Islam (1995). He is constantly perceived as a "Muslim," in other words, he is ascribed an identity he did not even have in his own country.[26]

As Sadik Al-Azm (1991) has pointed out, the West's entrenchment of "Muslim" as a superordinate identity, inescapable for anyone born into the fold, is a truly romantic ideology. Any romanticism, however, can be pernicious in its consequences. A similar argument is made by Edward Said in his *Covering Islam* (1981) and other works. Nor does such a position recognize the possibility of a difference between a person's subjective identity and the public stereotype. Speaking from Norway, I am struck by the fact that children of Muslims are perceived to be, ipso facto, Muslim. Any question of their own adherence to the faith seems not to arise as a possibility—whereas native youths are presumed to think for themselves and to stake out a course that may be different from that of their parents.

Research from other European countries (France, the Netherlands, and Britain) shows, however, that there may be a discrepancy between embracing a faith and having a faith ascribed to one. In a study in France, for example, 68 percent of youths of Algerian background said they did not adhere to any particular religion, and of the 32 percent who considered themselves Muslim, only 10 percent practiced Islam regularly (Ibrahim 1995).[27] No such study has been made in Norway, and should anyone dare to suggest it, it would probably be quelled in its inception as racist. Muslim is an inalienable identity, or should be, from the viewpoint both of believers and of nonbelievers. Sara is reported to have said that she would like to leave Islam when she was an adult. That choice was never to be hers; she was killed, fifteen years old, for a lesser heresy (though maybe her "whoring," her dancing with unrelated men, was seen by her male kinsmen as equivalent to her departing from Islam).

But to have an ethnic identity means, as Greenfeld and others have argued, that one is a certain person "every moment of one's life and in everything one does, whether one is aware of this or not" (2000). It also puts an end to discussion:

> She is a whore, she doesn't exist for us, she is dead for us, don't you understand! . . . But you are not Muslim, so you won't understand. My whole family has been disgraced, my life has been destroyed, my mother's life has been destroyed.

So raged the brother who had stabbed his sister in the back twenty-one times, hammering his fists at every word (*Dagens Nyheter*, February 11, 1997).

Yes, if Muslim is perceived as an *ethnic* identity, a primordial identity, then this would put an end to discussion. But it need not be so. There are many Muslims who would keep the dialogue going, who argue that not only is Islam compassionate and merciful but an emphasis on equality and freedom is an age-old value among Muslims. In other words, religion or other identifications are not exclusive. They do not close the conversation, but open it up, keep it going. If the human condition is one that exposes us all to certain existential problems and we nonetheless have to live with one another, despite all differences, then the path ahead is one that both enables us and compels us to stick together. It means plurality, yes; ethnic diversity, yes; but not making the *principle* of ethnicity and ethnic diversity the basis for our common endeavor. For that, the principle of civic liberties will do better. But if this is so apparent, why is the other principle so persistent?

We are speaking now not of nation-states that celebrate ethnicity, such as Drakulić's Croatia, but of Western liberal democracies. It is the ethos of multiculturalism that confuses and misleads, argues Greenfeld, *unless* there are strong countercurrents. This is an extremely important provision, because

> cultural perspectives which emphasize ethnic identity discount the individual as an independent social actor and the bearer of rights . . . and subordinate him or her to the group to which he or she *objectively* (namely

in terms of one's ascriptive characteristics and irrespective of one's will) belongs. Such a celebration of ascriptive characteristics denies the individual the freedom of choice and the right of self-determination, and makes an accident of birth, if not a census category, destiny. (2000:26)

By contrast, "'democracy' in Western discourse refers to the cultural and political perspective that asserts the primacy of the individual over the group and affirms individual liberty as an inalienable right." Of course, this also is ambiguous (27). Many of the world's nations (such as Algeria, North Korea, and Ethiopia) call themselves democratic, without adhering to this principle. What matters in assessing the prospects for individual freedom is the specific definition of "democracy" and the *meaning* of popular sovereignty in that society, not whether the society calls itself a democracy. This important point, Greenfeld notes, has not been given due attention.

> Like abstract notions of "truth" and "justice" . . . , adherence to "democracy" tells us nothing about the character and aspirations of a people. For it is possible to abide by the principle of popular sovereignty, that is, to apply the techniques of democracy, without actually vesting sovereignty in the people. It is this respect for the individual as the basis of the principle of popular sovereignty, not the principle as such . . . , which lies at the foundation of *liberal and constitutional* democracy . . . The idea of the human rights . . . favors, and is, therefore, associated with, a particular type of political, social and economic structure . . . The idea of the human rights implies the equality of all mature individuals under the law which guarantees to each of them the enjoyment of certain inalienable rights, specifically the right of self-determination or liberty. (Greenfeld 2000:28)

A qualification is in order here. The law can guarantee rights to people, but not enforce them. A liberal democracy like Norway ensures citizens their human rights, but falls pitifully short of upholding them in many cases. Aisha's story is a case in point. What is lacking is not popular sovereignty but adequate institution building that can deal with the facts that present themselves. The challenges are particularly pressing in our present multicultural societies. Take forced marriage as an example. Illegal by Norwegian law, forced marriage goes unpunished. There is no sanction, legal or otherwise, against parents who are found to have married their children by force. Liberal democracy is not a panacea. Liberal democracies like the Scandinavian ones may even be particularly inept at protecting citizens' human rights because of the conflict of principle between cultural rights and human rights. A champion of charity, the liberal Scandinavian does not like to take sides.

Membership in nation-states can be based on criteria of two different kinds— civic or ethnic. As for the ethnic, we have heard what it implies. Recall Drakulić's lament "I was pinned to the wall of nationhood." It is different with national identity in civic terms. This presupposes a *social contract.* It is an agreement entered into by the nation-state and the individual, not an inborn characteristic of immutable nature. Thus, civic citizenship can be replaced, changed, and assumed, depending on one's ability to fulfill the criteria. These criteria are not given in the blood. They are a matter of social contract.

Such is the ideal. The reality may be more complicated—as the next chapter will show. Contrasting civic and ethnic citizenship, Greenfeld links the broad appeal that *ethnic* nationalism has in the modern world to its ability to provide superior psychological gratification:

> It limits individuals' freedom, and by the same token relieves them of responsibility and offers a sense of tangible order . . . It is natural, what with the stress of anomie and the disconcerting indeterminacy of one's reality, to yearn for the comfort of the regulated world where one is never allowed more than what one can accomplish and where one's dignity is ascribed to one as a national birthright and assured by the membership in the dignified community irrespective of one's accomplishments. (2000:35)

In Greenfeld's analysis, therefore, the experience of modernity favors ethnic nationalism.

I distance myself from Greenfeld on this point. I see far less gratification and far more pressure and compulsion. Many of the people whose voices have been heard in this book—young people, women, even male leaders— seem to be forced into an unwanted choice through a conspiracy of state and community pressures. What Greenfeld seems to overlook, perhaps because she is presenting an ideal-type argument, is the fact that many of those who are sucked into ethnic nationalism do not want it but are given no choice. Rather than "psychological gratification," what many of them experience is a deep sense of disquiet and constraint, as well as an intense desire to break out and establish a different form of social contract with their rulers. Certainly, this is the message I have heard from the majority of people I have met around the world. They yearn for a better life, a dignified life based on a more equitable social order and respect for their autonomy, a life in which they can use and be rewarded for their competence and qualifications. It is this, rather than "the comfort of the regulated world where . . . one's dignity is ascribed to one as a national birthright" that is at stake. Indeed, I doubt that the majority of people in nondemocratic nations experience dignity as a birthright. It is more likely to be seen as a privilege of the elite.

Precisely on that account, I argue, migration to the West holds out such hope. Prosperity, and the increased freedoms it facilitates, is part—and a vital part—of the attraction of migration for many people. But there is more to it, and this "more" is intimately linked to the attractions of civic citizenship. But for whom? Again the uncomfortable question arises: who are the beneficiaries? And who stands to lose?

The inroads of ethnic nationalism all too readily deny many immigrants, and even their children, the benefits of civic citizenship. It is too early to assess the effects of such developments on liberal democracies, but the prospects are not encouraging.[28]

In chapter 21 we shall see the dual forms of citizenship, ethnic and civic, wage battle over who will decide over whom and to what effect. It is often assumed that dual citizenship is an advantage for those who hold it, even if it complicates matters for the nation-state. I shall show that it can indeed be an advantage, but only for some. Just as Aisha had no chance of benefiting from her citizenship in a liberal democracy cum welfare state, so Nadia, whom we shall meet next, came dangerously close to being swept up by the forces of ethnic nationalism and having her civic citizenship rendered null and void. Let us now turn to her story.

On October 3, 1997, Norwegians awoke to the news that Nadia, a Norwegian citizen, eighteen years old, had been kidnapped by her parents and taken to Morocco, where she was being held captive.[1] The alleged purpose was to have her married by force. It was Nadia herself who managed to sound the alarm by way of a phone call to a fellow employee at a store where she used to work, and where she had failed to show up on Monday, September 1, giving no notice. She was in a terrible state, telling how she had been drugged, beaten, and forced into a van that had transported her, in handcuffs, with her family to Morocco. Stripped of her passport, she was now held at her father's house, and she was desperate to be set free.

Her colleague contacted their boss, who went straight to the police, but when the police were slow to take action, he contacted the Ministry of Foreign Affairs.[2] They acted expeditiously. The Norwegian ambassador in Morocco was informed, and a rescue plan was conceived. The ambassador would try to negotiate with Moroccan local authorities and with Nadia's father for her release.[3]

Now there was every reason for Norway to engage itself, for not only was Nadia a Norwegian citizen, but her parents were too. Nadia's father had come to Norway in 1971 at the age of twenty and had held Norwegian citizenship since 1985. Her mother had joined him in 1978, also aged twenty, becoming a citizen in 1987. Norway does not recognize dual citizenship, so from the point of view of Norway, Nadia's judicial status and that of her parents were clear. Also, the crime, if so it was—and at this point there was much to indicate that a crime had been committed—had been perpetrated on Norwegian soil.[4] Hence, there was no question about Norway's right and duty to investigate the case and try to work out a solution.

But there was a hurdle, and it concerned citizenship. That one state does not recognize dual citizenship matters little as long as another state with which a citizen is affiliated does, and Morocco did. Morocco does not relinquish its hold on its citizens. The country practices what might be called ethnic citizenship, meaning: once a citizen, always a citizen, and citizenship is carried down to subsequent generations. This had serious consequences for Nadia. A Norwegian legal adult, she was transformed into a Moroccan child—for the legal age in Morocco is twenty, not eighteen as in Norway. Hence she came under her father's jurisdiction, since he was the undisputed legal head of his family. If he felt warranted to keep his daughter locked up, that was his business. All the Moroccan authorities could do was to help Norway locate the family, as they did.

A week of tense negotiations followed, conducted by phone between the ambassador and Nadia's father.[5] Time and again Nadia had to step in for her father because he became so enraged that he could not talk. Norwegians meanwhile followed the case with the utmost suspense, for Nadia's case, *Nadiasaken,* had become a national event, and the outcome was fraught with uncertainty. Several journalists and photographers were on the spot in Nadoor, the Moroccan city on the northern shore where Nadia was being held;[6] and a snapshot of Nadia, taken before her abduction, along with photos of her captors' house in Nadoor and an increasingly desperate ambassador, were a constant reminder of what was at stake in this transnational family drama that had become a matter of high politics.[7]

Three times Nadia's father promised to set her free, only to renege on his word—leading the ambassador, at one point, to call him a liar. A key point of contention concerned the father's demand for a guarantee of "free passage," meaning he would not be prosecuted on his return to Norway. This the ambassador could not and would not extend. The case was under police investigation, and it remained to be seen what conclusion they reached. But Nadia's father would not budge. The negotiations broke down. And when the embassy next lost contact with Nadia and heard that she had been removed to a remote village, not only the ambassador and his staff but the Norwegian public who was following the case day by day, hour by hour, felt a deep sense of desperation. Was all hope gone?

Because Nadia did not count as a Norwegian citizen in Morocco, not even the Norwegian foreign minister could make any headway in getting her released. He did tell the media of his concern, however, and it was reported that he planned to contact his counterpart in Morocco. But efforts faltered before Moroccan law. As confirmed by an eminent Moroccan lawyer consulted by the Norwegian Embassy, the father's authority over his children was indisputable. It probably did not help matters that Nadia's maternal grandfather was a prominent and wealthy patriarch, wielding considerable power in the local district where his granddaughter was being held. The chances of her release seemed dismal.

When hope was all but lost, however, Nadia suddenly reappeared in Oslo airport, her father having paid for her return ticket himself. The embassy and the Foreign Ministry were taken by surprise, as was everyone else. The only ones who had known about Nadia's return and had met her at the airport were her brother and a friend of his, along with a social worker who was a family confidant. Now the three of them escorted Nadia, unbeknownst to the media, to the social worker's apartment, where Nadia remained for several days. It was the social worker who finally broke the news.

Nadia, who has never granted an interview to the media, was reported to be exhausted but happy to be back in Norway. All she wanted was to rest and be left in peace. A week later she was reunited with her family when they too returned to Norway.

What was the reason for the father's change of heart? I believe two moves on the part of the Norwegian authorities were crucial. First, the police arrested Nadia's brother Samir, interrogating him for complicity in her abduction. According to Nadia, Samir had helped push her into the van and had used force to stifle her screams and get her handcuffed. Because Samir was only sixteen, and because the police did not think there was any risk of his leaking evidence (*bevisforspillelse*), he was not put behind bars (*i varetekt*) but allowed to go home. His passport was confiscated, however. Samir phoned his parents that night and warned them that he might be jailed. It is clear that this scared them.

But the decisive move, I believe, was the social welfare agency's suspension of all social welfare benefits to the family. The father had been entitled to disability benefits since 1990 (due to a heart condition), and the amount he received—168,000 kroner a year (about $19,080 in U.S. currency at the time) was considerable even by Norwegian standards.[8] In addition, his wife received 20,000 kroner ($2,270) in child benefits. The family also had a comfortable apartment granted by the municipality, for which they paid a token rent.

Now Nadia's parents might be seen as not really needing the money. They were well off by both Moroccan and Norwegian standards. In Nadoor they owned a house valued at one million Norwegian kroner ($115,000), which they kept as a vacation home, not renting it out (a fact that was raised in court). Moreover, Nadia's mother came from a very wealthy family. Her father had what was described by the defense as a palace; and indeed, to judge from the pictures, it was. So Nadia's parents might have lived comfortably in Morocco. But that was not what they wanted; they wanted to remain in Norway, and for that the disability pension was crucial.

How could the Norwegian authorities proceed to cancel the welfare benefits to Nadia's parents? On the grounds that they had failed to inform the authorities that they would be out of the country for more than a month. This constituted a breach for which it was possible to effectuate sanctions, which Norway now did—with the desired result. Nadia was set free.

But hardly had Nadia been reunited with her family than her case took on a new turn: she retracted everything she had said before. The story about her kidnapping had been all made up. She had gone to Morocco of her own accord to visit her sick grandmother. But when the family wanted to remain in Morocco longer than she did, she became desperate: she missed Norway, and so she pulled off the lie to marshal help.

She was deeply sorry, she said, for the turmoil she had caused and for letting her parents down by depicting them as criminals and child abusers. She had never realized what the import of her actions would be. She had been confused, and unable to distinguish right from wrong.

The social worker in whose home she lived for the first few days and a lawyer who had been assigned to assist her announced that Nadia was happy but exhausted, and that she only wanted to be reconciled with her family and to put the bad experience behind her. Her lawyer also said that he was optimistic about the future, meaning, as I understood it, that he thought the case had been resolved.

It goes without saying that this new turn of events caused quite a stir, and many wondered what was really going on. Some Moroccan and Pakistani youths I talked with complained that Nadia had let them down. She could have become a rallying point for others who were threatened with forced marriage, and now what had she done? Chickened out, for fear of reprisals. It was perfectly understandable why she had done so, but to brave things so long and then give in?

There were also debates in the media (some of which I participated in myself) regarding the plight of the second generation, especially with regard to forced marriage. These issues had been discussed before; but Nadia's case served as a catalyst, giving them added urgency and a human face.

Following Nadia's admission of lying, her parents were reported to be preparing a lawsuit for slander against two national newspapers and against the Ministry of Foreign Affairs. A sizable compensation would be claimed.

But it was not to be. A year later, Nadia's parents were brought to court by the Norwegian state on a charge of "having forcibly held someone against her will" (*frihetsberøvelse*), with a stipulation that the time period had exceeded one month, as it had in Nadia's case. The minimum sentence was one year in prison; the maximum, fifteen years.[9]

As amicus curiae as well as expert witness (*sakkyndig vitne*)[10] to the court, I attended the whole proceedings. I also met with Nadia's parents and her grandfather in the parents' home, in the company of a leader and mediator from the Moroccan community. The story that follows draws on this engagement.

But I know more than I can tell, since I was also present during a part of the trial that was closed to the public during Nadia's testimony. In addition, I withhold information that had been given me in trust by Nadia's mother. I also do not tell what I know from telephone conversations with the father's defense attorney or from private conversation with the Moroccan leader. My account is primarily a public account based on what was revealed in the court and in the media; the interpretations are, of course, mine. I obviously cannot reveal what was said during a part of the trial that was closed to the public during Nadia's testimony.

The trial lasted five days, with an extra day for the verdict. Witnesses for the defense were Nadia's grandfather, her brother, the brother's friend, the social worker, two Norwegian-Moroccan girls, a leader from the Moroccan community, and a couple of other family friends. Witnesses for the prosecution were Nadia, the ambassador, the police investigators, a psychologist whom Nadia had been seeing over the past year, and a couple of her Norwegian friends. In addition, the prosecution presented as evidence a tape of two telephone conversations between Nadia and her parents that had been recorded by the police with Nadia's help but without the parents' knowledge. Despite the defense attorneys' vigorous protest, the judge finally decided to allow the tapes.

Nadia's parents each had a lawyer (a man and a woman), whereas Nadia had a "support lawyer" (*bistandsadvokat*). A municipal court (*byretten*), the kind in which this trial was held, is presided over by a professional judge, who is assisted by two lay judges (in this case a man and a woman).

Two and a half days of the trial were spent on Nadia's parents' testimony, the proceedings slowed down by translation. The mother said she knew no Norwegian, though she did speak quite well, and her husband was quite fluent. But with what was at stake, it was only natural that they would seek the added assurance that translators provide.[11]

The parents' story more or less repeated what Nadia had told on her return to Norway: She had gone to Morocco of her own accord to visit her sick grandmother. Indeed, she had pleaded with them to let her go, against the warnings of Nadia's mother that she might lose her job by not being able to notify her boss; they had to leave in great haste. But so much does Nadia love her grandmother that she didn't care.

The parents conceded that there had been problems between Nadia and them at times. But they had never done anything but act in Nadia's best interests. They were trying to save her from herself and her bad Norwegian friends, they said. To that effect, they were willing to go to some lengths, naturally, but never to the point of beating her or kidnapping her or keeping her locked up. Nadia had always been free to do what she wanted. She had been a loved, even a spoiled, child. And what is more, in Morocco she had been free to go where she wanted; there had been no keys, no locked doors—as Nadia herself admitted in court. But, as she said, where could she go without her passport, without money, with informers all around? "The whole country had kidnapped me!"[12]

Faced with the necessity of having to brand their daughter a liar, the parents resorted to an age-old device—throwing the blame on others.[13] It was not Nadia's fault that she did what she did; she had fallen under Norwegian bad influence, both that of her schoolmates and that of some journalists who, the parents claimed, wanted to make money off of her. They had tricked her into inventing those lies in order to sell her story. Some of them were out to blacken the Muslim community by using Nadia as a ploy. Nadia's father also argued in court that the Norwegian authorities and the police had pressured Nadia to stick to her original stories of lies and deception.

According to Nadia's subsequent testimony, however, her parents also believed her to be subject to another kind of influence—jinns that had bewitched her. To her horror, she was subjected to various cleansing rituals in Morocco; some simply consisted of being given amulets to wear and magical water to drink. But some, described in the part of the trial that was closed to the public, were far more terrifying. Her parents, however, had made no mention of jinns or black magic. All they conceded was having given her a mixture of rosewater and cloves to drink in order to calm her down—a common remedy in Morocco. At no point did they present themselves as anything but modern, educated people—which indeed they were. Nor did the defense attorneys try to mount any kind of cultural defense based on the parents' supernatural beliefs, which they might not even have heard about before Nadia's testimony—although such beliefs are widespread among Moroccans in Norway. On the contrary, the defense tried to capitalize on the parents' standing as members of a prominent cosmopolitan family. The court was shown photos of the grandfather's mansion in Morocco, and of the stylish house belonging to Nadia's own parents. Bringing jinns into the picture could only have complicated this image, though it might have explained why the parents kept Nadia so long in Morocco: for the cleansing rituals to work, one must not cross the sea for a month, I am told by Moroccan-Norwegian friends.

But Nadia's parents told a different story of why they kept Nadia overseas for so long: they had acted in good faith. They thought they were in their full right to abide by Moroccan family law—in Morocco. Wouldn't any parent, even Norwegian parents, have wanted to do what they did—safeguard their own child? Time and again this theme featured in the parents' defense: they were not special; they were just ordinary people who did what parents must do: protect their children. It wasn't a matter of culture conflict but of common, universal concerns. They were law-abiding citizens who were tolerant of Norwegian culture; their mistake was simply that of assuming that their Moroccan citizenship applied in Morocco. Hearing them, I could not help but feel a certain resonance with their plight. They presented themselves as deeply caring people who had somehow been trapped, as indeed they had. The question was how it had happened and what their own role might have been. For that to be assessed, Nadia's testimony was crucial.

The cries were heartrending. I shivered as I sat in the hallway outside the courtroom during a recess, hearing from afar those desolate cries of someone in agony. Was someone being attacked? What was going on? Slowly the realization dawned on me that they might be coming from Nadia; yet they were not the cries of a young woman; they seemed subterranean, unreal.

But it was Nadia, who had come to testify against her parents in court. After two and a half days devoted to her parents' testimony, just half a day had been set aside for Nadia. A family tragedy that was bound to have no winners, only losers, was now being enacted in full view of the public. And Nadia's desolating cries as she entered the municipal court bespoke the price she was paying for her quest for freedom.

Bringing one's parents to court—especially one's mother—is something utterly abhorrent to Muslims (as to many others). It did not matter that it was not Nadia who had done so; the charge had been brought by the Norwegian police. In the eyes of the community, Nadia was a traitor and should be treated accordingly.

She made her entry from a door at the rear of the courthouse, avoiding the deluge of gazes that were sure to meet her had she entered from the front. For she was already a celebrity, through no wish of her own. Indeed, she had been in hiding for over a year, living at a secret address with police protection. And when she testified in court that very day, there were two policemen sitting guard behind her, just for security.

She entered the courtroom with a blanket over her face to avoid the public gaze, I thought. But it was not that; it was to avoid her parent's eyes, which would be staring at her from the back (she came through a side door). She had asked that they not be present in the courtroom, where they would have sat in the defendants' seats to the right of the witness stand. That would have meant she would then have to face them when she turned her head in their direction to answer the questions from the defense attorneys. Her request was granted, and the parents were seated in the translator's cubicle, but it was only a few yards away, and there was just a glass wall separating her from them.

She hadn't made it a condition of her testifying that they be absent from the courtroom proper; she would testify in any case. But she had pleaded, and her request had been granted. No one doubted what agony she must be going through. Nor did anyone doubt the bitter pain of her parents' hard-tested emotions. They hadn't seen each other for a year, parents and child—not since that day on which Nadia decided to tell the truth after all. As we have heard, she did so first in Morocco, but then repented to cover for her parents on her return to Norway, only to be overcome by fear that they might let her down again, and then who would heed her cries for help? She was also concerned about her little sister, whom she adored and who might one day come to share her fate, and about unknown others who were in the same plight. All this I know from her testimony in court.

So she had gone back on her cover-up story and had contacted the police, ten days after being reunited with her family. The police had not believed the cover-up in the first place and were, as she knew, already conducting an investigation of her parents. She offered to cooperate in gathering evidence against her parents.

Here she was—a slender, almost fragile-looking girl as she entered the courtroom, a black blanket covering head and face, her body slightly bent.

A HOPE FOR THE FUTURE

But as soon as she stood up in the witness stand, the blanket removed, she appeared steadfast and strong. She spoke with a clear voice, did not mutter, and answered every question coherently and lucidly. At times she broke down. The memory was too much for her. Some time into her testimony, her attorney suggested that she be allowed to testify sitting down, in front of the witness box. It must have been a relief, for when standing, she had felt the full force of her parents gaze. She had made no concession to them in the way she appeared. She was dressed in black pants and a black sweater, both tight-fitting but not immodestly so from a Norwegian perspective. The parents would probably not have agreed. Knowing that the way she dressed had been a point of contention between Nadia and her parents, I cannot help wondering whether she wore that outfit in silent defiance. But why should she not appear as she really was, when that was what the whole battle had been about—her right to be her own person?

I never turned to look at her parents throughout Nadia's testimony. But I know others who did. One journalist reported the father shaking his head in exasperation at times. The mother reportedly wept a lot. The next day Nadia's father asked to be allowed to speak, out of turn. He accused his daughter of being a liar. All she had said was false. How could any parent do to his daughter what she accused them of? Could anyone be so callous? But Nadia had brought shame on the whole family and herself; that was why she was desperate. She was no longer a virgin, and in Morocco a girl who is not a virgin before marriage has no future. She will be left to fend for herself, and end up in the streets.

In revealing that Nadia was not a virgin, Nadia's father publicized a secret that there was no reason for him to reveal, had he not wanted to. And thus he may be seen to have triggered the shame that could otherwise have remained undisclosed. Nadia had been more discreet. In the closed part of the hearing she had testified that she had told her mother, on the way to Morocco, that she had slept with a boy.[14] Now that her father repeated this in public, he exposed the disgrace, bringing it over himself, it might seem, by making the matter public. But perhaps he felt he had already been so disgraced by his daughter's misdemeanors that there was nothing to lose. Better reveal the depth of her fall and be done with it.

"Here in court," he said, shaking his head, "you think we are the ones who have committed a wrong. But Nadia cries because her honor is destroyed. Everything she tells you is just lies and falsehood. But I know she does not mean any of this. It is her accomplices who are making her do it. Nadia has forgotten the nine months in her mother's womb, the care and affection she received, her childhood, her upbringing until she came of age. Now we are repaid for the kindness we have shown as parents," he said, while the mother wept openly.

According to Nadia, what her father derided as "just lies and falsehood" had been a terrifying reality—her reality—of being beaten, forced, kicked, handcuffed, and transported like merchandise on an excruciating journey through Europe to North Africa. She was not even allowed to go out and relieve herself for the five days the journey lasted; after she tried to alert a border patrol officer in the Netherlands to come to her rescue, she was further restrained. The kidnapping itself had been a trauma. She came home from work on Sunday at midday; she had a cold, for which her father gave her cough tablets—or so she thought. She slept heavily until suddenly awoken by shrill cries of "Fire! Fire!" and by her brother's pulling her to her feet. They tumbled downstairs in panic, her brother supporting her, since she was drowsy and weak. Down in the yard stood the van with the doors wide open; she was pushed in before she could react, and beaten by her father when she cried out and tried to escape. He also threatened her with a knife. Not until they reached Tangier was she allowed to go out—to take a bath at the driver's home and be treated by a sheikh. [15]

According to Nadia, her parents had planned to marry her to a twenty-one-year-old Moroccan (whose picture her mother had showed her) so that he could get a visa to Norway and she would "become Moroccan." Indeed, this was what the whole battle had been about, her wish to be Norwegian against their insistence that she become Moroccan and become Muslim.

The retraction she had produced on her return to Norway was at her parent's instruction; it was their condition for setting her free. By taking the whole blame herself, she would ensure that they would not be prosecuted. Her concern for her younger siblings also contributed to her trying to pull off the cover-up. Should the mother be thrown in jail, who would take care of them?

That Nadia and her parents had long been at loggerheads is clear: six months before her abduction Nadia had contacted the child welfare agency regarding her father's ostensible abuse. Her father, she claimed, beat her and accused her of being "too Norwegian": she was not allowed to wear make-up, wear pants, go dancing, or have even a Pakistani boyfriend. Her father had gone to a café where she had worked and told some of the staff that he would kill them if they didn't make Nadia quit. This threat was confirmed by the people in question.

A HOPE FOR THE FUTURE

As a result, Nadia was placed under child welfare custody for three months and housed in a youth institution. She returned home only after her eighteenth birthday (when she became legally an adult) and with her father's assurance that he would not beat her.[16] Apparently the move was voluntary. But as Nadia said in court: the project (her word) of the child welfare agencies was not her own. They were set on reuniting her with her family, against her own will.

The problems did not go away; they resumed. Nadia's brother testified that he didn't love her anymore after she had said that she did not want to be a Muslim. Her parents testified that they had nothing against Nadia being "Norwegian"—she could do as she liked, even marry a Norwegian—but they didn't like her drinking and smoking and staying out late at night. Would any parent, even a Norwegian parent? Two girls who served as witnesses for the defense confirmed that Nadia's parents had given her full freedom, even to marry the Pakistani if she wanted; but they were naturally upset by her disgraceful behavior. Had she not been seen drunk in the street on occasion?

But Nadia herself told a different story. "Didn't you tell me I would have to stay in Morocco till I was married and had a baby and only then could return to Norway?" Nadia asked her mother in a taped telephone conversation that was presented in evidence in open court. "And didn't you threaten me that I would have to stay in Morocco till I rotted?"

"You misunderstood me, my daughter, I was only joking," said the mother.

"That's hardly a joking matter," said Nadia.

A crown witness for the prosecution was the ambassador, Arne Hønningstad. He painted a highly unflattering picture of Nadia's parents. The father, he said, had resorted to the most abhorrent threats, such as threatening to beat Nadia if Norway did not grant him "free passage." The mother had screamed that all Norwegian women were whores and that she was certainly not going to have her daughter become one of them. Five days into the negotiations, the ambassador told the court, he was afraid that Nadia might break down. She was clearly under terrible pressure. Through the telephone lines that had been connected to amplifiers in the embassy (with the Foreign Ministry's consent) so that other embassy personnel besides the ambassador could silently assist the negotiations and serve as witnesses, one could hear the clamor of angry voices. It was evident that Nadia was being threatened. Her voice quivering, she nonetheless said that she was fine. At this point, the ambassador told the court, he was afraid she might succumb to the "Stockholm syndrome"—a condition whereby a hostage comes to empathize with her captor.[17] But when, ferreting out how she really was, he interjected questions that demanded a "yes or no" answer, she affirmed her desperation. The ambassador's testimony was entirely in line with Nadia's.[18]

But one of the ambassador's allegations caused a public stir in Norway and was hotly contested by Nadia's mother: that she had called all Norwegian women whores. She claimed she did not even know what the word "hore" meant, so how could she possibly have said that? Seeing the woman mortified by the reported outrage of Norwegians at being thus described, I intervened on her behalf and told both the media and the court that "whore" is a common invective in Arabic, no big deal, almost an everyday swearword.[19] My explanation did help to get the woman off the hook, I believe, though she insisted she had never uttered the word.

A key witness for the defense was Nadia's maternal grandfather, a prominent and wealthy patriarch who wielded considerable influence in his home district in Morocco. A cordial man, he left in disgust: "I thought Norway was a democracy where there was justice before the law. But this is not democracy! The judges chose to believe a young girl over her family, they sided with her. That is injustice." He said he would go back to Morocco and tell the people as much; he would also file suit against the ambassador, who, the grandfather claimed, had vastly overstepped his powers. "He even offered to send a car to pick up Nadia—from her own family!"[20] But the worst, of course, was all the things the ambassador had said to the media, and now had repeated in court. The grandfather wanted his family's honor restored, and he was going to do it by suing the ambassador.

Had not Nadia gone to Morocco of her own free will to visit her sick grandmother? Had she not begged her parents to let her go, even though they had been concerned that she would let her employer down by not showing up for work? The grandfather's testimony on these points was in line with that of the parents. They had told the court how the decision to go to Morocco had been made impromptu on a Saturday evening. A telegram from Nadia's maternal uncle, telling the family, "Your mother is ill; urgent that you come," had arrived a few days before.[21] But there were no flights available to Morocco until two weeks later. So Nadia's father was thrilled when, by sheer good luck on Saturday, he met a man in a café who was going to drive to Morocco the next day; the man happened to have five seats free in his van—just enough to accommodate Nadia's family.[22]

Hence, the decision to go was made that very evening. Nadia came home late, rose early next morning to go to work, returned after a few hours, and

A HOPE FOR THE FUTURE

went back to sleep; so it was not until mid-Sunday that she was informed of the family's decision to travel that night. To her mother's delight she insisted on coming along. "I could not believe my ears when Nadia said she wanted to come," said her mother in court. But so much does Nadia love her grandmother that she was even willing to let her employer down, and risk losing her job. "I'll get it back," her mother reported her as saying. Yet the Norwegian state prosecutes the family for having forced Nadia to go, even kidnapping her! The grandfather was outraged. But when questioned about his wife's illness, he was at a loss. Well, she is sick all the time. How is she sick? Well, she has diabetes, and she faints and such things. Does she faint often? How could he know, he doesn't sit at home. And so on. It was a sad spectacle. Watching Nadia's mother watch her father was even sadder. Whether his exalted status had forbidden them, out of respect, to instruct him in their story, or whether he had forgotten his lines or just felt uncomfortable in court, I cannot tell. In any case, his testimony undermined the parents' story.[23]

Someone who might have corroborated the parents' story, the driver with whom they went to Morocco, could not be brought as a witness because he could not be identified, let alone found. The parents claimed to know nothing about him except for his first name, although they had spent five days together in the van. According to Nadia, they had also spent a night in his house in Tangier. The parents claimed that the man lived in the Netherlands, whereas Nadia named a certain suburb of Oslo.

Among other witnesses who came out for the parents was a social worker (a special friend of Nadia's brother, whose liaison contact she was). She said she could not imagine that the family would do anything bad to Nadia; she knew them to be kind and caring people. She also painted a detrimental picture of Nadia, as did two Moroccan girls—Nadia's friends, as they said—along with her brother and a friend of his. They all declared or implied that Nadia was a rather "loose" girl, fond of drinking, smoking, and staying out late at night.

But such habits, it seemed, were due to the bad influence of her school-mates. Time and again this point was stressed by witnesses of the defense: it was not Nadia but her schoolmates who caused her to fall.

In the end, the Norwegian state chose not to include a charge of forced marriage against Nadia's parents. For although Nadia was under the clear impression that they had a marriage in mind for her, there was no firm evidence of it. The charge was simply that of forcibly holding someone against her will (*frihetsberøvelse*), with a stipulation that the offense had exceeded one month, as it had in Nadia's case. But to have sent her parents to jail, even indirectly, even if she had not filed the case, is that something Nadia could have lived with? I argued "no" in court when I was asked to take the stand as a witness—actually a witness for the defense, though it had been conceded that I could function on behalf of the court, as an expert witness. So let me explain my role in this case.

About six months before the trial, I was contacted by Leidulv Digernes,[24] the lawyer for Nadia's father, asking whether I would be a witness for the defense in the impending court case. I was surprised. My position regarding the plight of girls like Nadia is well known in Norway. I had also written an op-ed article in a major newspaper—*Nadia og debatten som bør følge*, "Nadia and the debate that ought to ensue" (*Verdens Gang*, December 22, 1997). There I had argued that Norwegian politicians should pay serious attention to the problem of forced marriage and to the law on family reunification that underpins the practice. I had also described the reactions I had heard from immigrant youths to Nadia's case, some of them feeling that she had missed a golden opportunity (at that point in the story): with all the publicity her case had received; she would have been in an ideal position to serve as a central figure in a movement for the rights of young people as against received tradition. Instead, she had changed her story, letting it appear that she had gone to Morocco of her own will. Clearly, the young people I talked with believed she had been forced. But they understood all too well Nadia's plight and why she "had to" be reconciled with her parents. What was the alternative? Total ostracism. And yet some of them felt somewhat betrayed. She should have stood by them. She should have persevered.

I phrased these observations carefully in my article. I did not want to hurt Nadia. Nor did I make any charge against Nadia's parents, though whoever read between the lines might intuit that I was not convinced of their innocence. But I had to be careful, for it hadn't been easy getting the piece published. It had been turned down by two newspapers—for no good reason, as it seemed at the time, but I learned shortly afterward that Nadia's parents were preparing a lawsuit against those two newspapers for their coverage of the case. However, the fact that it had been turned did make me cautious.

So I had chosen my words carefully in a revised version that was published by *Verdens Gang* (Norway's best-selling daily). My aim was not to harm anyone. But the one who was hurt and who said so was Nadia. I did not know her. To this day I have never met her in person. She phoned me, however, clearly upset. She wanted me to know that her original story was true; in other words, she had not gone back on it, as I had written. She seemed in great haste and afraid to talk, as if someone could be overhearing her. She said she wanted to meet me, but I must not tell anyone about the phone call. We made an appointment for a few days hence, but exigencies on both sides prevented our making it. This was around Christmas 1997, three months after her return to Norway and ten months before her case came up in court. What I didn't know at the time was that she had already gone to the police, in secret, with her real story. She had not let her cohort down; she had stood by her story at enormous cost to herself; indeed, if anyone let her down, it was her peers who did when her case finally came up. Then there was complete silence from all those who might have rallied to her support or even shown in small, quiet ways that they cared, that they felt for her. But no immigrant youth spoke out in public. Those few that testified in court denounced her behavior. She was alone, totally alone, as Nasim Karim had been before.[25]

So when Nadia's father's lawyer asked me if I would be a witness for the defense: I could not believe he was serious. We talked, and I didn't expect anything more to come of it. I was doubly surprised when a week before the trial I received a letter from the court informing me that I must testify. Digernes was probably right to call me, for I did come to his clients' defense in a way, without letting Nadia down. Being a witness to their ordeal throughout the five full days the proceedings lasted—sitting close to them, sensing their plight, and knowing what they meant to Nadia and she to them—I developed a strong sympathy for her parents. But when I came to their defense, it was mainly for Nadia's sake.

As it turned out, my status in court was changed from that of witness for the defense to that of expert witness and amicus curiae. This was done at my own initiative. Realizing that as a witness I would be excluded from following the court case in its entirety, I asked for the change of status. The court seemed to welcome the move, since I was knowledgeable about Islam and North Africa. And so I could follow the court case in its entirety.

The jury took only three days to reach a verdict. Both parents were found guilty. Nadia's father was given a suspended sentenced of one year and three months, her mother one year. The father was also fined 15,000 kroner (about $1,700 in U.S. currency) and ordered to pay 60,000 kroner (about $6,800) in court costs (saksomkostninger) connected with bringing in witnesses from abroad, the defense lawyer's journey to Morocco, and so forth.

Nadia's parents thus received a sentence less than the legal minimum for the crime of which they were convicted. My own role may have had some significance here. As a witness I was asked to answer truthfully to every question but also to *bring up any matter that I judged to be of significance to the case.* And I did so, speaking at some length on what I judged would be the cost to Nadia and her family, should her parents, and especially her mother, be thrown in jail.

I was alarmed, I told the court, to find that Nadia, having had a lot of support among youths in the Moroccan community before the trial, had now lost it. Instead, she was harshly criticized by nearly everyone; and the reason I heard was that she was "throwing her parents in jail." People do not care about the fact that it is the Norwegian state that charged the parents. To them she is guilty, and of the most horrible deed—that of throwing her mother in jail. And elaborating on the mother's position in Islam, I tried to make it comprehensible why the reactions would be as they were. I also gave some objective reasons why the mother should be treated more leniently. As a wife in Islam she is subject to the "law of obedience," being duty-bound to obey her husband. So the mother especially should be given the benefit of the doubt.

My testimony lasted for three quarters of an hour. I was also questioned by the judge on the matter of relative guilt. I cannot remember exactly how the question was phrased, but I do remember searching for the words to say that I had found Nadia's testimony trustworthy, without these words sounding like an outright condemnation of her parents. But it was true: I did believe Nadia, who had provided a coherent and credible account, whereas her parents' stories were full of holes; it was hard to take them seriously.

In its published verdict, the court did make reference to my testimony. Regarding the mother, it also noted that as there was no evidence that she had beaten Nadia as the father had done, so she should receive a milder sentence.

All in all, the court granted that for the sake of the whole family, and in the hope of any family reconciliation, the parents must not be imprisoned. So it was necessary to go below the minimum legal sentence. But it was also necessary to establish a firm precedent and underscore the seriousness of the crime. The final sentence was in accordance with the prosecutor's procedure. He had pleaded forcefully for Nadia's case, asking the court to convict her parents while keeping the options for family reconciliation open.

The trial was an emotionally draining experience for me, which left me depleted at the end of each day. Even now, a year later, thinking back, I am haunted by a sense of despair. For although Nadia's parents were treated mercifully considering the severity of the crime of which they were found guilty, and although Nadia's words were believed—she was found to be truthful and courageous—the family tragedy in which they are enmeshed is devastating. Nadia's anguished cries as she entered the court house bear testimony to that, as did her mother's sorrowful weeping and even her father's hard-won composure. Back home in the family's apartment, a little boy and girl were waiting, a three- and a five-year-old, Nadia's siblings, whose lives were also being overturned. This remains her greatest sorrow—that she has become separated from them.

Nadia's parents were lucky compared to Mohammed Bashir and Sekina Khan, British citizens from Pakistan, who in March 1998 were sentenced, respectively, to twenty-four months' and six months' imprisonment in England for trying to abduct their daughter. Like Nadia's parents, the British Pakistani couple had drugged their daughter by giving her a drink that she thought was something else—in that case soda water. They then took her by car to the airport to spirit her out of the country, having bought a ticket for her beforehand. But she half woke up at the airport and cried out, bringing airport personnel to her rescue. (Her parents tried to convince her she was at the hospital which is why there were so many people around.)

Nadia's parents were more shrewd, according to Nadia. They knew it would be impossible to have her travel by air; she would have alarmed the crew. Hence that long, excruciating—as it must have been for all parties—journey through Europe. But Nadia's parents were also luckier in that there is every indication that their daughter hopes for some reconciliation with them in the future, if only for the chance to see her younger siblings. The daughter of Mohammed Bashir and Sekina Khan, on the other hand, was older and seemed to have lost all hope of reconciliation.[26]

We will look more closely at the verdict in the Nadia case in the next chapter for what it brings out in regard to citizenship. But let me end on a note regarding Nadia's good name. In its verdict, the court noted that here had been attempts by several witnesses to present Nadia in a disreputable light. Nevertheless,

> the court has a positive impression of Nadia as a clear-headed and bright girl. In the view of the court, Nadia deserves respect for the way she has managed to carry through with her testimony. The court cannot see that

evidence has been presented to indicate that her demeanor is any different from that of other Norwegian girls her age.[27]

In this opinion, the court followed the recommendation of the prosecutor, Bjørn Rudjorde, who had advocated that Nadia receive some form of redress (*oppreisning*) for the injustice she had suffered because of the massive attempts by some witnesses to blacken her reputation and portray her as a liar.

In the end, Nadia stood forth in recalcitrant independence, a solitary figure, devoid of friends within the Moroccan community, where she was perceived by many as a traitor. She even received threats to her life.

Her parents' attempts, corroborated by others, to make her appear the dupe of bad Norwegian friends who exerted an evil influence on her went totally against her own desire, which was to be perceived as a person in her own right. That was what the battle was all about for Nadia—to be her own person. But for her parents, the only way they could hope to salvage her good name and their relationship with her was by finding a scapegoat—an age-old human response to an unbearable loss.

22   *Welfare and Citizenship*

It was the matter of citizenship that decided Nadia's fate, in more than one way. Obviously, had she not been a Norwegian citizen, the Norwegian government could not have interceded on her behalf. But also, it was of the essence that her parents were Norwegian citizens. This is clear from the writ of the verdict. It states:

> The defense attorneys have argued for acquittal on the grounds that Nadia, according to Moroccan law, becomes legally adult (*myndig*) only at twenty years of age. Moroccan citizens are not freed from (*blir ikke løst fra*) their citizenship if they acquire another. Nadia therefore had dual citizenship. Her parents must therefore assume that she was a child/minor in Morocco, and that they were fully within their rights to keep her there against her will.
>
> The court does not agree. When the parents have taken the step of applying for Norwegian citizenship for themselves and their children, this implies both rights and duties. An application for citizenship means that

one has decided for oneself which state one wants to be most closely connected with, if not emotionally, at least judicially. That also means that one has to submit to (*innordne seg*) the rules applying in this state. The parents were well aware of what the legal age in Norway is. For a Norwegian citizen resident in Norway one cannot assume that Moroccan law should apply during short-term visits in that country, and especially not when she [Nadia] has been brought there against her will. The criminal offense (*det straffbare forholdet*) was initiated in Norway . . . Forcibly holding Nadia against her will was therefore in violation of the law.

Ignorance of the law (*rettsvillfaring*), which also has been claimed as grounds for acquittal, is likewise not applicable, according to the court. Forcibly holding a person against her will is illegal in most states, if not in all. As residents of Norway, and as actually Norwegian citizens, [Nadia's parents] must know the rules at least in this country.

Both the subjective and the objective conditions for sentencing (*domfelling*) are present, and the accused are sentenced according to the charge.

The verdict further states:

> The case arises from culture conflicts. But it is the parents who have chosen to live in Norway. After many years of residence here, they are fully aware of how Norwegian society functions, for better or for worse. That they wish to maintain the customs of their country of birth is unobjectionable, as long as these customs do not come into conflict with Norwegian law. Children can develop in ways that are different from what the parents hope for. But that is the risk in having children, and—not least—in letting them grow up in a different culture. The parents have made a choice as to which country their children will be molded by. That circumstance may have such consequences as resulting in the case currently before the court. Using violence and forcible deprivation of freedom of movement as an answer is unacceptable.
>
> The court also notes that the family continues to live in Norway and that they have two children below school age who will grow up here. Therefore, there must be aspects of Norwegian society that they, in sum, perceive as more positive than the negative ones.[28]

The verdict was a clear statement of what the Norwegian state demands of its citizens, according to the law. And it was historic. It was the first time that the Norwegian courts declared—and in blunt language—what citizenship entails. The reactions were predictable—outrage from members of the Muslim community and others who sympathized with Nadia's parents; and satisfaction from still others, some Muslims included, who felt it was necessary for the Norwegian state to put down its foot.

Mohammed Bouras, chairman of the Islamic Council (an association of about forty Muslim congregations) and himself a prominent member of the Moroccan community, declared: "This is an insult to all Muslims. It implics that we are bushmen who do not follow Norwegian laws and rules!" (*Dagbladet,* November 11, 1998). It was the issue of citizenship and the judge's emphasis on the duties involved in taking Norwegian citizenship that caused his wrath. He was also quoted as saying, "The charges and the verdict are an offense against the family and us Muslims. The judge is requiring us to respect Norwegian laws, but does not show us any respect" (*Arbeiderbladet,* November 11, 1998). Bouras had been a witness for the defense.

Others were quoted as saying, "This is directed against us Muslims! The Norwegian state does not care about Nadia. They are just using her as a pretext (*påskudd*) to oppose us."

It was clear that the verdict had added insult to injustice, according to many members of the Muslim community. Others agreed with them. "Justismord!—miscarriage of justice!" cried a Norwegian editor and friend of Nadia's parents, who had been a witness for them in court. "A declaration of war!" wrote a prominent journalist, Peter Normann Waage, who, like me, had sat through the whole trial. His concern was that by not making any concession to Nadia's parents, the court had not merely done them an injustice but had antagonized the Muslim community, and so reactions were bound to come. There was nothing wrong with the suspended sentence, as he saw it; it was the premises of the verdict that were unacceptable: "[Saying that] the parents ought to know how the Norwegian society functions and that it is they themselves who have chosen to live here—[is] a form of *besserwissen* (paternalism) that can only be like salt in open wounds," he wrote (*Dagbladet,* November 11, 1998).

Let us step back for a moment and look at the court's stance in a wider perspective to see what might justify it.

Nadia's parents had lived in Norway for a long time: the father twenty-eight years, the mother twenty years. By contrast, their residence in Morocco had amounted to only seventeen and twenty years respectively. Unlike many immigrants who are illiterate, or nearly so, they were well educated. Thus there were some grounds for expecting them to know better.

Nadia's parents were also not among the poor and pitiful who, as some might say, should be excused for their lack of knowledge, having come "unwillingly" to Europe only because of their lack of prospects back home. Nadia's parents were well off. They might have chosen to lead a prosperous life in Morocco, where they have a big house and a large, prominent family, and where the father could still receive his Norwegian disability pension. The reason he lost it at the time of Nadia's abduction was not that he went to Morocco but that he stayed away too long without notifying the social welfare agencies. The only benefit the family would lose, materially, by returning to Morocco would be the children's monthly allowances, but the cost of bringing them up in Morocco, as compared to Norway, would be so small as to compensate for the loss.

Thus the conclusion may be drawn that the family lives in Norway of its own will and because, as the court said, they judge the benefits of Norwegian society to outweigh the disadvantages.[29] What might be the benefits? There are free medical services and free education. With the father's heart disease, taking advantage of the Norwegian health care system was clearly to his advantage. As for schooling for their children, it is obviously highly important for them. They send Nadia's younger siblings, five and three years old (in 1998), to nursery school, and are clearly committed to their children's education.

Samir, their eighteen-year-old, might have been better off in Morocco. He has been in conflict with the Norwegian law, as has a disproportionate number of second-generation boys. In Morocco, there might be stricter surveillance from his extended family. But what, then, are the employment prospects for young males in Morocco? They are dismal.[30] Which is why many keep trying to make it to Europe as illegal immigrants—the only option for most. Every night, on the shores of Spain, scores of hopeful young men turn up, having braved the turbulent Gibraltar strait to seek a new future in Europe. Many are lost at sea,[31] and many others have their hopes thwarted by the Spanish police that patrol the beaches. Some make it all the way to Norway. Recently a dozen young stowaways were found on a boat. Some of them said this was not the first time they had tried to make it—and failed. But they would try again and again, until, God willing, they would get lucky.

So Samir is better off in Norway after all. If he does not manage to find employment, there is the cradle-to-the-grave safety net that secures him (and any family he might establish) a decent standard of living. Unlike many men in developing countries for whom marriage is becoming increasingly difficult as the costs connected with it supersede the grooms' potential income,[32] Samir is lucky: the *mahr* he will have to pay for his future bride will be minimal,[33] for he holds a trump card in his hand: citizenship in a European welfare state and, with it, the right to permanent residence abroad. The material and symbolic value of citizenship confers great prestige.

Making their abode in Europe today allows "the new immigrants," as they are called, to savor the best of several places and civilizations. Nadia's family goes to Morocco on long vacations, sometimes twice a year, while enjoying the comforts and securities of a welfare state. It is this that is called sojourning in immigration research: The "new immigrants" tend to stand with one foot in each camp, traveling back and forth between the new country and the old homeland. Nadia's parents fit this picture. They even have a beautiful residence in Morocco (with a complete wardrobe) waiting for them; they do not need to lodge with relatives.

The published verdict in the Nadia case made a distinction between emotional and judicial commitment, declaring that in taking Norwegian citizenship, the family had decided which state to abide by legally, even if they continued to be emotionally more connected with their native land. Perhaps this was true of Nadia's parents—that they had made this commitment. Yet they had not anticipated that caring for their daughter in the way they deemed necessary meant that they would come into conflict with Norwegian law.

Sojourning is vital for many immigrants to maintain their cultural identity and to remain in touch with kith and kin. But it has its costs, both from the point of view of the nation-state and for the children's life prospects. "Having to learn 'Ba, ba, little lamb' over and over again," is how one young man of Pakistani descent, put it to me. Children may be taken out of school from time to time to travel to the parents' homeland. Indeed, this became such a problem in Oslo's primary schools that the school authorities sought, and obtained, official sanction for a policy that would authorize the social welfare agencies to cancel child benefits to families that broke the rules. According to some school principals I have talked to, this policy had immediate results and alleviated the problem, though it did not solve it.

The problem is not, of course, that parents should not be entitled to take their children to their home country in order to teach them about their heritage and to nurture family ties. The problem is that it is done at the children's expense in many cases—if we grant that getting a proper education and being able to progress in school at a regular pace are of value. "When the third grandmother died, and the family had to go immediately to Pakistan for the forty-day mourning period, I put my foot down," said one principal in exasperation. "We have given up on immigrant parents," announced a Norwegian convert who is head of the Muslim Women's Organization, in a newspaper interview. What she seems to be expressing is her frustration that things are not going as they should, and that too many parents are ignorant of Norwegian society, distrustful of Norwegian society, and "living in another world."

This jibes with the reports I have heard from numerous teachers. With only a few exceptions, they complain of immigrant parents' lack of engagement with their children's school: most of them never come to parents' meetings (even when personally invited and assured that there will be interpreters), and many seem to have minimal knowledge of what the education is all about. Now this is not just an "immigrant" problem; native parents falter too, but the problem with immigrants calls for special attention due to their marginalization. Lack of trust clearly goes both ways here, and the losers are the children who—like Khalid—will have to try to make it in Norwegian society, irrespective of how the parents feel about their homeland. As with Nadia, who does *not* stand with one foot in each camp, or Aisha, so it is with many others: their life projects are not those of the parents, and unless the parents recognize that, everyone will suffer. The losses afflict us all.

The verdict in Nadia's case should be seen in this context. It seemed aimed at rectifying the situation by stating in no uncertain terms that taking up permanent residence in a country and becoming a citizen of that country entails a commitment, a social contract. For although the court did not use that term, that was what was at stake.

I myself have used the concept of the social contract over and over again in my engagement in the integration debate in Scandinavia. To me, that is what it is all about. That is also why I supported the premises of the verdict in Nadia's case, and said so in the media when interviewed about my response. I believe the state does need to insist that there are duties that go with citizenship or permanent residence, not just rights. This should be self-evident, though it is not. And it should be underscored for the sake of the collective interests we share as members of one state. In view of the immense cultural and ethnic diversity within all European states today, there is a need for some common glue, something to hold that cultural plurality together. There must be some rules of the game that apply to all, and in which we all can trust. For, as Michael Walzer notes (1997:23–24), "mutual toleration depends on trust, not so much in each other's good will as in the institutional arrangements that guard against the effects of ill will."

This trust is the more important in the face of the conflicts that are arising both within and among different immigrant groups, and, not least, between "immigrants" and "refugees" or asylum seekers. As anyone with a close knowledge of immigrant communities is aware (using the word "immigrant" in its broad sense), relations are often far from amicable and there is considerable tension within and among many of the ethnic groups that make up the new Europe. Racism and discrimination are not, as I have argued, a problem only between majority and minority; they can arise at every level and in all kinds of connections, unless there are strong counterforces that deter animosities and distrust. Walzer's words on toleration are instructive here.

> Tolerating and being tolerated is a little like Aristotle's ruling and being ruled. It is the work of democratic citizens. I don't think that it is easy or insignificant work. Toleration itself is often underestimated, as if it is the least we can do for our fellows, the most minimal of their entitlements. In fact, tolerance (the attitude) takes many different forms and toleration (the practice) can be arranged in different ways. Even the most grudging forms are very good things, sufficiently rare in human history that they require not only practical but also theoretical appreciation. As with other things that we value, we have to ask what is it that sustains toleration, how it works . . .
>
> I recognize that each regime of toleration must be singular and unified to some degree, capable of engaging the loyalty of its members. Coexistence requires a politically stable and morally legitimate arrangement. (1997:xi–xii)

Walzer presents what he calls an argument from necessity. I do the same, if from a different point of departure. My compelling concern is the concrete situation among the multiple parties in a small European country, as I know it firsthand. It is for this reason that I argue for an explicit social contract specifying rights and obligations, binding on the government as well as the people. Considering that a sizable number of immigrants to the West come from countries where supreme loyalty rests with the clan or family, and where democracy may be a bad word, there is all the more reason to emphasize a new form of allegiance that foregrounds civic identities and the obligations devolving on a citizen, not just the entitlements of citizenship.

The counterargument is sometimes presented that a social contract, of the kind I advocate, goes against human liberty since it includes an element of coercion (*tvang*), obstructing a person's freedom to choose for him- or herself. That is true. And yet I stick to my position.

As Michael Ignatieff argues with reference to human rights, the same is true of peaceful coexistence among "a colorful plurality": it requires a strong institutional framework for its realization. Building that institutional framework—creating the conditions whereby individuals are genuinely free to avail themselves of such rights as they want, without encroaching on the rights of others—is a necessity. And its best guarantee may be the rule of law. A strong state, not a weak state, may be the best guarantee of human rights and hence of that moral empowerment that stems from being able to exercise one's rights (Ignatieff 1999:23).

In this context, coercion is not a bad word as I see it, although it is often used as such by the advocates of "free will," whether liberal intellectuals or illiberal traditionalists who may both see their interests served by a lack of interference from the state. But who stands to gain and who pays the price? The argument from necessity compels us to take stock of winners and losers; it compels us to recall Eric Hobsbawm's argument about whom the government most needs to serve; and it is in line with Amartya Sen's notion of individual freedom as a social commitment (see below).

Children in democratic societies are subject to many forms of coercion, including elementary schooling. Many do not go of their own free will but because they have no choice. It is part of the social contract, enforced for the citizen's and society's good. A democratic welfare state demands of its citizens that they should be able to read and write and acquire competence in relevant fields of knowledge. To that end, the state is obliged to provide the necessary institutional arrangements. The Norwegian state may have had some such notions in mind when Parliament declared, in 1987, with respect to immigrants, that freedom of choice cannot be interpreted to mean that immigrants can choose to stand entirely outside the Norwegian society, for example by refraining "from learning Norwegian and acquiring knowledge about Norwegian society."

Yet when it came to acting on this principle, the Norwegian state failed to fulfill its part of the social contract. In stating that immigrants cannot choose to refrain from learning Norwegian and acquiring knowledge about Norwegian society, did the state think that a programmatic declaration was enough, that people would take care of themselves? Whatever the reasoning, facts have long since proved that an explicit social contract specifying rights and obligations of the government as well as the people is needed. Let me add that my plea for a social contract is supported by many immigrants I know who are distressed with the way things are going in Norway, feeling that the social fabric is being fractured and torn.

I find resonance for my view in this statement by Mohammed Bouras, chairman of the Islamic Council in Norway, in his book *Islam in Norway* (1998): "It is my dream that all Muslims in this country will respect Norwegian laws, Norwegian culture and traditions." Others I know harbor the dream that their respective communities of Vietnamese, Somalis, or Tamils will share in this same vision. But for that to happen, the Norwegian government must demonstrably fulfill its part of the social contract. Let me specify some of what I think needs to be done.

First and foremost is the matter of language. As the Nobel laureate Amartya Sen points out in his essay "Individual Freedom as a Social Commitment" (1990:51), "illiteracy is also unfreedom—not just the lack of freedom to read, but also the curtailment of all the other freedoms that are conditional on communication requiring reading and writing." It is my argument that the Norwegian government is curtailing precisely such freedoms for many immigrants by not taking seriously their need to be able to read and write (or at least to speak and understand) Norwegian. For illiteracy need not be configured as the inability to read—in the strict sense of the word. It can mean an inability to understand the national language in the country where one lives. How can immigrants, for instance, take part in the democratic process in Norway if they don't even know the language? How can they acquire and assess information of relevance to their lives if they are unacquainted with the lingua franca in the country where they live? As Peter Schuck (1989:55), a distinguished professor of law, observes,

> An effective society—one that can accomplish its common goals, facilitate the private ends of its members, and nourish its system of values—requires that newcomers achieve at least a modest degree of assimilation into its culture. At a minimum, this must involve attaining competence in the common language in which that culture expresses and changes itself, but it also demands some comprehension of the nation's institutions and traditions. If newcomers . . . fail to acquire the mastery of the language and social knowledge that citizenship requires, they jeopardize their own well-being and (if they are sufficiently numerous) that of their adopted society.

Am I perhaps making too much of a claim for the national language—Norwegian in this case? Can't immigrants also learn a lot and orient themselves through their native languages and by way of spoken communication? Yes, they can. But there is no denying that without knowing Norwegian they would be missing out on crucial sources of information to a degree that would inhibit their participation in society and often render them unable to carry out their functions.

Relevant here is a distinction Amartya Sen and Martha Nussbaum draw between "function" and "capability." (For an extended discussion, see Nussbaum 2000.) For function to translate into capability, certain politico-economic preconditions must be present. For as Sen notes (1990:49), "some of the most distressing problems of social ethics are deeply economic in nature." People must be provided with the conditions that actually enable them to perform their functions, that is, to turn them into capabilities.

The right to vote in democratic elections is a good example. How is this function to be translated into a capability unless people can amass the relevant information, assess it, and act on it? But these tasks require the skill, the capability, to orient oneself within a field of knowledge that, in Norway at least, makes extensive use of the national language. Indeed, the failure of a law of 1983—which gave immigrants the right to vote in elections after only three years of residence in Norway—to achieve what it intended, namely, increased participation, may be seen in this light. With limited language proficiency among a large part of the constituency, participation naturally falters.[34] For it is not just the right to vote that matters, but everything that makes people interested in, and capable of, carrying out their functions as citizens.

A case in point is the poor attendance at parent-teacher meetings and the fact that many children have to serve as translators for their parents, especially mothers, even after the parents have lived in Norway for years. The issues are linked. And they are highlighted by the exhilaration women are reported to have experienced when they are given the means to learn Norwegian. Indeed, as I have argued on many occasions, to deprive women of the opportunity to learn Norwegian—whether by the state's failure to provide the necessary facilities or resistance from spouses or kin—runs counter to an explicit tenet of one major religion, Islam. Not only are Muslims, women included, under an obligation to seek knowledge, but the mother, in Islam, is the maker of the child's future. She is entrusted, by being in charge of the child's upbringing, with the power and authority to prepare the child for life. This requires knowledge and competence and the ability to orient herself in the child's world.[35] It requires language and the ability to collect and assess the relevant information. For an immigrant mother in Norway, it means, simply, a working knowledge of Norwegian.

At times, when I have presented this argument, imams and mullahs have been in the audience. They have never questioned my position, probably because they find it unassailable. All the more reason for the Norwegian government and immigrants to act in concert to make parents capable of carrying out their parental functions. This is not to say that the only ones incapable in this respect are some immigrant parents. It is simply to make an argument from necessity with regard to language and the state's obligations to immigrant citizens and residents.

The importance of language can be illustrated in many ways. One example is provided by Camilla Kayed (1999), who in her research on divorce among Muslim women in Oslo discovered that some of them, though long-time residents, did not know they had an equal right to divorce in Norway; they had believed Norwegian law to be as restrictive as Pakistani or Moroccan law. In other words, lack of "language" coupled with segregation and marginalization disempowered these women from gaining knowledge of their basic rights. Language competence underpins many forms of participation. Here is another example: I was attending a "Stop the Violence" gathering in Oslo that drew hundreds of people (including several cabinet ministers), along with my friend Gol, a young Afghan-Norwegian. "Look, Gol!" I exclaimed; "there are hardly any immigrant parents here! Why d'you think that is?" (The event had received massive media coverage). The answer was not slow to come: "Because they don't know about it! They never read Norwegian newspapers or watch Norwegian news on TV!" (Wikan 2000b).

Gol's remark may have been an overstatement, but it contained a lot of truth. Why would people read Norwegian newspapers or watch Norwegian TV if they hardly even knew the language? I am referring here to those with little or no knowledge of Norwegian, and it is impossible to estimate their numbers. This is indeed one of the many facts that must be established. Clearly, however, a considerable percentage of the Norwegian population consists of functional illiterates, meaning those whose Norwegian is nonexistent or extremely poor. And many are also real illiterates in any language.[36]

The situation in Norway is not unique. "The school is betraying us new Swedes," said Mehmet Osmanovski, fifteen years old. Mehmet was born in Sweden, has a Swedish passport, and reckons himself a Swede, but he cannot speak Swedish fluently. He says, "It's really crazy that I have learned Swedish so poorly that I don't speak fluently. As soon as I go into town and open my mouth, people think I'm a foreigner.[37] I'm stigmatized because I don't sound like a Swede" (*Sydsvenskan*, February 7, 1997).

A Swedish-Turkish author and advocate in immigrant matters, Thomas Gür, supports Mehmet's view that he has been betrayed. Already in the 1980s, Gür sounded the alarm. "But it was not until 1993 that the politicians recognized as a fact what they had thought to be an impossibility: that children born in Sweden did not learn proper Swedish." Gür is harsh in his criticism of sociolinguists who recommend that broken Swedish—also known as kebab-Swedish—be given the status of a Swedish dialect: "That's romanticizing the problem. What is at stake is a language that marks one as underclass" (ibid.).

It is hard to say which is worse—having a language that marks one as underclass or having no language that can facilitate communication. But the former at least enables one to learn to read and write. Not so with many women of a certain West African community that a friend of mine (being married into it) knows well. Most of them are confined to what she calls *glattcelle*, prison cells with minimal equipment, an apartment with a television set and little else.[38] They cannot go out alone as they cannot read street signs or names on buses and trams. With their husbands away in Africa much of the time,[39] many suffer intensely from isolation. They are deprived of precisely those freedoms that Amartya Sen underscores as being conditional on reading and writing, and their bondage is even greater than it would in their own country, where at least they would be able to communicate orally.[40]

Another unfortunate factor in the current state of affairs is provided by leaders of Muslim congregations in Oslo, the mullahs and imams. Influential as they are in both judicial and day-to-day matters,[41] their knowledge of Norwegian is by all accounts pitiful. This was vividly brought home to me when I was invited by a Pakistani youth organization to participate in a seminar on "the role of the mother" in Islam. The organizers had specified that all discussion would be in Norwegian. Four speakers had been invited, three laypersons (including myself) and one imam. The audience consisted of a dozen imams and about a hundred others. As it turned out, the imam speaker knew no Norwegian; he had been imported from Denmark. And so he gave his speech in three other languages—Arabic, English, and Danish (the same speech three times). Judging from the expressions of the imams in the audience, they may not have understood any of the languages, perhaps knowing only Urdu and Punjabi. But it is significant that the highly committed youth organizers had evidently been unable to find a Norwegian-speaking imam among the fifty or so candidates in Oslo. That is not surprising—Oslo is only a stepping-stone in the careers of many who aspire to more prestigious positions in England, France, Germany, and elsewhere. But given the power and influence many of these imams wield, the situation is serious.[42]

What then can Norwegian authorities do? And what have they done to ameliorate the situation?

First, Norway has shown itself miserly when it comes to providing Norwegian language lessons for adult immigrants. Compared to Sweden, Norway—a much richer country—has offered only 750 hours for refugees and 500 hours for immigrants, as compared to 2,000 hours for both categories in Sweden. Only in late 1998 did Norway change its policies; it now offers 3,000 hours to adult immigrants and refugees who lack the equivalent of the Norwegian elementary school exam. Others are offered only 500 hours (if immigrants) or 650 hours (if refugees). These instruction hours are entitlements. There is no guarantee that people will make use of them, or that adequate facilities will be provided.

In 1996, the parliamentary leader of the Labor Party then in power announced that the party had decided to make Norwegian obligatory for all immigrants. Not only that, but each individual would be offered instruction according to his or her level and ability, and there would be no upper limit on the hours offered: everyone should be able to attain functional literacy in Norwegian, whatever it took. (The Conservatives and the Progress Party had already made similar pronouncements.)

I seized the occasion to congratulate the party (in an op-ed article) for its wisdom and humanity (Wikan 1996b). But there was a hitch, I said. What about the economics? Had the party any idea of the costs? To work that out, I suggested, one would need to have an assessment of the present state of literacy and illiteracy in the immigrant population as a whole. And what of mothers with children? Would the government offer to provide free nursery care to allow mothers to attend language classes? Or were families expected to solve such problems themselves? Since many of the men were unemployed, it shouldn't be necessary to provide nursery care in all cases, I pointed out. But my conclusion was that whatever it costs, Norway cannot afford not to act. The gains far outweigh the costs.

As it happened, nothing came of these good intentions; and I was not surprised. For the problem was, of course, quite overwhelming with a number of critical issues at stake: First, the problem of economics—appropriating the funds. Second, the problem of gender, or power, and "respect for their culture." How to handle men's frequent resistance to their women's being obliged to leave home to take language lessons? Third, what of the logistics of the case? Providing enough instructors and classroom space was only part, and perhaps even the easier part, of the problem. But what of transport facilities for the women if public transport was not available, or if some men insisted that "seclusion" must prevail: would their women have to go by taxi? And what of child care and nursery facilities? Fourth, the problem of equity: how would the "Norwegian" population react to large resources being spent—and in some cases being unequally spent (for example, to accommodate demands for "seclusion") on an immigrant population that is already costing the country too much, as many feel?[43]

Truly, the problems may seem overwhelming. But my own position remains that the cost of not acting to deal with the problems is the more serious. Commitments to human rights, to liberal democracy and social welfare, including gender equality and the rights of the child, all should compel Norway to make knowledge of Norwegian obligatory for all citizens and permanent residents, other than the very old and frail or those with special disabilities.

Given the premises of Norwegian immigration policy in the 1970s to mid '90s, as I understand them—that things would work themselves out if we were kind and generous to immigrants; and also, that immigrants had not come to stay—it is not surprising that Norway has been reluctant to make national language skills obligatory. And when it became undeniable that most had in fact come to stay (or sojourn), the dominant attitude seemed to be: Give immigrants time, and the language business will take care of itself. But that isn't happening. And the government's belated move to increase the number of Norwegian lessons offered from 500 or 750 per person to 500 or 3,000 per person proves that it isn't. It is doubtful, however, that increasing the hours alone will do the trick.

For some time there have been long waiting lists of people—particularly women—wanting to enroll in language courses. The number of courses offered falls far short of the demands, at least in the capital—an encouraging sign. Nevertheless, the indications are overwhelming that nothing short of making Norwegian compulsory will ever solve the problem of massive illiteracy among large segments of the population. Already, Sweden and the Netherlands are moving in that direction—which gives hope for Norway, since Norway tends to follow Sweden in such matters.

"Workfare" rather than "welfare" is the idea now. Applied to language learning it means that the right to welfare goes hand in hand with the duty (for refugees) to take language courses. In Norway, the right of municipalities to institute workfare has been in force since 1984 (for social welfare clients in general), but most opt not to. Moreover, even if workfare were nationally instituted to promote Norwegian language learning, what of those immigrants who do not live on welfare? The problems are many, and this is not the place to discuss them all. My point is simply that having facility in Norwegian should be a requirement of Norwegian citizens, and that means that the necessary public facilities must be available to teach it.

Regarding the case for women, many girls of immigrant background have pointed out to me that the mother is often the more restrictive of the parents, owing to her unfamiliarity with and fear of the surrounding society (see also Mørck 1996; Sandrup 1998). Illiteracy may nourish fear; and there is no need for a civilized society to curtail people's freedoms in this way. Rather, a civilized society must move in the other direction: toward an expansion of the human freedoms conditional on literacy.

"But why bother to learn Norwegian?" said a Kurd to me, "when you Norwegians do everything illiterates want?" He was referring to the translator services that are offered to residents and citizens even after twenty to thirty years in Norway. And he is right. Consider Nadia's parents, for example. Her father had an Arabic interpreter, her mother a Berber one, throughout the court proceedings. Every question and every answer was translated. And this father and mother had lived in Norway, respectively, for 27 and 20 years. Now a court hearing is a special case, in which nuances of expression are of the essence; so the need for translators is especially justified there. Not knowing is presented as legitimate, excusable. But should it be—for long-time Norwegian citizens?

The verdict in the Nadia case foregrounds citizenship as a social contract. It makes a case for citizenship as a social, moral, and legal commitment—not least for the sake of the children. Was that perhaps why the forebodings that the verdict would lead to increased hostilities between Muslims and "Norwegians," as some predicted, have not been borne out? To my knowledge, there is nothing to indicate worsened relations. Having made their point ("this is an insult against all Muslims!"), did most perhaps continue as usual? Or were they perhaps determined to show "the Norwegians" that they are not the irresponsible "bushmen" that the verdict seemed to imply, but responsible, committed fellow citizens? Is, perhaps, the argument from necessity winning out?

I would hope so. But it may also be that what is taking place is a refinement of the techniques of subversion. Even if the argument from necessity is winning out, it may not be resulting in what the verdict in Nadia's case had hoped for. "Necessity" may be configured as the need to be more astute, more imaginative. We shall return to the problem when we revisit Aisha's case. What can now be said is that Nadia's case served to intensify awareness of the law and to emphasize that there should be no second-class citizens: all should be equal under the law.

Nadia's story is not finished, however. Her parents appealed the verdict on the spot. And so the case would have to be tried again by a higher court.

I was with Nadia's parents the evening before the verdict was announced, visiting them at home; and as I talked with Nadia's mother, I asked her: "What will you do if you lose the case tomorrow?"

"Launch an appeal!" she said.

Knowing how distraught she had been and how the trial had weighed upon the whole family, including her little ones, and knowing of her husband's heart disease and her own foremost wish, as she had said, to be reconciled with Nadia, I remarked, "But then you will have to go through this whole ordeal again, meeting Nadia in court, sitting through it all."

She looked at me aghast: "You mean we will have to go through a new court case?"

"Oh, yes!" I said—realizing that it came as a shock to her. "What did you think?"

She had only thought that the lawyers would launch an appeal; that it was a matter of paperwork and not of harsh realities where she would again be called to do her part, and once more would be accusing her daughter publicly of lying and deception—and having the counteraccusation thrown at her.

Now it may not have been true that she did not know. Or she may have known but could not bear to think of the realities, so had barred them from her consciousness. But this was not the impression I gained. To me, she appeared truthful in her claim that she did not know that appealing the verdict meant—one more court case. And if so, this is the moral lesson I draw:

A highly educated and cultured person like Nadia's mother, with twenty years' residence in Norway and having children who are born and raised there, is also highly marginalized with respect to the larger society. She does speak Norwegian relatively well, but she moves in a world in which only limited and partial knowledge comes her way—knowledge that is sorely insufficient if she is to have "the freedom to assess [her] situation and the possibilities of changing it" (Sen 1990:53). The state cannot compel citizens to lead a certain kind of life. But it can open up possibilities whereby citizens are encouraged, and in some respects even required, to acquire knowledge of the larger society, with its basic institutions and "culture."

The Nadia case has been a lesson to all, immigrants and nonimmigrants, the public and the politicians, of the complexities of citizenship. However the appeal will end, issues have been brought to the fore that are of key significance. That, at least, is a vital step forward.

POSTSCRIPT   As fate would have it, the appeal was not to be. Nadia's father died of a heart attack in June 1999. The Norwegian state subsequently withdrew its charge against the parents—to her mother's great relief but to the chagrin of Nadia's brother, who, making use of a rarely used section of the law, wanted to appear in court in his father's stead and prove his innocence. The grounds for withdrawal were to facilitate a reconciliation between Nadia and her family and to spare them from further pain. I believe Nadia's father would have wanted it that way. Shortly before he died, he expressed his regret to a trusted person in the Moroccan milieu that he had to proceed with the appeal. He had no choice. His family's honor required it. Such is the problem with joint honor: it is not a matter of personal decision what to do. His prestigious family-in-law in Morocco having been dragged into the Nadia case (which had been publicized, even in Morocco), Nadia's father was trapped. Whatever his heart told him to do, he had to follow the dictates of the family honor.

His heart failed him, and he died. After his death, his son ascended to a position as head of the family. He is incensed with his elder sister and against any reconciliation. So the intentions of the court have not borne fruit so far. But perhaps Nadia and her mother and younger siblings meet secretly.

There are those who say that Nadia caused her father's death. But it may be well to remember that the time of one's death, according to Islam, is given at birth; it is foreordained. Nadia's case may well have broken her father's heart. But he died because his time was up.

Our journey into the Norwegian welfare society began with Aisha, and it is to Aisha that we now return—coming full circle. You will recall that the comparison provided with her father found them both trying to forge an identity according to their respective ideas of what a female, or a male, should be. Both were out to secure a good life for themselves; both wanted their freedom and to be respected for what they were. The Norwegian welfare state came to the father's rescue when he could not manage by himself—but it abandoned the daughter. It betrayed and deceived her, as Aisha herself said.

Why would Norway not stand by Aisha when it did stand by Nadia? There are several reasons. But before we ponder them, let us draw a lesson from the morality tale afforded by Aisha's story.

The welfare state is not a neutral actor, dispensing social justice and welfare. It is a political actor with an agenda that may play into the hands of some as against others. In this case it played into the hands of Aisha's father to the detriment of his daughter. The case precisely illustrates a central argument of this book: that a welfare society like Norway privileges some citizens above others. It is not neutral in its distribution of good and pain. If anyone needs an example, Aisha's story provides it. To think that a fourteen-year-old Norwegian girl, who fought for her right to have her integrity respected, using every available means to call for help, was ushered into a forced marriage because the authorities would not hear! Meanwhile her family—who must be seen as the guilty parties in this case,[44] in conjunction with the child welfare authorities—continues to lead the good life in Norway, enjoying material welfare and human liberties in good measure.

There were no defendants in Aisha's case, no "criminals" as in Nadia's case. But the conclusion is inescapable: The Norwegian welfare state produces winners and losers by the position it takes on such crucial matters as culture, gender, and the rights of the child.

It is my argument that the Norwegian welfare state has favored immigrant men (particularly if they were Muslim) as against women and children. It has done so in the best of causes—in the name of charity. It has done so in order to "respect their culture" and to honor Islam. If the authorities only knew what the real Islam, the true Islam, as many Muslims see it, demands of the human being. For Islam is compassionate and merciful, and it enjoins equality, according to many Muslims all over the world. To put it in Fatima Mernissi's words (1991:viii–ix),

If women's rights are a problem for some modern Muslim men, it is neither because of the Koran nor the Prophet, nor the Islamic tradition, but
simply because those rights conflict with the interests of a male elite . . .
But if there is one thing that the women and men of the late twentieth
century who have an awareness and enjoyment of history can be sure of,
it is that Islam was not sent from heaven to foster egotism and mediocrity.
It came to sustain the people . . . , to encourage them to achieve higher
spiritual goals and equality for all.

On the basis of the "vast and inspiring records of Muslim history so bril-
liantly completed for us by [several renowned] scholars," Mernissi further
concludes (viii–ix):

We Muslim women can walk into the modern world with pride, knowing
that the quest for dignity, democracy, and human rights, for full participation in the political and social affairs of our country, stems from no
imported Western values, but is a true part of the Muslim tradition.

So it was the Orientalist syndrome, as Edward Said (1978) has called it,
that was at play in this misconceived "respect for culture." Orientals—in
this case Muslims—were perceived as products of Islam, an Islam that was
backward in its nature—paternalistic, patriarchal, authoritarian, demanding
women's and children's submission for the sake of the family's honor. But
it must be said that "Orientals" too played up to this picture: it was the
work of many immigrant men who saw their interests served by precisely
this representation.

When Aisha was sacrificed, it was for her own good, as the child welfare
authorities saw it at the time—though I am not implying that "sacrifice" was
ever on their mind. But acknowledged failings deserve to be clearly named.
And it is to bring out the true nature of the tragedy that I use that word.

Remember Sara, and Anna, and Noreen, and the Turkish girl who was
stabbed twenty-one times in the back by her brother? They all had the
experience of coming under the protection of the child welfare agencies
at some point. And they all had the similar experience that the child welfare agencies refused to understand the severity of their plight. "They must
understand that once they have taken us away from our families because
we could not live with them, there is no going back," said Nasim Karim
when, in the aftermath of her own ordeal, she wondered what the child
welfare agencies might have done differently. Sara, as we remember,

had been reunited with her family, in this case delivered to her father's brother by a police escort when she refused to be removed from her foster family, afraid that her kinsmen might kill her (as they indeed did). Anna was terrified that the child welfare agencies would reveal her secret address to her family as they had warned her they would. And Nadia commented in court that the child welfare agencies had a "project" other than hers: to reunite her with her family after she had sought refuge with them on being mistreated by her father.

An example from another Scandinavian country, Denmark, is revealing. The anthropologist Anne Knudsen tells how one night on a ferry she met a Danish-Turkish woman who had run away from her husband after being beaten and otherwise mistreated by him. She was now on her way to Turkey to seek help from relatives. Knudsen, having established that she had no family who would help her in Denmark, asked her, "But aren't there any Danes who could help you, some social workers, for instance?" "Those!" replied the woman, her voice full of contempt, "they just think it's culture!" In Istanbul, on the other hand, she had some relatives who would understand because "they are modern human beings" (Knudsen 1994).

It reflects sadly on Scandinavia if some immigrant women feel they must turn to the Middle East to find "modern human beings"—Scandinavian social workers being so enamored with "culture" as to have embraced backward tradition. But such is the state of affairs in many cases. This is not to belittle the very important work that social welfare workers do, often under extremely difficult circumstance, but simply to point to a further constraint, "culture," which jeopardizes what they are seeking to achieve.

Social work has been characterized as a "feminized profession" (Culpitt 1992). Its officials and practitioners are primarily female. Perhaps this accounts in part for the "charitable" orientation of much social work. What remains to be explained is why "charity" should often come to mean authorization to mistreat female children—those of immigrants. For that was the effect, if not the intention, of much social work. To my mind, the explanation lies with the peculiar conjunction of antiracism and Orientalism that has plagued Scandinavian immigration policies.[45] This, as we have seen, was an ideology perpetrated from above—a sort of metanarrative that social workers, among others, were asked to buy into. It was believed to further the best of all interests, the interests of a separate cultural identity that immigrants must maintain if integration, not assimilation, is to be achieved. For the sake of the colorful community (*fargerike fellesskap*), difference must prevail. But it was a matter of celebrating collective differences, that is, group rights, over and above individual human rights. I doubt that the individual, for the most part, was even seen as existing apart from the group, especially if she was a child.

Anthropology has been criticized from within its own ranks (McHugh 1989; Spiro 1993) for having propagated a distinction between "the self" in the East and "the self" in the West as if they were of a fundamentally different nature: "collectivistic" versus "individualistic" are the terms used to draw the contrast. While the generalization holds some truth, it is overdrawn. All selves are relational, and all persons have some experience of themselves as unique individuals; the difference is therefore a matter of degree, and it crosscuts a simple paradigm of East versus West. But it seems to me that a romanticized notion of Eastern collective selves has found its way into much social work, at least in Scandinavia. From there, it does not take much to confound the welfare of the individual with that of the collectivity, as was done with such tragic effect in Aisha's case.

Welfare needs to be rethought as individual human welfare rather than as family or community welfare. So argues Amartya Sen, who has devoted much of his life to exploring and writing about the prerequisites for equity, democracy, and quality of life in the developing world. Perhaps, I would add, this has become even more important in our times when group thinking flourishes under the influence of ethnic identity politics. Individual freedom must be a social commitment, as Sen points out. But this implies certain challenges.

> It must be emphasized that . . . seeing individual freedom as a social commitment does not eliminate the necessity of facing problems of conflicts between groups and between individuals. As Ralf Dahrendorf has argued, we cannot even assess the future of social and political freedom without taking adequate note of the pervasive conflicts in modern society . . .
>
> Distributive principles deal with conflicts, rather than eliminating them. For example, if a principle of social justice gives priority to enhancing the freedom of the worst-off group, then that is a way of responding to the conflict, not a design for eradicating it. A major task of social arrangements is to recognize the conflicts of interest, and then, to seek a fair response to them, yielding more just distribution of individual freedoms. (Sen 1990:54)

The verdict in Nadia's case might be seen in this context: it addressed a deep-seated conflict of interest and sought to yield more just distribution

of individual freedoms, according to Norwegian jurisprudence and fundamental values. But in so doing it encroached on the rights of Nadia's parents, in the view of people who sympathized with them. (Remember Nadia's
grandfather's outcry: "I thought Norway was a democracy . . . But this is
not democracy! The judges chose to believe a young girl over her family,
they sided with her. That is injustice.") To quote Sen once again (1990:54),

> distributive principles of justice deal with conflicts, rather than eliminat-
> ing them. Indeed, if conflicts of interest are very sharp and extensive,
> the practical feasibility and actual emergence of just social arrangements
> may pose deep problems. [However,] if individuals as social persons have
> broader values and objectives, including sympathy for others and com-
> mitment to social norms, then the promotion of social justice need not
> face unremitting opposition at every move.

Let us now compare the cases of Aisha and Nadia and ask why distributive
principles of justice favored Nadia and not Aisha. The answers point to both
practical issues and principles that need to be resolved in order to enhance
the liberties of the worst-off group—in this case, girl children—and make for
a more equitable society.

Most important is the matter of citizenship seen in conjunction with legal
age. Aisha was a minor; Nadia was an adult from the point of view of Norwegian law. From this difference flowed a crucial set of consequences. The fact
that Nadia was a legal subject in her own right meant that the Norwegian
authorities could legitimize their intervention on her behalf with reference to
their own jurisdiction and international law. There was no conflict of interest
in that sense; even if Morocco did not recognize that Norway had any jurisdiction over Norwegian Moroccan citizens on Moroccan soil, it could still
acknowledge and respect Norway's position in that regard—that Norway,
given the views it had, was under an obligation to act.

Aisha's position was different. She too was a Norwegian citizen. But
she was a child. This alone was enough to vastly complicate the matter.
Parents have jurisdiction over their child. She is their charge. Attempting
a rescue operation of Aisha in a Middle Eastern country was not feasible
for Norway. Indeed, Norwegian authorities said as much. In one of the
documents I have seen, an authority to which her school had appealed
Aisha's case concludes that "because she has traveled with her family and
siblings to her [sic] homeland, Norwegian law and jurisprudence [rettspraksis]
do not apply to the family for the time being."

The words "her homeland" are worth noting here. Aisha had never had any other homeland than Norway; and there was ample evidence that that was how she perceived it. Assigning her a new homeland might have been just a slip of the pen. But the effect is to cushion Norway's disgrace in letting the child down. No wonder Norway cannot help her, when she has gone to her own homeland.

Nadia's case was also simpler for Norway, legally speaking, for it was thought to involve a crime. In fact, an international arrest order had been issued against Nadia's father in case he should leave Morocco. But with Aisha there was no crime, only hearsay of violence and infringement of the rights of the child. She was reputed to have been married by force, which her parents denied, saying she was only going to school in their homeland. But even if there had been evidence of marriage, what might Norway have done? The Norwegian police has no authority to investigate civil offenses in a foreign country. Moreover, the line between forced and arranged marriage can be difficult to draw. And while forced marriage is illegal according to both the Qur'an and Norwegian law, Norway does not hold the parent to account. The parent goes scot-free, whereas the spouse is designated the culprit. Take Nasim Karim's case. To have her marriage annulled in Norway, she had to file a suit against that pitiful husband of hers in a Pakistani village who was by all accounts as innocent as she. Thus, forcing a person to marry can be done with impunity for the parents in Norway.[46] If Aisha is suffering such a marriage in the Middle East, it is sad, but what can be done about it?

Aisha's plight was confounded because she was a child who didn't have a "case," but also, and more importantly, she did not manage to sound an alarm after her disappearance. That is another crucial difference between her and Nadia. Aisha has been silent after being taken to the Middle East. But even if she had managed to sound an alarm, what might Norway have done? Exerted pressure on her parents? Applied material sanctions in the form of withdrawal of social welfare benefits—as was done to good effect in Nadia's case? There may have been grounds for so doing, since Aisha's family too had overstayed its time abroad without proper notification. But no one checked into the matter, as far as I know, and the family continued to reap its benefits, leaving Aisha as the only loser.

The conclusion is inescapable: Aisha's plight, terrible as it was in human terms, seems inexorable given that the Norwegian authorities failed to help her while there was still time—in Norway.

A HOPE FOR THE FUTURE

Nadia had the satisfaction of being believed by the Norwegian authorities; Aisha was judged a liar. She screamed out her pain in letters to her teachers: "Do they think I'm lying? Don't they believe me? Do they think I've gone crazy?" It is a terrible thing for anyone not to be believed by the powers that matter, but particularly for a child. Aisha was not believed—and with fatal consequence. Nadia was, and it mattered greatly. "Nadia is happy that the court has found her truthful, though it does not heal her pain," commented her lawyer after the verdict was reached. (She herself has made no comment to the press.) Indeed, when she went back to the police to disclose her cover-up story, it was in part because she could not live by being a liar. But Aisha had to live with precisely that pain, of being perceived as a person given over to fantasy and imagination.

Dual citizenship highlights what is at stake in not believing a child. A child has more to lose than an adult. Aisha's case teaches one important lesson: act before it is too late. But then the child must be heeded and given the benefit of the doubt. It does not make the work of child welfare authorities easy. As Amartya Sen reminds us, conflicts of interest must be recognized in order to yield a more just distribution of individual liberties. Any assessment of what goes into enhancing the freedom of what Sen terms the worst-off groups must reckon with the fact that citizenship is under siege in the modern world. And since so many of the besieged are children, heeding children's voices matters more than ever.

An observation by Michael Ignatieff is relevant here. How are human rights, including children's rights, best protected? Ignatieff (1999:23) suggests that citizenship in a law-abiding state provides the clue.

> We need to appreciate the extent to which state sovereignty is . . . the best guarantee of human rights that there is. This is an unfamiliar, even controversial principle within a human rights community which for 50 years has looked on the state as the chief danger to the human rights of individuals. And so it has often proved. But this need not always be the case . . . For it can be said with certainty that the liberties of citizens are better protected by their own institutions than by the well-meaning interventions by outsiders. The rights that a person has by virtue of membership in a law-abiding state are usually the more valuable than the rights a person has by virtue of his membership in the human race, and the remedies which a

citizen has by virtue of his citizenship are more effective than those which inhere in international human rights covenants.

But what when a citizen is a member of not just one but of two states? And what when the laws of the two law-abiding states are in disjunction, as was true in Nadia's and Aisha's cases? The international community has a long way to go to deal with the perils of dual citizenship for those who are most in need of protection.[47] Documenting the hazards is a vital first step. Abating the perils by rethinking citizenship and taking a critical look at the so-called benefits of transnationalism and globalization is also urgent. Benefits there may be, but for whom? and under what circumstances? Rather than assuming that transnationalism is a good thing, consider the fates of Aisha and Nadia and others like them. We need critical analyses, not credos; and we need to scrutinize citizenship from the bottom up, not just from the top down. A "history according to winners and losers" (Scott 1985) is what I have in mind.

Last, in our comparison of the two girls, we turn to Norway's position in historical time and the learning of lessons. More than two years elapsed between Aisha's disappearance and the trial in the Nadia case. Something had been learned in the interval: an awareness of the problems of females of immigrant background who come into conflict with their families had intensified. Some intermittent cases of forced marriage had been reported, and the media were becoming ever more alert to the problem. Aisha's case was premature, in a way. This does not excuse Norway's betrayal of her, but it does make it more understandable.

So Nadia's case was a crucial step forward. But it was also, in a sense, well timed. Much of the groundwork regarding "culture" had been laid. An awareness was being built among politicians and public alike about the interface of culture with power and pain and the concomitant need to take a critical view of culture and welfare. Simultaneously, Norway was being exposed to increasing interethnic youth violence, impressing upon everyone the need for increased responsibility—on the part both of parents and of society. A verdict with premises like the ones in Nadia's case would, I believe, have been inconceivable a couple of years before. It remains to be seen what the next step will be, but I have no doubt that the *issue* next to be addressed must be family reunification.

It is family reunification that provides the impetus whereby many young people of both sexes are compelled to marry against their will. Again, it is a matter of doing harm in the name of charity. A well-intentioned law, giving a resident of Norway the right to bring in a spouse, is being subverted for another end—to provide visas to people who could not otherwise make it to the West.[48] To this end, not just happiness but lives may be sacrificed. Several Norwegian girls have met their deaths in Pakistan and other places for refusing a forced marriage. Others have escaped and are living in hiding, their lives threatened. But most will comply because the price of resistance is too high—ostracism by the family and the community (besides fear of losing one's life). Evidence from other European countries points to the same thing: going Nasim's or Nadia's way may cost more than it is worth.

Nasim Karim and Nadia stand out not only by their courage but also by being ahead of their times. As this is going to press, Norway is experiencing a sea change with regard to the problem of forced marriage: several young women are speaking out and bearing testimony to their ordeals or those of others they know. All do it anonymously, save for one, who decided to go public after first appearing in disguise. Her message is momentous: even freedom with a threat on one's life is better than the prison of forced marriage. She was forced into marriage, but escaped with a three-year-old child after four years. She is living in hiding—but happy. And she exhorts others to go her way.[49]

Again and again the message surfaces in these testimonies: the youngsters were used as means to obtain a visa for relatives or acquaintances in the parents' homeland. Statistical findings speak to the fact: not a single marriage contracted by Norwegian-born youths of Moroccan or Turkish descent in Norway over the three-year period 1996–98 was with a partner from Norway. In each instance, a spouse was brought in from the parents' homeland. Among Pakistanis in Norway, the percentage is almost as high; 85 percent of all marriages were with a person from Pakistan.[50] Thus marriage lines follow family, clan, or ethnic boundaries that are reinforced in the process, and not just among Muslims; many other minorities show a similar pattern.[51]

A note on ethnicity is relevant here. Ethnicity, as we have seen, need not refer to national identity; it can be a matter of other salient identities, such as clan, tribe, or subcaste, which take on ethnic significance because they are made to. In one tragic case I know, two Kurds in their early twenties, both Muslim, fell in love, married against the girl's parents' wishes, and are now fighting for their lives. Their offense? She is of Syrian, he of Turkish descent. Being Kurd or non-Kurd is not the question; what matters is which particular branch of Kurd one belongs to. Family reunification accentuates the conflict. The girl had been promised to her cousin in Syria as a child; he is eager for his visa. The legal spouse, the Turkish-Norwegian Kurd, has been offered a deal by the girl's family: pay 100,000 kroner (about $12,000 in U.S. currency) and the matter is closed. When he could not pay, the girl was captured and is at present in Syria. She will undoubtedly reappear. A letter from a lawyer informs her legal spouse that she wants a divorce— most probably, he believes, because she is under compulsion to bring in the cousin as a spouse. The point of the story is that when we speak of marriage among immigrants in Scandinavia as reinforcing ethnic boundaries, it is not even national identification that is at stake, but family, clan, caste, tribe, and the like.

Interethnic marriage facilitates integration, as Nathan Glazer points out in his incisive work *We Are All Multiculturalists Now* (1997). Interethnic marriage is both a reflection and a predictor of cross-cultural tolerance and integration.[52] In the United States, at least one-third of Asian and Hispanic immigrants, a large percentage of whom are recent arrivals, marry outside their ethnic group. Figures from Norway and other European countries run clearly in a different direction.[53] Hidden behind the trend is much human misery. But the mechanisms and gratifications that reinforce the pattern are obvious enough: "family reunification" provides visas to a liberal welfare state. Or in a word, *visuni:* the youngsters were used as means.[54]

When "girl" translates as "visa" or as "gilded paper" in common parlance,[55] there is cause for alarm. Family reunification must come up for scrutiny, and this is happening at last in Scandinavia.[56] Denmark, which has gone farthest, has instituted a new law whereby family reunification on marriage will not be granted to an applicant less than twenty-five years of age unless each party submits to an interview alone so that the authorities can attempt to verify that they are not being forced. Norway is considering to follow suit.

While the travails of forced marriage afflict people of either sex, the price for the female is higher. Divorce and remarriage are easier for the male; polygamy may also be possible in some cases (Kayed 1999).[57] Though divorce is equally obtainable for both parties under Norwegian law, Muslim law privileges the male. And since Muslims in Norway marry by both sets of law, obtaining a Norwegian divorce is not enough: divorce according to Muslim law is not just a felt need; it is imperative if the community is to acknowledge a woman as divorced, and if she is to have any hope of remarriage with a Muslim.[58] Forced marriage inhibits a woman's life chances far more than those of a male, as evidenced by a number of murders, or attempted murders, of females for refusing a forced marriage.[59] Males are more apt to comply, since less is at stake. For a Muslim male, marriage is not necessarily a final destination.[60]

A visa to Norway offers the prospects of permanent residence being granted after three years.[61] But the person will be eligible for all social welfare benefits immediately upon arrival in Norway. Permanent residence may be converted into citizenship after seven years' residence. Children attain Norwegian citizenship at birth if the mother is a Norwegian citizen. This has significance in the absence of marriage. If the parents are married, the child will be entitled to Norwegian citizenship from either parent, in accordance with the principle of descent (*nedstammingsprinsippet*). Norway also practices the principle of domicile: persons born in Norway are entitled to Norwegian citizenship at eighteen years of age, provided they have lived in Norway for at least seven years and have no criminal record. Those not born in Norway can apply on similar conditions. Norway does not accept dual citizenship.[62] A person accorded Norwegian citizenship should have the former citizenship annulled within a year of becoming Norwegian. Nadia's case shows that practice may be otherwise.

"Citizenship in Western liberal democracies is the modern equivalent of feudal privilege—an inherited status that greatly enhances one's life chances," observes Joseph Carens (1987). We have seen that this is a partial truth. To whom is it like a feudal privilege? Who wins and who loses by citizenship in a welfare state like Norway?

The discussion of citizenship in the literature on immigration suffers from a one-sided perspective that is all too frequent—that of adult males. Dual citizenship, it is assumed, enhances human freedom and facilitates integration. Make the acquisition of dual citizenship easier, not harder, seems to be the message. The more options, the better for people.[63]

Aisha's and Nadia's stories ring with a different message: that of the perils of dual citizenship. Rather than expanding their freedom, dual citizenship hobbled them. But more has been learned from their cases. Citizenship itself is under siege in this era of globalization. It is in need of life support. To safeguard the privileges that ought to be incumbent on citizenship in a liberal democracy, the nation-state needs to build institutions that provide a cushion against fates like Aisha's. Rendering stories like hers and Nadia's is a way to give deeply vexed moral and legal issues a human face and thus, hopefully, to marshal interest in putting them on the political agenda.

Citizenship needs to be reinvented as a social contract, in accordance with the principles spelled out in the verdict in Nadia's case. To that end, dual citizenship should be discouraged unless both countries involved offer an equal guarantee of respect for human rights, including the rights of the child. This may sound odd, given that Aisha was let down by a country—Norway—that endorses human rights. But that blatant failure does not invalidate the argument; rather, it underscores what is at stake: that entitlements must be turned into capabilities for the legal language to confer true benefits.

I suggest that citizenship in a modern welfare state cannot be combined with citizenship in a state that grants fewer and lesser rights, especially to the weaker members of the collective. Saying this might sound like whistling in the wind: what does it matter if Norway, say, does not accept dual citizenship as long as other states, with which Norwegian citizens are affiliated, do?[64] It matters in the sense of raising awareness—taking adequate note, in Amartya Sen's words—of the dangers inherent in transnationalism, of which the impact on children and women is only beginning to be explored. There is evidence that Norway is learning this lesson: One effect of Nadia's case has been to impress upon the authorities the need to follow up on a person's obligation to discard his or her foreign citizenship, once the person has attained Norwegian citizenship.[65] It may inhibit the adult's freedom and feel like an infringement of human rights. But it aids the child's rights, and adds to freedom, especially if the child is a girl.

Ample research the world over shows that there is particular reason to be concerned with female children. In the early 1990s, UNICEF undertook a series of studies in Asia on "the situation of the girl child." I was one of the researchers recruited for the task, in this case in Bhutan (Wikan 1991b). The aim of the UNICEF project was to gather data that might enhance the welfare of female children, who, by many indicators, fared badly in comparison with male children in some parts of Asia. But what of Europe in the new millennium? A "situation of the girl child" analysis may be as pertinent in UNICEF's own backyard as it was earlier in the so-called developing world. In his recent book *Development as Freedom* (1999), Amartya Sen argues that there is sound reason for judging development precisely in terms of the forms of freedom it permits citizens to have and enjoy. Aisha and Nadia show us that dual citizenship confers bondage on precisely those members of a liberal democracy that are in urgent need of having their freedoms protected and extended. If this book has served to highlight what is at stake for persons like them, it will have served its purpose.

I have sometimes been asked by foreigners: Why do immigrants in Norway bother to take Norwegian citizenship? What is in it for them, when all the benefits of the welfare state are theirs to be had by just becoming permanent residents? A study of Tamils points to an answer: "travel," said they, was what Norwegian citizenship afforded (Fuglerud 1999). It is much easier to travel on a Norwegian passport than on a Sri Lankan or a Somali one. And people do travel, not least those immigrants who have relatives spread through a vast diaspora.

But again a qualification is in order: Who travels? Who has the right to travel? Not all equally. A non-Western woman often needs her husband's or guardian's permission; without such permission, most Muslim or Hindu women cannot travel. Many young girls have their passports confiscated by their parents, even after coming of age, as did Nasim and Nadia. Retaining a person's passport is a way of keeping control over that person. Thus, having a Norwegian passport does not benefit all equally.

Apart from ease of travel, what other benefits does a Norwegian citizenship provide? The right to vote at national elections is one entitlement, but it is questionable what value it has. The rate of voting is on the decline among the whole population, but particularly among immigrants.[66] Then there is the right not to be deported if one commits a serious crime, although this right may apply also to noncitizens under certain conditions.[67] The conclusion seems inescapable: *citizenship* in an affluent welfare state isn't what enhances one's life chances; *residence* is the key.[68] Indeed, residence may work better to one's advantage, allowing one to enjoy the privileges conferred by citizenship in another country (which does not accept dual citizenship; Pakistan is a case in point) while savoring the fruits of the Norwegian welfare state.

But that conclusion is premature. Where would Nasim Karim or Nadia have been if they did not have Norwegian citizenship? For girls like them it is citizenship, not permanent residence, that counts. Without Norwegian citizenship, Nasim could hardly have been helped by the Norwegian embassy in Islamabad to find her way back to Norway. Without Norwegian citizenship, Nadia would not have been helped the way she was. But note that citizenship was a necessary but not a sufficient condition for the girls' quest for freedom. Had they been unable to escape or to sound an alarm, their citizenship would have availed them little. The same pertains to an increasing number of children who are being left by their families in Africa on the grounds that they have become "too Norwegian." Capable, as some of them are, of making their way to the Norwegian embassy in Kenya or Ethiopia, their chances of being helped are clearly better if they have Norwegian citizenship.

Citizenship in a European welfare state can be an asset, a resource. But to deliver its promises, citizenship needs to be reinvented and reinforced. Nadia's and Aisha's stories demonstrate what is at stake; their message carries over to the international arena. But on the domestic side too, there is reason for concern. Sara, Anna, Khalid, and others point to the predicaments of the child in a transnational world. They were citizens of a modern welfare state, as was the Norwegian-born son of the Pakistani father who cried, "My child is not *my* child, he is a Norwegian!" trying to impress upon the authorities their obligation to treat the son as a citizen, not an as-if citizen, by letting him learn proper Norwegian.

It should not be necessary for any father to say so much. His child's rights should have been naturally guaranteed. If this book has carried its message, it is that all children in a welfare society must have the same right to have their dignity and integrity respected. To that end, opportunities must be provided for all of them to develop and grow. Under the social contract, they must be provided with equal facilities to learn what they need in order to prosper and thrive. To that end too, parents and the state must relinquish their hold on children: As the verdict in Nadia's case said, "culture" provides no excuse for inhibiting a person's liberty to live the life she values.

Welfare needs to be rethought as individual human welfare, and to become a social commitment.

Social justice demands a renewed focus on the child. Citizenship can provide a valuable means of distributing social justice. A society worth living in is one that heeds Aisha's message.

Postscript: Aisha and the Long Way to Freedom

March 28, 2000. A message on my voicemail says, "Aisha is here with me. Please phone." I'm shaken to the core. For four years I have lived with that girl, though we never met. And I had given her up, given up any hope of seeing her. And now, the voice says, she is back.

I grab the phone, leave a message, then wait for what seems an eternity until the person calls back; she is Aisha's teacher from four years ago, and she was out at a meeting when I called. I despair at the thought that I might miss Aisha, that she might somehow disappear again. This thought is so strong with me that when, on the way to see her at the teacher's office, I pass a girl in the schoolyard who looks as though she might be Aisha, I'm almost tempted to run after her before she disappears. I feel like a child who is desperate not to miss a precious gift.

But there she is, a beautiful young girl—serene, composed. In retrospect, I realize my surprise that she should look so mature, so contained. But then, why would she not, with what she has gone through? Her story is harrowing, and I tell it with Aisha's permission.

Four years in captivity in the Middle East. Married by force last summer. Raped repeatedly since then—though she does not say so, it goes without saying. She only says that she doesn't think her husband loved her; he never showed her any affection. All he was interested in was getting to Norway by means of her.

She resents the man and wants to get rid of him. Wants to escape this whole life of violence and oppression. Which is why she is here, with the teacher. Can the teacher help her to escape? Time is short, for her husband is due to arrive any day. Her father has just told her that he has sent in the application for him to be reunited with Aisha. He is still in his homeland; the family—Aisha and her parents and siblings—came back to Norway a month ago. Aisha is frantic. She is desperate to escape the man, whom she clearly fears, desperate to attain freedom before it is too late.

Yet freedom . . . ? Her father and uncles have threatened to murder her if she does not play by the family's rules. She is terrified, but determined: She is sure they will shun no obstacle to attain their goal. But she will not shrink from her determination to escape at any cost.

The teacher contacts the shelter for women in Oslo, whose staff connect her with a lawyer. The meeting she attended with Aisha before I met them was with this lawyer. The immediate problem now is to find a shelter outside Oslo where Aisha will feel safe; she dares not stay in the shelter in Oslo for fear that her family may find her. She tells us that taxi drivers in Oslo (most of whom are immigrants) keep a watchful eye on all those who lodge in the shelter in Oslo, and she is sure someone would give her away. Shelter spaces are available in several places beyond Oslo, but they are costly: getting the social welfare office in Oslo to pay for Aisha is a first problem that the lawyer must solve. As things turn out, the problem is not solved by the time Aisha escapes, two days later—earlier than we had expected, but she is obviously terrified to miss her chance. She takes a tiny bag with one set of clothes and runs away in the early morning before her parents are awake. At 7:30 A.M. she is standing outside the teacher's office. And from there she goes to my home, where she remains for two days. She would have been welcome to stay longer, but she is afraid: the house is a bit remote, and although it has always seemed to me as safe as a castle, for Aisha it takes on a different aspect. She doesn't say so, but I intuit that every window, every door, provides a catastrophic possibility that a murderer may enter. At pains to contain herself and not to worry me, now that I have taken her under my wing, her fear is yet palpable and settles in my body too. The family has said they will certainly kill her if she runs away. A prison sentence is no deterrent for them. Suddenly the house, my house, feels totally exposed; and we agree that she has to move.

So we find a shelter for her outside Oslo; the social welfare office would not pay, insisting she should be in the shelter in Oslo. So I guarantee the payment, which is not high, and set to work to solve the larger problem— how to guarantee her safety over time so that she can lead a normal life. But after two days in her constant company, I admit I am totally depleted. Her fear is so intense, it is contagious. And I am warned by people in her parents' community to be cautious lest the family take revenge on me too.

As this is being written, I am optimistic that Aisha's life will be saved and her future too. With the inestimable help of mediators within the parents' local community, we are already attempting to achieve a solution. Aisha's uncles have been approached and won over. Next, their country's officials will be brought in vis-à-vis her father. For reasons that cannot be revealed here, much is at stake for the father. He may not fear imprisonment in Norway—Norwegian jails are considered luxury hotels by many—but jail in some Middle Eastern countries is another matter. And the team that is now working for Aisha is determined to have him sent to jail in his native land unless he guarantees Aisha's safety.

As a next step, her marriage will have to be annulled. To that end, she needs her passport and marriage certificate, which her father has kept. If he does not give them up voluntarily, the police will have to intervene. Meanwhile, the Norwegian embassy in the parents' homeland must be informed; they must be warned of the impending civil lawsuit that Aisha must file against her husband. The outcome, however, is certain.

The man she married will not be allowed to come to Norway. There will be no "family reunification" in this case. If ever a concept was misplaced, this is it.

Aisha faces a long way to freedom. She has to start by completing elementary school. Since she was removed from school in grade eight and taken to the Middle East, she has had no further education. (Interestingly, Aisha too traveled by car, not by air, just as Nadia did. Aisha tells the same story Nadia did, that her parents would never have risked taking a plane, fearing she would have sounded the alarm; car travel is safer if you want to transport a recalcitrant child or youth—who has a case—out of Europe.) She was kept in virtual captivity in her grandfather's house. Her parents and siblings were also there most of the time; only intermittently did her parents travel to Norway to do what it took to ensure that their social welfare benefits would not be cut. Twice the mother went to Norway to give birth to children, reaping the birth bonus (*fødselspenger*) of 32,000 kroner (about $4,000 in U.S. currency) per child, to which an unemployed woman is entitled.

As Aisha tells me her story, her parents' castigated her time and again in their homeland. They chastised her for being the reason they had to stay away from Norway: "It's only because of you . . . !" She was kept under strict control, never allowed to go out, save occasionally to the market or to visit relatives in the company of family members. Her time was spent in housework and in caring for her younger siblings; her only form of leisure was watching TV.

How did she endure it? Through the hope that she would one day be allowed to return to Norway. The chances were good; she was sure that a forced marriage was in store for her and, with it, the prospects of family reunification. "Merchandise, I was being used as merchandise," says Aisha. The fact that her father did not marry her off at sixteen (the legal marital age in his homeland) but waited until she turned eighteen only confirmed her expectation that "family reunification" was in store for her; the father was playing safe according to Norwegian family law so as not to have his plans thwarted.

Life sometimes plays havoc with the best-laid plans; and Aisha was determined it was not going to happen to her. So she conceived a strategy that she executed to perfection: she appeared the docile, complaisant, well-adapted girl in all her dealings with her parents. She gave them the comfort and security that she was content—and would never ever think of rebellion. Otherwise she might be kept in the Middle East—while her only hope of freedom lay in returning to the country of her birth.

On her return to Norway, she continued to play by the family's rules. They had come back in advance to prepare the application for family reunification for her husband. She was so successful that her parents acceded to her working in a drugstore some distance away from her home. It was this that permitted her, in due course, to steal some time in order to contact her former teacher. Her parents' permission to let her work had a practical purpose as well. Two conditions are contingent on achieving family reunification for a spouse in Norway: the applicant must have independent living quarters and a source of personal income. Letting Aisha work for a month or so fulfilled the formal requirements with respect to wages. But it was she who managed to convince her parents to let her work in the kind of business (a large department store, rather than a corner shop) from which she would be able to venture out to seek help, once her "husband's" coming was imminent. She did it by executing a carefully crafted role that she had been practicing for four years: be docile; appear content; give them every reason to trust you.

On the day when she appeared at her teacher's office—the day I first met Aisha—she had called in sick; that gave her a full day (before she had to rush home with the tram she was expected to catch) to plan for her escape with the teacher and me—although, as I see it, we were merely the willing helpers; Aisha was dead set on her goal. It was what she had been planning for since her departure from Norway four years ago; it was what had kept her spirits up all these years.

To my relief, Aisha had not become pregnant. She does not say much about her marriage; it is clearly too painful. But in response to my hesitant question, she tells me that a cousin helped her to get contraceptives. She is on the verge of tears when she mentions this cousin, who encountered a fate worse than hers: she was married to a man she despises in the Netherlands, a violent man, and has little hope of escape.

As I contact the Norwegian embassy in her parents' homeland to alert them of the application for family reunification that will be coming in for Aisha's husband, I learn to my surprise that the embassy did in fact try to come to Aisha's rescue in the spring of 1999, when she went there to have her passport renewed. But they did not succeed. Aisha was not cooperative. This was at a time when she had not yet married; and it's tantalizing to think what she might have been spared if she had found an escape at that point. What was the situation? What went wrong? A closer examination reveals the predicament of girls like Aisha and of the envoys of the Norwegian state who care and want to help.

When Aisha went to the embassy, with her family, to have her passport renewed, she was dressed in long attire and headscarf and appeared a traditional Muslim girl. She was demure and downcast. Having been alerted to her case a year before, an official at the embassy recognized her and beckoned her into a conference room, without her family, to give her a chance to speak out. She did not. He tried various tacks, in vain.

I asked Aisha why she had not responded in kind. Why did she let this chance go by? She was surprised. She had no inkling, she said, that that was what the official was trying to do—provide her with an escape route. She had wondered why he asked so many questions. She did feel there was something in the air, but what? And she would not, of her own initiative, have dreamed of confiding in him and asking for help. She did not trust anyone. That was the one thing she had learned in life: not to trust people. Had she not begged for help before, time and time again, and been turned down? And if she ever gave her family away, in their native land, she faced certain death—or that is what she believes.

Taken together, the stories told by the official in question and by Aisha testify to the problems both parties faced in trying to work out a solution, when what was at stake was the very survival of a young girl. An embassy envoy, naturally, must move with utter discretion and cannot be too direct in attempting intervention. In this case, what if Aisha were actually content and had reported the official to her family? The matter would have been different if she had taken the initiative. But if Aisha had suffered three long years in the Middle East, she was surely not to give in at this point. She tells me her heart jumped with happiness when her family took her to have her Norwegian passport renewed. That meant she was going to return to Norway! The end was in sight.

In Aisha's mind, there is one institution and one person that deserve no excuse—the child welfare authorities and the particular official who "had" her case and decided her fate. Again and again she reverts to the question: how can one person let's call her Britta—flout a child's right for protection and basic security? Yes, indeed, how is that possible? As Aisha tells her story, and as it is confirmed by her teachers, Britta had been amply warned of the dangers of reuniting Aisha with her family, once she had escaped and had been placed with a foster family. The evidence was overwhelming that Aisha was being subjected to violent treatment at home, and that her parents insisted on her conforming to traditional Muslim ways. It was also clear that Aisha suffered tremendously at home, and that her only hope of a livable life, as she saw it, was to be allowed to remain in her foster home. As she wrote in a letter to a teacher at the time:

> Dear _____:
> I have not been able to study for the English test. Yesterday, I had a meeting with the child welfare, my parents and my siblings. It was said in this meeting that I have to move home again on Monday. So yesterday, all I did was stay at home in [the town where the foster family lives] and cry.
> Just now, when I had found a little peace and was happy, then suddenly this happens. I don't believe I will be able to manage very well in school now when I have to move home.
> I don't understand why the child welfare cannot help me. Don't they believe in me?
> I hate the child welfare.
> I thought the child welfare was there to help children, but I was mistaken!!
> I have the feeling that the child welfare has betrayed me.
> I'll have to run away from home again, or else I'll run away from here before Monday.
> Love, Aisha

This was written in 1996. Aisha did run away before that Monday. But she was caught by the police and delivered to her biological parents.

Aisha's rage at this person who masterminded this operation is intense. And she derides the child welfare authorities for their seeming concern about her fate once she was in the Middle East: "They phoned to ask how I was. What could I say, surrounded by the whole family? 'Fine!' It reassured them."

One child's betrayal can become an eye opener for a society that thrives on concealment and taking the easy way out. Aisha is that child. She is both right and wrong in targeting one individual, Britta. Britta is responsible for her actions, but the child welfare authorities are responsible for instituting a system whereby one person gains the power to play havoc with the fate of a child like Aisha. I assume that Britta acted with the best intentions; I assume she was within her rights to do as she did. But a system that exercises its rights over children in any such ways needs immediate reform. And Aisha's case helps us to pinpoint the problems that are in most need of solution.

We had considered, Aisha and I, filing a lawsuit: the Norwegian child welfare authorities that sacrificed Aisha on the altar of culture were not to be exonerated. Loss of a normal childhood, loss of an elementary school education, forced marriage, rape—that was the price Aisha paid for the Norwegian welfare state's failure to stand by this citizen. And she would sue the state and demand compensation; the money mattered, for she needs to build a new life for herself. Indeed, the fact that she is no longer a child, legally speaking, is a disadvantage in her present situation. The state is obliged to look after children, provide them with shelter and the necessities of life, including a foster family or some kind of supportive network. But Aisha is out of the age bracket. Once too young, she is now too old. On contacting high officials in the Ministry of Child and Family Affairs on her behalf, one of the mediators and I received this message: they are extremely sorry, but Aisha is too old; she will have to become a social welfare client and hope for the best.

Material compensation would be important for Aisha, as well as public acknowledgment of the wrongs she has suffered on the part of the child welfare authorities. Her story would also serve as an example, as had Nadia's before her.

POST-POSTSCRIPT   But once again, life outdid us—if this time for the better. Aisha has had her marriage annulled and has been reunited with her family. They have accepted her right to a life of her own. She lives by herself, is even allowed to have a (Muslim) boyfriend from another ethnic community. Family reconciliation has been achieved with the help of mediators within the Muslim community, and they have achieved what Aisha and I (and others with us) had thought impossible—true family reconciliation, not mere "reunification."

We therefore dropped the idea of bringing the child welfare authorities to court; a lawsuit would only publicize her parents' misdemeanors.

So Aisha's story has a happy ending so far, all things considered. She is left without an elementary school education and finds it difficult to resume schooling. She has suffered traumas of many kinds that continue to haunt her. But she is alive and well and has proved herself a true survivor—an example to others and, one hopes, a catalyst to modern welfare societies with their commitment to the rights of the child.

Notes

A note on translations. All translations in the text and notes from Norwegian, Swedish, and Danish sources are my own.

1 David Grossman, interview in *Aftenposten,* February 14, 1996.

2 The aim of "situation analysis" is to collect the relevant information on an issue or in a field of inquiry, in preparation for developing a public policy. An "action plan," on the other hand, outlines policy on an issue and the series of steps that need to be taken to implement that policy.

3 I had done extensive fieldwork in Bali, Indonesia, and Bhutan.

4 Among the qualitative studies I especially benefited from were works by Jon Knudsen (1992), David Lackland Sam (1991), and Tor Aase (1992).

5 The book was published in Norwegian under the title *Mot en ny norsk underklasse: Innvandrere, kultur og integrasjon* (Oslo: Gyldendal, 1995). I deliberately put "norsk" (Norwegian) in front of "underclass" to underscore that immigrants are part of Norwegian society, and that part of the responsibility for the situation must therefore rest with the Norwegian government. I declined offers to have the book published in English because, unlike the present work, it was written specifically for a Norwegian readership.

6 I am told that shortly after my book was published, the word "underclass" in reference to immigrants started appearing in the Swedish media also.

7 I borrowed the concept "welfare colonialism" from Enrico C. Cortes Jr., a prominent activist and advocate of the poor, working in San Antonio, Texas. For an interview with Cortes, see Lavelle (1995).

8 I had published three books on Muslim societies and had a fourth in press (Wikan 1980, 1983, 1991a, and 1996a).

9 It bears mention that I had been invited to speak at conferences, seminars, or national conventions of five of Norway's seven political parties. I had turned down only one, that of the Progress Party.

10 With Farid and Mustapha, I have also had the occasion to meet with prime ministers, cabinet members, and even the King and Queen of Norway. Our meeting with the King was scheduled to last fifteen minutes. We had been informed that we would be given a clear signal when our time was up, but when after one hour there was still no signal, Laatiaoui bade a graceful farewell. We were impressed with the King's knowledge of and engagement with the issues. The Queen's meeting with us was also memorable. She came to the organization's quarters in Oslo's inner city, dressed in casual attire, and sat talking with the youths in a manner that made them feel totally at ease.

11 This same city council, under the chairmanship of Rune Gerhardsen, had the courage to commission the Oslo report on refugees, to which I refer extensively later.

12 For a masterly critique of this argument, see Cheryl Mattingly (1998).

13 Hege Storhaug, journalist and author, deserves major credit for having tirelessly worked on the issues since 1992, when she first reported Nasim Karim's story (chap. 13). She has undertaken several research journeys to Pakistan and written two books (1996 and 1998) besides a number of newspaper articles and full-page op-ed pieces. In 1999 she did the research for two television documentaries on forced marriage among Norwegian Pakistanis, which had a major effect on Norwegian society. The film included excerpts from a BBC documentary on violence against women in Pakistan and was shown just as Amnesty International published a devastating report on the same issue. The Norwegian documentaries, produced by and shown on Norwegian television (TV2) in September 1999, had far-reaching effects, both in encouraging youths to seek help and in creating a political demand for measures to deal with the problems. Major credit goes to Tonje Steinsland for her outstanding work on the films, and to Gerhard Helskog, director of the program *Rikets tilstand* (State of the nation) that produced them.

PART I   WELFARE FOR WHOM?

1 Ethnic minority families are reluctant to volunteer as foster families for fear of being perceived as disloyal to their own group and of triggering reprisals from the child's family. Many ethnic minority families are also deeply distrustful of the child welfare authorities and perceive their intercession in the internal affairs of the family as an affront.

2 It bears mention that alcohol is forbidden in Islam.

3 Forced marriage is also illegal in Islam.

4 My own engagement with the case began when the principal of Aisha's school got in touch with me in 1996, just after Aisha had disappeared. He told me he had tried to reach me (I was out of town at the time) when the interrupted phone call from Aisha alerted a teacher that she was in danger; he had hoped I might get some higher authority to intervene. I was then asked to conduct a joint seminar for the school staff and the child welfare officials who had handled Aisha's case. I was to discuss the situation of Muslim families in Norway but not to mention Aisha's case—that was too sensitive. Both the school personnel and the child welfare officials were deeply affected

by her disappearance. I was shown all the documentation on Aisha's case that the school had accumulated. I went public with the story in two full-page op-ed articles in a major national newspaper, in public lectures, in a radio address, and in several interviews. I also spoke with two cabinet ministers. I was pressured by journalists to identify Aisha's real name so that they could launch an independent investigation that might lead to her being returned to Norway. But the school was resistant, hoping Aisha's family could be persuaded to bring her back voluntarily, and fearing that publicity might result in harm to the girl.

5   For similar observations from Denmark, see Bertel Haarder (1997). Haarder quotes a radio interview with an immigrant who said, "Danes have a need for kindness without limits, because it apparently gives them egoistic, personal satisfaction." Haarder concurs: "That the kindness does harm is the price *they* [immigrants] must pay so that *we* can feel good about ourselves" (1997:97). For observations from Sweden, see Jonathan Friedman (1999).

6   For a harrowing example from India, see Veena Das (1995:55–83).

7   I borrow the expression from Ernst Bloch, who writes of "the right to reject [one's] uniform" (1976:158, cited in Finkielkraut 1995:104).

8   The right to vote in local and regional elections is extended to immigrants with at least three years' stay in the country in Norway, Sweden, Denmark, and the Netherlands.

PART II   THE NEW NORWAY

1   I am indebted to Wenche Werring for telling me the story.

2   I come from a small town on an island two hundred miles north of the Arctic Circle.

3   In California, in 1995, just over a third of the state's school-aged children spoke a language other than English at home (Cornelius 1995). The proportion is similar in Los Angeles, San Francisco, New York, and Miami (Zhou 1997:68).

4   In Norway as a whole, 6 percent of children in primary school were foreign-lingual in 1998, up from 3 percent ten years earlier. In just one year, 1997–98, there was an increase of 9 percent (Bjertnæs 2000:32).

5   Storhaug also shows how agents were operative from the start. Enterprising individuals set up shop and helped village men get to Norway, when other, more attractive European destinations had become more difficult to reach. The first Pakistani immigrants arrived as penniless tourists in the late 1960s, and Storhaug shows how the Norwegian government was taken aback, not knowing what to do with these visitors, who were visibly destitute. The solution adopted was to extend to them social welfare, rather than putting them on a plane and sending them back, as did some other European nations in similar cases. Regarding agents, my husband, Fredrik Barth, tells how, at a bus stop in North Pakistan in the 1970s, he ran into a man who, on hearing my husband was an anthropologist, declared, "I too am in the people business." He was helping people get illegally to the West.

6   Portes and Rumbaut (1996:271) caution against the use of "push-pull" as a model to explain the origins of immigration. Their point is that the model resembles a cost-benefit approach to immigration, as if immigration were an individual affair triggered by "factors of expulsion" (economic, social, and political hardships in the sending countries) and "factors of attraction" (comparative economic and political advantages in the receiving countries). Rather, what needs to be explained are differences *within* countries in propensities to migration, and here the critical analytical concept is that of social network. As the authors note, once migration gets going and the messages sent back to the place of origin are positive, the process tends to become self-sustaining; migration becomes the proper thing to do: "For the most part, the decision to migrate is group mediated and its timing and destination determined largely by the social context of networks established over time" (277–78).

7   For an observation to the same effect from Denmark, see Mørck (1996); from the Netherlands regarding Turkish mothers, see Lindo (1995:153–54, 162). Portes and Rumbaut (1996:240) point out that "one of the poignant features of immigrant adaptation to a foreign society is that the roles of parents and children are often reversed. In these situations, children become, in a very real sense, their parents' parents . . . , elders [being forced] to rely on their youngsters for guidance." I contend that this is particularly true of mothers, who, at least in Scandinavia, become dependent on their children to a much greater extent than fathers do, since males move in a public world and accumulate knowledge and competencies from which many women are debarred.

8   For an excellent analysis of "culture contested" see Baumann (1996), who explores the meanings of "culture" and "community" among a cohort of young immigrants, mostly males, in Southall, London.

9   Muslims in Norway comprise between 67,000 and 70,000 persons, or approximately 1.6 percent of the population in 1998. This is roughly equal to their proportion in Germany—1.7 percent. The numbers are estimates, however, as religious affiliation is not registered in Norway, as in most West European nations. One arrives at the count by an indirect method: the percentage of Muslims in Norway is assumed to be equivalent to their percentage in their countries of origin. By this procedure, 99 percent of Iranians, in Norway for instance, are registered as Muslims, whereas many are nonbelievers. Scholars of religion in Europe have coined the term "ethnic Muslim" to underscore that the official registers of Muslims count ethnicity rather than embraced belief (see Vogt 2000:7–8).

10 With respect to Canada, Frideres (1992:56) notes: "It is evident that over the past half century, Canadians have been opposed to a more liberal immigration policy. Attitudinal and public opinion data collected over this time period reveal consistent opposition by a majority of Canadians." Furthermore, "recent polls . . . suggest that prejudice and discrimination is on the upswing. Across Canada, Canadians are increasingly resisting those visible immigrants who do not blend in readily with the mainstream population" (64). As for Australia, "By the end of the 1980s, opinion polls consistently showed around 60 to 70 percent of Australians to be in favor of reducing immigration and opposed to multiculturalism" (Birrell 1994:117).

11 Hirschman (1996) discusses similar problems in the United States, where in 1980 the Bureau of the Census dropped the question about the parents' birthplace from the decennial census. "Although a new question on ancestry was added, the loss of the parental birthplace question meant that it was no longer possible to identify directly the children of immigrants in census data from 1980 and 1990. Ironically, this loss of critical information coincided with a wave of immigration from Latin America and Asia in the 1970s and 1980s. Tracking the progress or lack of progress of the children of new immigrants has become a more difficult task without adequate census data on the topic" (1996:54). As Hirschman also notes, "Local studies in particular cities and neighborhoods can provide deeply textured accounts of those immigrants and their children, but only census data hold the possibility of comparing specific immigrant streams across the country" (55). This comparative function is the more important in view of the heterogeneity of contemporary immigration and the variations in immigrant communities in the United States. The same would obtain for Norway.

12 A Pakistani-born child of a Pakistani-born father and a Norwegian-born mother of Pakistani descent, living in a Pakistani environment in Norway, is not considered an immigrant. Only if both parents were Pakistani-born would the definition apply.

13 The Norwegian government has recently become aware that "acquiring knowledge about the empirical aspects of the situation of [the children of immigrants] is especially important." The Norwegian Statistical Bureau now includes second-generation immigrants in a broader definition of "the immigrant population." Because the great majority of the second generation in Norway is still very young—in 1998, 90 percent were below twenty years of age—we still do not know very much about them (Bjertnæs 2000:10).

14 The term "race," which is commonly used for official statistical purposes in the United States and Britain, is unacceptable in Scandinavia. Here "race" is considered derogatory.

15 In Norway, "mother tongue" refers, in official parlance, to the language of either parent.

16 The situation is similar in Canada and the United States. In Canada, "immigrants from Third World countries are concentrated in the larger cities, even more than traditional immigrants from Europe and the U.S. . . . Seven out of ten immigrants (from the Third World) lived in Canada's three largest cities in 1986. And their numbers are increasing" (Stafford 1992:74–76). "Immigration to the United States is today an urban phenomenon and one concentrated in the largest cities. In 1993, less than 5 percent of legal immigrants went to live in nonurban areas, and more than half settled in just ten metropolitan locations . . . Given [the] past experiences and the propensity of major contemporary immigrations to remain clustered, there is little reason to expect a dispersal of recent immigrants and their children" (Portes and Rumbaut 1996:43–44, 53).

17 In 1997, 81 percent of Moroccans and 77 percent of Pakistanis in Norway were living in Oslo (Vassenden 1997:83), as against 7 percent of Bosnians. By comparison, in the

Netherlands, 60 percent of Moroccans and 56 percent of Turks were living in cities of more than one hundred thousand inhabitants, as against only 22 percent of the total Dutch population (Eldering 1997:337).

18 There are some exceptions to this pattern: some parts of Oslo's inner city have acquired special appeal to young people and families because of their colorful plurality and also, no doubt, the lower cost of living.

19 The implications are, however, far from clear. As Portes and Rumbaut (1996) show in their comprehensive study of the United States, the integration prospects of different ethnic groups, and groups within the groups, depend on a variety of factors relating to what immigrants bring with them to the new country as well as the context of their reception. Physical congregation may *further* the immigrants' integration in society, as it has, for example, with Cubans in Miami, or it may weaken it, as it has with Cambodians or Laotians. The critical variable is not congregation as such but cultural resources, socioeconomic position, and structural frameworks.

20 This figure is from December 1998 (*Aftenposten*, January 6, 1999). Broken down by age cohort, the five districts of Oslo with the highest proportion of non-Western immigrants (Gamle Oslo, Søndre Nordstrand, Grunerløkka-Sofienberg, Romsås, and Stovner) had 28–55 percent immigrant children aged 0–6; 32–67 percent aged 7–15; and 31–59 percent aged 16–19. Overall, the proportion of non-Western immigrants in these districts ranged from 18 percent to 33 percent (*Verdens Gang*, February 9, 1998).

21 For comparable observations from Denmark, see Mørck (1996:128).

22 In Fjell, a suburb of Drammen, 60 percent of the four thousand inhabitants are of immigrant background, mainly from Turkey; and the proportion is steadily rising. See Sandrup (1998) for an interesting study.

23 To give an idea of the rate of change, the proportion of non-Western immigrants in one district of Oslo rose from 16.1 in 1992 to 26.6 percent in 1996 (Brox 1998:5).

24 Two years later, a study by the Norwegian Statistical Bureau found that 50 percent of immigrants had arrived over the past 8.4 years, and 30 percent had come less than five years ago (Vassenden 1997:11, 63).

25 The cost of making it to Norway, though exorbitant, is much less than to the United States or Canada. A "package" to Norway (false visa, papers, ticket, etc.) from Sri Lanka, for example, costs the equivalent of about US$8,000 whereas one to the United States or Canada costs two-thirds more.

26 My presentation may give the impression that immigrants have more choice in the matter than they actually have. Many political asylum seekers are at the mercy of agents who might drop them in destinations where they had not wanted to be.

27 *Aftenposten* (February 7, 1998) reports: "One of those who has contributed to the flow of political asylum seekers from East Slavonia [to Norway] is the Serbian journalist Saša Dimitrijević. He is a correspondent in Norway for Radio Beograd and the daily *Politika:* 'I like to say that I am a patriot of Norway, and that I have done a lot of good advertising for Norway through my reports,' said Dimitrijević, but this time, it may

become a bit expensive for the government." His reporting about the liberalization of the Norwegian refugee policies had been instantly picked up by other news media in the former Yugoslavia.

28 Relevant here are not just the material benefits conferred on refugees and asylum seekers who reach Norway but also repatriation benefits for those who eventually return to their home countries. In the case of Bosnians and Kosovo Albanians, for example, Norway gave each person (adult or child) a sum fifteen times greater than Germany did; the Norwegian rate enabled a family of four to build a new house in Kosovo or Bosnia for only half of the amount they received.

29 The European Union International Center on Migration Policy in Vienna estimates that various mafia organizations cash in about US$8.5 billion a year by smuggling people into Europe (*Aftenposten*, December 11, 1998). The most prolific have been the Italian, the Albanian, and the Turkish mafias. Regarding Norway, the Chinese organized much of the human smuggling into the country until 1998, but former Yugoslavs and Iraqi Kurds have since taken over much of the activity; among their clients are many Tamils from Sri Lanka (*Aftenposten*, September 21, 1999). The cost of being smuggled from Iran or Iraq to Scandinavia was about US$6,000 in 1999, but it was also possible to get help for part of the way. A ticket from Göttingen in Germany to Denmark cost US$1,100, whereas the price to Sweden was $1,600 and to Norway $2,000. The reason for the higher price of being smuggled into Norway than into Sweden, which was the same distance away, was that Norway with its more liberal refugee policy was more attractive (*Aftenposten*, September 25, 1999). A new form of smuggling people that has recently evolved consists of establishing people on false identities in Norway and other countries. The agents earn the equivalent of US$6,000 (55,000 Norwegian kroner) for each person they manage to get into the country and establish with a false identity. A false passport and residence on false grounds costs 30,000 to 40,000 kroner ($3,400 to $4,500); thereafter the price is 15,000 kroner for further help to have one's permit renewed (*Aftenposten*, October 21, 2000).

30 One example is a group of six men who claim to be political refugees from Algeria, but the police are confident that they are from Morocco (among other things, they arrived aboard a Moroccan vessel with twelve other men who were detected to be Moroccans). But in order for the six to be sent back to Morocco, their Moroccan identity needs to be established. Since all the evidence the police has are the fingerprints of the men, the problem is nearly insoluble. Trafficking in false identities has become a matter of course among refugees. An Ethiopian who wanted to be smuggled from Germany to Norway tells how she was warned to give herself up as an Iraqi. If a refugee has been refused political asylum or residence on humanitarian grounds and all else fails, the person may go into hiding and remain in Norway by sharing a countryman's identity. Two Tamil brothers, for instance, shared a passport, bank account, and address, but not jobs; only one of them had legal residence in Norway. According to the police, such sharing of identity is quite common (*Aftenposten*, October 21, 2000).

31 In late 1999, the government modified its policies with regard to Iraqi Kurds, extending only temporary protection and denying the right to family reunification. As expected, this has elicited protests from those who come under the new rule, who regard it

as injustice that some of their countrymen are privileged to bring their families into Norway, whereas they cannot.

32 On lack of trust, see Fuglerud (1999:75–77): "In exile, relationships . . . are fraught with suspicion . . . In dealing with fellow countrymen, there is always the possibility that actions in Norway will have consequences in Sri Lanka. The refugees are not fleeing a common enemy, the violence is within as much as on the outside." Knudsen (1988) describes a similar situation among Vietnamese refugees, showing how self-presentation and control over biographical information become critical problems. Indeed, journalists are increasingly telling us how immigrants, refugees, and asylum seekers report each other up to the police and other authorities—for instance, for illegal entry into Norway and misappropriation of social welfare benefits.

33 As Brox observes (1998:103), "at the last major election, in September 1995, the only issue which seemed to mobilize voters was immigration."

34 On the two-minute limitation, let me interject a note to fellow anthropologists and others who might want to "go public." Was it worth it, I wondered, to spend so much time and energy just to be given two minutes to talk? I asked my husband and son for advice. My husband, an anthropologist, said no; my son, a student of media and communication, said, "Mama, do it." He was right. It was one of the wisest decisions I have ever made—to seize on those two minutes for all they were worth, though it took more nerve than I would have had without the encouragement.

35 Kåre Hagen (1997:7) observes that Julian Kramer (himself an anthropologist and immigrant) noted in 1982 (NOU 1987:8) that the way Norwegian authorities applied social assistance for integration purposes carried great risks of clientification. But "this had little impact . . . until Unni Wikan raised the same argument 14 [sic] years later."

36 The integration bonus amounts to 300,000 kroner (approximately US$34,000) per person over five years. Thus a family of six would receive on average 360,000 kroner per year (US$40,000)—roughly equivalent to an associate professor's salary.

37 There are, however, variations between different ethnic groups. A study by Sørlie (1994) found Pakistani refugees to have moved to the capital at a rate of 40 percent within four years, compared to only 6–7 percent for Latin Americans and Vietnamese. Among Tamils, a refugee group that has settled in the far north, only 7 percent of the men and none of the women who had come after 1976 were still found to be living there seven years later.

38 The sample comprised refugees from Chile, Iran, Somalia, and Vietnam, as well as Tamils from Sri Lanka and Kurds from various countries in the Middle East.

39 Kåre Hagen, one of the authors of the Oslo study, notes that it was financial concerns regarding the great expense of integrating refugees, and not sociopolitical concerns for their welfare and standard of living, that led the Oslo city council to commission the study. The politicians assumed that the actual cost of integrating refugees was much higher than the integration bonus that the Oslo municipality received from the state. Hence the survey could provide evidence to support financial claims on the state

(Hagen 1997:20). In particular, they wanted to gain knowledge about the variation in labor market participation and dependence on social assistance among different ethnic minorities (18). An assumption confirmed by the survey (and by a number of later studies) was that there are extreme variations in the cost of integrating various ethnic minorities.

40 Indeed, with an unemployment rate of 3.5 percent in Norway in 1995, as against Sweden's 8.5 percent, the fate of refugees in Norway was worse in relative terms. Djuve (1999:25), in a comparative study of integration of ethnic minorities in the Nordic welfare states, observes that although Norway has used more material resources than Denmark and Sweden in order to integrate refugees and immigrants into the labor market, there is no clear evidence that Norway has been more successful in doing so.

41 The rate for immigrants was 25 percent. The situation in Sweden was comparable: 30 percent of immigrants depend on social assistance as against 7 percent of native Swedes (SOU 1996:55).

42 "In trying to limit *labour* migration to a minimum, a country may find that the much more expensive *asylum-seeker* queue is growing" (Brochmann 1996:28). This is indeed what has happened in Norway, as in many other European countries. An example from Norway: Blom (1996), in a study of six groups of refugees that had come to Norway during 1987–92, found that 45 to 49 percent of the first arrivals were still on social welfare nearly ten years later. More than 60 percent of those arriving in 1990 were social welfare clients.

43 Hagen (1997:9) cautions that there is an inflationary component in the assessment of social assistance among refugees. Costs related to their establishment in Norway, especially housing costs, are not deducted from but are included in an overall assessment. (These are expenditures native Norwegians rarely have, though they too can obtain help in case of need.)

44 The study also found that only 20 percent of refugee parents obtained two sets of wages from work, compared to 70 percent of native Norwegians.

45 Tamils have the highest rate of employment and the lowest level of welfare support of all ethnic minorities in Norway (Fuglerud 1999:95)

46 In 2000, severe, organized misuse of disability pensions was detected in some immigrant groups. Life-long disability pensions could be bought for about US$10,000, with the help of doctors who were in on the deal. The Norwegian social welfare system was found to be practically without controls, based on trust, and lending itself to easy abuse by transnationals. For example, a Moroccan who received a disability pension in 1984 and subsequently moved to Morocco was found to be receiving child welfare benefits for eight children that no one had ever seen. Several families in Pakistan and elsewhere were living on the disability pensions of relatives long dead. The deaths had not been registered. These disclosures (made by the media) alarmed politicians, social welfare officials, and the public (immigrants included) alike. Measures are now being implemented to combat such exploitation by certain ethnic minorities.

47 Eldering (1997:337) further notes, "If those who are not working and are receiving benefits under the Sickness Benefits Act or the Employment Disability Act are added to the unemployed, one is forced to conclude that a very high percentage of first-generation immigrants, particularly Turks and Moroccans, is no longer economically active."

48 No Norwegian studies are available regarding the qualifications of boys of immigrant background versus native boys. For Great Britain, however, Lewis (1994:23) finds disturbing statistics: "In the age group 16–24, the proportion of Pakistanis and Bangladeshis with no qualifications whatsoever was 48 and 52 percent respectively, as against an overall 20 percent for all others."

49 Cf. also Eldering (1997:431): "Many traditional Turkish and Moroccan parents in the Netherlands decide to stop the schooling of their daughters after puberty, even if they have to pay a heavy fine." For similar observations from Belgium and Switzerland, see Cammaert (1992) and Hoffmann-Nowotny (1985:124).

50 For an incisive study of the language problem, see Christine Johansen (1999). Statistical studies from Norway are not available.

51 The case is from Fjell, a suburb of Drammen in which immigrants, the majority of them from Turkey, constitute 60 percent of the population (Sandrup 1998). For a report on the case, see *Verdens Gang*, August 30, 1997.

52 In Britain, a local teacher in Bradford, England's most populous Muslim community, pointed out as early as 1987 that "Muslims in the city would have less inter-cultural contact than would have been the case a decade earlier" (Lewis 1994:71). Describing the Tamil community in Norway, Fuglerud (1999:130) points to "numerous indications that migrants who have lived in Norway for fifteen years or more are increasingly turning their backs on Norwegian society in order to search for a sense of belonging in the exclusive company of fellow Tamils."

53 Movement is two ways. Immigrants also move out, as has happened in Oslo where there was an influx of native Norwegians to the colorful inner city. At the turn of the century, there was a distinct pattern of non-Western immigrants in Oslo moving out to certain suburbs that, as some observers warn, are becoming ghetto-like. In Sweden and Denmark, non-Western immigrants have long segregated themselves in certain suburbs that now have an immigrant population of 80 to 90 percent.

54 This attitude may have been one reason for the local authorities' decision to segregate Turkish children in a "Turkish-only" class: they hoped to deter further movement of Norwegians out of the community by enhancing the quality of classroom teaching.

55 Drug abuse among immigrants and children of immigrants shows a characteristic pattern: the drug is inhaled, not injected. Inhaling makes the drug intake easier to control and leads to fewer deaths from overdoses. Inhaling also lessens the risk of being detected, which is especially important among Muslims, for whom drug abuse is both sinful and shameful (al-Baldawi 1994).

56 Again, this aspect of the Norwegian situation is in no way unique. Research from the United States has found that "the longer youth were in the United States, the poorer

their overall physical and psychological health." Also, the more "Americanized" they became, the more likely they were to engage in risky behaviors such as substance abuse, violence and delinquency (C. Suárez-Orozco 2000:26). As Portes and Rumbaut (1996:243) observe, "the central question is not whether children of immigrants acculturate, but *to what sector* of American society they acculturate." The same probably holds for Norway. Note also their excellent discussion of what they call dissonant and selective acculturation (1996:243, 247ff).

57 Since the late 1990s there has been an explosive increase in theft and property crimes conducted by nonnatives, viz. political asylum seekers, in Norway. The great majority of the offenders come from Russia and Eastern Europe, especially Romania and the Baltic countries. In the summer of 2000, the American State Department warned American tourists to Norway to be aware of pickpocketing and other forms of theft in public spaces or on public transport.

According to police reports, much of this crime is organized by mafias in Russia and Eastern Europe. Many of the offenders enter the country as tourists, but if they are arrested, they present themselves as political asylum seekers, which guarantees that they will be allowed to remain in the country until their applications have been processed. The processing often takes more than a year, and in the meantime, if there is no hard evidence against them, the offenders may have freedom of movement in Norway as well as social welfare benefits. If an application is turned down, the applicant can appeal the decision, and Norway pays for the lawyer. There is evidence that some of those who are denied asylum and sent out of Norway reappear, sometimes several times. There is also evidence that youths and children below the minimum age for criminal prosecution are recruited by the mafias to commit crimes; but even these youngsters come in the capacity of political asylum seekers.

Problems of the kind I have been describing are becoming so severe in Scandinavia that Denmark, for instance, has found it necessary to isolate political asylum seekers from certain countries (which do not generally qualify as asylum-sending countries) in special locations while their applications are being processed. Norway is considering a similar policy but is concerned with the human rights implications.

58 Immigrants appear to be settling in Oslo at an increasing rate. An example are the Tamils, who have settled mainly in the far north and worked in the fish industries. Between 1995 and 2000, the number of Tamils in Båtsfjord and Vardø, the two most populous Tamil communities, decreased nearly 50 percent; those who left were heading for Oslo.

59 The study was undertaken by the Economist Intelligence Unit (*Aftenposten*, February 6, 1998).

60 The welfare state is so entrenched in Norway, and the economy so thriving, that it makes little difference whether the cabinet is socialist or conservative.

61 This is true. One may actually suffer a loss of income by working instead of collecting social welfare in some cases, as several studies have shown.

62 Many European scholars and researchers have also pointed to the unintended consequences of a cradle-to-grave safety net. Naser Khader (2000), a Dane of Palestinian-Syrian background, warns that many immigrants are unlearning their ability to help

themselves and are sinking into permanent welfare dependency. Bertel Haarder, former minister of education in Denmark and vice president of the European Union,
observes that Turks, the largest ethnic minority in Denmark, are managing more
poorly in Denmark than in other countries: In 1990, 50 percent of Turks in Denmark
were unemployed, compared to 23 percent in France. "It is not the Turkish culture
but the Danish culture that is flawed. It is in Denmark Turks have learnt not to do
anything for themselves." Haarder also notes how people may lose money by working instead of going on welfare (Haarder 1997:85ff, 81). Djuve (1999:34) suggests that
whereas social welfare has the positive effect of deterring poverty among most immigrants, "public assistance in itself may be a possible explanation of why immigrants
seem to have greater unemployment problems in Scandinavia than in other countries."

63 An earlier provision that a person applying for family reunification in Norway must
be able to document earnings and lodgings of a certain minimum level was lifted in
1999, thus distinguishing the Norwegian situation from that in England or the United
States.

64 A Lebanese told me how he had been advised, before coming to Norway, to which social welfare office in Oslo to turn to maximize his chances of generous benefits. Acting
on this advice, he was lodged in a four-star hotel until he could find an apartment in
the best part of town—this too paid for by the municipal welfare office. Another example: "You will meet Tamils in Colombo who know they will have more difficulties if
they end their journey at one Norwegian police station rather than another. Detailed
knowledge becomes a vital possession" (Fuglerud 1999:62).

65 Brox's observation is corroborated by a study by Blom and Ritland (1997). The standard of housing among immigrants was not poorer than among ethnic Norwegians
even though the disposable household income of immigrants was 58 percent lower
(184, 189).

66 The U.S. Supreme Court rendered a decision on May 17, 1999, on the same issue—the
rights of newcomers to equal welfare. A two-tier welfare system practiced by California
and subsequently accepted by fifteen other states after the 1996 federal welfare law
had authorized California's approach was deemed unconstitutional. California had
attempted to hold newcomers in their first year of residency to the benefit levels of the
states from which they had moved, and thus to discourage movement from one state to
another. The Supreme Court decision was based not on "the right to travel"—a much
critiqued phrase that does not appear in the Constitution—but on the Fourteenth
Amendment, which says, "No State shall make or enforce any law which shall abridge
the privileges or immunities of citizens in the United States." What is at stake is the
equality of all citizens, in the United States as in Norway.

67 In 2001, the Norwegian government is proposing to give up the policy of dispersing
refugees all over the country, including remote locations. Experience shows the policy
to be counterproductive: there is a consistent flow of refugees moving to the capital
and its surroundings, as well as to other urban areas in the south. Aslam Ahsan, an
immigrant from Pakistan and an important figure in Norwegian politics, has warned

that the government should enforce dispersal of recent immigrant arrivals to the capital, due to the severe social problems and ghettoization there (*Verdens Gang*, February 6, 1998).

68 Solid data on immigrants are not available, although one survey of eight ethnic minorities found Pakistanis, Turks, and Vietnamese to have a particularly low level of higher education. Many of the Vietnamese, however, are now enrolled in higher education programs. Iranians and Chileans came out on a level similar to that of Norwegians (Blom and Ritland 1997:172ff).

69 Norway has recently been criticized by the United Nations Refugee Commission in Geneva for discrimination against immigrants in the labor market.

70 An observation from Canada bears mention here: "In the past immigrants had an advantage over Canadians in competing for jobs, but changing factors are likely to mitigate against this in the 1990s. One contributing factor is the decline in the level of educational attainment of recent immigrant admissions" (Stafford 1992:80–83). Regarding the connection between higher education, Norwegian proficiency, and employment in Norway, there are intervening variables. Tamils, for instance, with an extremely high employment record, are often working in jobs where they do not need to know Norwegian.

71 Tamils are also the ethnic group with the lowest level of welfare support. In Oslo in 1995, only 1.3 percent of Tamils' income came from social welfare as compared to 41.7 percent among Somalis and 37.5 percent among Vietnamese. Indeed, the Tamil level of welfare support was lower than that among Norwegians (2 percent; Fuglerud 1999:95).

72 One example of such affirmative action is giving all minority-lingual five-year-olds in one district of Oslo free access to nursery school. (Children start school at six years of age in Norway.) It is done on a trial basis in the hope that it will enhance attendance. Another example is the provision of interpreter services to immigrants if needed, however long they have lived in Norway.

73 There are also, naturally, significant differences *within* minority groups. As Lewis (1994:22) reports in his socioeconomic profile of Pakistanis in Britain, the 1991 census found an unemployment rate of 28.8 percent for Pakistanis compared to 8.8 percent for the white community, but a 1981 study also found that between 7 and 10 percent of Pakistanis live in the most affluent suburbs.

74 I say this on the basis of my own fieldwork in different parts of the world, as well as by the reports of others. Would anyone question, for instance, that the Chinese have a work ethic that puts the general Norwegian attitude to shame? Or that Gulf Arabs or Egyptians are unlikely to abide by a Protestant work ethic? Such generalizations are not, of course, absolute. The point is simply that there are differences among peoples and within societies in the relative value placed on working and on leisure, and we cannot assume that culture plays no part in shaping such attitudes. In some countries where I have worked, prestige derives from giving orders and being able to enjoy leisure; to labor indicates low status.

75 Members of other disciplines, however, may be more candid. Eldering (1997:339) observes: "An important issue in the current debate in the Netherlands on the disadvantaged educational position of ethnic minority students is whether it is caused by cultural differences or by the parents' low educational level."

76 Hard data are not available from Norway to substantiate this point, but qualitative data indicate that many immigrants in Norway—as, no doubt, elsewhere in Europe or in the United States or Canada, for that matter—invest a large proportion of their savings in their original homeland, making them inclined to accept a lower standing of living in the host country than they otherwise would. People who have visited "Little Norway" in Gujerat, Pakistan, speak of the mansions and expensive cars with private chauffeurs enjoyed by many who in Norway live in cramped quarters in the "ghetto." Norwegian-Pakistanis interviewed in their residences in Pakistan sometimes compare their two lives in precisely these terms. The great majority of Moroccans in Norway—Berbers from the seaport city of Nadoor—invest their savings in property and businesses "down there," making Nadoor today "the richest town in Africa," in the words of some Norwegian-Moroccans. The same pertains to people of other nationalities—for example, Africans from Ghana and Gambia who are becoming very prosperous in their homelands. Thus to assess immigrants' standard of living only on the basis of their visible situation in the host country can give a very skewed picture. This is not to deny that many are suffering great economic hardship in Norway—warranting the term "underclass." But my use of that word in my 1995 book was meant to point to a general situation of marginalization and stigmatization, not just the economic side of people's lives—which is clearly more complex than I had then realized.

77 An example of how my position might be reversed: At a talk I gave at the Conservative Party's National Convention in 1996, I was criticized by two prominent members for having been against immigrant mothers who stay home with their children. I had mentioned that 50 percent of the children of immigrants lived in families where neither the mother nor the father was at work or at school, as against only 4 percent of native children who were in that situation. Whereas my intention had been to point to dismal inequality in children's life chances, it was misconstrued by at least one prominent person to indicate a discriminatory viewpoint.

78 What Appadurai (1985) writes of South India holds true for many other societies as well: being a benefactor to someone is a way of exerting dominance, while accepting gifts is a sign of accepted inferiority.

79 John Rawls, in his *Theory of Justice* (1971), regards self-respect as the most basic human need. See also Nussbaum (2000).

80 Compare Hirschman on the United States: "The incorporation of the new wave of post-1965 immigrants and their children is one of the most important challenges facing American society . . . [Yet] collection of immigration and emigration statistics is so poor as to be a national scandal . . . There have been no innovative efforts to collect survey data on a scale comparable to those launched to study other national issues, such as aging and retirement, youth employment, crime victimization, or drug use" (1996:80).

81 With the exception of Sweden, and to some extent France and Belgium, most European governments retained an "illusion of return." Rosemarie Rogers (1985) observes, "Measured against the absolute expectation that all migrants' sojourns in the host countries would be temporary, the European model of year-round labor migration must be judged unsuccessful. On the other hand, one can point out that such an expectation was never realistic . . . It is well known that there results some permanence even under the strictest rotation systems . . . ; why then should the incidence of migrants becoming permanent residents not be considerably larger under systems in which foreign workers are 'guests,' with flexible departure dates?"

82 Figures from Norway are not available, but the British situation provides an interesting example: "A total of 17,120 Pakistanis entered Britain between 1955 and 1960, compared to 50,170 in the 18 months preceding the 1962 legislation that closed the door on automatic entry for Commonwealth citizens" (Lewis 1994:17). But this need not mean that the immigrants saw themselves as taking up permanent residence. With regard to the Netherlands, Lindo (1995:147) observes that "[the] idea of being here only temporarily, to earn in a relatively short time the means to make for a better future back home, was not given up when they decided to call for their families to follow them. That their children would grow up and take root in Dutch society was a consequence of family reunification which was initially hardly thought through. Against all the odds, the image of the . . . immigrant as an 'international commuter' held out long in Dutch society. This is partly because the migrants themselves saw no reason to argue against it."

PART III   THE POLITICS OF CULTURE

1 Oslo Red Cross International is working actively to help children get back to Norway. Eva Khan, head of the organization, reports that in 1998 they were able to bring back six missing girls.

2 For Australia, see Wrede-Holm (2000); for South Africa, see Chambers (2000).

3 I find comfort in this statement by the psychiatrist Robert Stoller (1968:155, viii): "To introduce the term 'identity' or any of its semantic relatives, such as 'self' [or] 'self-representation' . . . is to assign a word to a quality, a feeling, a sense, for which no adequate word has yet been hammered out . . . I use the term more as an act of faith that there is a real 'thing' behind the word than from ability to prove that the 'thing' exists. Nonetheless, I can see in others and sense in myself clusters of fantasies, feelings, beliefs—whatever you wish—that make me aware that I exist and that I can find myself to be distinctly different from all other people in certain pretty clear-cut ways . . . [Yet] after much struggle, I cannot see, when actually observing a person, what is identity as different from self, . . . self-representation, and so forth. All the efforts at definition in the literature blur terribly for me in facing real life."

4 Erving Goffman's classic *The Presentation of Self in Everyday Life* (1959) was an early, and clearly one of the best, analyses to date of the complex processes whereby persons construct and project their identities. Otherwise, there is an immense literature on identity and/or self, which I choose not to go into here (but see Cohen 1994).

5   The celebrated author Amin Maalouf (1998:14) tells how, after he came from Lebanon in 1976 to settle in France, he has often been asked whether he feels "more French" or "more Lebanese." He always answers "both!" Does that then mean that he is half French and half Lebanese? Not at all. Identity cannot be split into halves, or thirds, or fractions: "I don't have many identities, I have only one, and it consists of all the elements that shaped it, according to one very special mixture, which is never the same from person to person." But what do you really feel deep in your heart? people ask. One assumes that deep down there is one valid identification, a kind of deep truth, a core that is determined at birth and that never changes. It is as if the rest of the person meant nothing at all, whereas every human being has multiple identifications.

6   Yalcin-Heckmann (1995:90–91) observes: "In the diaspora, some of the Islamic prescriptions gain a particular weight and new meaning. One case in point is the practice of veiling, or rather covering the hair and body in a particular style dictated by the Islamic fashion . . . Turkish migrants in Germany regard the headscarf as an index of ethnic and gender identity in a foreign context . . . In Germany, those women who do not wear a headscarf are widely seen as 'assimilated,' 'Germanized Turks,' or else as 'religiously liberal and modern Turks' . . . This disregards the meaning attached to various types of head wear by various generations of women in rural and urban Turkey."

7   To quote Amin Maalouf (1998:26, 14) again: "I have argued that identity is composed of a multiplicity of identifications, but it is equally important to keep in mind that identity is singular—there is only one identity, and we must enact it as a whole . . . My identity is that which means that I am not identical with any other person."

8   In retrospect, I find similar formulations by others. Maalouf (1998:92) writes, "Traditions are only deserving of respect to the extent that they are respectable, that is, only insofar as they respect the fundamental rights of all men and women." Bhikhu Parekh (1999:70) observes: "Respect for human beings does not necessarily entail respect for their cultures, for the latter might show no respect for human beings."

9   The op-ed editor, Per-Egil Hegge, commented on the first version he saw (which I had already rewritten many times) that it read like a dry academic exposition; he doubted that it would capture the public's attention. So I rewrote it yet again.

10 Cf. Richard Shweder (1998:48): "Anthropologists need to be part of . . . public policy discussions, if for no other reason than to defend, dispute or qualify the meaning and use of the idea of culture in these debates."

11 Cited in Laura Nader (1988:153).

12 On this point, see for instance Ebiri (1985), Lewis (1994), and Portes and Rumbaut (1996). Ebiri (1985:208) notes that the typical Turkish migrant was a skilled or semi-skilled industrial worker *more educated* than his fellow citizens who stayed at home. "He normally *earned more than the average income* in the sector in which he worked. He was, in short, a 'better than average' worker and socially more mobile." Lewis (1994:16–17) makes the following observation: "What is often unremarked in accounts of South

Asian migration is that migrants did not come from the poorest areas, but rather from places with a tradition of migration . . . People growing up in such emigration cultures compete with each other. Sending people away from home is an indicator of economic success and enormous social pride for families within their own communities." Cf. also Portes and Rumbaut (1996:10–12): "The very poor and the unemployed seldom migrate either legally or illegally; and unauthorized immigrants tend to have above-average levels of education and occupational skills in comparison with their homeland populations . . . The main reason why the poorest of the poor do not migrate across international borders is that they are not able to."

(This and the previous note were not part of the original op-ed article.)

13 This chapter is a much revised and abridged version of a chapter originally published under the title "Folk—ikke kulturer—kan møtes" in *Velferdssamfunnets barn*, 1994, edited by Tordis Dalland Evans, Ivar Frønes, and Lise Kjølsrød.

14 I develop the concept of resonance in regard to culture and translation in Wikan (1992).

15 Kottak (1991:17) defines culture as "distinctly human; transmitted through learning; traditions and customs that govern behaviour and beliefs."

PART IV   GENDER AND IDENTITY POLITICS

1 For my knowledge of Sara's case, I am indebted to Arne Ruth, former editor-in-chief of the Swedish daily *Dagens Nyheter*, who invited me to participate in a debate on February 10, 1997, to discuss the issues of integration that Sara's death, and the tragedies of others, had brought to the fore. Other participants were the late Swedish minister of integration, Lars Blomberg; the journalist and lawyer Jesús Alcalá; professor of economic history and author, Mauricio Rojas; and author and chair of the Swedish PEN club, Agneta Pleijel. In preparation for the debate I was sent a complete file of press clippings dealing with the various cases that I discuss in this chapter. It was also in this way that I was alerted to Anna's case, which I discuss in the next chapter. A one-and-a-half-page write-up of the debate was published in *Dagens Nyheter* on March 16, 1997.

2 Among those to whom Sara had confided her fears was her foster family when she had visited them two weeks earlier, but even they failed to realize the gravity of her situation.

3 There was also a third case involving a Kosovo-Albanian woman who was murdered by her estranged husband, but for some reason this did not capture the attention of the Swedish public. Perhaps a reaction of exhaustion had set in, due to the massive media coverage of other cases. The Kosovo-Albanian was a twenty-four-year-old mother of three children, whose husband had been imprisoned for three months for threatening to kill her and running away with their children. On his release, he wanted a reconciliation, but she wanted a divorce. "She had adapted well, whereas he was out of work. He couldn't accept that she wanted to be independent," said the social workers who dealt with her case. After committing the murder, he gave himself up to the police (*Svenska Dagbladet*, January 16, 1997).

4   The police, the social welfare agency, and the shelter for women had all been warned
    (by both anonymous and non-anonymous calls) that Varna was severely mistreated.
    "We did all in our might to help her, we knew her life hung on a thread," said Gunvor
    Wicklund, head of the shelter for women in Skellefteå, where Varna lived, "But she
    refused help for fear of being ostracized by her community" (*Expressen*, September 15,
    1997).

5   One form of sanction against boys who become "too Swedish" (or Danish, Dutch,
    Norwegian, etc.) is to send the boy to the parents' homeland for some time to teach
    him proper behavior. But the sanction is rarely used unless the boy has been in severe
    conflict with the law.

6   Alcalá (1997a) reports: "Sara resists, hides, and does all she can to avoid being removed
    to her father's brother. The social welfare agencies view her as 'not cooperative,' and
    call on the police." In their own words, "removal takes place with the help of the
    police" (Protocol of prosecutor, 1996.12.17). Alcalá asks: "What did the social welfare
    agencies think when they placed Sara with her father's brother? Hadn't Sara absolutely
    refused that solution?" Yes, she had, the welfare agencies admit, but family unity
    (*släktsamhörighet*) is important, and Sara's father's brother had promised to be kind (*snäll*)
    to her. As written in the protocol of the prosecutor: "Sara was afraid that something
    terrible might happen to her because of her father's and her uncle's disapproval of her
    way of being Swedish. However, while her case was being decided, her father's brother
    promised to protect Sara."

7   This conspiracy was revealed by Ingrid, a former common-law wife of another uncle
    of Sara's. She said that in 1995 there had been a meeting between the menfolk of Sara's
    family to discuss what to do about the problem of Sara—*problemet Sara*. On his return
    from the meeting, this uncle reported that they had decided to kill Sara, but had not yet
    agreed on who would do it. Since he was a bachelor without dependents, he thought
    he might be selected. Ingrid was told she must tell no one and must not warn Sara,
    or "they would fix her too" (Protocol of prosecutor, 1997.01.09). She complied out of
    fear: she knew that her then husband and his four brothers all beat their wives, but
    she could not believe they had definitely agreed to kill Sara. Only after the murder did
    Ingrid go to the police and tell them what she had known.

8   As Nalin Baksi, a Swedish member of Parliament of Kurdish background, said: "A
    seventeen-year-old boy does not proceed to kill his sister without being told to do so.
    He would never dare to do it on his own, for fear of his father." Thus she has no
    doubt that Sara's murder was plotted by the family. If the brother is not willing to act
    for the family, she said, he would be dead himself by being ostracized from his ethnic
    community (*Svenska Dagbladet*, February 8, 1997).

9   Under the heading "Männen i familjen borde åtalas" (The men in the family should
    be charged), Alcalá (1997a) took the Swedish police to task for not heeding Ingrid's
    testimony that the adult males of Sara's family had plotted Sara's murder. The police
    had not even interrogated Sara's father and his brother (Sara's custodian), save for a
    couple of minutes' talk with the latter. But this did not concern his threats against Sara,
    only Sara's life and personality. Sara was very independent, said the uncle, "so I tried

to set limits and raise her in the best way." Other than this remark, the uncle's answer to the question whether he had heard Hassan and Tareq threaten Sara is all that is noted in the prosecutor's protocol which consists of only half a page. Sara's father and his other brothers had not been interrogated at all. It is strange and incomprehensible from a judicial view point, wrote Alcalá.

"Even more strange, the information provided by Ingrid is not part of the protocol of the prosecutor [*förundersökningsprotokoll*]. The prosecutor did not want to include it in the charge. Why? What could have made the prosecutor disregard such an important testimony?

"For the sake of justice, for the sake of truth, and, not least, for Sara's sake, it is absolutely necessary that the criminal investigation be complete. Umeå Municipal Court must urge the prosecutor to complete the investigation. On my part, I hereby charge Sara's father and father's brother with a crime" (*Dagens Nyheter,* February 7, 1997). Alcalá's action had an effect, and the court followed up on his charge.

10 Interview with Charles Westin, professor and chair of the Center for Immigration Research, Stockholm University (*Dagens Nyheter,* February 12, 1997). See also op-ed piece by Professors Lundgren and Elden, "Voldsbrått mot kvinnor er inte något exotiskt" (Violence against women is nothing exotic; *Svenska Dagbladet,* January 21, 1997). They argue that violence against women in Sweden is downplayed and hidden under an ideological veneer of gender equality. A similar point is made by Charles Westin: "We must not forget that even Swedish men mistreat Swedish women and that our gender equality in many cases is a facade." He also notes that whereas Swedish men explain their violence as stemming from jealousy, the immigrants in the above cases speak of honor. In both cases, he observes, the abuse of power is at issue (*Dagens Nyheter,* February 12, 1997).

11 In several countries, honor crime is a legal category that justifies lesser punishment for violence against women. (See Cohen-Almagor 1996; Jehl 1999.)

12 It should be noted that honor crimes are also at times directed toward men as victims. Some recent Norwegian evidence indicates that of seven identified honor crimes, two have been directed against men (Hege Storhaug, personal communication).

13 Alcalá's pleas did have an effect. In the aftermath of Sara's death, the Iraqi-Kurdish association in Sweden mobilized to discuss the conflicts that triggered the tragedy and to create awareness among its members of women's rights and the need to respect Swedish law and basic values. But the official Swedish response was to downplay "culture" and highlight the universality of violence against women as the problem. It took another three years, and another tragic case, for the Swedish authorities to come out squarely against honor crimes.

14 For comparable observations from the Netherlands, see de Vries (1995:39), who describes gossip of "a fairly malicious nature" constraining the lives of many girls and young women. "Most girls live surrounded, to varying degrees, by compatriots who see it as their task to keep watch over the girls' behaviour: they must be chaste and remain Turkish, that is, not become 'Dutchified' (*vernederlandst*). Gossip will be directed not just at the girl but at her whole family, and once the family reputation has been tarnished, this may lead to further sanctions . . . such as beating, house arrest, an (early)

arranged marriage, or an interdiction on attending school." As many girls themselves put it, "they have a sense that someone is always 'looking over their shoulders,' that they 'live in an open prison,' and that their lives are being 'controlled by others.'"

15 This is in line with what de Vries observes from the Netherlands and Mørck from Denmark: "Many Turkish parents indeed discourage their daughters, in a more or less forthright manner, from developing close ties with Dutch people. Many dread that their daughters may become infected with Dutch, that is, unsuitable ideas" (de Vries 1995:41). Likewise in Denmark: "Most [Turkish] parents think it is best that their children do not have Danish friends, they should preferably have friends of the same religion" (Kerep 1995, cited in Mørck 1996:205). My own research indicates that girls as young as eight to ten are often not even allowed to take part in school outings, sports, or other extracurricular activities.

16 A mother's excessive beating may reflect the fact that she is responsible for the children's upbringing on a day-to-day basis, whereas the father is a more distant figure. The mistakes of the children, and especially the daughters, are visited upon the mother (cf. Shaaban 1991:24ff; Wikan 1980, 1996a).

17 The Syrian professor of English literature Bouthaina Shaaban (1991:75–76) observes: "To most Arab women, extended families mean one thing: extra male authority. I can think of many women who have been prevented from marrying men of their choice or from following up a certain career or profession because a cousin or a father's or mother's cousin didn't approve of their decision . . . Thus, extended families guarantee a tighter grip and exert efficient male domination over women."

18 Anna's going public with her story may actually have increased her chances of not being molested. Publicity may guard against assault in some cases. The religious leader of Assyrians (Syrian Christians) in Sweden said in an interview with the press that violence against women was totally unacceptable and, according to him, practically unknown within his community. I would not be surprised if he, or other leaders, would try to dissuade Anna's family from harming her, should they want to try.

19 Again, to quote Shaaban (1991:10) on Syria: "Today, young men's attitude to virginity is changing (though no man would openly admit this), and is becoming quite relaxed and understanding." An article in the Syrian law, however, "guarantees the man an immediate divorce and full reclamation of the dowry if his bride turns out not to be a virgin." It may well be that attitudes to virginity among many Syrians in Sweden are more rigid than among townspeople in Syria—in accordance with the reinforcement of tradition that often takes place in diaspora communities.

20 In a letter of November 1999, the department of culture and education in Oslo municipality asked the schools to help to distribute crisis manuals (*kriseguider*) warning girls over fifteen not to travel on vacation to the parents' homeland if they strongly feared that they might be married by force. The pamphlets had been published by the organization "Self-help for immigrants and refugees" (SEIF). In 1999, SEIF received about seventy requests for help from girls and boys who feared they might be married by force. They were of diverse background—Muslim, Hindu, Buddhist, Greek Orthodox, and Catholic. According to the leader of SEIF, Gerd Fleisher, "it is unfortunately the rule rather than the exception that youths have their passport taken away from them

as soon as they reach the parents' homeland" (*Aftenposten*, June 10, 2000). The crisis manual was written by journalist and author Hege Storhaug, who has researched the problem for ten years, and is extremely knowledgeable. Distribution of the manual led to protests from several immigrant politicians, who argued that it encouraged youths of immigrant background to break with their families. But the initiative of SEIF and Oslo municipality received support from the Ministry of Child and Family Affairs, which later engaged Camilla Kayed to write a similar crisis manual for them.

21 In 1999, after two cases of forced marriage that had received major media coverage (one concerning Jack and Zena; see Briggs and Briggs 1998), the British Parliament established a committee to look into the extent of the problem and propose measures to help combat it. It is officially estimated that at least one thousand Muslim girls of Asian background annually are married by force in Britain. But Asian women's organizations in Britain estimate the numbers to be much higher. According to Muhammad Sarwar, member of Parliament, forced marriage is one of the main sources of violence in British Muslim society (*Dawn*, August 5 and August 14, 1999). In 1999, 742 cases were registered in the district of West Yorkshire alone, according to Philip Balmforth. Balmforth, an officer of the West Yorkshire Police, is the Bradford area community officer. Bradford is the area with the highest population of Muslims in Britain.

22 The point is contested, however, and there are some Muslim religious scholars who argue that marriage between a Muslim woman and a non-Muslim man is permitted according to the Qur'an; what is forbidden is marriage with a heathen—hence a Christian or a Jew is acceptable.

23 Nasim's story first appeared in the press on November 11, 1992, six months after she came back to Norway. It was she herself who contacted the journalist Hege Storhaug. Nasim's story was featured over five full pages in the daily *Dagbladet*, replete with full-color photos of her as a bride, with the groom. A pseudonym, Sima, was used.

24 To have her marriage annulled, Nasim Karim had to go to court and file a civil lawsuit against her husband in Pakistan. Her father was not charged. Norwegian law exonerates parents or blood relatives in cases of forced marriage and targets instead the husband, who, in cases such as Nasim Karim's, is often as innocent as the bride. As evidence of force, Nasim Karim presented in court a video of her wedding that her mother had lent her; the video shows the bride weeping and in despair.

25 As of January 1, 2000, only three girls in Norway have had their marriages annulled by the Norwegian courts, though the incidence of forced marriage is high: an estimated 1,600 such marriages took place in the last few years of the twentieth century, according to an investigation by the Ministry of Child and Family Affairs in 1999. "Force" is used to mean that the persons concerned experience severe mental or physical pressure, not that the marriage is arranged, though the distinction can sometimes be difficult to draw. Most of those who are married by force regard the cost of ostracism from their families as more difficult to deal with than that of remaining in the marriage, though there is evidence of change since late 1999. (See n. 13, p. 230.)

26 For reasons I cannot disclose here, marriage according to Muslim law was not feasible at the time. The couple have remained together and now have two children.

1   On a similar situation in Germany, see Ursula Mehrländer (1985).

2   In several documents that I was shown in connection with my work on the situation analysis for the Ministry of Child and Family Affairs, the school authorities expressed their concern regarding the discrepancy between the child's spoken language and the national language in which many children received mother-tongue instruction.

3   See, for instance, Lindo (1995) for an incisive comparison between pupils of Turkish and Portuguese descent in the Netherlands. See also Eldering (1997) and Gibson (1997).

4   It is to the credit of the Norwegian government that it has come to realize as much. In January 1999, Parliament passed a new proposition regarding language instruction for children of immigrants. Mother-tongue instruction is to be eliminated after the fourth grade. For the first four years it is to be given only as a supplement and to help especially needy children gain facility in Norwegian and other subjects. The primary language of instruction will be Norwegian for all. As for the mother tongue, it is to be the child's *real* home language, whether spoken by the mother or the father. What will happen in practice remains to be seen, but already there is evidence of resistance from some school principals, who are continuing with mother-tongue instruction in their schools, though it goes by another name. Norway's change of policy is in line with that of several other countries that have come to realize, belatedly, that intensive instruction in the mother tongue may not be the best way to help an immigrant child acquire facility in the national language.

5   The very large number of dependents that Somalis in general have has caused suspicion among Scandinavian authorities as to their authenticity. In Denmark, in 1998, after DNA tests were introduced to check biological links, about 58 percent of those who agreed to be tested were found to have given false information. Norway is considering similar testing on condition that it be done on a voluntary basis. A precipitating cause was the case of a Somali woman with two children who managed to bring thirty-one relatives into Norway on family reunification in the course of five years (*Verdens Gang*, October 24, 1999).

6   Average fertility among Somali women in Norway is 5.5 children as against 3.6 for Pakistanis (the second highest) and 1.8 for native Norwegians (Vassenden 1997:54).

7   Many illiterate married women are not able to handle their own bank accounts, or even get to the bank. In several cases that I know of, husbands control the child allowances and birth bonuses that their wives receive from the state. All they need do is keep the wife's credit card.

8   Somalis are twelve times more likely to be unemployed than native Norwegians, as against five times more for immigrants in general (Blom and Ritland 1997:178). Eighty percent of the household income of Somalis derives from public assistance, as against 14 percent for native Norwegians, and 11 percent for Tamils. From Denmark, Haarder (1997:88) observes that nearly all the 10,000 Somalis in Denmark are unemployed. I mention these facts to highlight the very difficult situation of Somalis in some, perhaps most, European countries.

9 Interview with Hassan Keynan in the Finnish newspaper *Hufudstadsbladet* (August 8, 1998) in connection with his participation in the Åbo conference, "Variations on the Theme of Somaliness," arranged by the European Association of Somali Studies. Keynan also said that the Somalis in Finland were significantly more active than the Norwegian Somalis, a reference, I believe, to the more encompassing Norwegian social welfare system and its somewhat negative effect on self-help and initiative.

10 Most refugees to Western Europe today are from the middle or higher echelons of society (see part 3, note 12); members of the lower classes cannot afford the exorbitant fees charged by the agents who arrange the journeys.

PART VI   TOLERANCE VERSUS HUMANISM

1 This does not mean that one cannot say "we" and still make a plea for personal freedom and social justice. Take these words pronounced by an old Bhutanese village woman: "Tibet was colonized by China, Sikkim was colonized by India, but we, the Bhutanese, have been colonized by our own government." Thus she expressed her disdain of the class-infested politics that had just cost her her home, in a case of expropriation that was wholly unnecessary as she saw it and that only confirmed her life experience of "small" versus "big" people—the latter free to do as they see fit. Her "we, the Bhutanese" is not the all-embracing "We" of the Bhutanese nation. It is a small "we," her "we," the people with whom she identifies in this connection. Her sense of identification changes, as it does for all of us, but her sense of solidarity with others enables her to use the first-person plural to singular effect: Look at me, I am part of a "we" that has been exploited! Her plea for individuality and democracy, for personal freedom and social justice, makes it clear that hers is not a singular predicament but a singular case of a common plight (Wikan 1994a).

2 Walid al-Kubaisi observes: "Those who are critical of Islam and who wish to emphasize universal values, such as freedom of expression and human rights, are not only stifled by their own milieu. They are regarded as traitors by Norwegian authorities and Norwegian intellectuals. Muslims should be Muslim first, human beings second. Antiracist work prioritizes exotic culture, not human beings. I came here because I wanted to be in a place where there was freedom of expression. And that means that one criticizes one's own background. All authors, eastern and western, with any claim to pride, have done so" (*Dagbladet*, March 21, 1996).

3 "Multiculturalism" is a contested concept. As Cohen, Howard, and Nussbaum (1993:3–5) point out: "Over the past decade, a variety of movements, theories, and proposals have emerged under the banner of 'multiculturalism.' Special tensions arise between group rights and individual rights, and between feminism and multiculturalism. The aim must be 'to achieve,' in Susan Okin's words, 'a multiculturalism that treats all persons as each others' moral equals.' "

4 Trained as an engineer in Syria, al-Kubaisi's chances of employment have been severely compromised. Who would want to hire a "traitor" at the risk of being labeled a racist? However, after his first book, *Min tro, din myte* (My belief, your myth, 1996) was finally published and was nominated for a prestigious Norwegian book award,

al-Kubaisi has been able to make a career of writing. He has now published four more books, all written in a rich and beautiful Norwegian, a language he taught himself after coming to Norway. All his books have received excellent reviews. He also writes op-ed pieces and other articles.

5   The paradox is of course also that they overgeneralize with respect to "culture" and "nation."

6   Bouthaina Shaaban (1991:7) notes how "the supposedly warm and supportive family atmosphere at times turns into a male inferno."

7   Aamir Javed Sheikh, a Conservative Party politician in Norway, originally from Pakistan, received threats on his life and damage to his grocery store after publicly advocating that Norwegian language learning be made obligatory for immigrants. Such sanctions are not uncommon against immigrants who urge stricter measures of integration. Mørck, in her research in Denmark (1996), uses the word *meningsterror*, opinion terror, and gives ample evidence of the severity of the sanctions used. For evidence of similar mechanisms at work in the Netherlands, see de Vries (1995) and Lindo (1995). For Norway, see Bilgiç (2000).

8   From my work in Cairo I have made an extensive analysis of "the people's talk" and other forms of slander as social phenomena (Wikan 1980:144ff, 1996a:117ff).

9   Bilgiç (2000:41, 205) notes how issues such as honor, virginity, homosexuality, and cohabitation before marriage are much discussed *within* the Muslim community in Oslo, but outwardly only one voice is registered, the conservative. Anyone raising such matters publicly would be considered a traitor. A concrete example comes to my mind: when a journalist from the daily *Aftenposten* attempted to interview some Muslim youths on homosexuality, only three out of twenty would respond. A Muslim student later explained to me the reason for the reticence: the youths did not know what the Qur'an really said, so they were afraid to voice an opinion. In other words, personal views must give way to a collective truth, which is formulated by religious authorities. According to Bilgiç (2000:31–32), among Muslims in Norway there are no democratic institutions. Thus, whereas freedom of thought and expression within the Norwegian society facilitates social change, immigrant cultures have stagnated and defend their right not to change.

10 See Wikan (1990, 1991a) for an analytical discussion of the idea of the "enlightened moment." Sally Falk Moore's concept of the "diagnostic event" is similar (Moore 1994).

11 Let me give an example of how deep these feelings go. A Norwegian-Pakistani woman, about thirty years of age, told me that she and her sister, aged thirty-three, had been wedded to two brothers from Pakistan through an arranged marriage. The brides were highly educated; she is a student of law at Oslo University, and her sister studies at the London School of Economics. The grooms likewise were highly educated. The wedding was a big feast with about three hundred guests, held in a town in southern Norway. Everything proceeded according to plan until the crucial moment: the consummation of the marriages. The brides were adamant; thus far and no farther; they would not sleep with the grooms. To make a long story short, the marriages were finally

dissolved. Or, rather, they never actually took place, for without sexual consummation there is no marriage, according to Islam. The two grooms were understanding but distraught. The brides' father and several brothers—unusual for such a case—sided with the brides. But their mother almost had a nervous breakdown and took off for Pakistan along with the grooms. There is no need to elaborate on this story, save to make this point: when I asked my friend and informant why on earth she and her sister went along with the plans in the first place, she looked at me and said, "But what could we do? They had been trying to get us married since we were fourteen, presenting us with one candidate after the other. We had to say yes eventually, or they would think we were in love with someone." What is remarkable is that two such highly educated and independent girls should feel they had to give in. It indicates the pressure young people are under to comply with an arranged marriage. That is why, as one girl of immigrant background has said on Norwegian TV, she considers the distinction between arranged marriage and forced marriage *en bløff* (a bluff).

12 For a discussion of "veiling" in France, see Viorst (1996) and Benjnouh (2001); in Germany, see Ewing (2000) and Mandel (1996). In Scandinavia, Muslims are generally allowed to wear the headscarf in any public setting, and many do.

13 An interesting example of the way equality between men and women is regarded in Islam was provided by a Pakistani *sayyed* who addressed the Association of Muslim Students at the University of Oslo. Having underscored how gender equality is basic to Islam, he was challenged by a member of the audience and, after some reflection, nuanced his position thus: women have equal *value* to men, but their statuses and tasks are different.

14 For a lucid discussion of the point that gender equality is not against Islam, see the collection of essays edited by Afkhami (1995) and the works by al-Hibri (1999) and An-Naim (1999).

15 *Barn er selveiere.* Jervel spoke these words at the meeting convened by the minister of child and family affairs in which I participated in 1992 (see Introduction).

16 Marianne Lund (1998), who did fieldwork in the school, reports that the Muslim leader functioned as an intermediary, and we think that it was he who persuaded the father to let his daughter take the course.

17 Another example is "the new Christianity lesson," as it is popularly called; it encompasses other religions and ethics, but with the main emphasis on Christianity. By October 1999, nearly a year after the "world view" class had been introduced in Norwegian primary schools, only 134 of many Muslim children had been partially exempted at their parents' request. "It is a catastrophically low number, which worries us. We are surprised that not more parents exert their right to seek exemption," noted one Pakistani politician (*Aftenposten*, August 31, 1999). A protest demonstration was then convened by Muslim leaders, mobilizing several hundred people. How many parents proceeded to ask exemption for their children in the aftermath is not yet known. But school principals I have talked to tell me the numbers are minimal. The Muslim leaders argue that the reason so few ask exemption is that the parents have not understood that they have the right to refuse. But my educated guess tells me that the situation is more

complex, and that many parents simply do not object to their children learning about Christianity and other religions, as long as this does not amount to indoctrination. They are less set on marking their Muslim identity in every possible setting than are many of their leaders—in public. As with the father in the story above, once he had made his case, registered his protest, and received an apology and a reassurance of respect, the problem was solved. He certainly knew he had the right to refuse. However, Muslim leaders may easily change the overall picture by exhorting and advising parents to refuse. The politics of fear are operative at all levels. But resistance is also being registered — resistance against letting one's identity (or the identity of one's children) become unidimensional and hence counterproductive, given the exigencies of life in the real world.

18 Eidsvåg made this point at a UNESCO meeting on "universal ethics" in Lund, Sweden, June 3–6, 1999.

19 Compare Lewis (1994:198–99): "a lack of coordination and internal feuding among the 450-plus Pakistani organizations in Britain absorbs all surplus time and energy."

20 Aslam Ahsan for over a decade has been the leader of the Pakistani Resource Center for Children. A prominent politician, he is a controversial figure, particularly within his own Pakistani community. He has been severely criticized for advocating that learning Norwegian should be compulsory for immigrants and for his generally integrationist stance. He has arranged a tour for prominent officials from Oslo to Pakistan to acquaint them with the culture of many of the children with whom they deal. For nearly twenty years he has organized a Christmas party for lonely Norwegians—an extremely successful venture for which he is widely praised.

21 A concrete example would be the sultanate of Oman, where my husband, Fredrik Barth, and I worked in the mid-1970s. As particularly discussed by Barth (1983), a vast array of cultural differences are not translated into ethnic differences but, rather, downplayed in the cause of civic identities. The result, in Oman, is a well-functioning plural society with a great degree of interpersonal and intercultural tolerance among all parties. See also Wikan (1991a).

22 Keynan made this point at a one-day workshop on Somalis that he organized for teachers in Oslo at the invitation of the chancellor of schools (December 10, 1998).

23 On the dangers of playing up to the clan identities of Somalis, Keynan warns: "To try to 'understand' the Somali society by letting clan rivalries play a role in the negotiations with the authorities, is like playing with fire. Somalis themselves are experts in that game, that was why the Somali state collapsed" (*Hufudstadsbladet*, August 8, 1998).

24 Caste identities are not always magnified. Among Tamils in Norway, they are downplayed. "It is worth noting that marriage is the single occasion among Jaffna Tamils in Norway where caste considerations are admitted as legitimate and necessary. While *consciousness* of caste is always there, this is never openly made to carry interactive implications" (Fuglerud 1999:111). This is in stark contrast to the situation among Pakistanis.

25 A seminal article on Bradford's Pakistani communities, based on research in the early 1970s, reports how "an initial tendency towards fusion—in which pioneer settlers associated together regardless of their regional, caste or sectarian origins—gradually gave way, as numbers grew, to fission and segmentation; in this second stage of fragmentation ties of village-kinship and sectarian affiliation grew steadily more significant as the basis of communal aggregation" (Dahya 1974:77–95, cited in Lewis 1994:56).

26 A point made by the Danish Palestinian-Syrian Naser Khader is that "Muslim" to Danes denotes a single thing, whereas there are in fact many different kinds of Muslims. "There are atheist Muslims who only accept that they are Muslim by origin. There are cultural Muslims, practicing Muslims, fundamentalist Muslims, orthodox, ultraorthodox, and extremist Muslims, and these categories might be broken down further," Khader notes (*Aftenposten,* December 18, 2000). Walid al-Kubaisi (1996) makes the same point.

27 The study was conducted by the National Demographic Institute on a sample of thirteen thousand persons, who were followed closely over a nine-month period (Ibrahim 1995). On the many different views of the meaning and value of Islam among youngsters of Muslim parentage in the Netherlands and Britain, see Sunier (1995) and Lewis (1994).

28 Several immigrants in Scandinavia have expressed their concerns regarding antidemocratic processes at work in Muslim communities. Many have blamed imams—religious leaders—for looking after their own self-interests at the expense of integration and children's life prospects. Imams, they claim, promote segregation to enhance their own power, and propagate fundamentalism and authoritarian rule. Khalid Salimi, former leader of the antiracist movement in Norway and himself a Muslim, urged Norway as early as 1992 to stop its state financial support of Muslim congregations unless they were willing to change that form of rule. "Demand democracy and elections!" he said. "Much of what is happening in the mosques is totally against what most immigrants themselves wish." He urged members of the congregations to revolt (*Verdens Gang,* September 17, 1992). Mian Zahid Rizwani, editor of the *Awaz,* Norway's largest Urdu newspaper, was in line with Salimi when he warned: "Imams are misusing Islam's name to serve their own interests. The state's financial support of Muslim congregations, newspapers, and cultural activities serves to support the fundamentalist imams, and to destroy the conditions for children of immigrants growing up in Norway" (interview in *Dagbladet,* March 21, 1996). Afzal Abbas, leader of NIKON (Norwegian immigrant organization against crime and narcotics) supports Rizwani: He has no doubt that the Norwegian authorities are supporting the fundamentalists, who are brainwashing children (ibid.). Bilgiç (2000) and al-Kubaisi (*Dagbladet,* March 21, 1996), both Muslims, have also castigated the Norwegian state for its overzealous, naive support of fundamentalist forces through state funding. Naser Khader has coined the word "ghetto-Islam" to alert Danes to what he regards as a frightening phenomenon: the growth, within the "ghettos," of a form of Islam driven by fundamentalists and fanatics who, in his words, are just as hateful, intolerant, and militant as neo-Nazis. "I must honestly admit that I am deeply worried. The growth of ghetto-Islam fills me with silent fear. These people nurture a wholly implacable hatred of the West, of

Christianity, of democracy, of human rights—indeed, of western values in their totality. We need to recognize this, and to relate to it; otherwise things will go out of control" (*Aftenposten*, December 18, 2000).

1   A shorter version of the Nadia case was published in *Daedalus* (Wikan 2000a).

2   Nadia phoned her colleague on September 8, eight days after her abduction and three days after the family arrived at their destination. The store owner contacted the Ministry of Foreign Affairs on September 10. He also guaranteed he would pay for Nadia's ticket, as there is no provision for the state to do so on behalf of Norwegian citizens.

3   On September 27, seventeen days after the Ministry was informed about Nadia's case, the ambassador was instructed to take immediate action. Because her case was unprecedented and politically highly sensitive, it was necessary to develop a comprehensive strategy among several concerned parties before proceeding.

4   An international arrest order had been issued against Nadia's father in case he should leave Morocco.

5   Negotiations between the ambassador and Nadia's father began on September 28, one day after the ambassador had managed to get into contact with Nadia. (A secretary from the embassy, making herself out to be Nadia's friend, made the call.) Thus, by the time Nadia's case sprang into the media, negotiations had already been under way for five days.

6   The ambassador was later to praise the news media for their engagement and help with the Nadia case; they were able to furnish information that was important. The media also clearly set Nadia's rescue above all else, or they would have published the sensational news about her case earlier than they did.

7   In developing its strategy for Nadia's release, the Norwegian Ministry of Foreign Affairs consulted with high officials in Morocco at the Ministry of the Interior, the provincial administration, and the municipality. Nadia's case was also well publicized in Morocco.

8   In letters to newspapers, several Norwegians angrily demanded to know how one could obtain such an amount; they too were living on disability benefits but received much less. That immigrants receive higher social welfare benefits than native Norwegians is a complaint that is made from time to time in the media and has even been found to have some basis in fact. Disability benefits, like other forms of public assistance, are subject to the judgment and whim of individual officials working in municipal offices, which abide by different standards.

9   Nadia's parents were charged with violations of sections 223 and 224 of the Norwegian Criminal Code. The two sections deal essentially with the same issue. Section 223 covers forcibly holding someone against that person's will and, more specifically, the underlying intent or the reason the person is being held. Section 224 merely covers holding someone against that person's will, regardless of the reasons.

10 An expert witness—*sakkyndig vitne*—in Norway is an expert for the court, and hence should be neutral. He or she can follow the whole proceedings, unlike ordinary witnesses, who cannot attend the trial until they have testified. The expert witness may be called by the prosecutor or the defense; in Nadia's case I was called by the defense. The expert witness should be a resource for the court as a whole and, though the witness's neutrality may be suspected by the party that did not call him or her, is obliged to be as impartial as possible.

11 There were two interpreters, one in Berber for Nadia's mother, one in Arabic for her father. Since I know Arabic well, I could follow much of what was being said in the father's case (not all, for there are dialect differences between his Moroccan and my Egyptian), and even a part of the mother's speech, for Berber contains a host of Arabic words and expressions. It was quite clear to me that having translators provided the defendants with a certain flexibility, since misunderstandings and inconsistencies could be attributed to the translators, who also, in some cases, helped the defendants with their answers. The Norwegian Ministry of Justice has recently published a comprehensive study about communication and justice before the law, with special focus on immigrants (Andenæs and Gotaas 2000).

12 The issue here is one that surfaces time and again in stories of girls abducted to the Middle East or South Asia by their parents in the West: they have nowhere to go, they cannot possibly escape, even though their feet are not tied and the doors are not locked.

13 For an extensive discussion of such practices in the case of Egypt, see Wikan (1980, 1996a). Egyptians generally regard that individuals are easily swayed to act against their own best interests, and the saying "she/he/they manipulated her/him/me" is commonly used to excuse one's nearest and dearest. Moroccan friends in Norway tell me similar usages are common among them.

14 I can only guess that Nadia told her mother in an attempt to dissuade her parents from a forced marriage. The mother would know that the virginity test on the wedding night would have the whole family scandalized. Indeed, her mother suspected the truth of the story, for she told the court that she had planned to take Nadia to a doctor in Morocco to check on her virginity but that there had not been time.

15 Nadia used the word "imam," which is the common term in Norway for Muslim priests and would thus be understood by the court. In Morocco, healers who are presumed to be knowledgeable about Islam and to use Qur'anic amulets, holy water, and other forms of treatment are called sheiks. Nadia's parents conceded that she had received the treatment she described on this occasion.

16 As a Muslim girl, she could not live by herself. The whole family would have been ostracized. Muslim girls live with their parents or guardians until they get married.

17 The Stockholm syndrome is named after a bank robbery in Stockholm that resulted in the taking of hostages.

18 The ambassador also said that Nadia had had accomplices in the family. Understandably, he did not specify who they were, but I am inclined to think they may have been relatives on her father's side. Nadia herself told the court how her father's brother

had tried to intervene when her father beat her upon being informed that she had contacted the embassy.

19 Several Norwegian women, including some well-known public figures, voiced their complaints in no uncertain language. Their criticism was directed not just at Nadia's mother but also at other immigrants who enjoy the fruits of the Norwegian welfare society while deprecating its basic values of equality and freedom.

20 The grandfather is referring to the ambassador's offer to send a car to pick up Nadia at her parents' house in Nadoor, thus helping her reach the nearest airport from which she could fly home to Norway. The family was doubly insulted: that she would go with an unrelated man, the driver; and that anyone would think the family itself could not accompany her.

21 The grandmother's illness was of course a key issue during the trial. As evidence, the parents presented the telegram they had received from the brother of Nadia's mother: "Ta mère est gravement malade. Venez urgent." Yet Nadia's mother said she did not telephone her family in Morocco during the seven days it took them to get there; Nadia's father said he telephoned the day the telegram arrived. By the time they reached Morocco, the grandmother was quite well.

   The jury found the story less than plausible. As stated in the premises of the verdict, when a close family member is gravely ill, one usually uses a phone to convey the message. The telegram appeared to be part of a cover-up operation. Moreover, if the grandmother had been so ill, one would have expected the parents to make contact during the seven days.

22 This part of the parents' story rings less than true. From what I know, people traveling overland to Morocco usually have their cars loaded, for there is a constant stream of people who want to go, and recruiting passengers is a way of sharing costs and company. Thus, finding a driver who is about to go with a near-empty van would take more than sheer good luck.

23 Nadia testified in court that her mother's family had been in on the kidnapping, whereas her father's family was not informed. Indeed, her father's immediate reaction to the ambassador's first call had been that they must bring Nadia back to Norway, they had no choice. But the mother's family refused.

24 Leidulv Digernes was also, incidentally, Nasim Karim's lawyer in her civil suit to have her marriage annulled.

25 Nasim Karim was now living in England: otherwise she no doubt would have lent Nadia a hand.

26 *Søndagsavisen*, April 7, 1998. I am grateful to Hege Storhaug for bringing this case to my attention.

27 "Retten har et positivt inntrykk av Nadia som ei ryddig og gløgg jente. Etter rettens syn står det respekt av den måten hun klarte å gjennomfore si vitneforklaring på. Retten kan ikke se at det er sannsynliggjort at hennes væremåte er annerledes enn for andre norske jenter i samme alder." Judgment in court case nr. 98–3021 M/77, p. 9.

28 Judgment in court case nr. 98–3021 M/77, pp. 8–10.

29 Many have wondered why Nadia's parents chose to go to Norway at all. I have been told the following from what I take to be reliable sources: Nadia's parents married for love, against the wishes of the mother's family, who objected to their daughter marrying down, Nadia's father being of inferior rank. To escape the pressures of the family and make a new life for themselves, they came to live in Norway.

30 The weekly *Journal* reports that 84 percent of Moroccan males aged 20–29, and 71 percent aged 30–39, wish to emigrate to the West, and so do 68 percent of all young women. The desire to emigrate is especially high among urban people. Seventy percent of people with higher education want to migrate to the West (*Aftenposten*, March 18, 1998).

31 The Spanish police estimate that at least one thousand lives have been lost at sea over the past three years.

32 See Wikan (1995b) for an analysis of the expense of marriage in Cairo, Egypt, and the strategies used by young people to deal with it.

33 The *mahr* in Islam is a gift given to the bride on marriage; it can consist of money, gifts, or both and should become the property of the bride; but her male guardian sometimes appropriates a part or all of it. The *mahr* has become so inflated in many societies as to make marriage very difficult, and some states—for example, in the Gulf of Arabia—have instituted a legal maximum (which is often evaded; see Wikan 1991a). A groom who resides in the West is so attractive by virtue of his situation that the *mahr* he has to pay is generally very low. Conversely, the *mahr* for a bride resident in the West is inflated, except in the case of close relatives.

34 This is not to say that limited language facility is the only reason for the declining rate of voting; voting is on the decline also among the majority population. But the much lower rate of participation among non-Western immigrants calls for special attention. Developments in Sweden are parallel to those in Norway (Kval 1997).

35 For an excellent discussion regarding Turkish mothers in the Netherlands, see Lindo (1995). On Muslims in Bradford, England, see Lewis (1994:177, 187). On the Muslim mother's role as maker of the child's future, see Wikan (1980, 1996a).

36 Statistics from Norway on illiteracy among immigrants are not available. A study was undertaken in 1998 by the Norwegian Statistical Bureau regarding the educational level of immigrants who had arrived in Norway after 1990 (more than 50 percent of the total immigrant population), but the results have not yet been released. Data from the Netherlands are, however, instructive. "A representative survey among ethnic minorities in 1994 showed [that] . . . about half of the Moroccan men and 61 percent of the women interviewed have had no education [either in Morocco or in the Netherlands]." The percentages of illiterates among Turkish men and women were lower, but still considerable—20 and 38 percent, respectively (Eldering 1997:338).

37 The boy was living in Rosengård, a suburb of Malmö in southern Sweden, with an immigrant population of about 80 percent.

38 And this pertains not just to the women but also to the children in many cases. One four-year old girl was terrified of putting foot on the grass at a birthday party to which my friend had invited her. She was accustomed to the ground beneath her feet being hard and flat—like the floor in the apartment in which she spent all her time.

39 Many of the men sell merchandise, which they transport from Norway to Africa in vans; being generally unemployed in Norway and living on social welfare, they make extra money in this manner. Surplus gains are invested in property in Africa, which requires work and attention, and also sometimes in plural marriages; so a man can be gone for a long time, and the wife in Norway is left to fend for herself.

40 Another limitation is economic. West African women are known to be successful traders and entrepreneurs. But activity of this kind requires complex skills. In the Norwegian context, by contrast, the income of most African married women derives from two sources—monthly child allowances and a maternity payment provided by the state. The former is credited to the woman's bank account, the latter is deposited as a lump sum at the birth of each child (see also p. 223). Since few women know how to use a bank or how to get to one, the husband often takes charge of his wife's bank card, and the money ends up in his pocket. So the maternity payment, a considerable sum intended to aid both mother and child, is sometimes used for other purposes, such as the bride-price for a new wife or the purchase of property in the homeland.

41 For an account of the judicial powers of the imams in relation to marriage and divorce, see Kayed (1999).

42 And not just in Norway, as it turns out. Here is an observation cited by Lewis (1994:114): "An Indian Barelwi imam, resident in Britain for some 15 years, recently provided an insider's perspective on his fellow imams active in Britain. He painted a bleak picture: 'The majority . . . lack a thorough knowledge of Islam. Their knowledge is limited to the sectarian parameters . . . [they] do not know anything about the context in which they are resident. They can neither speak the English language nor are they acquainted with the socio-political context of the dominant British culture' (Raza 1991:32–33)." Lewis also notes that of the 70 ulama (used as a hold-all to include all mosque personnel) in Bradford, England's most populous Muslim community, "only half a dozen have a good command of the English language. A major disincentive to learning English is insecurity—economic and contractual" (1994:122).

43 Recall a point made in chapter 5 that the immigration "stop" had the unintended macro effect of channeling immigrants into routes (asylum, family reunification) that are more costly for the European nations, giving grounds for opinions that they come "to exploit our welfare state" (Brochmann 1996:137).

44 By calling Aisha's parents "guilty parties," I do not mean to imply that they were not acting for what they saw as Aisha's own good.

45 Antiracism and Orientalism are not the only factors inhibiting intervention. Practices harmful to children often remain hidden in the private or domestic realm, and detecting them becomes the more difficult when parents harbor a deep distrust of state

agencies and regard it as shameful to disclose family problems to others. This does not pertain just to immigrant parents, but "culture" may exacerbate the problem.

46 In a report on judicial regulation of forced marriage commissioned by the Norwegian Ministry of Interior, Hennum and Paul (2000:xi) observe: "As of today, marriages conducted with the use of force are punishable under the *penal law* governing the use of force. We propose that this law be formulated in stronger, pedagogical language, in which 'forced marriage' is explicitly stated as being a punishable offence. Further, the responsibility for making a complaint and taking up the case ought to be taken away from the young people being forced and placed on the prosecuting authorities." A law against forced marriage was reinstituted on January 1, 1995, having been canceled two years previously, as it was no longer deemed relevant under (indigenous) Norwegian circumstances. The punishment for forcing someone to marry, or contributing to such action, is now three years in prison, or six years in very severe cases. However, the law also states that if the crime is committed against someone of the person's immediate family, the state will not file a charge.

47 Brubaker (1989:5) observes that we lack a developed political theory of dual or multiple citizenship. Works recently published, such as Kymlicka (1995) and Shachar (2000) significantly enhance our understanding of what has come to be called multicultural citizenship—viz., the rights and duties incumbent on different co-existing cultural (ethnic, religious) minorities within a nation-state.

48 Arranged marriage is a time-honored tradition in many societies, and it may work out very happily in many cases, as I have observed in my own longitudinal work in Egypt, Oman, and Bali, and as many others have testified to. The line between arranged marriage and forced marriage is sometimes difficult to draw, but a reasonable criterion of forced marriage is that the person is under severe pressure, mentally or physically, to marry against her or his will. Forced marriage has been documented to be widely practiced in many groups or societies, hence family reunification is not its only impetus. What I, and many others, argue is that family reunification reinforces or even aggravates the practice—in a world where love marriage is becoming increasingly common among the educated sectors of society.

49 My information here derives from two documentaries on forced marriage shown on the Norwegian channel TV2 in September 1999 (see Introduction, n. 13). In preparation for the series, twenty-eight girls of immigrant background in Norway were interviewed. Several appeared anonymously in the series, and only one under her full name.

50 These statistical findings were provided by Norwegian Statistical Bureau in response to a request from the TV series mentioned above.

51 By January 1996, about 20 percent of non-Western immigrants who were married had a Norwegian spouse. The differences among the various national minorities, however, were extreme. Whereas 86 percent of married Thais had a Norwegian spouse, only 2.7 percent of Pakistanis and 2.6 percent of Vietnamese did (Vassenden 1997:71–73).

52 Glazer (1997:128) observes: "Intermarriage may well be considered the last step in

assimilation . . . Intermarriage is so crucial a final step because it does more than mark the attraction between two individuals—it marks the highest degree of social acceptance."

53 Statistics on marital patterns among Indians and Pakistanis in Britain, for example, show only 5 percent of them being married outside their national group (Coleman 1994). Statistics from Norway show little change in intermarriage across national boundaries for the first- and second-generation immigrants of the largest groups. Among Pakistanis above thirty years of age, the percentage married to native Norwegians is 3.9 percent as against 2.3 percent for those younger. Among other groups Turks, for example—there is no registered change (Vassenden 1997:73).

54 In connection with the TV series on forced marriage, there were interviews, conducted by Tonje Steinsland, with several young men in "Little Norway" in Pakistan, the region in Punjab from which most immigrants to Norway come. The men made no secret of the fact that *visuni*—visa—was their word for a marriageable girl in Norway.

55 Gilded paper—*gullkantet papir*—is an expression used of marriageable Muslim girls among some immigrants in Norway.

56 Interestingly, in Sweden, unlike Denmark and Norway, forced marriage has not become a political issue (Bredal 1999). As there is little to indicate that the lives of young women of immigrant background are much different in Sweden, one must seek elsewhere for an explanation. My guess is that honor crime was the "diagnostic event" (Moore 1994) that triggered concern with young women's fates in Sweden, whereas in Denmark and Norway forced marriage played a similar role. Recall Sara's case versus those of Nasim and Nadia. Sweden is now seeing its concern corroborated (see n. 13, p. 247). On June 24, 1999, a nineteen-year-old girl, Hanah, was murdered in cold blood in Iraqi Kurdistan for having become "too Swedish." The culprits were two of her father's brothers. Witnesses were the mother and a younger sister, Sara, who managed to escape and get back to Sweden. In danger of her life, Sara reported the murder to the Swedish police, and stood as witness in court when her uncles were tried in December 2000. They had returned to Sweden, believing they were safe since the murdered girl's father had claimed responsibility for the crime and had received a nominal sentence in a Kurdish court. The uncles were sentenced to life imprisonment.

57 Polygamy is proscribed by Norwegian law, but the actual coexistence in Norway, as in most Western European nations, of two sets of law, one civic, the other Islamic Shari'ah, means that polygamy is easily practiced (Hennum and Paul 2000; on France, see Okin 1999). Even though Norwegian law is paramount in theory, respect for Islam coupled with sheer ignorance on the part of several European nations opens the way for polygamy and other illegalities. Norway is presently investigating the problem in order to try to combat it.

Three ministries (Justice, Interior, and Child and Family) have joined forces in this matter. But the problem is complex, and the best intentions may backfire. To illustrate: A mother is allowed to settle in Norway if her child's father is a Norwegian citizen. But this means that a man can bring in several wives if they bear his child. To combat the practice, the Ministry of Justice now wants to forbid the foreign wife to settle in

Norway if the husband is already married. But a new citizenship law, to be introduced shortly, will give the children of Norwegian fathers Norwegian citizenship. (Until now, citizenship at birth was conferred only if the mother was a Norwegian, if the parents were not married.) The father can automatically bring the child into the country, whereupon the mother can follow as a matter of course on family reunification. The government deplores the situation: "We did not think about the effect of the new law in regard to polygamy." The new regulation also fails to anticipate that the couple can divorce. Again, the mother will be admitted on family reunification. There is also concern in Norway that women might become victims in the battle against polygamy. It is important to secure their rights.

The Ministry of Child and Family Affairs has threatened to rescind the right of imams to contract marriages on the basis of extensive evidence that they permit, and in some cases even encourage, polygamous marriage (*Aftenposten,* July 24, 1999). (See also Kayed 1999.)

58 Being able to remarry a Muslim is important for women, since Islam, in the view of most Muslims, does not permit marriage for a female with a non-Muslim.

59 In Britain, in the district of West Yorkshire alone (as noted on page 249, n. 21), 742 cases have been registered in which Asian females ran away from their families and sought refuge because of threats of forced marriage. And the numbers are rising every year. Philip Balmforth, the Bradford area community officer of the West Yorkshire Police (who are in charge of handling such cases), observes: "Up until a few years ago when coroners began getting suspicious, we had a number of 'suicides,' where Asian girls who left home were said to have set themselves on fire. The families would all tell the same story: 'She had been sad, she was so depressed, we should have taken her to see a doctor.' In some cases, families have commissioned searches by bounty hunters, kidnappings and forced one-way trips to Pakistan. In extreme cases, the families have punished their daughters by beating them, throwing acid in their faces, and burning them to death." Balmforth also notes that girls who are forcibly taken to Pakistan, even if they are English-born, fall out of British jurisdiction once they are back in their parents' native land (*Herald Tribune,* October 20, 1997).

60 That males are also in need of help is evident from their use of the "crisis telephone" (*krisetelefon*) that was instituted in Oslo to help youths who feared forced marriage. One third of the calls in the year 2000 have come from males. Apparently, the problems of males with regard to forced marriage have been seriously underreported.

61 In her study of divorce among Muslim women in Norway, Kayed (1999) discovered that the three-year limit was a factor that sometimes led a husband to divorce his wife just before she would obtain permanent residence. In the case of battered women, Norway has, in some cases, extended permanent residence to the woman even if she was divorced before three years so that she would not be doubly disadvantaged.

62 Other European nations that do not accept dual citizenship include Sweden, Denmark, and Germany.

63 Hammar (1989:81) observes that "most legal experts and statesmen agree that dual citizenship should be avoided, and several international agreements have been concluded

to achieve this objective." Nonetheless, the number of persons holding dual or multiple citizenship has increased substantially in recent decades, and will probably continue to increase. The case for dual citizenship, generally argued by liberal intellectuals (many of whom are political scientists, political philosophers, and anthropologists) is that the prohibition of dual citizenship is one of the principal obstacles to naturalization among many permanent residents of Western societies today (see Carens 1989:47) and that citizenship is an inherently egalitarian ideal that implies full legal and political equality among citizens; hence naturalization of permanent residents should be facilitated.

64 In Sweden, with a population of roughly eight million, the number of dual citizens had been estimated as over 100,000 by 1989 (Hammar 1989:83). This is despite the fact that Sweden requires a person to relinquish his or her former citizenship upon acquiring Swedish citizenship. Similar conditions apply in Norway, Denmark, and Germany.

65 In the aftermath of Nadia's case, a member of Parliament raised the issue that failure to relinquish one's former citizenship should meet with sanctions. Nadia's case had made it clear that the formal requirement was a sleeping law: it was not being enforced. If the law is to work, there must be international agreement among nation-states. In the case of Nadia and of Aisha, their parents' formal relinquishment of their original citizenship would have meant little, as their native lands might claim them as ethnic citizens in any case.

66 It should be noted, however, that naturalization does lead members of *some* immigrant groups to vote. About 30 percent of Britons in Norway who acquire Norwegian citizenship use their votes, whereas Chileans with Norwegian citizenship virtually never vote (Kval 1997:200ff).

67 If a man has fathered children in Norway with a Norwegian citizen, he may seek, and sometimes obtains, exemption from deportation.

68 Hammar (1989) has coined the term "denizens" for privileged noncitizens. Brubaker concludes, on the basis of studies of six European countries, that "citizenship status is in fact relatively insignificant as a basis of access to social services . . . In the area of economic and social rights, . . . citizenship matters relatively little, while status as a permanent resident . . . matters a great deal" (1989:155, 160). "The main line of division in each of our countries, is not between citizens and non-citizens, but between denizens and other foreigners" (1989:27). Schuck (1989) speaks of the "devaluation of citizenship" as weakening democratic institutions, and yet it can be seen as an enlargement of liberal principles of inclusiveness and equality. "Ad hoc enlargement of immigrant rights may obstruct rather than clear the path to full membership" (Brubaker 1989:5).

References

Aardal, Bernt, and Henry Valen. 1995. *Konflikt og opinion*. Oslo: NKS-Forlaget.

Aase, Tor. 1992. *Punjabi Practices of Migration: Punjabi Life Projects in Pakistan and Norway.* Oslo: Scandinavian University Press.

Abu-Lughod, Lila. 1991. "Writing against Culture." In *Recapturing Anthropology: Working in the Present*, edited by R. G. Fox, 137–60. Santa Fe, NM: School of American Research Press.

Afkhami, Mahnaz. 1995. *Faith and Freedom: Women's Human Rights in the Muslim World.* Syracuse, NY: Syracuse University Press.

Al-Azm, Sadik. 1991. "The Importance of Being Earnest about Salman Rushdie." *Die Welt des Islams* (Leiden) 31:1–49.

————. 1995. *Mot hevdvunne sannheter.* Oslo: Cappelen.

al-Baldawi, Riyadh. 1994. *Exil, kultur och drogmissbruk.* SIMON (Sveriges invandrare mot narkotika). Stockholm: Allduply Offsettryck.

Alcalá, Jesús. 1997a. "Männen i familjen borde åtalas." *Dagens Nyheter*, February 7.

————. 1997b. "Inte ett mord, en avrättning." *Dagens Nyheter*, February 8.

al-Hibri, Azizah Y. 1999. "Is Western Patriarchal Feminism Good for Third World/ Minority Women?" In *Is Multiculturalism Bad for Women?* edited by Joshua Cohen, Matthew Howard, and Martha C. Nussbaum, 41–46. Princeton, NJ: Princeton University Press.

al-Kubaisi, Walid. 1996. *Min tro, din myte.* Oslo: Aventura.

Amersfoort, Hans van, and Rinus Penninx. 1994. "Regulating Migration in Europe: The Dutch Experience, 1960–92." *Annals of the American Academy of Political and Social Science* 534:133–46.

Andenæs, Kristian, and Nora Gotaas. 2000. *Kommunikasjon og rettssikkerhet: Utlendingers og språklige minoriteters møte med politi og domsstoler.* Oslo: Unipub.

Anderson-Levitt, Kathryn M. 1997. Editor's Preface. *Anthropology and Education* 28 (3): 315–17.

An-Naim, Abdullahi. 1999. "Promises We Should All Keep in Common Cause." In *Is Multicuturalism Bad for Women?* edited by Joshua Cohen, Matthew Howard, and Martha C. Nussbaum. Princeton, NJ: Princeton University Press.

Anwar, Mohammed. 1998. *Between Cultures: Continuities and Change in the Lives of Young Asians.* London: Routledge.

Appadurai, Arjun. 1985. "Gratitude as a Social Mode in South India." *Ethos* 13 (2): 237–45.

———. 1988. "Putting Hierarchy in Its Place." *Cultural Anthropology* 3:36–49.

Appiah, K. Anthony. 1994. "Identity, Authenticity, Survival: Multicultural Societies and Social Reproduction." In *Multiculturalism,* edited by Amy Gutman, 149–63. Princeton, NJ: Princeton University Press.

———. 1997. "The Multiculturalist Misunderstanding." *New York Review of Books,* October 9, pp. 30–36.

Aspelund, Grete. 1998. "Den handlende skolen." Master's thesis. Oslo: Institutt og museum for antropologi, Universitetet i Oslo.

Austin, J. L. 1975 [1962]. *How to Do Things with Words.* Cambridge, MA: Harvard University Press.

Barth, Fredrik. 1983. *Sohar: Culture and Society in an Omani Town.* Baltimore: Johns Hopkins University Press.

———. 1993. *Balinese Worlds.* Chicago: University of Chicago Press.

———. 1994a. "Enduring and Emerging Issues in the Analysis of Ethnicity." In *The Anthropology of Ethnicity: Beyond Ethnic Groups and Boundaries,* edited by H. Vermeulen and Cora Govers, 12–31. Amsterdam: Het Spinhuis.

———. 1994b. "A Personal View of Present Tasks and Priorities in Cultural and Social Anthropology." In *Assessing Cultural Anthropology,* edited by Robert Borofsky, 349–61. New York: McGraw-Hill.

———, ed. 1998. *Ethnic Groups and Boundaries: The Social Organization of Culture Difference.* Boston: Little, Brown, 1969. Reprint, Prospect Heights, IL: Waveland Press.

Baumann, Gerd. 1996. *Contesting Culture: Discourses of Identity in Multi-ethnic London.* New York: Cambridge University Press.

Baumann, Gerd, and Thijl Sunier, eds. 1995. *Post-migration Ethnicity: De-essentializing Cohesion, Commitments, and Comparison.* Amsterdam: Het Spinhuis.

Béji, Hélé. 1982. *Désenchantement national.* Paris: La Découverte.

Benjnouh, Lára Samira. 2001. "Å bare eller ikke bære: hijab, tro og tradisjon blant unge muslimske kvinner." Master's thesis. Oslo: Institutt for sosialantropologi, Universitetet is Oslo.

Bilgiç, Sükrü. 1993. "Fra ei ung utenlandsk jente til de norske sosialarbeidere." *Det nye Oslo,* pp. 6–14.

———. 2000. *Integering: Fra teori til praksis.* Oslo: Kulturbro forlag.

Birrell, Robert. 1994. "Immigration Control in Australia." *Annals of the American Academy of Political and Social Science* 534:106–17.

Bjertnæs, Marte Kristine. 2000. *Innvandring og innvandrere 2000.* Oslo/Kongsvinger: Statistical Analyses 33.

Bloch, Ernst. 1976. *Droit Naturel et dignité humaine.* Paris: Payot.

Bloch, Maurice. 1994. "Language, Anthropology, and Cognitive Science." In *Assessing Cultural Anthropology,* edited by Robert Borofsky, 276–83. New York: McGraw-Hill.

Blom, Celine H. 1998. "Jeg tenker norske tanker: Et studium av ungdom med migrasjonsbakgrunn i Oslo." Master's thesis. Oslo: Institutt og museum for antropologi, Universitetet i Oslo.

Blom, Svein. 1996. *Inn i samfunnet? Flyktningekull i arbeid, utdanning og på sosialhjelp.* Oslo/Kongsvinger: Statistical Analyses 5.

————. 1997. "Bokonsentrasjon blant innvandrere i Oslo." In *Tett eller spredt: Om innvandrernes bosettingsmønstre i Norge,* edited by Ottar Brox, 44–62. Oslo: Tano Aschehoug.

Blom, Svein, and Agnes Aall Ritland. 1997. "Levekår blant ikke-vestlige innvandrere." In *Innvandrere i Norge. Hvem er de, hva gjør de, og hvordan lever de?* edited by Kåre Vassenden. Oslo/Kongsvinger: Statistical Analyses 20.

Borofsky, Robert. 1994. "Introduction." In *Assessing Cultural Anthropology,* edited by Robert Borofsky, 1–28. New York: McGraw-Hill.

Bouras, Mohammed. 1998. *Islam i Norge.* Oslo: Milennium.

Bredal, Anja. 1998. *Arrangerte ekteskap og tvangsekteskap blant ungdom med innvandrerbakgrunn.* Oslo: Kompetansesenter for likestilling.

————. 1999. *Arrangerte ekteskap og tvangsekteskap i Norden.* TemaNord 604. København: Nordisk Ministerråd.

Briggs, Jack, and Zena Briggs. 1998. *Jack and Zena: A True Story of Love and Danger.* Leicester, UK: Ulverscroft.

Brochmann, Grete. 1996. *European Integration and Immigration from Third Countries.* Oslo: Scandinavian University Press.

Brox, Ottar. 1998. "Policy Implications of the Settlement Patterns of Immigrants: Some Norwegian Experiences and Viewpoints." In *OECD Proceedings: Immigrants, Integration and Cities; Exploring the Links.* Oslo: Norsk institutt for by og regionforskning.

Brubaker, William Rogers, ed. 1989. *Immigration and the Politics of Citizenship in Europe and North America.* Includes articles by editor: "Introduction," 1–27; "Citizenship and Naturalization: Policies and Politics," 99–128; "Membership without Citizenship: The Economic and Social Rights of Noncitizens," 145–62. Lanham, MD: University Press of America.

Cammaert, Marie-France. 1992. "Fighting for Success: Berber Girls in Higher Education." In "The Insertion of Allochthonous Youngsters in Belgian Society," edited by Eugeen Roosens, special issue, *Migration* 15:83–102.

Carens, Joseph H. 1987. "Aliens and Citizens: The Case for Open Borders." *Review of Politics* 49 (3): 251–73.

————. 1989. "Membership and Morality: Admission to Citizenship in Liberal Democratic States." In *Immigration and the Politics of Citizenship in Europe and North America,* edited by William Rogers Brubaker, 31–50. Lanham, MD: University Press of America.

Chambers, David L. 2000. "Civilizing the Natives: Marriage in Post-Apartheid South Africa." *Daedalus* 129 (4): 101–24.

Clifford, James. 1988. *The Predicament of Culture.* Cambridge, MA: Harvard University Press.

Cohen, Anthony P. 1994. *Self-Consciousness: An Alternative Anthropology of Identity.* London: Routledge.

Cohen, Joshua, Matthew Howard, and Martha C. Nussbaum. 1999. "Introduction: Feminism, Multiculturalism, and Human Equality." In *Is Multiculturalism Bad for Women?* edited by Joshua Cohen, Matthew Howard, and Martha C. Nussbaum, 3–5. Princeton, NJ: Princeton University Press.

Cohen-Almagor, Raphael. 1996. "Female Circumcision and Murder for Family Honour among Minorities in Israel." In *Nationalism, Minorities, and Diasporas: Identities and Rights in the Middle East,* edited by Kirsten E. Schulze and others, 171–87. London: Tauris.

Coleman, David A. 1994. "Trends in Fertility and Intermarriage among Immigrant Populations in Western Europe as Measures of Integration." *Journal of Biosocial Science* 26:107–36.

Cornelius, Wayne A. 1995. *California's Immigrant Children.* San Diego: Center for U.S.-Mexican Studies, University of California, San Diego.

Culpitt, Ian. 1992. *Welfare and Citizenship: Beyond the Crisis of the Welfare State?* London: Sage Publications.

Dahya, Badr. 1974. "The Nature of Pakistani Ethnicity in Industrial Cities in Britain." In *Urban Ethnicity,* edited by Abner Cohen, 77–118. London: Tavistock.

Das, Veena. 1990. "What Do We Mean by Health?" In *The Health Transitions: Social, Behavioral, and Cultural Developments,* edited by J. Caldwell and others. Canberra: Australian National University Press.

————. 1995. *Critical Events: An Anthropological Perspective on Contemporary India.* New Delhi: Oxford University Press.

de Vries, Marlene. 1990. *Roddel nader beschouwd.* Pub. no. 40. Leiden: COMT.

————. 1995. "The Changing Role of Gossip: Towards a New Identity? Turkish Girls in the Netherlands." In *Post-migration Ethnicity: De-essentializing Cohesion, Commitments, and Comparison,* edited by Gerd Baumann and Thijl Sunier, 36–56. Amsterdam: Het Spinhuis.

Dhahir, Omar. 1995. "Danmark kalder mig muslim." *Politiken,* June 14.

Djuve, Anne Britt. 1999. *Integrering: Etniske minoriteter og de nordiske velferdsstatene.* Oslo: FAFO-rapport 304.

Djuve, Anne Britt, and Kåre Hagen. 1995. *"Skaff meg en jobb!" Levekår blant flyktninger i Oslo.* Oslo: FAFO-rapport 184.

Djuve, Anne Britt, Kåre Hagen, and Torkel Bjørnskau. 1996. "Fra behov til budsjett." En evaluering av Oslo kommunes kriteriebaserte budsjettfordeling mellom bydelene. Oslo: FAFO-rapport 210.

Djuve, Anne Britt, and Hanne Cecilie Pettersen. 1997. *Virker tvang? Erfaringer med bruk av økonomiske sanksjoner i integreringsprogrammer for flyktninger.* Oslo: FAFO-rapport 234.

Drakulić, Slavenka. 1993. *The Balkan Express: Fragments from the Other Side of the War.* New York: W. W. Norton.

————. 1996. *Cafe Europa: Life after Communism.* New York: W. W. Norton.

Ebiri, Kutlay. 1985. "Impact of Labor Migration on the Turkish Economy." In *Guests Come to Stay: The Effects of European Labour Migration on Sending and Receiving Countries,* edited by Rosemarie Rogers, 207–30. Boulder, CO: Westview Press.

Eldering, Lotty. 1997. "Ethnic Minority Students in the Netherlands from a Cultural-Ecological Perspective." *Anthropology and Education* 28 (3): 330–50.

Ewing, Katherine Pratt. 2000. "Legislating Religious Freedom: Muslim Challenges to the Relationship between 'Church' and 'State' in Germany and France." *Daedalus* 129 (4): 31–54.

Fadiman, Anne. 1999. *The Spirit Catches You and You Fall Down: A Hmong Child, Her American Doctors, and the Collision of Two Cultures.* New York: Farrar, Straus and Giroux.

Fardon, Richard. 1990. *Localizing Strategies: Regional Tradition and Ethnographic Writing.* Edinburgh: Scottish Academic Press.

Favret-Saada, Jeanne. 1980. *Deadly Words: Witchcraft in the Bocage.* Cambridge: Cambridge University Press.

Finkielkraut, Alain. 1995. *The Defeat of the Mind.* New York: Columbia University Press.

Freeman, Gary P. 1994. "Can Liberal States Control Unwanted Migration?" *Annals of the American Academy of Political and Social Science* 534:17–30.

Frideres, James S. 1992. "Changing Dimensions of Ethnicity in Canada." In *Deconstructing a Nation: Immigration, Multiculturalism, and Racism in '90s Canada,* edited by Vic Satzewich, 47–68. Halifax, NS: Fernwood Publishing.

Friedman, Jonathan. 1999. "Rhinoceros II." *Current Anthropology* 40 (5): 679–94.

Fuglerud, Øyvind. 1999. *Life on the Outside: The Tamil Diaspora and Long-Distance Nationalism.* London: Pluto Press.

Gangdal, Jon. 1998. "Somaliere og irakere topper asylsøkerstatistikken i Oslo." *Oslo-politiets magasin,* no. 1, March.

Geertz, Clifford. 1968. *Islam Observed.* New Haven, CT: Yale University Press.

————. 1973. *The Interpretation of Cultures.* New York: Basic Books.

Gibson, Margaret A. 1997. "Exploring and Explaining the Variability: Cross-National Perspectives on the School Performance of Minority Students." *Anthropology and Education* 28 (3): 318–29.

Glazer, Nathan. 1997. *We Are All Multiculturalists Now.* Cambridge, MA: Harvard University Press.

Goffman, Erving. 1959. *The Presentation of Self in Everyday Life.* Garden City, NJ: Doubleday.

Greenfeld, Liah. 2000. "Democracy, Ethnic Diversity, and Nationalism." In *Nationalism and Internationalism in the Post Cold-War Era,* edited by Kjell Goldman, Ulf Hannerz, and Charles Westin, 25–36. London: Routledge.

Grünfeld, Berthold, and Kjell Noreik. 1991. "Uførepensjonering blant innvandrere i Oslo." *Tidsskrift for Norsk Lægeforening* 111 (9): 1147–50.

Haarder, Bertel. 1997. *Den bløde kynisme: og selvbedraget i Tornerose-Danmark.* Copenhagen: Gyldendal.

Hagen, Kåre. 1997. *Innvandrere og sosialhjelp: Kunnskapsstatus og utfordringer for videre forskning.* Oslo: FAFO-notat 7.

Hammar, Tomas. 1989. "State, Nation, and Dual Citizenship." In *Immigration and the Politics of Citizenship in Europe and North America,* edited by William Rogers Brubaker, 81–95. Lanham, MD: University Press of America.

Harris, Nigel. 1995. *The New Untouchables: Immigration and the New World Worker.* London: I. B. Tauris.

Heide-Jørgensen, Vibeke. 1996. *Allahs piger.8 innvandrerpiger fortæller om livet og kærligheden.* Copenhagen: Aschehoug.

Hennum, Ragnhild, and Rachel Paul. 2000. *Rettslig regulering av tvangsekteskap og bigami.* Oslo: Institutt for kriminologi, Universitetet i Oslo.

Hirschman, Charles. 1996. "Studying Immigrant Adaptation from the 1990 Population Census: From Generational Comparison to the Process of 'Becoming American.'" In *The New Second Generation,* edited by Alejandro Portes, 54–81. New York: Russell Sage Foundation.

Hjärpe, Jan. 1997. "Kan kultur och religion orsaka mord?" *Göteborgposten*, February 16.

Hobsbawm, Eric. 1993. "The New Threat to History." *New York Review of Books*, December 16, pp. 62–64.

Hoffmann-Nowotny, Hans-Joachim. 1985. "The Second Generation of Immigrants: A Sociological Analysis with Special Emphasis on Switzerland." In *Guests Come to Stay: The Effects of European Labour Migration on Sending and Receiving Countries*, edited by Rosemarie Rogers, 109–34. Boulder, CO: Westview Press.

Hovland, Arild. 1996. *Moderne urfolk: Samisk ungdom i bevegelse*. Oslo: Cappelen Akademisk Forlag.

Ibrahim, Youssef M. 1995. "Europe's Muslim Population: Frustrated, Poor, and Divided." *New York Times*, May 5.

Ignatieff, Michael. 1999. *Whose Universal Values? The Crisis in Human Rights*. Praemium Erasmianum Essay. The Hague: Foundation Horizon.

Ingold, Tim. 1993. "The Art of Translation in a Continuous World." In *Beyond Boundaries: Understanding, Translation, and Anthropological Discourse*, edited by Gisli Pálsson, 210–30. Oxford: Berg Publishers.

Jehl, Douglas. 1999. "Arab Honor's Price: A Woman's Blood." *New York Times*, June 20.

Jensen, Leif, and Yoshimi Chitose. 1996. "Today's Second Generation: Evidence from the 1990 Census." In *The New Second Generation*, edited by Alejandro Portes, 82–107. New York: Russell Sage Foundation.

Johansen, Christine. 1999. "En studie av motkultur i en mekanikerklasse på yrkesskolen." Master's thesis. Oslo: Institutt og museum for antropologi, Universitetet i Oslo.

Kahn, J. 1989. "Culture: Demise or Resurrection?" *Critique of Anthropology* 9 (2): 5–25.

Karim, Nasim. 1996. *Izzat: For ærens skyld*. Oslo: Cappelen.

Kayed, Camilla. 1999. "Rett, religion og byråkrati: En studie av skilmisse blant muslimer i Norge." Master's thesis. Oslo: Institutt og museum for antropologi, Universitetet i Oslo.

Keesing, Roger. 1989. "Exotic Readings of Cultural Texts." *Current Anthropology* 30 (4): 459–69.

———. 1994. "Theories of Culture Revisited." In *Assessing Cultural Anthropology*, edited by Robert Borofsky, 301–12. New York: McGraw-Hill.

Kerep, Laila. 1995. "Jeg kommer fra Konya." *Politiken*, October 15.

Kermode, Frank. 1966. *The Sense of an Ending: Studies in the Theory of Fiction*. London: Oxford University Press.

Keynan, Hassan. 1995. "Somalia: The Great Escape." *UNESCO Courier*, September 28–30.

Khader, Naser. 2000. *khader. dk: sammenførte erindringer*. Copenhagen: Aschehoug.

Kleinman, Arthur. 1998. "Experience and Its Moral Modes: Culture, Human Conditions, and Disorder." In *The Tanner Lectures on Human Values*, vol. 20, edited by Grethe B. Peterson. Salt Lake City: University of Utah Press.

Knudsen, Anne. 1994. "Forvandlede kroppe." *Kvinder, Køn & Forskning*, no. 2.

Knudsen, Jon. 1988. *Vietnamese Survivors: Processes Involved in Refugee Coping and Adaptation*. Bergen: Department of Social Anthropology, University of Bergen.

———. 1992. "Ensomhet og anonym trygghet: Vietnamesiske ungdommer i Norge." In *Unge flyktninger i Norge*. Oslo: Kommuneforlaget.

Kottak, Conrad Philip. 1991. *Anthropology: The Encyclopedia of Human Diversity.* 5th ed. New York: McGraw-Hill.

Kroeber, A. L., and Clyde Kluckhohn. 1963. *Culture: A Critical Review of Concepts and Definitions.* New York: Random House.

Kumar, Loveleen. 1997. *Mulighetenes barn: å vokse opp med to kulturer.* Oslo: Cappelen.

Kuper, Adam. 1999. *Culture: The Anthropologists' Account.* Cambridge, MA: Harvard University Press.

Kval, Karl-Eirik. 1997. "Valgdeltagelse og stemmegivning." In *Innvandrere i Norge. Hvem er de, hva gjør de, og hvordan lever de?* edited by Kåre Vassenden, 37–91. Oslo/Kongsvinger: Statistical Analyses 20.

Kymlicka, Will. 1995. *Multicultural Citizenship.* Oxford: Clarendon Press.

Lavelle, Robert, ed. 1995. *America's New War on Poverty: A Reader for Action.* San Francisco: KQED Books.

Leach, Edmund. 1969. *Genesis as Myth and Other Essays.* London: Cape.

Lewis, Philip. 1994. *Islamic Britain: Religion and Identity among British Muslims.* London: I. B. Tauris.

Lien, Inger Lise. 1997. *Ordet som stempler djevlene: holdninger blant pakistanere og nordmenn.* Oslo: Aventura.

Lindo, Flip. 1995. "Ethnic Myth or Ethnic Might? On the Divergence in Educational Attainment between Portuguese and Turkish Youth in the Netherlands." In *Post-migration Ethnicity: De-essentializing Cohesion, Commitments, and Comparison,* edited by Gerd Baumann and Thijl Sunier, 144–64. Amsterdam: Het Spinhuis.

Lönnaeus, Olle. 1997. "När hedern är viktigare än lagen." *Sydsvenskan,* February 11.

Lund, Marianne. 1998. "Fremmed i skolen? En studie av minoritetsspråklige elevers faglige og sosiale situasjon på en norsk skole." Master's thesis. Oslo: Institutt og museum for antropologi, Universitetet i Oslo.

Lundgren, Eva, and Åsa Elden. 1997. "Voldsbrått mot kvinnor er inte något exotiskt." *Svenska Dagbladet,* January 21.

Maalouf, Amin. 1998. *Identitet som dreper.* Oslo: Pax.

———. 2000. Lecture, Faculty of Humanities, University of Oslo, October 18.

Mandel, Ruth. 1996. "A Place of Their Own: Contesting Spaces and Defining Places in Berlin's Migrant Community." In *Making Muslim Space in North America and Europe,* edited by Barbara Metcalf, 147–66. Berkeley and Los Angeles: University of California Press.

Mattingly, Cheryl. 1998. *Healing Dramas and Clinical Plots: The Narrative Structure of Experience.* Cambridge: Cambridge University Press.

McHugh, Ernestine Louise. 1989. "Concept of the Person among the Gurungs of Nepal." *American Ethnologist* 16 (1): 75–86.

Mehrländer, Ursula. 1985. "Second-Generation Migrants in the Federal Republic of Germany." In *Guests Come to Stay: The Effects of European Labour Migration on Sending and Receiving Countries,* edited by Rosemarie Rogers, 135–58. Boulder, CO: Westview Press.

Mernissi, Fatima. 1991. *The Veil and the Male Elite.* Reading, MA: Addison-Wesley.

———. 1996. *Women's Rebellion and Islamic Memory.* London: Zed Press.

Michaels, Walter Benn. 1995. *Our America: Nativism, Modernism, and Pluralism.* Durham, NC: Duke University Press.

Mikaelsen, Gro. 1998. "Lagspill og andre samspill—et studie av idrett som verktøy for integrasjon blant ungdommer med ulik sosial og kulturell bakgrunn." Master's thesis. Oslo: Institutt og museum for antropologi, Universitetet i Oslo.

Miles, Robert. 1992. "Migration, Racism, and the Nation-State in Contemporary Europe." In *Deconstructing a Nation: Immigration, Multiculturalism, and Racism in '90s Canada*, edited by Vic Satzewich, 21–46. Halifax, NS: Fernwood Publishing.

Moore, Sally. 1994. "The Ethnography of the Present and the Analysis of Process." In *Assessing Cultural Anthropology*, edited by Robert Borofsky, 362–74. New York: McGraw-Hill.

Mørck, Yvonne. 1996. "Køn, kulturel loyalitet og multikulturalisme: Perspektiver på etnisk minoritetsungdom." Doctoral thesis. University of Copenhagen.

Nader, Laura, 1988. "Post-interpretive Anthropology." *Anthropological Quarterly* 61 (4): 149–59.

NOU (Norges Offentlige Utredninger). 1987. *Flyktningers tilpasninger til det norske samfunn.* Oslo, no. 8.

Nussbaum, Martha C. 1999. "A Plea for Difficulty." In *Is Multiculturalism Bad for Women?* edited by Joshua Cohen, Matthew Howard, and Martha C. Nussbaum, 105–14. Princeton, NJ: Princeton University Press.

————. 2000. *Women and Human Development: The Capabilities Approach.* Cambridge: Cambridge University Press.

Obeyesekere, Gananath. 1990. *The Work of Culture: Symbolic Transformation in Psychoanalysis and Anthropology.* Chicago: University of Chicago Press.

Okin, Susan Moller. 1999. "Is Multiculturalism Bad for Women?" In *Is Multiculturalism Bad for Women?* edited by Joshua Cohen, Matthew Howard, and Martha C. Nussbaum, 9–24. Princeton, NJ: Princeton University Press.

Østby, Ingvild. 2000. "Avdeling Stjernen: En studie av barn med ulik kulturell bakgrunn i en norsk kommunal barnehage." Master's thesis. Oslo: Institutt for sosialantropologi, Universitet i Oslo.

Parekh, Bikhu. 1999. "A Varied Moral World." In *Is Multiculturalism Bad for Women?* edited by Joshua Cohen, Matthew Howard, and Martha C. Nussbaum, 69–75. Princeton, NJ: Princeton University Press.

Paul, Robert A. 1990. "What Does Anybody Want? Desire, Purpose, and the Acting Subject in the Study of Culture." *Cultural Anthropology* 5 (4): 431–51.

Portes, Alejandro, and Rubén G. Rumbaut. 1996. *Immigrant America: A Portrait.* Berkeley and Los Angeles: University of California Press.

Portes, Alejandro, and Richard Schauffler. 1996. "Language and the Second Generation: Bilingualism Yesterday and Today." In *The New Second Generation*, edited by Alejandro Portes, 8–29. New York: Russell Sage Foundation.

Rawls, John. 1971. *A Theory of Justice.* Cambridge, MA: Harvard University Press.

Raza, Mohammad S. 1991. *Islam in Britain: Past, Present, and the Future.* Leicester, UK: Volcano.

Rogers, Rosemarie. 1985. "Post–World War II European Labor Migration: An Introduction to the Issues." In *Guests Come to Stay: The Effects of European Labor Migration on Sending and Receiving Countries*, edited by Rosemarie Rogers, 1–28. Boulder, CO: Westview Press.

Rosaldo, Renato. 1989. *Culture and Truth.* Boston: Beacon Press.

Said, Edward W. 1978. *Orientalism.* London: Routledge.

————. 1981. *Covering Islam.* London: Routledge.

Salimi, Khalid. 1994. "Anti-rasisme er arbeid for individets rettigheter." *Dagbladet,* October 3.

Sam, David Lackland. 1991. *Tilpasning av innvandrere: En psykososial undersøkelse blant unge innvandrere i Norge.* Bergen: Hemilrapport, no. 2.

Sandrup, Therese. 1998. "Sin mors datter—et studie av tyrkiske og pakistanske jenter og kvinner i en norsk drabantby." Master's thesis. Oslo: Institutt og museum for antropologi, Universitetet i Oslo.

Satzewich, Vic, ed. 1992. *Deconstructing a Nation: Immigration, Multiculturalism, and Racism in '90s Canada.* Halifax, NS: Fernwood Publishing.

Scott, James. 1985. "History According to Winners and Losers." *Senri Ethnological Studies* (Osaka) 13:161–210.

Sen, Amartya. 1990. "Individual Freedom as a Social Commitment." *New York Review of Books,* June 14, pp. 49–52.

————. 1999. *Development as Freedom.* Oxford: Oxford University Press.

Shaaban, Bouthaina. 1991. *Both Right and Left Handed: Arab Women Talk about Their Lives.* Bloomington: Indiana University Press.

Shachar, Ayelet. 2000. "Positioning Rights in a Multicultural World: On Citizenship and Multicultural Vulnerability." *Political Theory* 28 (1): 64–89.

Shore, Bradd. 1996. *Culture in Mind: Cognition, Culture, and the Problem of Meaning.* Oxford: Oxford University Press.

Schuck, Peter H. 1989. "Membership in the Liberal Polity: The Devaluation of American Citizenship." In *Immigration and the Politics of Citizenship in Europe and North America,* edited by William Rogers Brubaker, 51–66. Lanham, MD: University Press of America.

Shweder, Richard A. 1998. "The Free Exercise Project: Multiculturalism and the Law." *Anthropology Newsletter* 39 (9): 45–46.

Sørlie, S. 1994. "Innvandrere og flyttemønsteret." *Regionale trender,* no. 1. Oslo: Norsk institutt for by- og regionforskning.

————. 1997. "Hvor bosetter innvandrere seg?" *Regionale trender,* no. 1. Oslo: Norsk institutt for by- og regionforskning.

SOU (Statens Offentliga Utredningar). 1996. *Vägar in i Sverige.* Bilaga til Innvandrarpolitiska kommittéens slutbetänkande. Stockholm: SOU no. 55, Arbetsmarknadsdepartementet.

Spiro, Melford. 1993. "Is the Western Conception of 'Self' Peculiar within the Context of the World Cultures?" *Ethos* 21 (2): 107–53.

Stafford, James. 1992. "The Impact of the New Immigration Policy on Racism in Canada." In *Deconstructing a Nation: Immigration, Multiculturalism, and Racism in '90s Canada,* edited by Vic Satzewich, 69–92. Halifax, NS: Fernwood Publishing.

Star, Alexander. 1997. "Don't Look Back: A Proposal for Our Roots-Obsessed Culture." *New Yorker,* February 3, pp. 81–83.

Stewart, Frank. 1994. *Honor.* Chicago: University of Chicago Press.

Stoller, Robert J. 1968. *Sex and Gender.* London: Hogarth.

Storhaug, Hege. 1996. *Mashallah: en reise blant kvinner i Pakistan.* Oslo: Aschehoug.

REFERENCES

————. 1998. *Hellig tvang: unge norske muslimer om kjærlighet og ekteskap.* Oslo: Aschehoug.

————. 2000. "Innvandringen kom helt naturlig." *Dagbladet,* September 27.

Stortingsmelding. 1987–88. Om innvandringspolitikken. Oslo: Kommunaldepartementet, no. 39.

————. 1996–97. Om innvandringen og det flerkulturelle Norge. Oslo: Kommunaldepartementet, no. 17.

Strauss, Claudia, and Naomi Quinn. 1994. "A Cognitive/Cultural Anthropology." In *Assessing Cultural Anthropology,* edited by Robert Borofsky, 284–98. New York: McGraw-Hill

Suárez-Orozco, Carola. 2000. "Identities under Siege: Immigration Stress and Social Mirroring among the Children of Immigrants." In *Cultures under Siege: Violence and Trauma in Interdisciplinary Perspective,* edited by Anthony Robben and Marcelo Suárez-Orozco. New York: Cambridge University Press.

Suárez-Orozco, Marcelo M. 2000. "Everything You Ever Wanted to Know about Assimilation, but Were Afraid to Ask." *Daedalus* 129 (4): 1–30.

Suhrke, Astrid. 1996. Foreword. In Grete Brochmann, *European Integration and Immigration from Third Countries.* Oslo: Scandinavian University Press.

Sunier, Thijl. 1995. "Disconnecting Religion and Ethnicity: Young Turkish Muslims in the Netherlands." In *Post-migration Ethnicity: De-essentializing Cohesion, Commitments, and Comparison,* edited by Gerd Baumann and Thijl Sunier, 58–76. Amsterdam: Het Spinhuis.

Tamir, Yael. 1999. "Siding with the Underdogs." In *Is Multiculturalism Bad for Women?* edited by Joshua Cohen, Matthew Howard, and Martha C. Nussbaum, 47–52. Princeton, NJ: Princeton University Press.

Vassenden, Kåre. 1997. "Innvandrerbefolkningens demografi." In *Innvandrere i Norge. Hvem er de, hva gjør de, og hvordan lever de?* edited by Kåre Vassenden, 37–91. Oslo/Kongsvinger: Statistical Analyses 20.

Viorst, Milton. 1996. "The Muslims of France." *Foreign Affairs* 75:81.

Vogt, Kari. 1996. *Kommet for å bli: Islam i Vest-Europa.* Oslo: Cappelen.

————. 2000. *Islam på norsk.* Oslo: Cappelen.

Walzer, Michael. 1997. *On Toleration.* New Haven, CT: Yale University Press.

Wierzbicka, Anna. 1993. "A Conceptual Basis for Cross-Cultural Psychology." *Ethos* 21 (2): 205–31.

Wikan, Unni. 1980. *Life among the Poor in Cairo.* London: Tavistock.

————. 1983. *Imorgen, hvis Gud vil—kvinneliv i Cairos bakgater.* Oslo: Norwegian University Press.

————. 1990. *Managing Turbulent Hearts: A Balinese Formula for Living.* Chicago: University of Chicago Press.

————. 1991a [1982]. *Behind the Veil in Arabia: Women in Oman.* Chicago: University of Chicago Press.

————. 1991b. *The Girl Child in Bhutan.* Thimphu: UNICEF.

————. 1992. "Beyond the Words: The Power of Resonance." *American Ethnologist* 19 (3): 460–82.

————. 1994a. "Local Communities, Aid Ideology, and the Bhutanese State." In *State and Locality,* edited by Mette Mast, Thomas Hylland Eriksen, and Jo Helle-Valle, 41–70. Oslo: Norwegian Association for Development Research.

————. 1994b. "Folk—ikke kulturer—kan møtes." In *Velferdssamfunnets barn,* edited by Tordis Dalland Evans, Ivar Frønes, and Lise Kjølsrød, 125–32. Oslo: ad Notam Gyldendal.

———. 1995a. *Mot en ny norsk underklasse: innvandrere, kultur og integrasjon.* Oslo: Gyldendal.

———. 1995b. "Sustainable Development in the Mega-City: Can the Concept Be Made Applicable?" *Current Anthropology* 36 (4): 635–54.

———. 1996a. *Tomorrow, God Willing: Self-Made Destinies in Cairo.* Chicago: University of Chicago Press.

———. 1996b. "Vårt grunnleggende menneskesyn." *Dagbladet,* September 16.

———. 1997. "Nadia—og debatten som bør følge." *Verdens Gang,* December 22.

———. 2000a. "Citizenship on Trial: Nadia's Case." *Daedalus* 129 (4): 55–76.

———. 2000b. "Kampen mot barneranerne." *Aftenposten,* March 20.

Wolf, Eric. 1994. "Perilous Ideas: Race, Culture, and People." *Current Anthropology* 20 (2): 10–15.

Wrede-Holm, Vivien. 2000. "Multikulturalisme som likhet og ulikhet: En studie fra Australia." Master's thesis. Oslo: Institutt for sosialantropologi, Universitetet i Oslo.

Yalcin-Heckmann, Lale. 1995. "The Predicament of Mixing 'Culture' and 'Religion': Turkish and Muslim Commitments in Post-migration Germany." In *Post-migration Ethnicity: De-essentializing Cohesion, Commitments, and Comparison,* edited by Gerd Baumann and Thijl Sunier, 78–98. Amsterdam: Het Spinhuis.

Zhou, Min. 1997. "Growing Up American: The Challenge Confronting Immigrant Children and Children of Immigrants." *Annual Review of Sociology* 23:63–95.

232n. 7; powerlessness of, 8–9, 27–28, 84; protecting rights of, 22, 213–14, 220; sacrificed for culture, 24–28, 69–71; social contract and, 197; social welfare use and, 47–48; violence against, 69–70, 158. *See also* family reunification; schools; violence against women; youth; *specific cases*

child's best interest: autonomy in, 158; complexities of, 125; as defense in trial, 178; ignored in action plan, 5; as key, 8–9; misapplication of, 100, 120; sacrificed in name of culture, 24–28, 69–71; sojourning as counter to, 194–95

child welfare authorities: complicity of, 22–23, 71–72, 94–95, 208–9; criticism of, 70, 112–14, 226–28; difficulties facing, 100–101, 213; distrust of, 230n. 1; immigrant men favored by, 207–8; placements by, 20, 27, 94, 100, 183. *See also* social workers

Chileans: educational issues and, 241n. 68; employment of, 58, 133; number of, 35; voting of, 264n. 66

Christian Democratic government, immigrant policy under, 40

Christianity: as culprit, 99–101, 103, 106; curriculum issues and, 158–59, 253–54n. 17; on marriage, 104; on violence against women, 248n. 18. *See also* Anna (Christian of Syrian descent)

Citanović, Mladen, 45, 103–4

citizenship: in Aisha's case, 24, 217, 220; benefits of, 219, 264n. 68; civic type of, 169–70, 190–92, 194–95; devaluation of, 264n. 68; dual type of, 173–74, 213, 214, 217–18, 261n. 47, 263–64nn. 63–65; ethnic type of, 160–68; gaining Norwegian, 217–18, 262–63n. 57; giving up foreign, 218, 264n. 65; language's role in, 198–99; legal age and, 211–12; in Nadia's case, 173, 190–94, 205–6, 217–19, 220, 264n. 65; protecting children's rights and, 213–14; reconsideration of, 220;

sacrificed to culture, 27–28; as social contract, 195–97, 204–5, 217–18, 220

clientification, concept of, 236n. 35

Clifford, James, 76

coercion, implicit in social contract, 197

Cohen, Joshua, 251n. 3

collectivity: choices in, 142; education devalued in, 143–44; as identity component, 159; individuality subsumed by, 117–19, 142–45, 147–48, 209–10. *See also* communities; traditions and customs

"colorful community" (*fargerike fellesskap*): components of, 209–10; educational issues and, 51; institutional framework for, 197; "traitors" to, 145; use of term, 6, 25. *See also* multicultural society

communism, individuality under, 118–19, 120, 147

communities: individuals juxtaposed to, 161; segregation of, 51, 238nn. 52–53. *See also* collectivity; "colorful community" (*fargerike fellesskap*); multicultural society; urban areas

conflicts of interest, approach to, 210–11, 213

Conservative Party, 202, 242n. 77

Cortes, Enrico C., Jr., 229n. 7

countryman, use of term, 162–63

crime: forced marriage as, 107, 168, 212, 249n. 24, 261n. 46; ghetto-Islam and, 255–56n. 28; increase in, 239n. 57; kidnapping as, 177–89, 256n. 9; participants in, 53; relative guilt in, 188. *See also* violence; violence against women; *specific stories*

Croatia, nationhood in, 165

cult of time-honored beliefs, origins of, 141

cultural cafés, 132

cultural pluralism: challenge of, 82–83; dangers of, 144–45; definition of, 31–32; documents on, 73–74. *See also* identity politics; multicultural society

cultural relativism: discussion of, 79–88; use of term, 146

cultural values, use of term, 86

culture: agency absent in, 83–84, 87; categorization by single, 72–73; children's sacrifice in, 24–28, 69–71; custodians of, 150; as defense for betrayal, 121–23, 145, 220; as defense for violence, 79–80, 83, 95–98, 107; definitions of, 34, 75–78, 80–83, 85–87, 245n. 15; education vs., 143–44; equality and, 27–28, 72, 121–23; foster placements and, 20; human rights and, 12, 27–28, 73–74, 128–29; in immigration debate, 45–46; law's preeminence over, 70–71, 73–74, 191–92; as lens for experience, 84–85; masking implicit in, 155–60; meeting/collision of, 83, 84, 87, 113, 145; as obstacle, 75–77; parents and government in complicity with, 5–6; politics of, 25–27, 63; as process, 77–78; as race, 37, 81–83, 113, 144–45; reconsideration of, 77–79, 87–88; religion's link to, 106; respect and, 63, 77–78, 145–46; role in identity politics, 25–27, 154–55; as sacrosanct, 147; society vs., 154–55; sojourning's role in maintaining, 194–95; speaking out against, 120; stagnation of, 252n. 9; as taboo subject, 59; value of work in, 58, 62–63, 241n. 74; *Volksgeist* linked to, 140–41; as way of distributing pain, 28. *See also* family honor and shame; identity politics; traditions and customs

customs. *See* traditions and customs

Dagbladet (newspaper), 8, 192, 249n. 23
Dagens Nyheter (newspaper), 95, 245n. 1
Dahrendorf, Ralf, 210
Danes, number of, 35. *See also* Denmark
Danish language, 201
Das, Veena, 28, 120, 150
Declaration of the Rights of Man, 141, 161
decolonization, cultures and, 140–41. *See also* identity politics
democracy: definition of, 168–69;

prerequisites for, 210–11. *See also* citizenship; liberal democracy

denizens, use of term, 264n. 68

Denmark: asylum seekers in, 36, 41, 239n. 57; DNA testing of immigrant children in, 250n. 5; dual citizenship not recognized by, 263n. 62, 264n. 64; equality in, 231n. 5 (pt. 2); family estrangement in, 104–5; family reunification in, 216; "ghetto-Islam" in, 255–56n. 28; Muslims as perceived in, 255n. 26; right to vote in, 231n. 8; runaways in, 209; segregated communities in, 238n. 53; unemployment in, 49, 239–40n. 62, 250n. 8

de Vries, Marlene, 59, 247–48nn. 14, 15

Dhahir, Omar, 166

difference: among Muslims, 255n. 26; among Pakistanis, 32–33, 241n. 73; cultural, 82, 86–88, 141, 144–45, 209–10; definition of, 164; discourse on, 160; in employment, 34, 58, 237n. 45; individual, 141; respect for, 82–83, 84; in settlement decisions, 38–39, 234n. 19, 236n. 37. *See also* diversity; ethnic minorities

Digernes, Leidulv, 186, 187, 258n. 24

Dimitrijević, Saša, 234–35n. 27

disability pensions, 48, 49, 237n. 46, 238n. 47. *See also* Nadia's case

discrimination: accusations of, 242n. 77; among immigrant groups, 196; against immigrants, 241n. 69; increase in, 232n. 10; as risk, 2

"distant-cultural" (*fjernkulturell*), use of term, 37

diversity: dangers of, 144–45; ethnic type of, 160–65. *See also* difference; ethnic minorities

divorce, 200, 216–17, 263n. 61

Djuve, Anne Britt, 59, 237n. 40, 239–40n. 62

Drakulić, Slavenka: on ethnicity, 165, 169; on first-person plural, 117–19, 120,

142; on identity politics, 153–54; on
individuality, 142, 147; as influence, 13
Drammen: "ghetto" problems in, 39,
234n. 22; language issues in, 238n. 51
drug abuse, 21, 53, 238n. 55

East Europeans: crime and, 239n. 57;
unemployment of, 48. *See also specific
groups*
Ebiri, Kutlay, 244–45n. 12
education: absence of, 57, 241n. 70;
"bilingual," 124–25, 126; culture vs.,
143–44; desire for, 49–50, 102; need
for, 64; in social contract, 197. *See also*
schools
Egypt: arranged marriage in, 261n. 48;
blame shifting in, 257n. 13; "people's
talk" in, 252n. 8
Eidsvåg, Inge, 160
Elden, Åsa, 247n. 10
Eldering, Lotty, 238nn. 47, 49, 242n. 75
elections: immigration debate preceding,
44–46; participation in, 259n. 34, 264n.
66; right to vote, 28, 199, 219, 231n. 8
employment: differences by ethnic group,
34, 58, 237n. 45; discrimination against
immigrants in, 241n. 69; in informal
economy, 131; as key component,
64–65; social wefare vs., 55, 239n. 61;
Trondheim study of, 43–44. *See also*
unemployment; work (as concept)
Employment Disability Act, 49, 238n. 47
English language, 124, 201
enlightened moment, use of term, 154
equality: belief in, 25, 35, 45, 58, 64; culture
and, 27–28, 72, 121–23; as immigration
policy goal, 70–71; Islam on, 156–57,
207–8, 253n. 13; moving around on
welfare and, 240n. 66; prerequisites for,
210–11
essentialism, shortcomings of, 72–73
Ethiopian, as asylum seeker, 235n. 30
ethnicity: construction of, 163–67, 215–16;
diversity in, 160–65; statistics on, 32–33
ethnic minorities: cultural politics
and, 25–27, 63; differences among,

59; differences within, 241n. 73;
employment differences among, 34,
58, 237n. 45; foster placements and,
20, 27, 230n. 1; numbers of, 34–35;
official recognition of, 33; settlement
differences among, 38–39, 234n. 19,
236n. 37; status of, 48. *See also* culture;
identity politics
ethnic Muslim, use of term, 232nn. 9–10
ethnic nationalism, concept of, 169–70
ethnic underclass. *See* underclass
European Association of Somali Studies,
251n. 9
European Union: appeal of, 159–60;
asylum-seeking conventions in, 40;
marginalization of immigrants in, 60;
return to homeland myth in, 65–66,
243n. 81
European Union International Center on
Migration Policy, 235n. 29
experience, as replacement for culture, 86
expert witness, neutrality of, 177, 187, 257n.
10
Expressen (newspaper), Anna's story in, 100

family honor and shame: as defense for
killing, 92–93, 95–97; forced marriage
linked to, 108–14; girls' oppression due
to, 99–107; as legal category, 247nn.
11–12; in Nadia's case, 181–82, 184,
206; politics of fear and, 150; privacy
and, 260–61n. 45; as public face, 156;
virginity as necessity in, 102–3, 248n.
19, 257n. 14
family reunification: in Aisha's case, 20,
22, 221–24, 226, 227–28; changes in (for
Kurds), 235–36n. 31; DNA testing and,
250n. 5; forced marriage reinforced
in, 42, 216–17, 261n. 48; illegalities
in, 152–53; law on, 216, 224; Nadia's
case and, 186, 188, 206; and polygamy,
262–63n. 57; reconsideration of,
214–16; requirements for, 240n. 63;
visas attained through, 215–16
fatwa, 107, 151
Favret-Saada, Jeanne, 25

fear: of abuse and death, 103, 222; politics of, 148–60; of racism, 61, 121–23; silence enforced by, 6, 25

feminization, of social work, 209–10

fine arts, culture linked to, 85

Finkielkraut, Alain: on Europe's appeal, 159; on identity, 26; on identity politics, 139–41, 153–54; on individuality, 142, 143; as influence, 13; on multiculturalism, 146, 147–48; on race as culture, 144–45; on rights, 129

Finland, Somalis in, 251n. 9

Fleisher, Gerd, 248–49n. 20

Florida, languages in, 231n. 3

"foreign-cultural" (*fremmedkulturell*), use of term, 37

foreigner (*utlending*), use of term, 38

France: immigration halted in, 39; religious identity in, 166; unemployment in, 239–40n. 62; veiling in, 156, 253n. 12

freedom: absent in identity politics, 141–42; beliefs in, 21, 98, 210–11; constraints on, 75, 197–98, 201, 206, 213, 218; gender issues in, 94, 146, 201; as immigration policy goal, 70–71; possibilities for, 168

Freeman, Gary P., 39–40

Fremskrittspartiet. See Progress Party (*Fremskrittspartiet*)

Frideres, James S., 232n. 10

"From a Young Foreign Girl to the Norwegian Social Workers" (Bilgiç), 80, 120–23

Fuglerud, Øyvind, 41, 55, 236n. 32, 238n. 52

Gambians, ethnic vs. civic identity of, 162–63

gender: divorce issues and, 216–17; freedom and, 94, 146, 201; identity politics linked to, 139–40. *See also* men and boys; violence against women; women and girls

gender equality, Islam and, 156–57, 207–8, 253n. 13

gender roles: differing norms for, 99–100; identity politics and, 156–58;

nurses and, 151–52; opportunities for changing, 129–35. *See also* family honor and shame; immigrant families

Gerhardsen, Rune, 13

Germany: cultural markers in, 244n. 6; dual citizenship not recognized by, 263n. 62, 264n. 64; immigration halted in, 39; Muslims in, 232n. 9; repatriation benefits in, 235n. 28; veiling in, 156, 253n. 12

ghetto, use of term, 39. *See also* urban areas

"ghetto-Islam," concept of, 255–56n. 28

Gibson, Margaret A., 59

gift relationship, issues in, 62–63, 242n. 78

girls. *See* women and girls

Glazer, Nathan, 216, 261–62n. 52

globalization, 214, 217

Goethe, Johann Wolfgang von, 144–45

Goffman, Erving, 243n. 4

gossip, as constraint, 101–2, 247–48n. 14. *See also* "people's talk"

Great Britain: identity in, 255n. 25; kidnapping case in, 189; language issues in, 52, 238n. 52; marriage patterns in, 249n. 21, 262n. 53; native vs. immigrant boys in, 238n. 48; permanent vs. temporary residence in, 243n. 82; "race" in, 233n. 14; unemployment in, 49; voting in, 264n. 66; within-group differences in, 241n. 73

Greenfeld, Liah: on democracy and diversity, 160–61, 167–68; on ethnic diversity, 163–64; on ethnic identity, 165, 167; on ethnic nationalism, 169

Grossman, David, 66, 229n. 1

Gülsum (Turkish Dane), 104–5

Gür, Thomas, 201

Haarder, Bertel, 231n. 5 (pt. 1), 239–40n. 62, 250n. 8

Hagen, Kåre: on equality, 58; on integration bonus, 236n. 35, 236–37n. 39; on social welfare, 57, 237n. 43; on society, 64; on underclass, 59

Hammar, Tomas, 263–64n. 63, 264n. 68

Hanah (Kurdish Iraqi), murder of, 262n. 56

headscarf. *See* veiling

health care, as benefit, 193

Hegge, Per-Egil, 244n. 9

Helskog, Gerhard, 230n. 13

Hennum, Ragnhild, 261n. 46

Hirschman, Charles, 233n. 11, 242n. 80

Hjärpe, Jan, 96, 97

Hobsbawm, Eric, 11, 13, 19, 61, 197

homelands: advice against traveling to, 103, 248–49n. 20; boys sent to, 246n. 5; identification of individual's, 211–12; investment in, 21, 72; money returned to, 242n. 76; myth of return to, 65–66, 243n. 81

homosexuality, survey regarding, 252n. 9

Hønningstad, Arne (ambassador to Morocco): accusations against, 184, 258n. 20; rescue attempts by, 174; testimony of, 183–84, 257–58n. 18

housing, 54, 56, 131, 240n. 64

Howard, Matthew, 251n. 3

humanitarian values: beliefs in, 21–22; failure of, 119; in immigration policies, 41, 71; in multicultural society, 135; paradox in, 24–28; tolerance juxtaposed to, 140, 146

human rights: beliefs in, 21, 98, challenge to, 106–7; child's loss of, 22; culture and, 12, 27–28, 73–74, 128–29; enforcement of, 168–69; institutional framework for protecting, 197, 213–14, 220; right to travel as, 57; universalizing approach to, 15–16

identity: concept of, 74–75, 243nn. 3–4, 244n. 5–7; construction of, 113, 166; culture as, 154–55; defense of, 106; definitions of, 72–73, 159, 163–67; Norwegian, 153

identity politics: civic citizenship vs., 161–63; culture's role in, 25–27, 154–55; discourse on, 160; fear as basis of, 148–54; female behavior as key to, 156–58; individuality subsumed under, 139–42;

167–69; masking implicit in, 155–60; repressiveness in, 141–45; settlement choices and, 38; terminology in, 37–38

ideologue, accusations of, 8, 10–11. *See also* racism, accusations of

Ignatieff, Michael, 73, 161, 197, 213–14

illiteracy: fear's link to, 204; financial issues and, 250n. 7; studies of, 259n. 36; as unfreedom, 198; as widespread, 128–29, 200

imams and mullahs: language issues and, 201–2; and polygamy, 262–63n. 57; shortcomings of, 260n. 42; use of term, 257n. 15

immigrant(s): areas settled by, 38–39, 46, 54, 56–57, 233–34n. 17, 234nn. 19, 20, 23, 236n. 37, 239n. 58; asocial behavior by, 24–25; benefits for, 193–94; betrayal of, 139–48; definition of, 35–37, 72, 163, 232n. 10; dual lives of, 65–66, 194–95, 213, 243n. 81; government knowledge of, 6–7; input from, 12; making demands on, 4; marginalization of, 60; opportunities for, 105, 129–31; organizations for, 161–62; as public responsibility, 59, 65; resourcefulness of, 81, 244–45n. 12; restrictions on, 159–60; terms for, 37–38; time of arrival of, 39–40, 234n. 24; tolerance and trust among, 42, 196, 236n. 32. *See also* asylum seekers; languages; refugees; respect; social welfare; unemployment; *specific groups*

immigrant families: implications of extended, 248n. 17; power structure in, 23, 26–27, 96, 148; role reversals in, 232n. 7; stresses on, 105. *See also* children; family honor and shame; family reunification; men and boys; Muslim children and families; women and girls

immigration: agents' role in, 231n. 5 (pt. 2); approach to understanding, 12–14; assumptions about, 33–34; attempt to stop, 39–40, 42, 60, 260n.

immigration (*continued*)

43; context and contingency of, 15–16; cost of, 234n. 25; models of, 232n. 6; open discourse on, 2; as subversion, 41

immigration policies: antiracism and Orientalism in, 209–10; approach to, 1–2; changes in, 40; cultural relativism and, 146; debate on, 44–46; decentralization in, 46, 54, 240–41n. 67; family reunification under, 235–36n. 31; goals and objectives in, 70–74; premises of, 61–64, 65; shortcomings of, 64–66, 72–73

Indians: marriage patterns of, 262n. 53; number of, 35

individuality and individualism: agency in, 83–84, 87; antigeneralization and, 147; antiracism's emphasis on, 82; human rights' link to, 73–74; masking of, 155–60; respect of, 98, 142–43; as right, 142–43, 161; standing up for, 119, 124, 126; subsumed in collectivity, 117–19, 142–45, 147–48, 209–10; subsumed in identity politics, 139–42, 167–69

individual responsibility: call for, 4, 83; context of learning, 118–19; for learning language, 204

integration: bonus for municipalities for, 46, 236n. 35, 236–37n. 39; citizenship issues in, 217; components of, 127; culture as deterrence to, 83; fostering respect in, 158–59; as immigration policy goal, 71; intermarriage and, 216, 261–62n. 52; social contract concept and, 195–97

international law, 73–74, 211, 212

Iranians: educational issues and, 241n. 68; as Muslims, 166, 232n. 9; number of, 34, 35; unemployment of, 58

Iraqis: as asylum seekers, 41; killing of female, 91–98; mafia's smuggling of, 235n. 29; number of, 35

Islam: on alcohol, 230n. 2; approach to, 8, 79; compassion in, 151–52, 207–8; as culprit, 99–100; defense of, 106; on drug abuse, 238n. 55; on equality, 156–57, 207–8, 253n. 13; on girls' swimming, 148–50, 151; identity based in, 166–67; language issues and, 125; on marriage, 104, 110, 212, 230n. 3, 249n. 22, 252–53n. 11, 263n. 58; mother's position in, 188, 199–200, 201–2, 204; on seeking knowledge, 199–200; on sexual relations, 111; on veiling, 74, 156, 244n. 6, 253n. 12

Islamic Council, 192

Italy, asylum seekers in, 36

Izzat—For the Sake of Honor (Karim), 107. *See also* Karim, Nasim

Jervell, Jacob, 158

Jews, as ethnic minority, 33

journalists, 11, 117–18. *See also* media

justice, definition of, 184

juvenile delinquents, terminology for, 21

Karim, Nasim: citizenship of, 219; context of, 215; on culture conflict, 145; escape of, 71; father of, 72; forced marriage annulled by, 212; on foster placement, 208; on multiculturalism, 146; Nadia compared to, 187, 258n. 25; stories of, 13, 107, 108–14, 249n. 23

Kayed, Camilla, 200, 248–49n. 20, 263n. 61

kebab-Swedish, status of, 201

Keesing, Roger, 144

Kerep, Laila, 248n. 15

Keynan, Hassan: on females under patriarchy, 147; on men's complaints, 132, 133–34; on opportunities for change, 129–31, 134–35; on Somali identity, 164, 254n. 23; on Somalis in Norway vs. Finland, 251n. 9; stories of, 13

Khader, Naser, 239–40n. 62, 255n. 26, 255–56n. 28

Khalid's case: as example, 220; language issues and, 124–29

Khan, Eva, 243n. 1

Khan, Sekina, 189

Klassekampen (newspaper), 7

Kleinman, Arthur, 28

knowledge: absence of, 6–7; culture's link to, 80; Islam on seeking, 199–200; as replacement for culture, 86. *See also* education

Knudsen, Anne, 209

Knudsen, Jon, 236n. 32

Kosovo Albanians: murder of female, 245n. 3; number of, 35; repatriation benefits for, 235n. 28

Kottak, Conrad Philip, 245n. 15

Kramer, Julian, 236n. 35

Kurds: as asylum seekers, 41; attempted killing of female, 92; changing policy on, 235–36n. 31; ethnicities of, 215–16; language issues and, 204; number of, 34; self-identification of, 165; tradition frozen for, 104; unemployment of, 58

Kvæns (Finnish speakers), as ethnic minority, 33

Laatiaoui, Mustapha, 13, 230n. 10

labor migration: Aisha's father under, 42; resourcefulness in, 244–45n. 12; shift to asylum seeking, 39–40, 237n. 42

Labor Party, 40, 202

languages: diversity of, 32, 231n. 4; identity politics and, 139–40; implications of first-person plural, 117–19, 120, 139, 142–43, 251n. 1; importance of, 200; marriage issues and, 50; national vs. mother tongue, 125–26, 250n. 2; necessity of learning, 198–99; new policy on, 250n. 4; political correctness and, 2, 3; in schools, 38–39, 50–52, 124–29, 220, 250n. 4; in trial court, 178, 257n. 11. *See also* Arabic language; Berber language; Danish language; English language; "mother tongue"; Norwegian language; Punjabi language; Swedish language; Urdu language

Latin Americans: areas settled by, 236n. 37; interethnic marriage of, 216; language issues and, 52

law: as basis for respect, 192, 208; expectations about, 192–94; on family reunification, 216, 224; on forced marriage, 107, 168, 212, 249n. 24, 261n. 46; as institutional framework, 197–98; on polygamy, 216, 262–63n. 57; as preeminent over culture, 70–71, 73–74, 191–92; on right to vote, 199. *See also* immigration policies; international law; social contract

Leach, Edmund, 141

Lebanese: housing advice from, 240n. 64; killing of female, 92, 94

Lewis, Philip: on imams' shortcomings, 260n. 42; on language issues, 125; on native vs. immigrant boys, 238n. 48; on organizations, 254n. 19; on resourcefulness, 244–45n. 12; on within-group differences, 60, 241n. 73

liberal democracy: ethnic diversity juxtaposed to, 160–63; multiculturalism in, 167–69; respect in, 142–43; social contract in, 169–70

Lien, Inger-Lise, 164–65

Lindo, Flip, 59, 243n. 82

Lund, Marianne, 253n. 16

Lundgren, Eva, 247n. 10

Maalouf, Amin, 155, 159, 244nn. 5, 7, 8

mahr, definition of, 194, 259n. 33

marriage: annulment of, 113, 223, 227, 249nn. 24–25; arranged type of, 252–53n. 11, 261n. 48; caste considerations in, 254n. 24; cost of, 193–94, 259n. 33; extended families and, 248n. 17; interethnic type of, 216, 261–62n. 52; Islam on, 104, 110, 212, 230n. 3, 249n. 22, 252–53n. 11, 263n. 58; for love, 155–56; patterns of, 37, 49–50, 102, 215, 261n. 51, 262n. 53; virginity as necessity in, 102–3, 248n. 19, 257n. 14

marriage, forced: advice for avoiding, 103, 248–49n. 20; in Aisha's story, 20, 22, 94, 212, 221–25; arranged marriage as, 252–53n. 11; context for, 214–15; crisis telephone for support against, 263n.

marriage, forced (*continued*)
60; death for refusing, 215, 216, 263n. 59; definition and number of, 249n. 25, 261n. 48; discourse on, 147, 154, 176–77; escape from, 71, 215; family reunification's role in, 42, 216–17, 261n. 48; forbidden in Islam, 230n. 3; law against, 107, 168, 212, 249n. 24, 261n. 46, media coverage of, 215, 230n. 13, 249n. 21, 261n. 49, 262n. 54; in Nadia's case, 173–75, 182, 185; in Nasim's story, 71–72, 107; Noreen's story of, 108–14; protection from, 28; publicizing of, 14, 230n. 13; as sacrifice, 24–28

media: on Anna's story, 100; on forced marriage, 215, 230n. 13, 249n. 21, 261n. 49, 262n. 54; on girls as nurses for male patients, 152; grammar of, 117–18; on housing, 131; immigration debate in, 45–46, 103–4; increased viewing of, 52; lawsuit against, 186; Nadia's case and, 174–77, 178, 186–87, 256nn. 5–6; restrictions on, 43, 53; role in asylum seeking, 234–35n. 27; on Sara's killing, 91–92, 93; on school curriculum, 158–59; on Somali men's struggles, 132; on swimming requirement, 149–50; as watchdog, 11, 214. *See also* publicity and publication

men and boys: crisis telephone for, 263n. 60; cultural cafés for, 132; favored by child welfare authorities, 207–8; finances controlled by, 250n. 7, 260n. 40; gender role changes and, 132, 133–34; identity politics' impact on, 148–54; immigrants assumed to be, 33–34; language issues and, 124–28; native vs. immigrant, 238n. 48; nurses' care for, 151–52; opportunities for, 20–21, 27–28, 105, 108; organizations focused on, 162; sanctions against, 94, 246n. 5; violence against, 247n. 12. *See also* employment; social welfare; unemployment

Mernissi, Fatima, 156, 207–8

Michaels, Walter Benn, 144

Middle Eastern immigrants. *See specific groups*

"Migrapolis" (TV program), 155–56

Ministry of Child and Family Affairs: Aisha's case and, 23, 227; crisis manual supported by, 248–49n. 20; forced marriage investigated by, 249n. 25; polygamy investigated by, 262–63n. 57; reticence of, 12; situation analysis for, 3–5, 250n. 2

Ministry of Culture, Aisha's case and, 23

Ministry of Education, on girls' success in school, 49–50

Ministry of Foreign Affairs, Nadia's case and, 173, 175, 177, 256nn. 2, 3, 7

Ministry of Interior: forced marriage and, 261n. 46; polygamy investigated by, 262–63n. 57

Ministry of Justice: on communication issues, 257n. 11; polygamy investigated by, 262–63n. 57

minority, composition of, 26. *See also* ethnic minorities

"minority-lingual" (*minoritetsspråklig*), use of term, 37

misconceived humanism, concept of, 166

Le Monde (newspaper), 46

Mørck, Yvonne, 248n. 15, 252n. 7

Moroccans: areas settled by, 233–34n. 17; as asylum seekers, 235n. 30; blame shifted by, 178, 257n. 13; disability pensions for, 48; educational issues and, 238n. 48; illiteracy of, 259n. 36; immigration rate of, 259n. 30; language issues and, 125, 126; marriage patterns of, 215; money returned to homeland of, 242n. 76; number of, 35; social welfare use of, 237n. 46; supernatural beliefs of, 178–79; unemployment of, 49, 193–94, 238n. 47. *See also* Nadia's case

Morocco, Nadia's case and, 173–75, 178–79, 185, 190–94, 206, 256n. 7, 258n. 22

"mother tongue": determining child's, 125–26; policy on, 250n. 4; proper instruction in, 124–25; use of term, 37, 233n. 15. *See also* languages

Mubashir, Noman, 155–56

multicultural citizenship, concept of, 261n. 47

multicultural society: challenge of, 82–83, 87; commitment to, 62; concept of, 145–46; confusions in, 167–69; criticism of, 146–48; discourse on, 160; female behavior as key to, 156–58; goal of well-functioning, 1–2; humanitarian values in, 135; human vs. cultural rights in, 12; patterns of behavior in, 24–25; terms for, 6

municipalities, integration bonus for, 46, 236n. 36, 236–37n. 39

Muslim children and families: author's talk on, 4; discourse among vs. without, 252n. 9; identity politics faced by, 34, 157–58; language issues and, 52, 125, 238n. 52; misperceptions of, 134; number of, 232nn. 9–10. *See also* family honor and shame; Islam

Muslims: antidemocratic processes among, 255–56n. 28; differences among, 255n. 26; divorce among, 200, 216–17; identity of, 34, 157–58, 166–67; polygamy among, 216, 262–63n. 57; on verdict in Nadia's case, 192. *See also* family honor and shame; Islam

Muslim Women's Organization, 195

Nadia's case: Aisha's case compared to, 211–14; appeal in, 205–6; background of, 182–83, 192–94, 209, 259n. 29; citizenship in, 173, 190–94, 205–6, 217–19, 220, 264n. 65; forced marriage in, 173–75, 182, 185; grandmother's illness and, 184–85, 258nn. 21–22; kidnapping and release in, 173–75, 182, 258n. 23; negotiations in, 174, 256n. 5; parents' trial in, 177–82, 183–87, 188–89, 204; politics and, 174, 256n. 3; reputation in, 181, 185, 189–90; social

welfare issues in, 175–76; timing of, 14, 176–77, 214; verdict in, 187–88, 190–92, 195, 210–11

Når overmakten blir for stor (report), 5

Nasim. *See* Karim, Nasim

National Demographic Institute, 255n. 27

"national interest doctrine," concept of, 26

nationalism, collectivity infused with, 118

nation-state: citizenship vs. residence in, 219; ethnicity as distinct from, 165; sovereignty and, 168, 213–14. *See also* citizenship; law; rights

"natives," silence of, 9

Netherlands: educational issues in, 238n. 49, 242n. 75; forced marriage in, 225; gossip as constraint in, 247–48n. 14; illiteracy in, 259n. 36; immigrants in urban areas of, 233–34n. 17; language issues in, 126, 203; permanent vs. temporary residence in, 243n. 82; right to vote in, 231n. 8; taboo subjects in, 59; unemployment in, 49

New York, languages in, 231n. 3

New York Times (newspaper), 49, 55

Noreen (character): as example, 139–40; story of forced marriage, 108–14

Norway: as destination, 40–42, 235n. 29; as example, 1–2, 14, 15–16; generosity of, 25, 55; geography of, 31; king and queen of, 53, 230n. 10; population of, 31–36; resources of, 54, 63–64. *See also* child welfare authorities; citizenship; crime; education; employment; equality; languages; law; Oslo; politics; public policy; quality of life; welfare society

Norwegian, definition of, 153, 163

Norwegian embassy personnel: in Aisha's case, 225–26; in Nadia's case, 174, 183–84, 257–58n. 18; in Noreen's case, 112

Norwegian immigration bureau (*Innvandrerdirektoratet*), 43–44

Norwegian language: lessons in, 202–4; limited knowledge of, 38–39, 50–52,

models, 232n. 6; on resourcefulness, 244–45n. 12; on settlement choices, 234n. 19

Rushdie, Salman, 146, 151
Russia, crime and, 239n. 57
Ruth, Arne, 245n. 1

Said, Edward, 166, 208
Salimi, Khalid, 8, 10–11, 82, 255–56n. 28
Sami: customs of, 85; as ethnic minority, 33
Sara (Iraqi female): as example, 139–40, 220; killing of, 91–98, 106, 208–9; Nasim and Nadia compared to, 262n. 56; religious identity and, 167
Scandinavia: family reunification in, 216; social contract debate in, 195–97; veiling in, 156, 253n. 12. *See also specific countries*
schools: affirmative action applied to, 241n. 72; children's absence from, 194–95; cultural relativism and, 146; culture and performance in, 59, 242n. 75; curriculum dispute and, 158–59, 253–54n. 17; enrollments in/dropouts from, 49–50; as free for immigrants, 193; language issues in, 38–39, 50–52, 124–29, 220, 250n. 4; parental involvement in, 134, 195, 199–200; swimming class required by, 148–50, 151
Schuck, Peter, 198, 264n. 68
SEIF, on forced marriage, 248–49n. 20
self-censorship, 118. *See also* publicity and publication
self-respect, 63, 242n. 79. *See also* respect
Sen, Amartya: on freedom, 197, 198, 201, 206, 213, 218; on function and capability, 199; as influence, 13; on welfare, 210–11
sex segregation, enforcement of, 151–52
sexual intercourse, as defense for killing, 91
sexuality: cultural norms for, 123; Islam on, 111; survey regarding, 252n. 9
Shaaban, Bouthaina, 248nn. 17, 19, 252n. 6
Shachar, Ayelet, 156
Shahid's story, language issues and, 127–28
sheik, use of term, 257n. 15

Sheikh, Aamir Javed, 128, 252n. 7
Shweder, Richard, 244n. 10
Sickness Benefits Act, 49, 238n. 47
silence: Aisha's, 24, 212; breaking of, 7, 11, 61, 107; as enemy, 2, 160; as political cover-up, 61–66; reasons for, 6, 9, 25, 154; state's complicity in, 121–23
situation analysis: findings of, 5–7; goal of, 229n. 2; request for, 3–5
slander, uses of, 150, 252n. 8
social class: individuality and, 142; language issues and, 126; of refugees, 133–34, 251n. 10. *See also* underclass
social contract: citizenship as, 195–97, 204–5, 217–18, 220; in liberal democracy, 169–70; state's failure of, 197–98
social welfare: in Aisha's case, 222; birth bonus in, 223; components of, 54–55; dangers of, 55, 133–34, 239–40n. 62; immigrant use of (general), 21–22, 27–28, 47–48, 193–94, 237nn. 41–44, 241n. 71, 258n. 19, 260n. 40; as individual vs. community, 210–12; misuse of, 237n. 46; for natives vs. immigrants, 56–57, 256n. 8; politics of, 207–8; publicizing issue of, 45–47; reconsideration of, 220; steered use of, 39; suspension of, 175–76, 194; Trondheim study of, 43–44; underclass as effect of, 60. *See also* disability pensions
social workers: collective/individual issues and, 209–10; culture as defense of, 121–23, 209; difficulties facing, 100–101; role of, 11; state's alliance with, 120. *See also* child welfare authorities
society: concept of one worth living in, 60–61; distributive principles of justice in, 210–14; ethnic diversity defined by, 164; identity construction in, 74–75; role in identity politics, 154–55; rules of, 64–65, 133, 195–96; sharp focus on specifics in, 33; unequal cost of, 28; willingness to adjust, 11–12. *See also* welfare society
sojourning, concept of, 194–95

solidarity: grammar of, 120; as immigration policy goal, 70–71; repressiveness of, 142–43 trust: lack of, 236n. 32; necessity for, 195–96, 225

Turks: areas settled by, 233–34n. 17, 234n. 22; attempted killing of female, 92, 94, 99, 100; constraints on female, 247–48nn. 14, 15; cultural markers of, 244n. 6; disability pensions for, 48; educational issues and, 238nn. 48, 54, 241n. 68; illiteracy of, 259n. 36; language issues and, 50, 51, 126; marriage patterns of, 215, 262n. 53; number of, 34, 35; resourcefulness of, 244–45n. 12; tradition frozen for, 104–5; unemployment of, 49, 238n. 47, 239–40n. 62

underclass: emergence of, 59–61, 64, 128; language as marker of, 201; use of term, 7, 45, 47, 229n. 6. *See also* respect; social welfare; unemployment

unemployment: benefits for, 56–57; due to alcohol, 20–21; educational issues in, 57; gender differences in, 131; immigrant rate of, 46–49, 54, 237n. 40; stigmatization of, 55; underclass as effect of, 60, 64

UNESCO: culture vs. education under, 143–44; Declaration of the Rights of Man and, 141, 161; *Volksgeist* linked to, 140

UNICEF, on "girl child," 218

United Nations Convention on Human Rights, 73–74

United Nations Refugee Commission, 241n. 69

United States: "immigrant" definition and public opinion in, 233n. 11; integration in, 242n. 80; interethnic marriage in, 216; language issues in, 52; "race" in, 233n. 14; risky behaviors in, 238–39n. 56; settlement choices in, 233n. 16, 234n. 19; unemployment in, 49; welfare law in, 240n. 66. *See also* California; Florida; New York

universal values: argument for, 15–16,

25In. 2; of individuality, 143. *See also* antigeneralization

urban areas: "ghetto-Islam" in, 255–56n. 28; "ghetto" problems in, 39, 127, 234n. 22; non-Western and native movements in, 238n. 53; segregation of, 51, 238nn. 52–53; as settlement choice, 38–39, 233–34nn. 16, 17

Urdu language, 124, 125, 201

values/norms: adherence to, 101; disagreements over, 86–87; immigrant vs. native, 99–100. *See also* traditions and customs

Varna (Iraqi female), killing of, 92–93, 94, 246n. 4

veiling, 74, 156, 244n. 6, 253n. 12

Verdens Gang (newspaper), on Nadia's case, 186

Vietnamese: areas settled by, 38, 236n. 37; educational issues and, 241n. 68; marriage patterns of, 261n. 51; number of, 34–35; social welfare use of, 241n. 71; trust among, 236n. 32; unemployment of, 58

violence: against children, 69–70, 158; increase in, 53–54; of youth, 13–14, 53–54, 132, 193. *See also* crime; *specific cases*

violence against women: causes of, 99–107; culture as defense for, 79–80, 83, 95–98, 107; downplayed, 247nn. 10, 13; family honor as defense for, 92–93, 95–97; immigrant organizations and, 162–63; increase in, 52–53; kidnapping as, 177–89, 256n. 9; as manly act, 96, 97; media coverage of, 215, 230n. 13, 249n. 21, 261n. 49, 262n. 54; murder as, 91–98, 106, 208–9, 245n. 3, 246n. 4, 262n. 56. *See also* Aisha's case; Anna (Christian of Syrian descent); Karim, Nasim; marriage, forced; Nadia's case; Noreen (character); Sara (Iraqi female)

virginity, 102–3, 181, 248n. 19, 257n. 14

visas, forced marriage as means to, 216–17, 262nn. 54–55

Vogt, Kari, 152
Volksgeist, concept of, 140–41

Waage, Peter Normann, 192
Walzer, Michael, 15, 195–96
war, collectivity infused with, 118
welfare colonialism, concept of, 7, 229n. 7
welfare society: Aisha's father in, 21–22,
    27–28; definition of, 19; failure of, 119;
    goals of, 57; immigrants in, 231n. 5 (pt.
    2). *See also* social welfare
West Africans: economic situation of,
    260n. 40; language issues and, 201
Westin, Charles, 247n. 10
whore, use of term, 91, 167, 184, 258n. 19
Wicklund, Gunvor, 246n. 4
Wolf, Eric, 76
women and girls: authorities' disbelief
    of, 213; beatings by, 248n. 16;
    culture's definition and, 78;
    family honor's cost to, 99–
    107; language issues and, 104,
    201–3, 232n. 7; living situation
    of, 257n. 16, 260n. 38; with
    many children, 131, 250n. 5;
    marginalization of, 205–6; as

nurses for male patients, 151–52;
    opportunities for, 129–31, 134–35;
    oppression of, 34, 100–107, 156, 201–2,
    219, 247–48nn. 14, 15; shelter for,
    222; state's betrayal of, 119, 120–23,
    226–28; status of kidnapped, 178, 257n.
    12; swimming class requirement for,
    148–50, 151; terminology for, 216,
    262nn. 54–55; undermined in action
    plan, 5. *See also* citizenship; social
    welfare; violence against women
work (as concept): social class and, 133–34;
    value of, 58, 62–63, 241n. 74. *See also*
    employment; unemployment
workfare, language issues and, 204

Yalcin-Heckmann, Lale, 244n. 6
youth: crisis telephone for, 263n. 60; cul-
    ture's definition and, 80–81; response
    to Nadia's case, 186–87, 188; sanctions
    on, 27, 94, 246n. 5; survey of, 252n. 9;
    violence of, 13–14, 53–54, 132, 193
Youth Against Violence (*Ungdom mot vold*),
    13
Yugoslavs: dialogue among, 160; mafia's
    smuggling of, 235n. 29; number of, 35